Documenting Fashion

Film and Fashions

Series Editor: Pamela Church Gibson

This series explores the complex and multi-faceted relationship between cinema, fashion and design. Intended for all scholars and students with an interest in film and in fashion itself, the series not only forms an important addition to the existing literature around cinematic costume, but advances the debates by moving them forward into new, unexplored territory and extending their reach beyond the parameters of Western cinema alone.

Titles in the series include:

Shoe Reels: The History and Philosophy of Footwear in Film
Elizabeth Ezra and Catherine Wheatley (eds)

Fashion on the Red Carpet: A History of the Oscars®, Fashion and Globalisation
Elizabeth Castaldo Lundén

Documenting Fashion
Elena Caoduro and Boel Ulfsdotter (eds)

https://edinburghuniversitypress.com/series-film-and-fashions

Documenting Fashion

Edited by Elena Caoduro and
Boel Ulfsdotter

EDINBURGH
University Press

Edinburgh University Press is one of the leading university presses in the UK. We publish academic books and journals in our selected subject areas across the humanities and social sciences, combining cutting-edge scholarship with high editorial and production values to produce academic works of lasting importance. For more information visit our website: edinburghuniversitypress.com

© editorial matter and organisation Elena Caoduro and Boel Ulfsdotter, 2023, 2024
© the chapters their several authors, 2023, 2024

Grateful acknowledgement is made to the sources listed in the List of Illustrations for permission to reproduce material previously published elsewhere. Every effort has been made to trace the copyright holders, but if any have been inadvertently overlooked, the publisher will be pleased to make the necessary arrangements at the first opportunity.

Edinburgh University Press Ltd
13 Infirmary Street
Edinburgh EH1 1LT

First published in hardback by Edinburgh University Press 2023

Typeset in 12/14 Arno and Myriad by
IDSUK (Dataconnection) Ltd

A CIP record for this book is available from the British Library

ISBN 978 1 4744 7616 4 (hardback)
ISBN 978 1 4744 7617 1 (paperback)
ISBN 978 1 4744 7618 8 (webready PDF)
ISBN 978 1 4744 7619 5 (epub)

The right of Elena Caoduro and Boel Ulfsdotter to be identified as the editors of this work has been asserted in accordance with the Copyright, Designs and Patents Act 1988, and the Copyright and Related Rights Regulations 2003 (SI No. 2498).

Contents

List of figures	vii
Acknowledgements	x
Notes on contributors	xi
Introduction	1
Elena Caoduro and Boel Ulfsdotter	

Part I: Film

1. Fashion documentaries and the tension between celebratory and critical approaches   11
   Elena Caoduro
   Expanding interview 1: Elena Caoduro in conversation with Lorna Tucker, director of *Westwood: Punk, Icon, Activist* (2018)   32
2. 'The Helen Rose originals are fabulous': the fashion featurette and fashion show as sites of industrial reflexivity   39
   Julie Nakama
3. The fashion of east and west in German cinema newsreels (1950–65)   57
   Sigrun Lehnert
4. 'Third way' teenage fashion: housewives' films documenting ideals of middle-class youth culture in 1950s Sweden   81
   Mats Björkin
5. A maverick on the streets: Bill Cunningham and the documentary process   102
   Karen A. Ritzenhoff
6. Extending the exhibition narrative: making sense of non-fiction fashion footage   122
   Boel Ulfsdotter

Expanding interview 2: Boel Ulfsdotter in conversation with
Alexandra Palmer at Royal Ontario Museum, Canada   144

Part II: Television
7   Documenting fashion history: television and the temporalities
    of cultural remembrance   159
    Jihane Dyer
8   Italian ready-to-wear fashion through Cori-carousels   182
    Giulia Caffaro
9   Fashioning self-care: *Queer Eye*, affect and makeover culture   203
    Elizabeth Affuso

Part III: Digital media
10 From newsreel to 'see now, buy now': a genealogy of the
    fashion show live stream   227
    Rebecca Halliday
11 Documenting fashion in the era of Instagram: a critical reading
    of Asri Bendacha's *Follow Me* and Chiara Ferragni's *Unposted*   248
    Marco Pedroni

Index   269

Figures

1.1 This screenshot is captured from a transition between chapters in *McQueen* (Ian Bonhôte and Peter Ettedgui, 2018). The skull harks back to pagan mythology, the gothic motifs so dear to the designer, but also his struggles with past traumas and mental health issues   19

1.2 *McQueen* (Ian Bonhôte and Peter Ettedgui, 2018) utilises computer animation to create a collage of negative reviews of McQueen's shows and accusations of misogyny   20

1.3 This still image from *The True Cost* (Andrew Morgan, 2015) depicts the inhumane working conditions in Bangladeshi factories producing garments for western high street fashion brands   24

E1.1 Lorna Tucker on a Greenpeace boat, shooting Vivian Westwood during the Save the Arctic campaign. Courtesy of Lorna Tucker   36

3.1 Bormann model in a morning gown, *Der Augenzeuge* no. A79, 1959   66

3.2 Parisian chic at Leipzig trade fair in GDR, *Der Augenzeuge* no. B14, 1957   69

3.3 Designer Heinz Schulze-Varell at his studio, *Neue Deutsche Wochenschau* no. 423, 7 March 1958   70

3.4 Emilio Schuberth's model at the Brandenburg Gate, *Welt im Bild* no. 100, 26 May 1954   72

4.1 *Tonårsmodet*, Husmors Filmer 1954, © Petter Davidson. Composite of images by author   94

5.1 Bill Cunningham amongst his filing cabinets in his tiny artist's loft on the top floor of Carnegie Hall. Screen capture from *Bill Cunningham, New York* by Richard Press (2010)   104

5.2 Bill Cunningham worked with analogue technology, shooting pictures on film rolls that needed to be developed for him to process. Here he is looking at a film roll that would then be digitised so he could work on his layout for the *New York Times* Style section. *Bill Cunningham, New York* (2010). Screen capture by author 107

5.3 Bill Cunningham wanted to be 'bird-like', free to explore, not bound by fiscal commitments when he took photographs at fancy galas as well as on the street. Here he is at the end of Bozek's 2018 documentary, *The Times of Bill Cunningham*, spreading his arms like wings. Screen capture by author 116

5.4 Fashion on the street: Bill Cunningham captures the latest fashion trends in Manhattan while photographing two young African American men who smile at his lens. Screen capture by author. *The Times of Bill Cunningham* (Mark Bozek, 2018) 117

6.1 Screenshot from *How Was It Made? Constructing Balençiaga's Historically Inspired Evening Dress*. Exhibition video featuring Ying Wang, 2017. © Victoria and Albert Museum, London 129

6.2 Screenshot from *Fashion Unpicked: The 'Wet Collection' by Mary Quant*. Exhibition video featuring curator Stephanie Wood, 2019. © Victoria and Albert Museum, London 131

6.3 *Christian Dior* exhibition with historical film projection inside the case. Royal Ontario Museum (ROM), Toronto, 2017. Photo: Alexandra Palmer. Courtesy of the Royal Ontario Museum, Toronto. © ROM, Toronto 134

6.4 Screenshot from *Christian Dior: Behind the Scenes at Royal Ontario Museum*, 2017. Karla Livingston, technician, mounting Saadi by Christian Dior for the exhibition. Exhibition video. Courtesy of the Royal Ontario Museum, Toronto. © ROM, Toronto 140

E2.1 *Christian Dior* exhibition with archival film seating area. Royal Ontario Museum (ROM), 2017. Photo: Alexandra Palmer. Courtesy of the Royal Ontario Museum, Toronto. © ROM, Toronto 147

E2.2 *A Chanel Tie Embroidered by Joseph Wong*, ROM, 2020. Composite of screenshots from video with donor conversation. Courtesy of the Royal Ontario Museum, Toronto. © ROM, Toronto 149

8.1	Eleonora Rossi Drago posing during the shooting of the Cori-carousel series *Agente Segreto*, 1967, GFT Archive (folder 2892, vol. 4), Turin/AsTo	190
8.2	Advertising Cori A/W 1973/74: Catherine Spaak performing in the Cori-carousel series *La Casa dei Vip*, 1973, GFT Archive (folder 2894, vol. 6), Turin/AsTo	196
8.3	One of the pictures selected for the Cori advertising campaign A/W 1973/74: Catherine Spaak performing in the Cori-carousel titled 'Sylva Koscina', *La Casa dei Vip*, 1973, GFT Archive (folder 2894, vol. 6), Turin/AsTo	196
9.1	Post by @tanfrance featuring the French tuck. 2020. Accessed 16 October 2020	213
9.2	Selfie by fan @diarmuidferry featuring the French tuck and the #qehiptip. 2020. Accessed 18 October 2020	213
9.3	Still from an @jvn IGTV video showing how to cleanse your face with Biossance Elderberry Jelly Cleanser. 2020. Accessed 5 October 2020	217
9.4	Post by @tanfrance in a robe promoting his Etsy collaboration. 2020. Accessed 19 October 2020	218
11.1	Bendacha begs for followers on the streets of Dubai. *Follow Me*, Asri Bendacha, 2017. Screenshot by author	253
11.2	This illustration is intended to show the use of low-resolution amateur videos from the 1980s (recorded by Ferragni's father) in the documentary as a visual strategy to emphasise authenticity. *Unposted*, Amoruso, 2019. Screenshot by author	258

Acknowledgements

This edited collection originates from the symposium 'Sewing Reality: Fashion and Non-Fiction Media' organised at the University of Bedfordshire, UK in June 2018. The event received the support of RIMAP, the Research Institute of Media, Art and Performance. Elena Caoduro would like to thank Alexis Weedon, Jane Carr, Priyanka Savita and Karen Randell and her former Beds colleagues for their help in the organisation and running of the "Sewing Reality' symposium. Many thanks are also due to all participants for their inspiring papers and the debates and discussion that followed.

We extend a heartfelt 'thank you' to Pamela Church Gibson who believed in this ensuing book project since giving a keynote address at that event; her support during the editing process was fantastic. The manuscript received research support funding from the School of Arts, English and Languages at Queen's University Belfast and we are particularly thankful for this help. Most importantly, we express our sincere gratitude to all contributors who have worked patiently and tirelessly, sometimes in the most difficult circumstances. Special thanks go to Gillian Leslie and Sam Johnson who chaperoned this project to completion.

Belfast and Gothenburg, May 2022
Elena Caoduro and Boel Ulfsdotter

Notes on contributors

Elizabeth Affuso is Academic Director of Intercollegiate Media Studies at the Claremont Colleges, where she teaches Media Studies at Pitzer College. Her work has been presented at conferences such as SCMS, Flow and Console-ing Passions. She is co-editor with Avi Santo of the special issue of *Film Criticism*, 'Films and Merchandise' (2018), and with Suzanne Scott of *Sartorial Fandom: Fashion, Beauty Culture, and Identity* (forthcoming). Her work on beauty, fashion, fandom and consumer culture has been published in *JumpCut*, *The Routledge Companion to Media Fandom* and *Point of Sale: Analyzing Media Retail*.

Mats Björkin is Professor of Film Studies at the University of Gothenburg. His publication with Amsterdam University Press, *Post War Industrial Media Culture in Sweden 1945–1960: New Faces, New Values* (2021), analyses how discourses on automation and pedagogy related to uses of media technologies in Swedish industry and the public sector during the 1950s. His research focuses on the economics and organisation of audio-visual media during the 1950s, and today.

Giulia Caffaro is Doctor of Philosophy in History of Architecture at the Department for Life Quality Studies and a member of the Cultural Fashion Communication International Research Centre at the University of Bologna. Her research focuses on the Gruppo GFT company, of which she studies the cultural exhibitions realised for Pitti Uomo and for many other institutional contexts during the 1980s as new media for the cultural validation of ready-to-wear fashion and 'made in Italy' itself. She writes reviews, interviews and critical texts about history of design and cultural communication, with particular attention to the enhancement of Italian heritage among international networks.

Elena Caoduro is Lecturer in Media Analysis at Queen's University Belfast. Her research interests include memory and nostalgia studies, representations of terrorism in film and television, and the relationship between fashion and media industries. She is co-editor of *Mediated Terrorism in the 21st Century* (with Karen Randell and Karen Ritzenhoff) and her work on fashion films, analogue nostalgia and European cinema has been published in edited collections and journals such as *Comunicazioni Sociali*, *NECSUS: The European Journal of Media Studies* and *Alphaville: Journal of Film and Screen Media*.

Jihane Dyer is a Techne AHRC-supported PhD candidate working between the Museum of London and Royal Holloway, University of London, on the project 'Wearing the City: Fashion and Clothing in the Curation of Urban History'. Her research interests focus on fashion museology, historiography and urban geography.

Rebecca Halliday is an Assistant Teaching Professor in the Department of English at the University of Victoria and the adviser for its Professional Communication minor. Her research examines the impact of digital and social media across the arenas of fashion, urban life, performance and politics, with a focus on users' material and immaterial interactions with fashion content. She is the author of *The Fashion Show Goes Live: Exclusive and Mediatized Performance* (2022), and her work has appeared in journals such as the *International Journal of Fashion Studies*, *ZoneModa*, *Comunicazioni Sociali*, *Imaginations* and *TranscUlturAl*, as well as in edited volumes. Rebecca holds a PhD in Communication and Culture from York University, Canada, and previously taught in the School of Professional Communication and the School of Fashion at Toronto Metropolitan University.

Sigrun Lehnert is an independent scholar in Hamburg, Germany. She received her PhD at the University of Hamburg with a project about German newsreels and television newscasts in the 1950s. Her ensuing book, *Wochenschau und Tagesschau in den 1950er Jahren*, was published by UVK Verlag in 2013. Her research interests are German film and television history, newsreels, documentaries, archiving, and film heritage. Blog and website: www.wochenschau-forschung.de.

Julie Nakama is an independent scholar and her research interests include American film history, production cultures, gender studies and material culture studies. Her first book project, *Shopping the Look: Hollywood Costume Production and American Film Consumption, 1960–1969*, analyses the relationship between the production culture of costume departments in post-studio era Hollywood and American fashion and beauty cultures. She has published essays in *Networking Knowledge* and the edited collection *Like One of the Family: Domestic Workers, Race and In/Visibility in The Help*.

Marco Pedroni is Associate Professor of Sociology of Culture and Communication at the University of Ferrara (Italy). He is the author of *Coolhunting* (2010), a co-editor of *Moda e arte* (Fashion and Art; 2012) and *Fashion Tales: Feeding the Imaginary* (2017), and the editor of *From Production to Consumption: The Cultural Industry of Fashion* (2013). His works have been published in peer-reviewed journals such as *Fashion Theory, Poetics* and *Journal of Consumer Culture*. He is a co-editor of the *International Journal of Fashion Studies* published by Intellect. As a fashion scholar, his research interests range from trend watching to digital media, creative professions and cultural intermediaries, with a special focus on bloggers and influencers.

Karen A. Ritzenhoff is Professor in the Department of Communication at Central Connecticut State University. She is affiliated with the Women, Gender, and Sexuality Studies Program and cinema studies. In 2021 she published two co-edited books: *Mediated Terrorism in the 21st Century* (with Elena Caoduro and Karen Randell), and *Afrofuturism in* Black Panther*: Gender, Identity, and the Re-Making of Blackness* (with Renée T. White). In 2019 her co-edited book *New Perspectives on the War Film* (with Clémentine Tholas and Janis Goldie) was published by Palgrave Macmillan. Also in 2019, *Teaching Dystopia, Feminism, and Resistance across Disciplines and Borders*, her co-edited collection of essays on *The Handmaid's Tale*, was published. In 2015 she co-edited *The Apocalypse in Film* with Angela Krewani, *Selling Sex on Screen: From Weimar Cinema to Zombie Porn* with Catriona McAvoy and *Humor, Entertainment, and Popular Culture during World War I* with Clémentine Tholas-Disset. Her latest work deals with Stanley Kubrick and feminism.

Boel Ulfsdotter is Reader in Film and Media Studies at the Faculty of Arts and Humanities at Gothenburg University, Sweden. Her areas of research are rooted in narrative and aesthetic perspectives of female subjectivity related to dress and *mise en scène* in all visual culture, with a preference for non-fiction cinema, exhibition practices and popular television. Recent publications include 'Genius and Taste: Sara Danius' Couture Gowns as Extended Power-dressing' in *International Journal of Fashion Studies* (2021); and 'Embodying Female Dissent in *Sanditon*: The Case of Esther Denham's Two Bodies' in *Journal of Film, Fashion & Consumption* (2022). She previously published the co-edited twin volumes *Female Authorship and the Documentary Image: Theory, Practice and Aesthetics* and *Female Agency and Documentary Strategies: Subjectivities, Identity, and Activism* with Edinburgh University Press in 2018. Boel Ulfsdotter is a formally trained dressmaker and freelancing fashion and visual arts critic.

Introduction

Elena Caoduro and Boel Ulfsdotter

'Be bold, be you'. With this catchy motto SHEIN, the ultrafast fashion brand – known for its innovative use of social media, for the accusations of its plagiarism and for the damage it causes to the environment – launched its own reality show, *Shein X: 100K Challenges*, at the end of August 2021. Available on their app and on YouTube, the four-part reality show follows thirty designers competing to win a lucrative collaboration, a cash prize and the showing of their collection at SHEIN's fashion week in Los Angeles. The initiative not only demonstrates the resourceful marketing strategies it now uses to target generation Z consumers, but also the long-standing relationship between fashion and the media industries. Fashion and media have flirted with each other in a symbiotic relationship since the dawn of modernity and this synergy has been mutually influential. It is sufficient to think of the ways in which television dramas have inspired catwalks and collections, and how designers have created costumes for feature films, or loaned their iconic garments to red carpet premieres and awards ceremonies. In tandem with these developments, the act of documenting fashion has been present since the emergence of the medium of film: from British and American actualities showing what was in vogue at the time, to German and French newsreels capturing fashion shows. The tradition continues into our own days: first with fashion blogging and vlogging, now with Instagram stories, reels and live-streamed fashion shows.

Documenting Fashion offers a critical view on the power of factual media to shed light on fashion, celebrity and consumer culture. The book invites its readers to consider fashion as an object of mediated fascination and responds to the real lack of scholarly works dedicated to the ways in which the documentary moving image frames fashion. In fact, while the scholarship dedicated to the intersection of film and fashion is fast increasing, the interest in this field has primarily focused on expressions related to fiction and to narrative storytelling. From an academic point of view, these works have examined, among other topics, the construction of femininity and masculinity through costuming, the definition of national identities through cinematic clothing, and the haptic pleasure of fashion in film. The Arts and Humanities Research Council (AHRC) research project 'Archaeology of Fashion Film' (2017–19), with its aim of investigating 'the epistemologies and contexts of contemporary digital fashion film and its precursors' (Evans and Parikka 2020: 323), inspired our effort to excavate long-entangled histories, but also to connect different media beyond the canonical feature films. This edited collection brings together, for the first time, a series of chapters that examine the documentary methods operating within fashion documentaries, newsreels, short films, advertisements, exhibitions, television reportage, reality TV, streaming videos and social media.

Non-fiction material in the cutting edge between film and fashion has, however, remained an understudied topic, with only a few scholarly works shedding light on, for example, early cinema's attention to the fashion world (Evans 2013), still and moving images in fashion archives (Palmer 2008), and celebrity, awards and fashion studies (Lundén 2020). In his monograph *Fashion Film: Art and Advertising in the Digital Age*, Nick Rees-Roberts (2018) dedicates one chapter to the fashion documentary, considering case studies produced for the big and small screen and providing a pioneering overview of the genre. Individual titles of fashion documentaries have been the focus of a number of articles (see for instance Szymanski 2012; Hui 2015; Joseph 2015). Similarly, reality television and its engagement with makeover culture, design, sewing and modelling competitions has accrued some scholarly interest (Ouellette 2016; Witsell 2016). *Documenting Fashion* reassesses the role of non-fiction media in shaping our understanding of fashion across multiple media platforms and different national contexts. It aims to create an open space for dialogue between fashion and documentary studies, drawing from methodologies and approaches such as media and cultural studies, ethnography, audience research, marketing and public relations. The volume indicates the fruitful outcome of such a problematisation across disciplines, while simultaneously inferring documentary fashion film's ongoing academic development as a separate field of scholarly study.

The chapters in this volume show that works belonging to this particular subgenre represent a spectacular window into the inner workings of fashion curation, fashion history in televised form, fashion journalism, department stores and fashion subcultures. Given the boom of non-fiction media about fashion and the political potential of fashion documentaries it has demonstrated, *Documenting Fashion* moves beyond these productions to broaden the representation of different types of discursive approaches to this topic. Covering a vast array of forms, from ironic takes or more explicit critiques of consumer society to hagiographic portraits of iconic figures, the chapters in this volume confirm that the fashion documentary now merits our full attention.

The first section of the volume examines the documentary film from different angles. Chapter 1 lays the basis for understanding the synergies between fashion and documentary, considering the contemporary boom in feature documentaries about designers, fashion professionals and ethical issues related to the fashion industry in the twenty-first century. In 'Fashion documentaries and the tension between celebratory and critical approaches', Elena Caoduro considers a large corpus of non-fiction films dealing with a variety of issues, behind-the-scenes reportage of operations inside fashion magazines and department stores, the genius artistry of fashion designers, but also investigative exposés about fast fashion, modelling agencies and pressures of the fashion system. These fashion documentaries display an inherent tension between a celebratory mode, which hints at depicting a hagiographic portrayal of the fashion icon or institution, and a more critical and political approach to the documentary subject. By paying close attention to two films, *McQueen* (Ian Bonhôte and Peter Ettedgui, 2018) and *The True Cost* (Andrew Morgan, 2015), as exemplary case studies of the spectrum, Caoduro analyses the fashion documentary in its contradictory effort of museification and glorification of its heritage, and demythologisation of its own industry. In Chapter 2, '"The Helen Rose originals are fabulous": the fashion featurette and fashion show as sites of industrial reflexivity', Julie Nakama considers the medium of the featurette, a predecessor of the 'making of' documentary to investigate post-war marketing strategies. In the 1950s, the MGM costume designer Helen Rose defined a certain American, middle-class, feminine style with her dress designs. During her career at MGM, she also designed and sold ready-to-wear clothing through exclusive department stores and specialty shops. After Rose left MGM in 1966, she continued to market fashion through her retail label, and one of her most effective marketing devices was the fashion featurette. In these short promotional films, Rose described her design process and showcased her work to both promote her own brand and offer viewers a window into film costuming practices. Nakama argues that Rose deployed the fashion featurette as a space through which the industry represented itself to itself, but also to showcase the craft of costume design to the film industry itself and the wider fashion retail industry. In Chapter 3, 'The fashion of east and west in German cinema newsreels (1950–65)', Sigrun Lehnert examines the medium of newsreel as a predecessor to modern-day fashion journalism on television. Considering the different aesthetics and narrative strategies of newsreels from East and West Germany during a crucial period of the Cold War, Lehnert outlines the rich variety of reports and the role of fashion and media industries in supporting ideologies. The chapter argues that newsreel reports about fashion worked as extravagant entertainment, but, more importantly, they also served as orientation and signposting for audiences in a world divided by the Iron Curtain. Chapter 4 also pays attention to the immediate post-war era, focusing on Sweden's socio-historical context. In 'Third way teenage fashion: housewives' films documenting ideals of middle-class youth culture in 1950s Sweden', Mats Björkin addresses the expansion of consumerism in Swedish society at the end of the Second World War through an analysis of 'housewives' films', a novel format which combined marketing and information. Although advertisement driven, these films put emphasis on an efficient lifestyle and are representative of the household rationalisation scheme, encouraged by the political climate of the time which prompted women to work part-time while continuing to be the main homemaker. Björkin focuses on one particular instalment, titled *Tonårsmodet* [Teenage Fashion] and shedding new light on an understudied aspect of Swedish fashion and its textile industry. In Chapter 5, 'A maverick on the streets: Bill Cunningham and the documentary process', Karen Ritzenhoff considers the New York fashion photographer Bill Cunningham and his photographic work on the streets of the Big Apple. By comparing the two feature documentaries dedicated to the photographer – Richard Press's *Bill Cunningham New York* (2010) and Mark Bozek's documentary *The Times of Bill Cunningham* (2018) – Ritzenhoff examines Cunningham's self-proclaimed definition of 'fashion historian', rather than fashion photographer, in her analyses of the films' documentary process, including Cunningham's use of analogue technologies for documentation. Ritzenhoff ultimately connects Cunningham with Dziga Vertov's *cinéma vérité* and argues that one of Cunningham's most enduring legacies is the popularisation of street glamour, foregrounding the democratisation of street fashion blogging and social media. Chapter 6, 'expanding the exhibition narrative: making sense of non-fiction fashion footage', introduces the complex relationship between documentary and curatorship within the museum context. Boel Ulfsdotter argues that since the 1990s, museums and galleries have become increasingly important venues for fashion displays, and with them the inclusion of documentary media to enhance the museification of fashion. The documentary method and act of remediation involved in fashion exhibitions, however, remains uncharted in relation to traditional museology. Drawing on scholarship about evidence, authorship, representation and issues of interpretation, Ulfsdotter unpacks the discursive remits of documentary media as an aiding narrative exponent of the fashion exhibition. The first section also contains two interviews with practitioners involved in the documentation of fashion today: Lorna Tucker on her unauthorised fashion documentary on Vivienne Westwood, and senior museum curator Alexandra Palmer on the topic of the ongoing museification of fashion.

The second section of *Documenting Fashion* discusses the fashion documentary image in the context of television. In Chapter 7 Jihane Dyer considers the BBC's exploration of fashion histories in a series of TV documentaries broadcast between 1999 and 2014. These multi-part documentary series have selected, reanimated and repackaged fashion history into mass-mediated acts of cultural remembrance that resonate with the contemporary cultural landscape, transplanting memories across generations and geographies, projecting the past onto the present and vice versa. Dyer maintains that this genre possesses an ability to mediate a uniquely affective engagement with cultural memory due to fashion's unparalleled relationship to the body. By theorising the fashion history documentary as a specific technology of cultural remembrance, her approach to the study of fashion in non-fiction television builds upon a recent emergence of literature joining cultural memory studies with media scholarship and asks how the study of fashion and material culture might introduce new perspectives for documentary makers, scholars and other cultural memory projects. Chapter 8 is dedicated to a series of shorts for the television advertising programme *Carosello*, the first Italian TV show dedicated to the promotion of consumer goods, broadcast since 1957. In 'The Italian ready-to-wear fashion through Cori-carousels' Giulia Caffaro draws attention to the Gruppo Finanziario Tessile, a key player in the Italian ready-to-wear fashion industry, and its production of shorts between 1964 and 1973 promoting new female identities. These carousels demonstrate how companies constructed femininity using clothes and their modes of expression, but mainly through the representation of new role models, those created by new mass media celebrities. Caffaro articulates the reasons why the collaboration between the ready-to-wear fashion industry and the Italian media channel became so successful. Chapter 9, 'Fashioning self-care:

Queer Eye, affect and makeover culture', focuses on Tan France and Jonathan Van Ness, the fashion and grooming experts on the 2018 Netflix reboot show *Queer Eye* (2018). Elizabeth Affuso frames the logic of the new makeover show within the culture of self-care and its making of grooming and fashion transformations into a tool of caring for the self and the outward projecting of that same care. In this chapter, Affuso also reassesses the role of fashion and beauty experts within reality TV media and discusses how this positionality differs from the role of the expert within documentary media more broadly. This contribution evaluates the historic function of gay men as arbiters of taste within fashion culture and the larger implications of this for gender, sexuality and care work.

The final two chapters of *Documenting Fashion* consider the fashion documentary image in relation to digital cultures. In Chapter 10, Rebecca Halliday examines fashion show live streams, produced by mainstream brands, inviting consumers to purchase items online concurrently with the show. Analysing Tommy Hilfiger's collaborations with fashion celebrities Gigi Hadid (TommyxGigi) and Zendaya (TommyxZendaya), Halliday argues that, rather than relying on the more standard and close-cropped toe-to-head shots of individual models used to produce consumer desire, these fashion shows utilise panoramic and aerial shots to create a more spectacular user viewing experience, drawing attention to the mediatised event itself rather than the collection. In Chapter 11, Marco Pedroni explores the role of influencers through a comparative and critical analysis of two fashion documentaries: Chiara Ferragni's *Unposted* (2019) and Asri Bendacha's *Follow Me* (2017). Ferragni, a leading actor in the fashion and marketing industry, is presented along with Bendacha, a film-maker external to the fashion world. The aims of the documentaries might differ, with Ferragni's will of self-consecration as a pop icon, and Bendacha semi-ironically unveiling the commodification of digital personae, but both address the commercialisation of the self and the audiences; the monetisation of everyday practices displayed via social media; female empowerment; digital entrepreneurship; the democratisation of access to the fashion world; and the commodification of authenticity. These topics, Pedroni argues, become evidence of the power of digital influencers to shape, directly or indirectly, the evolution of the contemporary fashion imaginary.

In place of a proper Afterword we should like to add that *Documenting Fashion* is not meant to be the last word on the relationship between fashion and documentary, the ultimate and comprehensive catalogue of the connections between fashion and the documentary image. Quite the opposite. However, as this is the first book-length study, we have attempted to summarise and conflate present thoughts and methodologies about the mutually fruitful relationship from scholars engaged in a variety of disciplines, from film and media studies to communication, design, history and journalism. At the time of writing this introduction we are still living in a global pandemic brought about by the Covid-19 virus; since its onset in the first months of 2020, the limitations and challenges affecting fashion and media consumption and their industries have created both turmoil and change. We hope that the present edited collection will serve to bear witness to these synergies and elicit further reaction, responses and research in these areas.

References

Evans, Caroline. 2013. *The Mechanical Smile: Modernism and the First Fashion Shows in France and America, 1900–1929*. London and New Haven, CT: Yale University Press.

Evans, Caroline and Jussi Parikka. 2020. 'Introduction: Touch Click and Motion: Archaeologies of Fashion Film after Digital Culture'. *Journal of Visual Culture*, vol.19, no. 3, 323–39. DOI: 10.1177/1470412920966015.

Hui, Calvin. 2015. 'Dirty Fashion: Ma Ke's Fashion "Useless", Jia Zhangke's documentary *Useless* and Cognitive Mapping'. *Journal of Chinese Cinemas*, vol. 9, no. 3, 253–70. DOI: 10.1080/17508061.2015.1082746.

Joseph, Alex. 2015. 'Second Looks: Two Films about Fashion by Frederick Wiseman'. *Fashion Theory*, vol. 20, no. 1, 103–16, DOI: 10.1080/1362704X.2015.1078137.

Lundén, Elizabeth Castaldo. 2020. *Fashion on the Red Carpet: The Oscars and Globalisation*. Edinburgh: Edinburgh University Press.

Ouellette, Laurie. 2016. *Lifestyle TV*. New York: Routledge.

Palmer, Alexandra. 2008. 'Untouchable: Creating Desire and Knowledge in Museum Costume and Textile Exhibitions'. *Fashion Theory*, vol. 12, no. 1, 31–63. DOI: 10.2752/175174108X268136.

Rees-Roberts, Nick. 2018. *Fashion Film: Art and Advertising in the Digital Age*. London and New York: Bloomsbury.

Szymanski, Adam. 2012. 'Bill Cunningham New York and the Political Potentiality of the Fashion Documentary'. *Film, Fashion & Consumption*, vol. 1, no. 3, 289–304. DOI: 10.1386/ffc.1.3.289_1.

Witsell, Emily. 2016. '"One day you're in and the next day you're out": Making *Project Runaway* Work from Bravo to Lifetime'. In *The Lifetime Network: Essays on 'Television for Women' in the 21st Century*, edited by Emily L. Newman and Emily Witsell, 54–73. Jefferson, NC: McFarland.

Part I

Film

Chapter 1

Fashion documentaries and the tension between celebratory and critical approaches

Elena Caoduro

Documentaries are hitting a golden age: a boom of theatrical features, and a frenzy of factual television and video productions made available by streaming services and digital channels. For Bill Nichols (2015: xi), this distinct period in documentary film-making is due to the 'proliferation of new ways to make, structure, and distribute documentaries'. More specifically, Thomas Austin and Wilma de Jong (2008: 1) point out that these significant changes at the turn of the new millennium reshape the 'technological, commercial, political, and social dimensions of documentaries'. There is a big appetite for factual content, character-driven stories and experimental modes of narration, and fashion has ridden this wave, increasing its presence in the media and feeding the demand for factual fashion-focused content.

Over the past fifteen years, documentaries about fashion have flourished, to the extent that one could speak of a new subgenre. The fashion documentaries engage with a variety of subjects: designers (Valentino Garavani depicted in *Valentino: The Last Emperor* by Matt Tyrnauer, 2008; Guo Pei in *Yellow is Forbidden* by Pietra Brettkelly, 2018; Frida Giannini in *The Director: An Evolution in Three Acts* by Christina A. Voros, 2013); editors, stylists, photographers and other fashion industry professionals (Franca Sozzani in *Franca: Chaos and Creation* directed by her son, Francesco Carrozzini, 2016; André Leon Talley in *The Gospel According to André* by Kate Novack, 2017; *Helmut Newton: The Bad and the Beautiful* by Gero von Boehm, 2020); but also institutions and fashion-related events (*The First Monday in May* by Andrew Rossi, 2016; *Scatter My Ashes at Bergdorf's* by Matthew Miele, 2014). Concurrently, issues related to labour and the environmental and human impact of the fashion industry have come to the fore (*Girl Model* by Ashley Sabin and David Redmon, 2011; *Alex James: Slowing Down Fast Fashion* by Ben Akers, 2016), as well as representations of the relationship between fashion and identity and the body (*Suited* by Jason Benjamin, 2016 and *A Perfect 14* by Giovanna Morales Vargas, 2018), to cite just a few). This brief list is not a comprehensive categorisation of fashion-focused documentaries, it merely illustrates the extent of the phenomenon. These documentaries are very different from one another in terms of style, narrative content and scope, and yet they all seem determined to penetrate the mystery behind the fashion industry's secrets. In terms of distribution, this huge growth in conventional documentary films about fashion has allowed them to be made readily available through theatrical release, or directly via DVD or SVOD.

In this chapter, I investigate the reasons for the emergence of the fashion documentary as a subgenre in the first decades of the new millennium, outlining some tendencies within this heterogeneous group. As well as tracing the contextual factors that brought about the widespread availability of fashion-focused factual content, I argue that fashion documentaries display a tension between a celebratory mode, which hints at depicting a hagiographic portrayal of the fashion icon or institution, and a more critical approach to the documentary subject. These two tendencies may appear in the same documentary film and ought to be understood as a spectrum of dispositions, rather than a dichotomy of opposing forces. In fact, according to Adam Szymanski, 'the fashion documentary, because of its concern with production processes, carries an inherent political potentiality' (2012: 293). As discussed later in the chapter, even documentaries that glorify the careers of designers or other distinguished fashion figures can display critical glimpses that put the industry in a less flattering light. And conversely, those documentaries which act as exposés of the social and economic consequences of different sectors connected to the fashion industry feature celebratory moments of fashion-related activism, social movements and strategies of political change which aim at redressing unjust practices. By paying close attention to two films, *McQueen* (Ian Bonhôte and Peter Ettedgui, 2018) and *The True Cost* (Andrew Morgan, 2015), as exemplary case studies of the spectrum, I present an analysis of the fashion documentary's contradictory effort of museification and demythologisation, and how it relates to traditional documentary discourse. In other words, I argue that the fashion documentary attempts to crystallise and honour fashion heritage, while at the same time it lifts the veil on submerged stories, less well known processes and uncomfortable truths.

Defining the fashion documentary

Fashion documentaries seem to escape any neat classification as a genre. The differences among them are not solely related to the type of subject under scrutiny but pertain also to the applied medium: fashion documentaries vary from feature films released in cinemas to television documentaries and other online streaming formats, including webseries. Scholars seem to agree on the main characteristics of this heterogeneous group of factual storytelling modes: fashion is not simply the common turf, it is the 'making of' fashion that binds them together. In his analysis of *Bill Cunningham New York* (Richard Press, 2010), Szymanski explains that the choice of focusing on the production of fashion is itself illustrative of the aura that the industry possesses (2012: 293). Similarly, Nick Rees-Roberts (2018: 84) adds that it is the 'staging of labor', the witnessing of the process from sketch to finished garments or collections, which links these films. The other shared characteristics of the fashion documentary, and to some extent of other non-fictional recounting of fashion, including factual entertainment, is the interest in events that take place behind the scenes. The fashion documentary, regardless of its focus on celebratory or critical approaches, unveils the dynamics and processes of 'making fashion' that are part of the know-how of fashion professionals but are considered generally unknown to the general public. For example, *Dior and I* (Frédéric Tcheng, 2014) traces the first eight weeks after the arrival in Paris of Raf Simons as artistic director of Dior. With help from his assistant Pieter Muller, Simons has limited time to create his first collection with the aim of honouring the sartorial heritage of the French brand and at the same time renewing it. The tribulations – from accessing the archive, designing, selecting materials and eventually putting together a show – are captured. The doors of this iconic French institution open to reveal the stress of the process, and equally the discomfort of Simons with the public relations aspects of his job.

As discussed in the introduction, it would be more correct to talk about a re-emergence of the fashion documentary if one considers its genealogy and relationship with fashion actualities, newsreels and industrial films. It is interesting to note that in France the chronology of the development of cinema and fashion shows is almost simultaneous, with the Lumière brothers showing their films to paying crowds in 1895, and the first fashion shows being organised in Paris at the end of the century. Caroline Evans (2011) draws attention to this relationship and considers the French-filmed fashion shows, 'the walkies', as a cinema of attractions, displaying a fascination both for human movement and female display, but more importantly a conflation of fact and fiction. In her analysis, Evans traces the development of fashion shows and newsreels from the 1910s to the 1930s as a promotional material genre which remained relatively static despite the rapid technological and stylistic development of those decades in cinema. This early attraction tradition is perhaps still present in present-day documentaries, preserved in the moments of suspension of narrative, when the pleasure of the fashion show or garments takes centre stage through the close-ups and parades of fashionable creations. The long history of the entanglement between fashion and factual storytelling has produced a variety of examples, which some of this collection's contributions cover, demonstrating the evolution of this 'static genre'. There are of course illustrious examples of fashion documentary features in the twentieth century, such as *Notebook on Cities and Clothes* (Wim Wenders, 1989), a documentary about Japanese designer Yuhji Yamamoto, and *Made in Milan* (Martin Scorsese, 1990), about Giorgio Armani, among others. However, it is really at the end of the first decade of the new millennium, probably with *Valentino: The Last Emperor*, which had its premiere at the Venice Film Festival in 2008, that a new and fruitful season of fashion documentaries emerged.

The reasons for this renewed interest are multiple. It is important to recognise that the re-emergence of the fashion documentary coincided with the popular breakthrough of the digital fashion film.[1] This was due to the accessibility and availability of new technologies, cheaper digital cameras, faster Internet connections and the proliferation of social media and other platforms for sharing audio-visual material. Moreover, the documentary genre boom has certainly played a role in the fashion-interested audience's desire for more factual content, especially in light of their 'increased fashion literacy' (Rees-Roberts 2018: 78). It was this widespread popularity and knowledge of fashion that initially fed the increased availability of fashion documentaries. It is sufficient to think of the vast popularity of fashion exhibitions in museums around the world. Stella Bruzzi and Pamela Church Gibson (2013: 6) noted that 'the "blockbuster" fashion exhibition has become one of the most interesting phenomena of the past ten years', with *Alexander McQueen: Savage Beauty* creating long queues around the Metropolitan Museum of Art in New York. Furthermore, reality television has helped push 'fashion' into more homes. In the early 2000s, makeover shows such as *What Not to Wear* (BBC, 2001–7) and reality competition shows such as *The Great British Sewing Bee* (BBC, 2013–present) cemented the interest in fashion and personal appearance, foreshadowing the rise of the fashion documentary.

According to Bronwyn Cosgrave, a journalist and producer of the documentary *Manolo: The Boy Who Made Shoes for Lizards* (Michael Roberts, 2017), the popularity of feature-length fashion documentaries can be attributed partly to the near-demise of long-form journalism, and to fashion's global march (Socha and Theodosi: 2019). First bloggers and then vloggers and influencers have made the creative process and the scenes backstage at shows and on the runway (apparently) more accessible to the general public, thus becoming the new gatekeepers of fashion trends, replacing traditional fashion journalists as the arbiters of what is in vogue. The short videos or social media posts by these professionals create a hunger and a curiosity to explore the larger picture, to understand the history and heritage of particular designers or fashion houses and institutions, thus generating a growing audience for factual fashion content.

A celebratory approach to fashion documentaries

With the fashion documentary becoming more commonplace in the past decade, scholars have started paying attention to the functions and agency behind these productions, and examining how to evaluate the fact that even if they are not presented as straightforward PR (public relations) vehicles they more often than not possess a promotional component. Rees-Roberts notes that 'the 2010s signal the rise of the made-to-measure "infomercial" film, whose raison d'être is simply to promote institutions, labels, or designers' (2018: 79). Similarly, for Myles Ethan Lascity, these documentaries appear 'to straddle the line between objective storytelling and public relations messaging' (2021: 141). This celebratory approach, which is present particularly in fashion documentaries with a biographical focus, require a taxonomy based on a scale with different degrees. There are of course cases of commissioned films which function more as vanity projects.[2] *Scatter my Ashes at Bergdorf's* is a key example of a combined presentation of advertisement and non-fiction with its history of this revered New York department store. The documentary parades a long list of celebrities, personalities and artists who shopped, worked for or are fond of the institution and thus ultimately provide video endorsements and positive reviews of their experiences at the Bergdorf Goodman store. This documentary, which can be better compared to a long-form advertisement, presents minimal elements of criticality, beside casting some doubts on the future of shopping experiences, urban planning in New York City and the role of shopping departments in the twenty-first-century modern city.

Nonetheless, a degree of criticality or a critical potential is inherent in the genre and the celebratory approach does not have to be understood necessarily as a pejorative characteristic; in fact, these are only rarely fan-serviced films. Fashion documentaries which tend to privilege a celebratory approach present a narrative with low risks of offending or creating outrage, since they are often offered a guarded and artificial access to the subject's private and public persona. Beyond the rare cases of commissioned films, these documentaries succeed by having access to archival material and nurturing mutually beneficial relationships with the brand, their workers or former employees, thus favouring a hagiographic, even mythological, portrayal of the designer, photographer or editor. For example, Carrozzini's *Franca: Chaos and Creation* was released a short time after the death of the renowned editor-in-chief of *Vogue Italia*, Franca Sozzani, and the documentary comes across as an affectionate eulogy directed by Sozzani's son, where he collated the personal and professional successes of his mother. These complacent documentaries are comparable to the approach of other biographical genres, such as some contemporary music documentaries. With the director rarely intervening, no in-depth explanation or questioning, these ad hoc *cinéma verité*/direct cinema style documentaries play it safe by airbrushing out any criticality. In their introduction to *The Music Documentary: Acid Rock to Electropop*, Robert Edgar, Kirsty Fairclough-Isaacs and Benjamin Halligan (2013: 19) argue that:

> Such a biographical focus offers an individualized mode of expression that supposedly allows the real celebrity an authentically mediated, self-articulated voice that rests precariously on the commercial and promotional activity of their brand. This trend has emerged in the firmament of an intensified celebrity culture in which, for better or for worse, the music documentary has taken its place.

As with the music documentary genre, the level of access granted by the subject of the documentary and their entourage, along with the positionality of the director, play a crucial role in the degree of appraisal of the film. The question of its outright documentary value, however, remains to be discussed and accessed, and applies to similar types of fashion documentaries as well.

The list of documentaries focusing on fashion designers continues to expand. This is because designers are becoming as publicly familiar as the clothes they design. As Pamela Church Gibson (2012: 196) does not fail to notice, designers are now a recognisable brand and 'may share the desire to be perceived as artists'. The fashion documentary thus contributes to the process of mythologisation which is inherent to the designer's art, recounting narratives of origin, 'rags to riches' or 'falling from grace' storylines. Although not dealing with a designer, *Diana Vreeland: The Eye Has to Travel* (Lisa Immondino-Vreeland, Bent-Jorgen Perlmutt and Frédéric Tcheng, 2011) offers a stylish portrayal of a larger-than life character, Diana Vreeland, legendary fashion editor at *Harper's Bazaar* and later *Vogue*. The documentary celebrates her long career in the publishing industry, dictating the trends of the period, and treats her life as a visual spectacle in a similar way to other documentaries featuring fashion designers.[3] The 'mythologisation' effect that Church Gibson is referring to may thus be interpreted in two ways: through their celebratory approach, fashion documentaries contribute to the spectacularisation of a certain fashion label and, at the same time, implicate its museification. For art and cultural management experts Federica Antonaglia and Juliette Passebois-Ducrois, these processes 'highlight the efforts made by the brand to emphasise the creative talent and charisma of its art directors' (2020: 130). By celebrating the heritage of the institution or the fashion house, the fashion documentary works towards the museification of its brand – in other words, towards the creation of a canon, a tangible heritage beyond their own archives, to be preserved for posterity and made available to the general public. The fashion documentary helps the fashion 'brand' to acquire cultural value and artistic dignity, whether this is a designer, a fashion house, establishment or institution. If fashion aspires to be considered as 'high art', being the subject of a documentary is ultimately an opportunity to polish its image, and its association with film can hopefully remove any stigma of frivolity and excess.

McQueen: celebrating a fashion genius

Recounting the life of an exceptional figure in the fashion industry has its advantages: the creations, personal experiences and ideas of these personalities are already out of the ordinary, making it easy for a director to engage with them. On the other hand, a documentarist could waver at the superlative nature of these works of art for fear of producing a tarnished or overly celebratory film. Ian Bonhôte and Peter Ettedgui's *McQueen* masters the original material well, doing justice to the art of the late fashion designer Lee Alexander McQueen. The documentary is a compendium of the personal and artistic journey of one of the greatest fashion creatives, able to unify sartorial talent with a rebel vision and smart managerial choices in creating the successful brand Alexander McQueen. The film traces McQueen's life from his debut in the fashion world to his premature death, dividing the principal passages of his life into five chapters, each named after one of his collections. Traditional elements of factual storytelling – interviews with relatives, friends and collaborators – are mixed with archival footage, broadcast material as well as home videos. *McQueen* is elegantly edited and explores different narratives, not only that of the designer's career and fame within the fashion world, but also his family trauma: McQueen's childhood sexual abuse by his sister Janet's husband, and his struggles with anxiety and depression. As a posthumously produced documentary with a respectful approach, the film does not gloss over the dark moments in the designer's complicated life.

Bonhôte and Ettedgui appropriate the skull, an iconic symbol of the McQueen brand, as an elegant but engrossing image, and shift its appearance from chapter to chapter in computer-animated transitions. Marking both McQueen's developing aesthetics and his deteriorating mental health, the skull fluctuates against a black background decorated with different patterns and motifs featured in the five representative collections narrated in the documentary: 'Jack the Ripper Stalks His Victims', 'Highland Rape', 'Search for the Golden Fleece' (his first collection for Givenchy), 'Voss' and 'Plato's Atlantis'. Displayed on a pedestal with the camera panning around it, the skulls hint at the process of 'artification' and museification of luxury fashion as this iconic symbol both preserves the fashion brand and reinforces its timeless impression. The gloomy interstitial skull sequences, therefore, celebrate the art of Alexander McQueen and crystallise it for posterity as an achievement designated for and worthy of museum exhibition. The high quality of these animated transitions clashes with the low quality of the VHS home videos – authentic testimonies of McQueen's private life – which also appear in the film. The signs of film degradation are not erased in post-production and are left so as to fulfil two functions. First, the maintenance of the indexicality of the analogue tape produces an effect of authenticity, allowing the viewer to participate in an intimate viewing of a family film. Second, conflating the highly aestheticised images of the skulls with the grainy texture of home videos and the behind-the-scenes camcorder footage by co-workers reproduces faithfully the aesthetics of McQueen's fashion, with both low- and highbrow references, and his own biography, taking him from a working-class background to the head of a luxury fashion company (Figure 1.1).

Fashion documentaries – tension between approaches

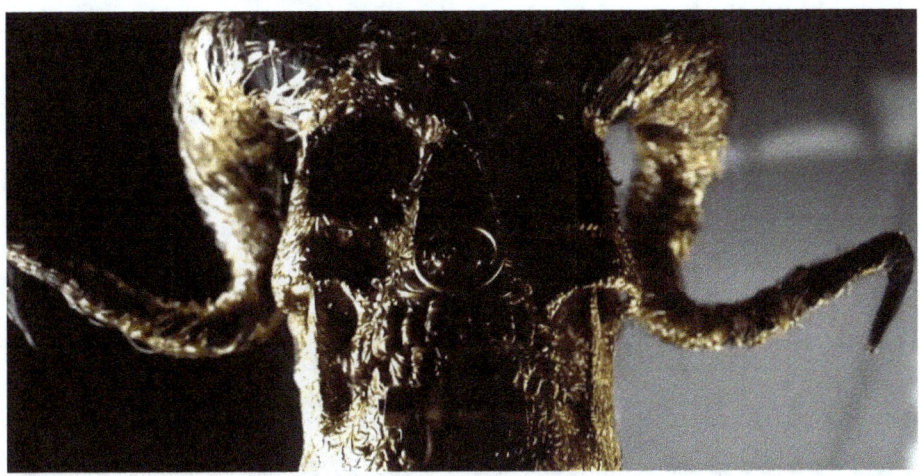

Figure 1.1 This screenshot is captured from a transition between chapters in *McQueen* (Ian Bonhôte and Peter Ettedgui, 2018). The skull harks back to pagan mythology, the gothic motifs so dear to the designer, but also his struggles with past traumas and mental health issues

Music composed by Michael Nyman punctuates *McQueen*, including an original track called 'Lee's Sarabande', which was commissioned by the designer himself in 2006 and is meant to express the sentiments of joy and melancholy with musical notes. It is precisely this track which becomes the central theme of the film, along with themes from *The Piano* (Jane Campion, 1993) an extract from Nyman's 1986 opera *The Man Who Mistook His Wife for A Hat*, and other tunes with medieval instruments and electronic experiments. According to composer and broadcaster Robert Worby, 'Nyman is a collector, an assembler of clutter, a guardian of the forgotten ... His references are gathered from sources well outside the dominant culture; fuelled by an insatiable curiosity he deliberately seeks out the arcane, the overlooked and the abandoned' (2017: xi). Similarly, McQueen operates by interweaving highbrow and folk/popular references, with critics hailing or disparaging this clash of styles (Figure 1.2).

The most emotional segments in the one hour and fifty-one minutes of the documentary are the interviews and archival footage with those closest to the designer: his mother Joyce, sister Janet and his mentor and friend the fashion editor Isabella Blow, whose suicide, as well as the gruelling work involved in keeping his fashion empire running, aggravated his ongoing anxiety and depression. Still photographs offered by family members and amateur videos capturing holidays and moments of personal life emphasise

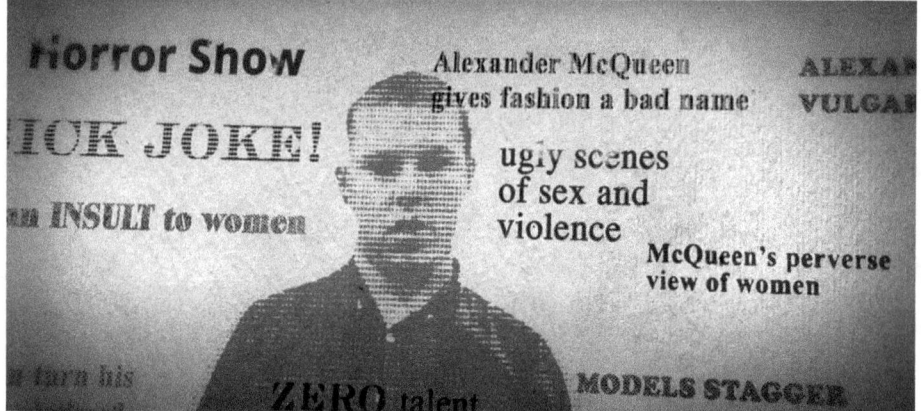

Figure 1.2 *McQueen* (Ian Bonhôte and Peter Ettedgui, 2018) utilises computer animation to create a collage of negative reviews of McQueen's shows and accusations of misogyny

the 'normality' of Lee Alexander McQueen, hence bringing his figure closer to the experiences of the general audiences, who are foreign to the fashion world. The 'talking head' fragments, tightly framed to further stress the moment of recollecting fond and painful memories, lay bare the affection but also the grief felt for Lee Alexander McQueen. They are also a reminder that when the documentary is about someone who has died, the narrative is often determined by the people who lived alongside the subject. The film reflects their story. Strangely, there are some noticeable absences: the designer's long-term partner, the film-maker George Forsyth, and Sarah Burton, first collaborator and now in charge of the Alexander McQueen brand. This last blank space is, however, intentional, because the directors did not want to make a film about the company and its fashion image, but about the man behind the brand. Ettedgui said, 'Had there been a very open channel or communication or co-operation between the brand and us, I think we would've probably wound up making a brand film, which was not what we wanted to make' (Turner 2018). Similarly, there are no interviews with celebrities and models, fans of McQueen's creations, because the aim was to capture personal recollections of the man, small anecdotes, and first-hand stories from those who were close to the subject, only friends, family and colleagues. This highly personal stylistic decision by Bonhôte and Ettedgui underlines once again the scope of the fashion documentary to open a window onto an undisclosed system and reveal its workings behind the scenes, even as far as the private sphere is concerned, of figures from the world of fashion. At the same time, by following a chronological order and dividing the film (and McQueen's life) into chapters named after some of his most notorious collections, the documentary not only celebrates the designer but, most importantly, crystallises his works in a museification effort to bring his designs closer to the public in a new exhibition space: cinema and home screens.

A critical approach to fashion documentaries

Halfway through *The Devil Wears Prada* (David Frankel, 2006), Miranda Priestly (Meryl Streep), the editor-in-chief of the fictional fashion magazine *Runway*, launches into a long irate monologue, illustrating the importance of all segments of the fashion industry chain. When her junior personal assistant Andrea Sachs, Andy (Anne Hathaway), dismisses and seems to ridicule the mentioned fashion items by calling them 'stuff', Priestly claims:

> That blue represents millions of dollars and countless jobs and it's sort of comical how you think that you've made a choice that exempts you from the fashion industry when, in fact, you're wearing the sweater that was selected for you by the very people in this room from a pile of 'stuff'.

Priestly's reaction to her assistant's indecision between two belts further valorises the complexity of designing, manufacturing and marketing garments. It also, to an extent, highlights the value of fashion industry workers whose work might be perceived as vain and frivolous, but actually produces meaning and economic turnaround. What this fictional film, but also other fashion documentaries, especially those with a celebratory approach, dismisses is an explicit discussion of industrial processes.

The 'making of fashion' is a crucial theme in fashion documentaries, since the very act of shadowing designers, editors and stylists in their day-to-day activities reveals the mysteries of the world of fashion and lifts its aura of representing an elitist and unknown sector. According to Adam Szymanski (2012: 293–4), the fashion documentary 'offers its viewers an opportunity to see how materials are assembled in such a way that through the abstract nature of creativity they become culturally defined as "fashion"'. When one considers fashion documentaries about designers, the role of craftmanship behind haute couture creations is only briefly acknowledged. Artisans become the unsung heroes of luxury fashion as they maintain centuries-old traditions and make tangible the process of manufacturing. In *The Last Emperor*, the highly skilled seamstresses in Valentino's atelier showcase their skill at draping and constructing a couture gown completely by hand. One of them is observed as she stretches against a wall, exhausted. In *Dior and I*, instead, the *petites mains* (literally 'little hands') seem initially confused when introduced to head designer Raf Simons, who comes from an industrial design background and knows neither how to cut nor how to sew fabric by hand. Exhaustion, overwork and mental health issues emerge as moments of narrative tension in these documentaries, and yet they are not explored at their fullest, remaining moments of critical potential. Where is the silk produced? How do cotton farms operate? It is Pietra Brettkelly who offers a more critical glimpse into fashion labour and its ethical dilemmas in her documentary *Yellow is Forbidden*. In a scene taking place at a hand embroidery manufactory, Chinese couturier Guo Pei meets with the manager of the shop and inspects the material. An argument erupts about the price charged for elaborate embroidery and the time and quantity of material needed. The designer succeeds in negotiating a better price for the job, but the camera lingers for a moment on the face of the manager as she frowns, thinking of the risks of overwork for her embroiderers and the possibility of completing this commission at a loss.

These examples underline the power relations between the various contributors involved in 'making fashion' and show that the critical approach can emerge even in documentaries which are predominantly celebratory of the designer's artistry. Irony and tongue-in-cheek dialogues are certainly common strategies to undercut the hagiographic mode present in many documentaries celebrating the life and career of various fashion figures. The critical approach, however, is more prominent when the documentary functions as a window onto the exploitation of labour, specifically in manufacturing, and shows how human rights related to the garment industry are connected with environmental justice. The question of how the fashion industry contributes to environmental disasters, including water and air toxicity, and how social identities, such as gender, race and class, play a role in fashion/industrial labour have been addressed by a growing number of documentaries. Since the beginning of the new millennium, films such as *T-Shirt Travels* (Shanta Bloeman, 2001), *China Blue* (Micha X. Peled, 2005), *The Last Train Home* (Lixin Fan, 2009) and *Cotton Road* (Laura Kissel, 2013) have attempted to shed light on the human and environmental costs of fashion. Interestingly, these films cast shadows on the supply chain of raw material and finished garments for high street fashion brands, especially fast fashion brands. A higher degree of criticality seems therefore more prominent when the attack is against fashion intended as a commodity, emptied of any artistic allure.[4] *China Blue*, for example, discusses the world of blue jeans factories, where teenagers struggle to survive the harsh working environment in order to meet the target agreed with western retail companies. Here the blue jean simply represents the final product of industrial labour, obtained through unfair working conditions, and is not treated as an iconic garment, fruit of technological innovation in terms of cutting, dying or designing.

In their monograph *Film and Everyday Eco-Disasters*, Robin L. Murray and Joseph K. Heumann (2014: 46–66) define these documentaries as 'clothing industry films', documentaries which illustrate social, economic and environmental injustices linked to the growing fast fashion industry. These titles are factual exposés; employing traditional documentary style with voice-over narration, they seem to respond to a more conscious consumer culture eager to understand the long journey of a fashion garment, from raw material to finished items on a shop's shelf. Whereas documentaries with a predominantly celebratory approach focus on the jet-setting lifestyle of many fashion figures (from purchasing textiles around the globe, to fashion weeks' catwalks and exotic holidays), these latter works display a strong interconnectedness among countries concerned with couture fashion, in contrast to others revealing the harsh experiences of exploitation of (fashion) factory workers. By exposing exploitative production practices, especially in the fast fashion industry, and the common efforts to pursue global environmental justice, these documentaries embrace transnationalism to enable the audience to 'see their global connectedness' (Chu 2010: 129). These film-makers recognise geographical specificities, but at the same time they are keen to represent commonalities in order to foster a sense of global interconnection, especially among the underprivileged. In short, the critical approach within fashion documentaries, although present on some occasions in more hagiographic and celebratory films, is concerned primarily with high street fashion, rather than couture. Of course, the discussion about raw material and the environmental impact affects all sectors of the fashion world, but from this corpus of films the major culprits appear to be those companies producing cheap clothing that replicates catwalk trends.

The True Cost: documenting the ugly truth of fashion

Among the growing number of titles criticising the exploitation, inequalities and environmental damage of the fast fashion industry, Andrew Morgan's 2015 documentary *The True Cost* has emerged as a powerful exploration of the economic, social and environmental cost of the fashion industry, an industry that is worth trillions of dollars but is also the third most polluting industry after agriculture and fuel. The documentary investigates the impact that the global fast fashion industry has on consumers and communities around the globe, but also on the workers involved. Covering a vast array of locations – fashion headquarters in London, runways in Japan, cotton farms in Texas, street protests in Cambodia, factories in Bangladesh and the Copenhagen Fashion summit, the leading business event on sustainability in fashion – the documentary exposes human suffering and environmental damage, things that are usually not reflected in fast fashion garments' price tags. Morgan, a fashion outsider, begins his exploration with just a few questions and embarks on a journey through each segment of the garment supply chain, from design to cotton farming. The opening scene is illustrative of the film's argument: through parallel editing, the viewer is exposed to two contrasting environments. Images from high street shops with consumers browsing through baskets and shelves packed with new collections of clothes are intercut with images of unsafe working conditions in garment factories and waste material in landfill sites (Figure 1.3). *The True Cost* has a central thesis: that the fashion industry and in particular the fast fashion brands characterising the high streets of many countries have become unsustainably dangerous to the planet and its inhabitants.

Figure 1.3 This still image from *The True Cost* (Andrew Morgan, 2015) depicts the inhumane working conditions in Bangladeshi factories producing garments for western high street fashion brands

The documentary's underpinning thesis is supported by interviews with different experts and research data from non-governmental agencies. It is suggested that because of middle-class wage stagnation, consumers are delighted to purchase an array of cheap clothes manufactured in low-wage countries with a poor record of working conditions, workers' rights and environmental protection. At the same time, manufacturers face the challenges of delivering complete products quickly at lower and lower prices. *The True Cost* makes explicit the economic implications of this tightening dilemma. With images from the 2013 Dhaka garment factory collapse in Bangladesh, where more than one thousand workers died when an eight-floor commercial building called Rana Plaza collapsed, Morgan explains that workers find themselves between a rock and a hard place as they face difficult working conditions, their wages get squeezed and their activism or union protests are suppressed by local governments in order to befriend foreign investors. Neoliberal economist Benjamin Powell intervenes in the debate, arguing that sweatshops represent a positive asset for low-income countries because they provide monetary influx and much-needed foreign earnings, contributing to the economic development of the country. Although this position appears quite reasonable, Morgan does not challenge it, nor does he question Powell's statements by casting doubt on the distorted effects of foreign investments or the dubious ethics of profiting from desperate manufacturers seeking contracts with foreign companies. Counterarguments to the documentary's thesis are not presented, and in this case evidence is not properly articulated, evaluated or addressed. In her review of the documentary, anthropologist Rebecca Prentice remarks that Morgan's film fails to grasp the incoherence at the heart of neoliberal capitalism: 'that market-based problems are only ever answered with market-based solutions. Unless we figure out a better way to regulate global labour standards, the true cost of the garment industry will continue to be borne by workers and their communities' (2016: 61). As a result, viewers are left with a shallow analysis of the economic impact of manufacturing fast fashion garments in developing countries. Moreover, the documentary proceeds at a fast pace without reflecting on a specific region or area. In its attempt to encompass a variety of points of view, the film lacks the depth of similar documentaries examining economic policies, such as Stephanie Black's *Life and Debt* (2001), about the impact of the International Monetary Fund and the World Bank's imposed restructure of Jamaica's system, or Zara Hayes's *Clothes to Die For* (2014), which solely focuses on the collapse of the Rana Plaza industrial complex.

The important contribution of Morgan's work stems from its attempt to connect the human and social costs with the environmental impact of the fashion industry. The documentary provides glimpses into the costs of intense cotton farming, the use of pesticides and the water and air pollution caused by the leather and textile industries, while, at the same time, it does not forget the issue of textile waste and the general environmental hazard generated by its disposal. This section of the film, however, veers towards the conspiratorial, as the narrator reminds the viewer about corporations endangering communities and their environment by putting profit above all else. The argumentation of *The True Cost* appears fallacious at certain points, despite the clear central argument, because there is a lack of sufficient evidence; nor is the narrator's attitude fully accounted for. Morgan is not presenting a personal journey of change in his consumption, like, for instance, Alex James, musician turned cheesemaker and wool producer, as he demonstrates in his documentary *Alex James: Slowing Down Fast Fashion*. Nor does Morgan provide a judicious and objective voice-over narration. The documentary is therefore moved by a strong ethos but fails to provide solutions. Counter-examples are mentioned but become overwhelmed by the destructive way in which the fashion industry operates. Safia Minney, founder and CEO of the fair-trade fashion brand People Tree, is a rare figure trying to change the system. She explains how her company avoids being caught up in fast fashion's traps. It is interesting to note how even this type of documentary, with its predominantly critical approach to the fashion industry, is underpinned by moments of celebratory portrayal. In this case the work of activist-consultant Livia Giuggioli, an executive producer of the documentary, along with the *Guardian* journalist Lucy Siegel, is showcased with great emphasis. In his review for the *Los Angeles Times*, Martin Tsai (2015) claims that interviewing the executive producer is a faux pas which undermines the documentary's credibility. Her intervention certainly stands out from other 'talking heads' moments; it is visually celebrated because it is intercut with scenes of disasters, environmental and human. Morgan depicts a grim portrait of working conditions around the globe, devastated landscapes and destroyed families, whereas the interviews with sustainability experts, such as Giuggioli, are serene and well lit. The solutions proposed by Giuggioli, but also by an organic cotton farmer from Texas– a more conscious and ethical approach to consumer behaviours – are the only positive moments in an overall depressing picture.[5] *The True Cost* oversimplifies globalisation processes, stating well-known truths about pollution and inhumane working conditions, and counteracts defeatism by glorifying the activism of Giuggioli and other personalities, including animal-rights advocate and fashion designer Stella McCartney. Their contributions offer some hope for the future, but, by having their interviews contrasted with images of clashes in Cambodia or news footage of the collapsed Rana Plaza factory, their interventions pale in comparison.

Conclusion

Being a visual medium with strong links to contemporary society and issues, fashion is an excellent object of study for documentary investigations. In this chapter I have explored the characteristics of this heterogeneous corpus of films, which emerged as a significant phenomenon at the beginning of the new millennium. Technological changes, a hunger for factual content and a more widespread fashion literacy have produced this boom, which does not show any sign of stopping. The proposed distinction between 'celebratory' and 'critical' does not aim to demarcate a clear categorisation of the genre, but rather it outlines some tendencies which have been taking shape over the past two decades. These approaches ought to be interpreted as coexisting modes with mutual influences. *McQueen* and *The True Cost* exemplify this wide spectrum of fashion documentaries, films which display both approaches to different degrees, but also a tension between the celebratory and critical modes. This tension could also be interpreted as an opposition between individuality and collectivity. While the celebratory approach tends to focus on a specific subjectivity, a person or institution, reflecting an interest in capturing on screen the individuality or the romantic celebration of fashion heroes, the critical approach draws attention to the collective nature, the industrial power of the fashion system.

Future developments of the fashion documentary seem hard to predict. However, it is worth noticing how the celebratory approach is moving beyond the celebration of leading figures in the sector; it is displaying a material turn, shifting to a celebration of iconic garments. I am thinking of documentaries such as *One Man and His Shoes* (Yemi Bamiro, 2020), tracing the history of the Air Jordan sneaker and its followers, or the TV mini-series *Worn Stories* (Netflix, 2021), which recounts the personal stories behind specific everyday garments. These examples display a departure from the more traditional celebratory narrative, where crucial events (the launch of a new collection, a museum retrospective, a new magazine cover) are intertwined with the biography or personal life of an artist, or a professional fashion figure. These more recent examples of fashion documentaries honour the materiality of the garments and the social and cultural significance of clothes. The celebratory or hagiographic documentary remains a favourite approach as it discusses fashion, often haute couture, in order to elevate the cultural capital of a brand in a museification effort, crystallising its history for posterity. These latter examples continue, in part, the tradition, removing the focus on the personal development of a designer, photographer or stylist, and yet they visualise the stories behind clothes and accessories, recognising in them a valuable status.

The emergence of a large group of films investigating the social, environmental and economic consequences of the fashion industry signals the necessity for some reflection, through non-fiction practice, about the ways in which the fashion industry operates. *The True Cost* takes away any artistic aura from the industry, contextualising fashion among other damaging enterprises of late capitalism. The critical approach to fashion documentaries works as a force that demythogisises the fashion industry, showcasing the real impact of unhealthy working environments and removing the excitement and appeal of the finished product. In doing so, I would argue, this exemplary film sets the tone (or the road) for a potential new investigation dedicated to the hidden stories of fashion. If fast fashion companies or unsustainable agricultural practices connected to fashion appear to be the focal point of these recent types of cinematic exposés, what happens in the milieu of high fashion, so celebrated in other documentaries, warrants closer and more critical attention. The issues of diversity, the physical and mental health of the different actors involved (from models to fashion professionals), 'greenwashing' campaigns and the reality of producing ready-to-wear lines could potentially become the terrain to explore in a new generation of fashion documentaries. If the celebratory mode has produced an exemplary list of white, often male, western figures to be canonised on the fashion Olympus, the future of fashion documentaries calls for new critical voices and new unheard voices to be admired.

Notes

1. It is beyond the scope of this chapter to discuss the definition of this spurious notion. Here I am referring to the popularity of the online short film about fashion, an interstitial medium in between advertisement and art which promotes the launch of new collections. For further discussions about digital fashion films, see Needham (2013), Uhlirova (2013) and Caoduro (2017).

2. There are different degrees of involvement in the projects. They range from the case of *Made in Milan*, the short documentary about Giorgio Armani shot by Martin Scorsese in 1989, which has as producer the ready-to-wear brand Emporio Armani. *The September Issue* (R. J. Cutler, 2009) chronicles the development of the autumn issue of *Vogue US* and is an interesting case, being commissioned by Condé Nast Entertainment, a production studio and distributor of film and television, but also a division of the global mass media company behind the fashion magazine *Vogue* and its global editorial director, Anna Wintour, the subject at the very centre of the documentary.
3. Even this celebratory documentary contains an element of criticality, though not fully explored. For example, when Vreeland's son says, 'I grew up wishing I had any mother but this mother', the documentary misses an opportunity to engage further about personal aspects of her biography, including her harsh remarks towards her daughter for her unconventional beauty.
4. It is worth mentioning a film such as *Gomorrah* (Matteo Garrone, 2008), which is not strictly a documentary but is based on the non-fiction book by investigative journalist Roberto Saviano: for once, a critical gaze is cast on 'Made in Italy' fashion. Through the storyline feature of the tailor, Franco (Toni Servillo), the film illuminates the complex relationship between Italian couture fashion, factories using illegal workers and organised criminality.
5. Giuggioli explains the failures of fast fashion brands to minimise their impact on the environment. More specifically, the documentary refers to an episode when the Italian-British activist challenged the sustainability director of H&M regarding their unresolved issue of giving fair living wages to the manufacturers of their garments abroad.

References

Antonaglia, Federica and Juliette Passebois Ducros. 2020. 'Christian Dior: The Art of Haute Couture'. In *The Artification of Luxury Fashion Brands: Synergies, Contaminations and Hybridizations*, edited by Marta Massi and Alex Turrini, 113–39. London and New York: Routledge.

Austin, Thomas and Wilma de Jong. 2008. 'Introduction: Rethinking Documentary'. In *Rethinking Documentary*, edited by Thomas Austin and Wilma de Jong, 1–10. Maidenhead: McGraw-Hill Open University Press.

Bruzzi, Stella and Pamela Church Gibson. 2013. 'Introduction: The Changing Fashion Landscape in the New Millennium'. In *Fashion Cultures Revisited: Theories, Explorations and Analysis*, 2nd edn, edited by Stella Bruzzi and Pamela Church Gibson, 1–8. Abingdon and New York: Routledge.

Caoduro, Elena. 2017. '"Women's Tales": Postfeminist Adventures into Consumerville'. *Comunicazioni Sociali: Journal of Media, Performing Arts and Cultural Studies*, no. 1, 37–42.

Chu, Kiu-Wai. 2010. 'From *My Fancy High Heels* to *Useless* clothing: "Interconnectedness" and Eco-critical Issues in Transnational Documentaries'. *International Studies in Communication & Culture*, vol. 2, no. 2, 127–44.

Edgar, Robert, Kirsty Fairclough-Isaacs and Benjamin Halligan. 2013. 'Introduction: Music Seen: The Formats and Functions of the Music Documentary'. In *The Music Documentary:*

Acid Rock to Electropop, edited by Robert Edgar, Kirsty Fairclough-Isaacs and Benjamin Halligan, 1–21. New York and London: Routledge.

Evans, Caroline. 2011. 'The Walkies: Early Fashion Shows as a Cinema of Attractions'. In *Fashion in Film*, edited by Adrienne Munich, 110–33. Bloomington: Indiana University Press.

Gibson, Pamela Church. 2012. *Fashion Celebrity Culture*. London: Bloomsbury.

Lascity, Myles Ethan. 2021. *Communicating Fashion: Clothing, Culture, and Media*. London and New York: Bloomsbury.

Murray, Robin L. and Joseph K. Heumann. 2014. *Film and Everyday Eco-Disasters*. Lincoln: University of Nebraska Press.

Needham, Gary. 2013. 'The Digital Fashion Film'. In *Fashion Cultures Revisited: Theories, Explorations and Analysis*, 2nd edn, edited by Stella Bruzzi and Pamela Church Gibson, 103–11. Abingdon and New York: Routledge.

Nichols, Bill. 2015. 'Foreword'. In *Contemporary Documentary*, edited by Daniel Marcus and Selmin Kara, xi–xvii. London and New York: Routledge.

Prentice, Rebecca. 2016. 'Review of Andrew Morgan (2015) *The True Cost*'. *Anthropology of Work Review*, vol. 37, no. 1, 60–1.

Rees-Roberts, Nick. 2018. *Fashion Film: Art and Advertising in the Digital Age*. London and New York: Bloomsbury.

Socha, Miles and Natalie Theodosi. 2019. 'Why Fashion Documentaries Are Ready for Their Close-up'. *WWD*, 4 September. Available at https://wwd.com/fashion-news/fashion-features/fashion-documentaries-flourish-multiply-1203238309/ (accessed 30 May 2022).

Szymanski, Adam. 2012. '*Bill Cunningham New York* and the Political Potentiality of the Fashion Documentary'. *Film, Fashion & Consumption*, vol. 1, no. 3, 289–304.

Tsai, Martin. 2015. 'Review: The True Cost Exposes Hidden Cost of Cute, Cheap Fashions'. *Los Angeles Times*, 28 May. Available at https://www.latimes.com/entertainment/movies/la-et-mn-true-cost-movie-review-20150529-story.html (accessed 30 May 2022).

Turner Christopher. 2018 'Lee Alexander McQueen: Piercing together a Portrait of the Fashion Genius'. *InMagazine*, 27 July 2018. Available at https://inmagazine.ca/2018/06/july-august-2018-cover-story-lee-alexander-mcqueen-piecing-together-a-portrait-of-the-fashion-genius/ (accessed 30 May 2022).

Uhlirova, Marketa. 2013. '100 Years of the Fashion Film: Frameworks and Histories'. *Fashion Theory*, vol. 17, no. 2, 137–58.

Worby, Robert. 2017. 'Foreword'. In Pwyll ap Siôn, *The Music of Michael Nyman: Texts, Contexts and Intertexts*, xi–xii. London and New York: Routledge.

Audio-visual references

Alex James: Slowing Down Fast Fashion. Directed by Ben Akers, 2016. Journeyman Pictures.
A Perfect 14. Directed by Giovanna Morales Vargas, 2018. A Perfect 14 Pictures.
Bill Cunningham New York. Directed by Richard Press, 2010. First Thought Films.
China Blue. Directed by Micha X. Peled, 2005. Teddy Bear Films Inc. and ITVS.

Clothes to Die For. Directed by Zara Hayes, 2014. Quicksilver Media.
Cotton Road. Directed by Laura Kissel, 2013. Council of International Education, Fulbright Scholars Program, The Fledgling Fund, The South Carolina Humanities Council.
Diana Vreeland: The Eye Has to Travel. Directed by Lisa Immondino-Vreeland, Bent-Jorgen Perlmutt and Frédéric Tcheng, 2011. Gloss Studio.
Dior and I. Directed by Frédéric Tcheng, 2014. Cim Production.
Franca: Chaos and Creation. Directed by Francesco Carrozzini, 2016. Disarming Films.
Girl Model. Directed by Ashley Sabin and David Redmon, 2011. Dogwoof and Carnivalesque Films.
Gomorrah. Directed by Matteo Garrone, 2008. Fandango, Rai Cinema, Sky.
Helmut Newton: The Bad and the Beautiful. Directed by Gero von Boehm, 2020. Lupa Film and Monarda Arts.
Life and Debt. Directed by Stephanie Black, 2001. Tuff Gong Pictures.
Made in Milan. Directed by Martin Scorsese, 1990. Emporio Armani.
Manolo: The Boy Who Made Shoes for Lizards. Directed by Michael Roberts, 2017. Nevision Studios One.
McQueen. Directed by Ian Bonhôte and Peter Ettedgui, 2018. Misfits Entertainment and Salon Pictures.
Notebook on Cities and Clothes. Directed by Wim Wenders, 1989. Centre Pompidou, Centre de Creation Industrielle, Road Movies Filmproduktion.
One Man and His Shoes. Directed by Yemi Bamiro, 2020. Break Em Films.
Scatter My Ashes at Bergdorf's. Directed by Matthew Miele, 2014. Berney Films and Quixotic Endeavors.
Suited. Directed by Jason Benjamin, 2016. A Casual Romance Productions.
The Devil Wears Prada. Directed by David Frankel, 2006. Twentieth Century Fox.
The Director: An Evolution in Three Acts. Directed by Christina A. Voros, 2013. RabbitBandini Productions.
The First Monday in May. Directed by Andrew Rossi, 2016. Condé Nast Entertainment, MediaWeaver Entertainment and Relativity Media.
The Gospel According to André. Directed by Kate Novack, 2017. Thunderbird Releasing Ltd.
The Great British Sewing Bee. Broadcast by BBC Two 2013–20, and BBC One 2020–present.
The Last Train Home. Directed by Lixin Fan, 2009. Eye Steel Film, Telefilm Canada, ITVS.
The Piano. Directed by Jane Campion, 1993. CiBy 2000 and Jan Chapman Productions.
The September Issue. Directed by R. J. Cutler, 2009. A&E IndieFilms and Actual Reality Pictures.
The True Cost. Directed by Andrew Morgan, 2015. Untold Creative.
T-Shirt Travels. Directed by Shanta Bloeman, 2001. ITVS.
Valentino: The Last Emperor. Directed by Matt Tyrnauer, 2008. Acolyte Films.
What Not To Wear. Broadcast by BBC Two 2001–3, and BBC One 2004–7.
Worn Stories. Produced by Netflix, 2021.
Yellow is Forbidden. Directed by Pietra Brettkelly, 2018. Avrotros &Svt and Libertine Pictures.

Expanding interview 1
Elena Caoduro in conversation with Lorna Tucker, director of *Westwood: Punk, Icon, Activist* (2018)

Elena Caoduro [EC]: *What is your relationship with fashion and, more generally, the fashion world?*

Lorna Tucker [LT]: I never was into fashion as a kid. It was more when I was 19, after I had my first daughter. Actually, I got scouted to model when I was 17, but then I wasn't really interested. That was the first time I even knew anything about fashion because, where I came from, people didn't really read *Vogue*. It was more kind of Adidas tracksuits and baseball caps and a bit of Reebok classics. Kids looked up to glamour models. It was the era when girls wanted to grow up to be footballers' wives, which is actually really depressing when you look back at it. I was very much into just wearing what everyone else wore, as most teenage girls do to fit in. It was interesting. Because once I was scouted to model and I was on shoots and I used to see how the models used to put their outfits together, I think that's when I really started to get and have an interest in fashion. But also, I started to understand about quality and the difference between buying cheap fabrics that won't last to just buying ethical cotton. The dressing up part of modelling was something that was extremely fun for me, because I couldn't really afford clothes; I didn't have a wardrobe. Like the majority of teenagers, I had a pair of jeans and a couple of tops, a jumper and that was it. It was really fun and I kind of fell in love with it, dressing up and seeing how outfits are put together. It took me till I was as much older to actually understand what fitted me and what suited me.

EC: *How do media and fashion relate, in your opinion?*

LT: I'm anti media fashion because of the one take-out I had. I wasn't a model for long. That's a big misconception about me. When *Westwood* came out, the press said I was a supermodel or I've gone from modelling into film-making, but I didn't. I was only modelling for two years, and I wasn't a very good model and I think that was more to do with the fact that I had a lot of pressure on me to be too thin. I'm naturally quite a curvy woman, I'm 5'11, size 10, and the minute I was scouted I was shown pictures in magazines of girls that were almost skeletal or introduced to other models that were painfully thin. And told that's what I was meant to look like. That really messed me up for a long time. I didn't read fashion magazines when I was younger prior to modelling. Media has a negative impact in portraying unrealistic expectations of what is beautiful. What I've really enjoyed more so lately, especially in the last five years, is that there's a definite shift happening about body positivity and diversity and that makes me really excited for the next generation behind me coming up. Just starting to take ownership of our own body, which has been really liberating. But also the negative representation of what society is. There were always those one or two designers that did use people of colour, that did use women that weren't anorexic looking. The mental health aspect of fashion is what concerns me; that there needs to be a lot more responsibility. The kind of models they use, what they're putting out, what fashion magazines are showing to represent society. I started making short films, music, videos, fashion films a bit later; it really was like a guerrilla form of film-making. I'd be sitting on a skateboard, and someone was pulling me along, filming models dressed, borrowing clothes from fashion designers. It was coming from a model in that sort of desperation, but I felt such a responsibility, knowing what I knew about the industry and the system. I try to use non-models or people that didn't fit the stereotypical model bracket.

At the back end of doing *Westwood* and seeing how much fashion waste there is and Vivienne [Westwood]'s talking about fast fashion, made me reconsider the system, the very nature of the business. I wanted to do the Vivienne Westwood documentary, not because she was a fashion designer, which everyone would like, but because of the injustices. None of my documentaries were about fashion. They were about human rights abuses. They were exploring what leads people to commit crimes and I've been really into historical things. And that I would like to lift up female voices and so, the thing that really interested me with Vivienne was her activism. I had been frustrated that grants to study art had been stopped, that college wouldn't be funded anymore by the government. I was really angry and didn't know what to do with that frustration. When I met Vivienne, she was talking about environmental causes, which I didn't have much knowledge about, and she was sharing with me her story. We had a chat when I was filming something for the band Queens of the Stone Age with her. And she had told me that she had been a single mum and that she would have loved studying fashion, but she couldn't afford to and she didn't think she'd be able to make money in it. We talked about how long it took for her to make money as a fashion designer and just it was more hearing the personal side of her life made me inspired. There could be a message for the whole new generation of kids that wanted to study fashion or art or had dreams of doing anything at all. There's not a straight road to success, but here was this larger-than-life character: Vivienne was like in her 70s with see-through dresses and six-inch high heels, looking absolutely gorgeous. As a woman, we know the pressure that's on us as we get to a certain age, we are meant to disappear or not wear bikinis and stay away from certain clothes because it's not acceptable. So, she was kind of a living embodiment of rejecting these norms.

It was more the kind of inspirational story aspect about Vivienne that engaged me, but also it was the contradictory nature of her life. On the one hand, she urged the fashion industry to clean up and be more ethical, but then she was running a fashion company, and it's impossible to be ethical. You can't make a profit by paying people absolutely fairly, like Katharine Hamnett who stopped because she realised she could stretch her business only to a certain point. Do everything locally, make small. You can try and make a business as much ethical as possible, but even the fact that you're sending clothes out all over the world, putting on shows and getting models, out is not environmentally sustainable. I was really amazed watching Vivienne's frustration and her fight to protect the planet, whilst running her fashion empire. But it was also exhausting.

EC: *How did you research the topic? What do you remember about the production of the documentary?*

LT: I was doing mad jobs in order to fund my first feature doc, *Amá* (2018), which was about how Native American women have been sterilised without their knowledge. While doing that, I had been offered to do a documentary series about political prisoners in America. I was put in contact with Vivienne because she was a big supporter of the political movement there. I was embedding myself within different communities to find out what happened. She was really interested in finding out the stories we were hearing. I did a few little things with her, and I was really inspired by her life. I think with all of my documentaries I always try and go into my film-making without doing research. This is probably because I left school very young. Going into documentary for me has been the biggest learning experience. I didn't go to film school; I learnt how to camera operate on YouTube. I can get researchers to bring me all the details and we kind of weave that into the film. The film is like a journey; the viewer will learn at my pace and therefore you're not preaching to the converted.

I had a few conversations, personal conversations with Vivienne, and then I did a little Google search just to look at the timeline of her story. But I wanted to find out about her life story through her. I wanted to go where she was born and find out what was going on when she was growing up. I wanted to speak to people who were in the fashion industry at that time or working for magazines and ask them what was going on at this particular time, instead of me researching and using archival footage. I embedded myself within the company, I filmed the process from the sketches to the pattern cutting and brought the viewer in alongside me. I just wanted to have heart and depth. I wanted to show that Vivienne Westwood wasn't just Vivienne Westwood, but hundreds of amazing people that make up an amazing company, like the pattern cutter from East London.

Fashion is supposed to be fun, and I've got a really silly sense of humour. In the film, I get called up a lot, for being naive, for saying the wrong things. It was a really interesting film to make and I was very lucky because of the people that helped me make that film. I needed to be supported behind the scenes, because it had the potential of being something really special. But I needed it to keep everything small so as not to distract everyone, so they could forget we were there, and I didn't want to give an impression of bringing a big film crew with booms and everything. Halfway through it, it started feeling quite special, so we kind of added together some scenes. There was a day, and I remember it clearly, when I felt like we'd followed a couple of cycles of the fashion lines and it got to the point where everyone had forgotten we were filming, so we were really able to show everyone's amazing personalities. We partnered with Passion Films and working with them was great because they helped in selecting, cutting and taking scenes out. I was really proud of it, and then we found out Passion had submitted it to Sundance without telling us because they just didn't want me panicking. It was never going to be ready or perfect enough for me.

EC: *What happened after the release of the Westwood documentary?*
LT: I think that people didn't get the feminist aspect of it, of what I was doing. But then maybe that's because I didn't do it properly. I was really happy with its reception, and I was a bit gutted that Vivian didn't like it, but I'd been warned for a year from a lot of people that were close to her. I understood that she always wanted it to be just about her activism (see Figure E1.1). But I was

Figure E1.1 Lorna Tucker on a Greenpeace boat, shooting Vivian Westwood during the Save the Arctic campaign. Courtesy of Lorna Tucker

always there, saying we can't make it just about your activism, otherwise people won't care about your activism or fashion. One needs to make people care and supportive and then they'll get behind someone's activism. Her feedback on it was so uncreative in a film sense, 'I don't like that shot with me', 'I don't like this'. Next thing, you start getting the lists of things that they want to change. I would never want to see a film of myself, so, I completely understood her. But that's when I had to remind everyone that it was my film and I was really proud of it, and I didn't want to lose all those things that I felt would inspire young artists to follow their passions. Obviously, I was a bit gutted when she tweeted against it on its premiere at Sundance, but again, also I expected nothing less. I'd just spent four years filming and editing a film about a punk icon. If she had said a really amazing comment about it, it would have been a fluff piece. It had to be a promo for her and I didn't want to make it in that way. I wasn't making an advertisement; I was making a film about an inspirational woman. The festival circuit was great. Sundance was the first festival for me, and the most amazing part of that was meeting other film-makers. After a year of touring, *Amá* came out, which actually was my first film, although the second to be released. Then I decided I wanted to take a year out, just to work on script commissions and a script I'd written which was picked up by the British Film Institute. *Westwood*, for me, will always be the film where I shift from guerrilla film-making and doing everything on my own, to proper documentary. It was the first time I was working with producers and with a crew, cinematographers other than myself; working with editors, and not having to do it all myself.

EC: *What do you think of fashion documentaries as a genre?*
LT: I'm naturally drawn to films where people have to overcome difficulties. I have my own thoughts on what truly makes someone incredible. I really was into *Halston* (2019) by Frédéric Tcheng, he did such a great job with that, and I loved his other fashion films. I love fashion when it's bringing me back to the old days, even going back to the thirties. And then, there are these amazing fiction films like when Tom Ford did *A Single Man* (2009). If I sit down to watch a documentary, it has to be something more than just a fashion documentary about pretty clothes. I want larger than life characters, unique stories. Otherwise, I get bored fast.

EC: *What do your works have in common? How are your projects for musicians similar to fashion documentaries?*
LT: If you want to get to the heart of people, you have to shut up and listen, and watch things unfold. But I intervened and I talked a lot, as I get very excitable. I remember the first time I went away filming bands; I came back with footage full of me, talking to people. It's all about the characters that interested me, very strong-willed personalities, built up over time to be the best. They had an element of silliness and naughtiness about them and a lot of them had overcome a lot of hardship. Moving from concert videos to *Amá* and *Westwood*, music felt super important for me, because I wanted it to lift emotion and I wanted to do something unusual. I didn't want to use punk music in *Westwood*. She's inspired by classical music, so I wanted to lift the film with incredible classical operatic music to get under your skin. Dan Jones composed the music, and he was amazing. The film I'm doing now, about homelessness, features a lot of music because it's a documentary about a big issue. The film explores how to end homelessness, but I've written it as a character-driven documentary and we've been using a lot of music, for instance Björk, urban music.

EC: *Is there any particular artistic figure that you would like to shoot a documentary about?*
LT: So many, but how do I make them as an entertaining film that doesn't hit you on your nose? I'm attached to a project for a documentary on Katharine

Hepburn; it was supposed to happen this year, but because of Covid it has been postponed. So inspirational, she never gave up and it involves a lot of fashion and beauty, but also, it's showing the dark side of fashion, beauty and celebrity. It's very timely because of Britney Spears and how women are built up only to be pulled down.

Audio-visual references

Amá. Directed by Lorna Tucke,. 2018. UK.
A Single Man. Directed by Tom Ford, 2009. USA.
Halston. Directed by Frédéric Tcheng, 2019. USA.
Westwood: Punk, Icon, Activist. Directed by Lorna Tucker, 2018. UK.

Chapter 2

'The Helen Rose originals are fabulous': the fashion featurette and fashion show as sites of industrial reflexivity

Julie Nakama

Beginning in the late 1950s, the spaces of costume design and exhibition in Hollywood began to shift to reflect the new realities of the industry and diminishing opportunities for costume designers as the studio era was drawing to a close. By the 1960s the extravagant costumes of Hollywood's Golden Era had essentially disappeared. As a result, costume designers had to create new spaces to exhibit their work, and the fashion featurette and fashion show became sites to exhibit both the process and products of their labour. The fashion featurette was an extra-textual promotional short designed to offer a behind-the-scenes view of costume design. It gave viewers a glimpse into the film-making process and promoted costume design as an art form. The fashion show functioned similarly in two ways. First, it occurred as a non-narrative space within a narrative film that consciously took the practice of fashion as its subject. Second, it occurred as an extra-textual promotional event. In the 1960s and 1970s the department store fashion show became a popular space for Hollywood costume designers to promote their retail design interests. The fashion featurette and fashion show offered costume designers the opportunity to promote their craft to both industry insiders and retail audiences in ways that anticipated later practices within production cultures and also foreshadowed the rise of the fashion film. This chapter will examine the work of two Hollywood costume designers, Helen Rose and Edith Head, to explore how each used the fashion featurette and fashion show to promote their work during a period in which costume design was increasingly devalued in the film industry.

Helen Rose and MGM

Rose was a costume designer at MGM from 1943 to 1966. She was known for creating elegant, understated costumes that were the epitome of 1950s upper-middle-class suburban femininity. She is often associated with actresses like Elizabeth Taylor and Grace Kelly, having designed wedding gowns for both actresses. Rose began her career designing vaudeville chorus girl costumes for the Lester Costume Company sometime in the late 1910s, before moving to the Ernie Young costume house, where she gained a strong reputation for designing theatrical costumes. At these theatrical houses Rose mastered the difficult art of chiffon design, which she would put to extensive use during her years as a film costume designer. In 1929 she moved to Los Angeles and began a brief assignment at Fox Studios before leaving to design costumes for the Ice Follies, a position she held for fourteen years until MGM courted her with an offer to replace their star designer, Adrian. Rose assumed the position of head designer, where she remained until her retirement from the film business in 1966. During her career at MGM she also designed and sold expensive ready-to-wear clothing through exclusive department stores and speciality shops. After she left MGM, she continued to market upscale fashion through her retail label (Lee 2000: 733–5). Rose's twin footing in the worlds of costume and fashion was not entirely unique, but she was extremely successful at both, and her designs were widely copied offscreen.

During the late 1950s and 1960s Rose designed the costumes for a number of films that featured female protagonists somehow engaged with the fashion industry. One of these films, *Designing Woman* (Vincente Minnelli, 1957), is loosely based on Rose's life, and she is credited with the story idea. The film is about a fashion designer named Marilla, played by Lauren Bacall, who also becomes a costume designer. To promote the film, MGM made a short interview-style featurette with Rose discussing her career and designs for the film. The short begins with a stock footage aerial shot which flies over the studio compound to capture the enormity of the campus. It then cuts to an exterior shot of the wardrobe department before moving into an interior shot of Rose's office. She enters and sits at a desk next to a stack of costume sketches and a set of crystal inkwells. In the staged piece, Rose answers pre-recorded questions that are not audible in the film. The short was created as a mock interview and fashion show for distribution to television networks, and the pauses indicate where Rose has left space for the interviewer. While the questions are lost, Rose's responses are a lasting testimony to her design philosophy. She provides candid insider titbits mixed with real costuming strategies. In response to a question that seems to be about what happens to the clothes after they appear onscreen, Rose says that they are sent to department stores, to movie theatres for lobby display, or to actors for personal appearances. Rose then displays costume sketches from *Designing Woman* and discusses details of particular costumes. A live model then enters the room wearing a gown from the fashion show scene in the film. In answer to a question ostensibly about the possibility of a retail line, Rose demurs, 'One of these days, who knows?'. At the end of the interview Rose provides her overarching design philosophy, stating that clothes should be 'chic, styled, flattering but basically simple'.

The Rose featurette offers an example of the behind-the-scenes look at costume production that accompanied promotional materials for films during the studio era. This example is striking because it provides a concise snapshot of the complex work of the costume designer. The film grants a glimpse into the design process through costume sketches and a brief fashion show that reveals the finished product. It also hints at a potential excursion away from film work and into retail fashion, which Rose would indeed take up later in her career. At the same time, however, the film effaces the labour of the costume designer and the wardrobing department. Rose's office is depicted as a stately room with large windows and plantation shutters. The crystal inkwells are displayed but sewing machines, bolts of fabric and sketchbooks are nowhere in sight. In keeping with Rose's design philosophy, the short offers a version of labour that is 'chic, styled, flattering, but basically simple'. The featurette functions rhetorically to promote a certain version of the production culture of the costume department at MGM during the period. Rose's grand office stands in deep contrast to the conditions facing costume designers a decade later, when slashed budgets forced designers to become mobile, resourceful and adaptable.

While Rose may have presented a sanitised version of costume design in MGM's featurette, she expressed the labour of the craft onscreen in other ways. For example, several scenes in *Designing Woman* show Marilla engaged in the labour of costume design in ways that are perhaps more representative of the work involved in designing clothes than that presented in the featurette. In the film, Marilla is preparing for a major fashion show to market her designs. In one scene she juggles a slew of duties. She selects fabric, pins a dress, approves designs, manages a staff of seamstresses and discusses a business opportunity. Marilla is portrayed as a dynamic, confident artist and businessperson. She has her own money and a collection of eccentric New York friends. Rather than sitting behind a desk, she is engaged in every part of the process from design to sale and is most in her element during the fashion show. Because of Rose's involvement with the film, it is tempting to understand Marilla as a surrogate for Rose whose version of the costume designer challenges the one put forth by the MGM featurette.

Other films that Rose designed similarly engage a fashion-based storyline to explore the craft and business of fashion. In *The Courtship of Eddie's Father* (Vincente Minnelli, 1963), a prominent character works as a fashion consultant. The plot for *Made in Paris* (Boris Sagal, 1966) revolves around Maggie, played by Ann-Margret, a buyer for a department store. The film is essentially a showcase for Rose's designs, as well as a peek into the creative labour behind fashion, as we see Maggie at work throughout. The film features a fashion show as a non-narrative container for additional costumes. Maggie echoes Rose's design philosophy, remarking on the differences between photographic design and real-life design and the importance of clean and flattering styles. One scene from the fashion show features a woman in a flowing gown whose undulating movements conjure an early film performance of the *Annabelle Serpentine Dance*, an Edison film from 1895. The reference to the serpentine dance removes the fashion show from the narrative arc of the story and places it within the realm of the fashion film, which Marketa Uhlirova has identified as a genre of non-fiction film (Uhlirova 2013a). In the 1960s, Rose designed films whose narrative pretence barely masks their real function as fashion films. Thus, Rose effectively repurposed the non-narrative fashion-show-within-a-film and extra-textual fashion show featurette to deploy these texts as sites of industrial reflexivity. These examples all point to Rose's keen promotional insight and business savvy. In addition to the fashion featurette, she used the films themselves as vehicles to advance her own design career and personal brand. In this, Rose anticipated what John Caldwell (2008) would later describe as the self-reflexive work of production cultures.

Production cultures and industrial reflexivity

In his foundational text *Production Culture: Industrial Reflexivity and Critical Practice in Film and Television*, Caldwell examines the film and video industry in Los Angeles both as an object and as a cultural activity, mainly through the labour of below-the-line workers (Caldwell 2008). Caldwell is interested in the ways that the media industry represents the products and processes of labour to itself in forms like behind-the-scenes documentaries, trade shows and trade literature. These objects signal how workers within the industry contextualise their labour. In Caldwell's sense, industrial reflexivity manifests in extra-filmic texts. Adapting Caldwell's formulation, I argue that, in addition to those texts, non-narrative spectacles like the fashion show in *Made in Paris* also represent the products and processes of fashion design. Behind-the-scenes fashion documentaries and fashion shows do similar work, but films about fashion as creative labour speak to both popular audiences and industry insiders.

Adapting Caldwell this way also works as a corrective to case studies of production cultures which tend to privilege mechanical or technological positions like gaffers, camera operators and sound engineers. These are occupations that are traditionally gendered male and, while women do work in these fields, the self-reflexive imagery regarding below-the-line work is gendered in ways that do not acknowledge contributions to craftwork within the industry that are traditionally gendered female, specifically costume production, whose workers Helen Warner considers as belonging to a 'symbolically female professional community' (Warner 2018: 37). For example, within the demos and trade images that Caldwell studies, he writes that figures of women have appeared in promotional imagery in stylised ways generally designed to either visualise technical capabilities or to act as seductive elements for advertising the product. Caldwell says, 'Feminism appears to have made few inroads in the gender consciousness of those who design for the digital practitioner trades' (Caldwell 2008: 137). Similarly, Caldwell's discussion of trade machines and mechanical gear acknowledges the industry's gendered approach to labour in its imaginings of itself. Demo tapes that exhibit gear and techniques 'regularly create pictures of alienated, male trauma' and celebrate the notion of the tortured male (Caldwell 2008: 167). While Caldwell specifically refers to digital practitioner trades, the larger field of production culture studies similarly often fails to recognise professions that are traditionally gendered female.

Including onscreen depictions of creative labour in costume and fashion reorganises how we conceptualise industrial reflexivity. Helen Rose provides an interesting case study because her designs are emphasised as non-narrative moments of excess within fiction films to the degree that they demand a reconsideration of their function in the film. As films about fashion production, they display and promote both the creative labour of fashion design and its products. Caldwell argues that 'the social performance of show making itself' must be considered in order to fully understand film and television as media forms (Caldwell 2008: 81). Analysing the fashion show both on screen and off takes up Caldwell's charge. This practice is significant as an example of the sort of industrial self-reflexivity that Caldwell theorises. Caldwell examines trade shows and insider literature as means through which the industry defines itself to itself. With costume, however, the onscreen fashion show becomes a site through which costume designers and wardrobe departments could promote their behind-the-scenes labour through explicit visual displays unmotivated by narrative. The representations of the fashion industry through female characters who worked within it further speaks to the ways in which these films were aware of the relationship among costume and fashion and created depictions that can be read as modes of self-reflexivity that considered two audiences – the filmgoers and the fashion industry itself. The behind-the-scenes fashion featurette and onscreen fashion show both provide insight into the creative labour of costume design. As the studio era ended, however, designers like Rose moved into the retail realm and took their fashion shows with them. Though these were seldom recorded and preserved, the offscreen fashion show provides an alternative exhibition site through which to analyse the production culture of costume designers.

The fashion show, early cinema and Edith Head

As Caroline Evans has demonstrated, fashion shows and film came into being nearly simultaneously (Evans 2011: 110). Evans notes that the structure of the fashion show reveals something about the cultural and industrial structures that give it context. For example, she analyses a specific fashion show that was mounted in Paris in 1925 by the designer Jean Patou. The show featured American models and Evans draws a connection between the athletic, standardised physique of the American women and the aesthetics of modernism, specifically modernism's 'tubular forms and mechanical bodies' and compulsion for standardised repetition (Evans 2008: 250). In other words, Evans suggests that Patou's fashion show was a spectacle that mobilised modernism's aesthetic by mapping it onto the bodies of women, yet it did so in a way that also kept alive the notion of individuality. The fashion show provided a space to both materialise aesthetics and also sell it through the paradoxical promise of mass-produced singularity. Evans notes that the fashion show superficially offered the allure of exclusivity to Patou's audience, comprised of private clients and department store buyers, who knew very well that they would purchase the designs with plans to mass produce 'knockoffs' or copies. The French designer knew this as well; thus, the whiff of exclusivity was merely a way to offer French fashion legitimacy to American mass-produced retail fashion. The fashion show functioned in a very similar way for Hollywood designers, who hoped to turn their onscreen designs into lucrative retail businesses by reproducing knockoffs of their screen designs while at the same time parading their uniqueness down the catwalk.

In other ways, the fashion show and film share a lineage. Catherine Hindson has pointed to the ways that early film took fashion in movement as its subject (Hindson 2013). Hindson charts the development of the serpentine dance, which was performed and filmed in various iterations, most famously by Loïe Fuller. The serpentine dance was an exhibition of fashion, film and movement the emerged with the birth of motion pictures. The fashion show, as well, had particular affinities with the 'cinema of attractions' and Evans suggests that long after film developed the narrative patterns that would move it away from spectacle and into plot-driven storytelling, fashion shows continued to function along the lines of attraction and spectacle (Evans 2011: 110). As the early film industry developed, so too did the relationship between fashion and film not only as a means to sell fashion commodities, but also as a way to draw 'respectable' middle-class women into movie theatres. Michelle Finamore details the history of the fashion featurette and the fashion newsreel and their inclusion in programmes during the early 1910s. For Finamore, fashion shorts and filmed fashion shows worked to attract female spectators to movie theatres (Finamore 2013: 132–86). Because they were often associated with Parisian couture, high-end department stores and sophisticated European designers like Paul Poiret, these fashion shows legitimated cinema-going as a middle-class pastime that could even be pedagogical in its pleasures.

Moving into the 1930s, 1940s and 1950s, fashion shows continued as a means to display couture goods offscreen. Onscreen they served a similar purpose. Charlotte Herzog argues that the filmed fashion show 'translated luxuriant mise-en-scène into hats, gloves, purses, shoes, lingerie, coats, and dresses, and even directed women to the stores where affordable equivalents could be purchased' (Herzog 1990: 136). Herzog terms this 'powder puff' promotion, or a technique whereby the sales pitch is buried in the medium's tremendous capacity to attract and entertain. Herzog sees the circuit between spectator, screen and store as fairly direct. The movies trained women in what to wear, how to wear it and where to buy it. The fashion show functioned as part of that circuit in bringing clothes offscreen and into the real material world of spectators. As Evans suggests, the fashion show promised exclusivity on the surface and yet was always undergirded by the mechanism of mass production. Thus, fashion show mimics the cinematic apparatus itself and its ability to interpolate at the levels of both individual spectator and mass audience. As fashion shows took to the road, the venues for this mode of consumer address became dispersed as designers like Rose, Marjorie Best and Edith Head began to exhibit their designs in department stores and civic clubs.

In the 1970s, Rose retired from her retail business and embarked upon a phase of her career that solidified her as Hollywood costume royalty. In 1970 the Arizona Costume Institute threw a gala dinner to honour the contributions of costume designers to the world of fashion. Rose was honoured alongside industry heavy hitters like Edith Head, William Travilla, Dorothy Jenkins and Ray Aghayan. These designers had all crossed over from the film world to fashion and their work marks the confluence of costume and fashion. During this period Rose also wrote an unpublished novel and an autobiography, *"Just Make Them Beautiful": The Many Worlds of a Designing Woman* (1976). She came out of retirement to promote the book through her fashion show, 'The Glamorous Wonderful World of Helen Rose', which toured department stores. Several years later Rose wrote another book, *The Glamorous World of Helen Rose* (1983), in which she shared more of her insights on her life in design.

Other Hollywood figures took to the fashion show circuit as part of a post-Hollywood career strategy. During the 1970s and 1980s, Edith Head toured her fashion shows across the country. Head's fashion shows are documented in archival programmes and advertisements in print media. Like Rose, Head toured in support of book publications and included designs from her film work that also translated into retail fashion. One show occurred in the afternoon of 8 May 1978 in Horne's department store at the corner of Penn Avenue and Stanwix Street in downtown Pittsburgh, Pennsylvania. The regional department store was the oldest department store in Pittsburgh, and one of the oldest in the country, having opened in 1849 ('Store Planned', 1990). However, by the late 1970s the store was struggling, as retail outlets had long begun their move into suburban malls, and larger national conglomerates had begun to acquire smaller regional outlets. Head's appearance at the downtown store marked not only the final chapter of her celebrated career, but also the end of a particular kind of shopping experience rooted in urban spaces and perhaps still dimly associated with the sensual pleasures of shopping at department store palaces during the turn of the century.

Head appeared with a collection of her movie costumes, which she staged as a fashion show on a makeshift runway between the bedding and drapery departments at Horne's. Head showed gowns she had designed for Dorothy Lamour, Ava Gardner, Rosalind Russell and Carole Lombard, among others. The gowns were worn by models made up to look like the stars who wore the originals. As they paraded down the runway Head narrated the event with insider titbits on the gowns and the actresses who made them famous. Photographs of the event show spectators seated in folding chairs, lining the runway and applauding with their eyes cast upwards at models such as the ersatz Carole Lombard. This Lombard wore what Head called the 'oldest and most famous' of her creations, a white satin dress with a white fur-trimmed cape. Head claimed that Lombard wore the gown at a cocktail party where she famously met Clark Gable.[1]

Sketches exist of the Lombard gown Head showed that day, and the gown itself still appears from time to time at costume exhibitions. Recently, an auction house in Beverly Hills exhibited a sketch of the gown alongside a still of Lombard wearing a similar gown in one of her films, though pointedly it was not the same gown.[2] In fact, the provenance of the gown is somewhat muddled. It is unclear if Head designed the gown for Lombard to wear in a film or for Lombard's own personal wardrobe. Was the gown that Head showed at Horne's department store really Lombard's, or was it something else? What is certain is that in 1976 Head designed the wardrobe for a biopic titled *Gable and Lombard*. In the film Jill Clayburgh plays Lombard and indeed wears the gown that Head exhibited that afternoon at Horne's. Nowadays when the gown appears in exhibitions of Head's work, it is at times attributed to Carole Lombard and other times attributed to Jill Clayburgh playing Carole Lombard. Despite this ambiguity, the gown gained such an afterlife and association with Lombard that in 1998 it appeared as part of a line of porcelain dolls the Head estate commissioned from the doll artist Robert Tonner. The dolls were crafted in the images of actresses wearing Head creations. The Lombard doll wears the dress that Head designed for *Gable and Lombard*, if not for Lombard herself (Guerin 1998). The Tonner doll again strengthened the association between Head, the dress and Lombard, even if this association was particularly tenuous. Amidst all these iterations, the gown that Head called 'the most famous' dress in Hollywood was actually a recreation of a Lombard dress designed for an actress playing Lombard and reiterated enough over time to become a Lombard dress again, if it ever was to begin with. The life of this particular Lombard dress illustrates the complex circuit among fashion, costume, star, market and public that characterises film and fashion in the post-studio era. This version of the Lombard dress would seem a far cry from what Charles Eckert describes in his essay 'The Carole Lombard in Macy's Window' (1990 [1978]). In that essay, Eckert describes a gown that Lombard wore in *Rumba* (1935). That gown, designed by Travis Banton, was copied for resale in shops shortly after the film's release. Eckert describes a relationship between film and filmgoer in which an idealised female spectator sees a dress she likes onscreen and wants to buy it for herself. Like Herzog, Eckert imagines a direct circuit between film, spectator and object. However, this relationship was perhaps never so simple and by the time of the show at Horne's department store, this relationship involved not only spectator and object, but a more complex network of social, affective and moral impulses that played out through the fashion show.

The commercial and civic function of fashion shows

In the 1960s, youth culture defined fashion trends and the fashion show underwent changes for certain fashion cultures. For example, a London fashion show in the mid-1960s might feature models dancing to rock and roll music whilst wearing the latest in hip Carnaby Street fashions, the location that served as the fashion centre of swinging London. A fashion newsreel from 1967 features models in futuristic fashions 'suitable for the best dressed ladies in the year 2000' (VIDCAT 2010). The clothes are space age designs made of transparent plastics and geometric prints. At the end of the fashion show, the women get into a spaceship to visit their friends in the 'outer space suburbs'. These types of fashion shows highlighted the forward-looking energy of youth fashion movements in Europe. However, in malls, department stores and ladies' lunches in the United States, the fashion show remained a stable showcase for accessible fashions for middle-class women. In Hollywood, Edith Head used the fashion show to display and circulate her own creations. Of the studio designers of the period, perhaps Head was the most masterful in using the fashion show as a means to promote her own brand and maintain relevance during a period in which costume designers were becoming less crucial within the world of film production. Beginning in the early 1960s and extending through the 1980s, Head staged fashion shows across the country.

Edith Head had a long career in Hollywood. She started at Paramount Studios in 1924 and moved to Universal in 1967 where she remained until her death in 1981 (Turim 1990: 227). By the time she went to Universal,

Head's film work had lessened substantially, and she was often a nominal presence at the studio. Instead she concentrated on work for television, as many film costume designers did, and on curating her fashion shows. Head hosted fashion shows from the early 1960s through to March of the year she died, 1981 (Head 1980–2). In addition to the fashion shows, Head wrote two instructional books on dressing, designed patterns for *Vogue*, designed military uniforms for the Coast Guard, and relentlessly promoted Hollywood glamour. For Head, the fashion show served a pedagogical function still related to commerce, but also related to Head's more encompassing project of educating women on the power of dressing. She largely enacted this project through her two books, *The Dress Doctor* (1959) and *How to Dress for Success* (1967), which she often promoted through civic club fashion shows.

In 1963 Head participated in at least two fashion shows for civic clubs. She was the special guest at a spring luncheon and fashion show for the Blessed Sacrament Mothers' Club. The event was called 'Springtime Fantasies' and was held in the Blossom Room of the Roosevelt Hotel in Hollywood. In July of that year she was in San Francisco at the Serra International Convention to present 'The Hollywood Story', a fashion show featuring her film costumes from Paramount Studios. The event was preceded by a light lunch of California tomato soup, salad, petits fours and coffee. Head was billed as the star, and she narrated the show with snippets of information about the gowns. When Head toured with her costumes, she often treated the fashion shows as an opportunity to promote her book, which she frequently provided for the attendees. As well as narrating, she might also give a short talk on how to dress for different occasions; thus the fashion shows began to take on a pedagogical function, in the vein of her books. The shows often consisted of a display of costumes described in the language of nostalgia. The gowns evoked old Hollywood but also served as evidence of Head's success in the industry. With eight Academy Awards and forty years of experience behind her, Head used the costumes as proof of her expertise as a designer. She then parlayed her knowledge of proper wardrobing conventions into book sales.

Performativity in the everyday

In 1967 Head published *How to Dress for Success*, which she also promoted alongside her fashion shows. The book is essentially an instruction manual for the presentation of the self in various situations and with particular goals in mind. In this way her premise is not entirely different from that of editor-in-chief Helen Gurley Brown in the pages of *Cosmopolitan* magazine. Head's advice is practical and entirely centred on creating an impression for another person. Unlike Brown, however, one senses that the goal of fashion and clothes for Head is not personal pleasure, but to dominate situations and relationships through the deployment of relentlessly appropriate dress. Head relied on her fashion shows to testify to her ability to create glamorous and, above all, situationally appropriate outfits. This is perhaps not surprising as Head spent her career using clothes rhetorically to craft characters in relation to a particular set of circumstances. For Head, the key to dressing is being able to first identify the situation accurately. In the chapter titled 'How to Dress to Get a Man . . . and Keep Him', Head advises women to first identify what sort of man they are dealing with.

The book continues on in similar detail through stylistic treatments of everything conventionally in the purview of a woman's world, including the husband, the family and the self. Success generally meant looking younger, slimmer and more attractive. Head's sartorial prescriptions seem outmoded now; however, her writing astutely identifies the significance of crafting a public self capable of navigating the social world. Her advice is firmly didactic because Head felt that fashion was a language that could be learnt and, furthermore, could be extremely beneficial to any adherent willing to take the time to study it. In this way, Head's fashion instruction becomes a kind of moral imperative for enjoying a 'successful' life. This is very much echoed in her fashion shows, which were often set among civic clubs and charity events. Head's books and fashion shows, then, offer an intersection between the fantasy and nostalgia of Hollywood costume, the milieu of civic duty, and the moral imperative of dressing successfully during a period in which there was great interest in parsing the personal and private selves.

Head wasn't the only one thinking about the moral implications inherent in crafting the public self. In 1959 the sociologist Erving Goffman published *The Presentation of Self in Everyday Life*. Influenced by the writings of Georg Simmel, Goffman argued that the presentation of the self is connected to a kind of moral imperative that occurs when an individual presents themselves to others. They present themselves via an array of signifying social characteristics that convey who they are. By entering into this 'information game', as Goffman terms it, they also enter into a social contract with others whereby they are indeed who they claim to be. By upholding their end of the contract, they put a moral obligation on others to value and treat them 'in the manner that persons of [their] kind have a right to expect' (Goffman 1959: 13). In other words, Goffman argues that fashion and self-presentation function rhetorically, as external codes that anchor how an individual wishes to engage with the public sphere. In their fashion shows, both Rose and Head sought to provide clothes that were already imbued with specific cultural associations and could thereby offer their wearer an intact coded message that drew on particular notions of white middle-class femininity.

Another important concept for Goffman is performance, which he argues is defined by influence. Goffman writes, "'performance' may be defined as all the activity of a given participant on a given occasion which serves to influence in any way any of the other participants" (Goffman 1959: 15). Performances are given for audiences, observers or co-participants and are used rhetorically to influence some thought, action or outcome. For Goffman there are essentially two poles of performance, cynicism and sincerity. The cynic recognises the value of performance but does not adhere to its rules and may furthermore take pleasure in knowing that others are morally obligated to do so. The sincere performer, on the other hand, faithfully observes the social contract and believes in his or her performance with the full faith that others will as well. Thus, we may say that the cynic delights in unmasking, while the sincere performer dutifully wears the mask in order to preserve social bonds. It should be noted that Goffman subtly aligns sincerity with middle-class values and the strong desire to leave social feathers unruffled.

With Goffman's concept of performance in mind, Head's fashion shows raise the question of what kind of influence Head wished to have, and for whom. With such an impressive command of fashion during a time of fantastic changes, why did Head remain within the safe confines of the costume fashion show? One of the reasons may be that Head still believed in the primacy of fashion and the power of the gown precisely during this period which was beginning to question these values. We can consider the milieu of Head's fashion shows – civic organisations and charity events – as 'sincere' environments. Head promenaded her costumes through years of ladies' lunches at hotels and convention centres. These lunches were, by definition, social events in which reputations were important and therefore masks were firmly in place. The fashion lunches were designed with philanthropy in mind and the audience, generally the wives of local businessmen, was considered in this light as well. With this setting in mind, it is possible to speculate on the potentially cynical capacity of the costumes within the fashion shows for the gathered audience.

Goffman notes that the cynic understands the rules of performance but refuses to adhere to them. Here consider Head's fashion shows and their ability to unmask performance as they delivered a thoroughly mobilised experience. The fashion show was comprised of moving pieces in more than one way. The costumes were unmoored from their settings within films and the attendees watched the shows in places characterised by their transitory natures like hotels and convention centres. This temporal and spatial displacement allowed spectators to view the costumes from a different vantage point, a place of fantasy in which the gowns and the spectators' affective responses governed the rules of engagement. This setting established a space in which the gown-as-performer become 'highly sacred' and shifted the focus of the social engagement from something interpersonal to something between subject and object (Goffman 1959: 22). The spectator need not perform in this context because performance shifted to the object. Furthermore, the counterpart to the performance became the narrator, in this case Head. Goffman refers to the 'profane' peddler who must move the performance from place to place. Thus, the setting and objects become highly sacred while the peddler becomes profane. In her fashion shows Head exhibited a kind of profanity in her twin desires to engender particular moral responses, such as giving to charity, and to peddle her own book and image. In this split between the sacred and profane we can also identify a split between sincerity and cynicism wherein the spectators take pleasure in the unmasking of performance and willingly support it through their charitable responses.

What Goffman describes in these two dichotomies can also be described as a fascination with surface and performativity as well as a keen interest in slippages of those things. In the world of underground and avant-garde film, two film-makers played with Hollywood costume and the spectacle of the fashion show in ways that seemed counter to the values and goals of Head's fashion shows. In 1963 Jack Smith directed *Normal Love*. The film is a lushly sensual collage of vignettes that recall various moments of western painting, adventure films and pop art. It is without dialogue and set to a vaguely orientalist musical soundtrack. One of the stars of the film is Mario Montez, a figure in the queer underground film scene of the 1960s who was also associated with Andy Warhol. Montez crafted himself in the image of Maria Montez, the glamorous star of several Universal adventure films in the 1940s including *Cobra Woman* (1944). Montez often designed his own costumes and did so for *Normal Love*. Ronald Gregg notes that Montez established his own costume house, Montez-Creations, and crafted his elaborate costumes from thrift store finds (2013). Drawing from the imagery of Hollywood, Montez reimagined and reworked scavenged materials into glittery, sequined, glamorous gowns that he wore both in films and on stage with The Ridiculous Theater Company. Donning the gowns and makeup became part of the pleasure of mounting productions and this joy can be seen in the way Smith, for example, allows his camera to revel with the characters in the delight of costume, makeup and imagination. The performances in *Normal Love* convey genuine adoration for the glamour and excess of classic Hollywood costumes as spectacles. The visibility of their construction brings attention to the equally constructed nature of the costumes that Head showcased in her fashion shows. If there is a difference between the two sets of work, it is perhaps only a matter of material, not spirit.

Somewhat similar to Smith, the photographer and film-maker William Klein made a number of films during the 1960s that worked through notions of irony. His 1966 film *Who Are You, Polly Maggoo?* (1966) cast a satirical eye towards the fashion industry. Klein himself was a well-regarded fashion photographer whose photo essays for *Vogue* were early forays into what would become known as street photography. *Who Are You, Polly Maggoo?* tells the story of a young French model who is followed by a television crew and interviewer. The interviewer tries time and again to get to the 'real' Polly behind the model. He doesn't succeed and the film is ultimately a send-up of the vacuity of the fashion industry, replete with a Diana Vreeland-esque figure whose snobbery is unmatched. The opening scene of the film features a fashion show set in a cave. The spectators watch, stacked on scaffolding erected against the walls of the cave, and the models appear in absurd creations made of sheet metal. While the narrative seems to indict the fashion industry, it is still a stylish film that can nowadays be considered alongside other films of the French New Wave. Thus, the film slips from satire to something of genuine concern and works on multiple levels of appreciation and contempt.

These two films from Smith and Klein seem at odds with Head's fashion projects, and yet, Head's deployment of, and enthusiasm for, the costume fashion show somehow plays nicely with Smith's contortion of film costume and Klein's commentary on the fashion show. All three seem aware of the possibility for costume to doubly articulate sincerity and cynicism and to dwell in both surface and subversion. All three also treat the ideas of performance, work and play as intertwined concepts. Head's treatment of the fashion show as both a business opportunity and charity event combines notions of work, leisure, and responsibility. Similarly, Smith's treatment of the costume as a place of fantasy and play is undergirded by the amount of work that Montez undertook to create extravagant costumes out of second-hand materials. And Klein's satire of the fashion industry relies on the idea that fashion and fashion modelling are not legitimate forms of work, but rather leisure-time pursuits.

Conclusion

The fashion featurette, department store fashion shows and avant-garde costume films of the 1960s all anticipate what Marketa Uhlirova has characterised as the fashion film. Uhlirova describes the fashion film as a mostly non-narrative genre that combines fashion and the moving image as part art film, part marketing and part fashion show. While fashion has been showcased in moving images since their development, Uhlirova differentiates the fashion film as a form that emerges from, and is controlled by, the fashion industry. In what she calls an emerging 'fashion-moving-image culture', these fashion films often put the body in movement through different spatial and temporal configurations such that fashion, movement, space and time themselves become the subject matter (Uhlirova 2013b: 149). Uhlirova has also traced the historical genealogy of fashion films over the last hundred years in formats like actualities, newsreels, filmed fashion shows and behind-the-scenes documentaries, dating the term to at least 1911 when it was used in connection with Pathé newsreels (Uhlirova 2013b: 153).[3] Uhlirova's essay traces the fashion film as an historical construction, but like the fashion featurette and show, it is also as an object that challenges the relationship between narrative and non-narrative spaces that offer expressions of industrial reflexivity. There are connections among the fashion featurette, fashion show and the fashion film as performative expressions of labour. With that in mind, could we consider the Rose films historically as 'fashion films'? Can they be linked through their treatment of fashion as myth and process? The benefit of merging the genres may be in nuancing the ways we think about the historical genealogy of fashion and film. Because these two objects have such a long, intertwined history, representations of costume and fashion-creation as creative labour within symbolically female production communities might be one way to begin parsing the historical relationship between fashion and film. That is, we can think about fashion and film as a process rather than an object and as a space of industrial reflexivity that occurs when a film consciously draws attention to the process of fashion and costume production through narrative and non-narrative means. Defining such a space might encourage critical thinking about production labour in relation to onscreen images rather than as trade narratives divorced from their created objects. Locating sites of industrial reflexivity within non-narrative spaces can tell us something about how aesthetic, industrial and cultural meanings are connected through film. Identifying these spaces will help us further parse the historical relationship between fashion and film so that we may trace their connections from the sewing room up and through the screen.

Notes

1. See 'Horne's photographs', which appeared in the *Daily News*, McKeesport, PA, Tuesday, 9 May 1978.
2. The sketch sold for $1,800 in 2009, Julien's Auctions, Beverly Hills, CA. http://www.liveauctioneers.com/item/6458914.
3. Uhlirova very specifically does not conflate the fashion film and advertising, noting that designers and brands were slow to adopt the digital format initially because of technological limitations (2013b: 150). Original source for the early use of the term 'fashion film' in Leese (1976: 9).

References

Caldwell, John. 2008. *Production Culture: Industrial Reflexivity and Critical Practice in Film and Television*. Durham, NC: Duke University Press.
Eckert, Charles. 1990 [1978]. 'The Carole Lombard in Macy's Window'. In *Fabrications: Costume and the Female Body*, edited by Jane Gaines and Charlotte Herzog, 100–21. New York: Routledge.
Evans, Caroline. 2008. 'Jean Patou's American Mannequins: Early Fashion Shows and Modernism'. *Modernism/modernity*, vol. 15, no. 2, 243–63.
Evans, Caroline. 2011. 'The Walkies: Early French Fashion Shows as a Cinema of Attractions'. In *Fashion in Film*, edited by Adrienne Munich, 110–34. Bloomington: Indiana University Press.
Finamore, Michelle Tolini. 2013. *Hollywood before Glamour: Fashion in American Silent Film*. New York: Palgrave Macmillan.
Goffman, Erving. 1959. *The Presentation of Self in Everyday Life*. New York: Anchor Books.
Gregg, Ronald. 2013. 'Fashion, Thrift Store and the Space of Pleasure in the 1960s Queer Underground Film'. In *Birds of Paradise: Costume as Cinematic Spectacle*, edited by Marketa Uhlirova, 293–304. London: Koenig Books.
Guerin, Polly. 1998. 'The Edith Head Collection – Spotlight on Hollywood Glamour Dolls'. *Doll World Magazine*, vol. 22, no. 2.
Head, Edith. 1980–2. Programs for fashion shows, 'Edith Head Papers, Programs 1980–1982', in Margaret Herrick Library, Special Collections.
Head, Edith and Jane Kesner. 1959. *The Dress Doctor*. New York: Little, Brown.
Head, Edith and Joe Hyams. 1967. *How to Dress for Success*. New York: Random House.
Herzog, Charlotte. 1990. '"Powder puff" Promotion: The Fashion Show-in-the-Film'. In *Fabrications: Costume and the Female Body*, edited by Jane Gaines and Charlotte Herzog, 134–59. New York: Routledge.

Hindson, Catherine. 2013. 'Dancing on Top of the World: A Serpentine through Late Nineteenth-century Entertainment, Fashion and Film'. In *Birds of Paradise: Costume As Cinematic Spectacle*, edited by Marketa Uhlirova, 65–77. London: Koenig Books.

Lee, Edith C. 2000. 'Helen Rose'. In *International Dictionary of Films and Filmmakers*, vol. 4, edited by Sara Pendergast and Tom Pendergast, 733–5. Detroit, MI: St. James Press.

Leese, Elizabeth. 1976. *Costume Design in the Movies: An Illustrated Guide to the Work of 157 Great Designers*. New York: Frederick Ungar Publishing.

Rose, Helen. 1976. *"Just make them beautiful": The Many Worlds of a Designing Woman*. Santa Monica, CA: Dennis-Landman Publishers.

Rose, Helen. 1983. *The Glamorous world of Helen Rose*. Riverside, CA: Rubidoux Printing Co.

'Store Planned for Pittsburgh'. 1990. *The Vindicator, the People's Paper*, Business section, 20.

Turim, Maureen. 1990. 'Designing Women: The Emergence of the New Sweetheart Line'. In *Fabrications: Costume and the Female Body*, edited by Jane Gaines and Charlotte Herzog, 212–28. New York: Routledge.

Uhlirova, Marketa, ed. 2013a. *Birds of Paradise: Costume as Cinematic Spectacle*. London: Koenig Books.

Uhlirova, Marketa. 2013b. '100 Years of the Fashion Film: Frameworks and Histories'. *Fashion Theory*, vol. 17, no. 2, 137–57.

Warner, Helen. 2018. 'Below-the-(Hem)line'. *Feminist Media Histories*, vol. 4, no. 1, 37–57.

Audio-visual references

Annabelle Serpentine Dance. Directed by W.K.L Dickson and William Heise, c. 1895.

Designing Woman. Directed by Vincente Minnelli, 1957. MGM.

Made in Paris. Directed by Boris Sagal, 1966. MGM.

Normal Love. Directed by Jack Smith, 1963. MGM.

Rose, Helen. 'Interview', *Designing Woman*, DVD special features, 1957. MGM, distributed by Warner Brothers Archive.

The Courtship of Eddie's Father. Directed by Vincente Minnelli, 1963. MGM.

VIDCAT. *Vintage Fashion Newsreel: 1967 Astro-Fashion*, 2010. Available at https://www.youtube.com/watch?v=3JxXnQRxLGw (accessed 31 May 2022).

Who Are You, Polly Maggoo? Directed by William Klein, 1966. Delpire Productions.

Chapter 3

The fashion of east and west in German cinema newsreels (1950–65)

Sigrun Lehnert

Introduction

Almost immediately after the Second World War, it once again became important to be well dressed. After years of limitations due to the war effort, fashionable clothing became the key to social acceptance and professional success in the era of the German 'Wirtschaftswunder' (economic miracle). Furthermore, the fashion industry was important for the growing economy, industry and export trade. How could people find out what was now 'in fashion' and which style was now being worn in the major fashion capitals? Cinema and film provided images of a new modern life, in which fashion played a significant part in Europe. Before television was established in Germany at the end of the 1950s, cinema newsreels were the only medium to provide news and trends through moving images. In the 1950s, people visited a cinema at least once a week to watch the latest film and the newsreels in the interludes.[1] By using moving pictures underscored by music and sound, newsreels gave viewers the impression of attending an illustrious fashion show or of being in the designer's studio, for example. In addition, the media represented the current political and cultural conditions in East and West. A comparison of the West German and East German newsreels reveals different perceptions of fashion and the demands on fashion in the contrasting systems of the two German states.

The fashion report in the West German newsreel *Neue Deutsche Wochenschau* (NDW) no. 19 from June 1950 is particularly impressive and may serve as a first example. It starts with the illuminated facade of the hotel 'Atlantic', accompanied by jazz music, and shows French designer Jacques Fath's fashion show at the popular Hamburg Hotel. The underscored music stems from the feature film *Gilda* (Charles Vidor, 1946).[2] In that film, Rita Hayworth wears long black gloves, just as the first model in the report does. In this way, the newsreel appeals to the audience's knowledge of film and encourages the viewers to decipher and interpret the music's meaning (Chion 1994). Although the effect of the newsreel on spectators in the 1950s is no longer verifiable,[3] it is likely that the newsreel's strategy of communication had the potential to shape the viewer's opinion and, in the longer perspective, the national image. As the newsreel reports were internationally exchanged, fashion was also an ambassador for and a symbol of the modernity of its country of origin.

The newsreel reports in general served as a seismograph, measuring the fluctuating trends and showing social and cultural developments in the East and the West. Its wide range of fashion themes, and the way in which they are presented, reveals the high importance of fashionable clothing in the 1950s and 1960s. There are special reports on clothing for leisure and everyday life, evening wear, hats or shoes, women's and men's or children's fashion. The reports' tonality, however (due to the spoken commentary and the music), differs considerably between the newsreels from the East and the West. Due to the different economic systems in West and East Germany, the political and technological competition (especially in the synthetic fibre industry) are portrayed in the fashion reports – although these cannot be described as political or technical at first glance. The competition between the East and the West is visible through the comparison of West and East German newsreels.

These issues have gained even more relevance over time, as these newsreels are now being used in television documentaries and as templates for feature films portraying German life in the 1950s or 1960s.[4] They are even used in music videos, for example in the video for the song 'Das Model' from the pop group Kraftwerk (1978). Thus, the presentation of fashion in 1950s newsreels was indeed crucial as they shaped the cultural memory and image of the period. The discourse pertaining to the cultural memory of a certain group or society shapes its self-image and is passed on to the next generation. It is based on traditions and includes culturally specific goods such as texts, images or customs (Assmann 1988: 9–19). In addition, the fashion reports discussed in this chapter are also indicative of the zeitgeist – as were the produced feature films with stories about models and fashion (Ganeva 2018: 145–177), which possibly followed on from the newsreel in the cinema programme.

Research on German post-war newsreels has mostly been more general, covering the whole history, a particular time period or concentrating on a country or territory (Jordan 1996; Schwarz 2002; Kleinhans 2013); specific topics have received less attention.[5] This chapter explores how newsreels informed and aesthetically impressed the viewers about the latest fashion in East and West Germany and how the differences between East and West were manifested through the comparison of the representation of this cultural and social phenomenon. In order to stress the importance of the topic, I will present the wide variety of newsreel presentation on the topic of 'fashion' in the years 1950–65. It is not only the most interesting decade of the economic resurgence, but the first of the divided German states, with contrary economic and political systems, during the Cold War. Each German state aimed to be representative of the whole Germany. My aim is to find out (1) how fashion was portrayed in the reports by cinematic means, and (2) what the newsreel films show about the relationship between West Germany and East Germany (or also respectively the west and the east) through the example of fashion. It is necessary to mention that West Germans usually could not see the East German newsreels nor East Germans the West German newsreels. It is all the more interesting that there are differences, parallels and overlaps in the newsreel presentations.

Methodology frame

The following analysis is based on the theoretical approach introduced in *Visual History* by Gerhard Paul (2012). According to Paul it is not a method, but a scientific attitude: Paul understands images (including film) not only as sources, but also as research objects whereby not only their content should be considered, but also their design, which is how I will deal with the aesthetics of the fashion reports under discussion here. In contrast to historical image research, the emerging field of visual history is thus based on a multilayered concept of the image, which understands images as signs and sources, as media that generate meaning and interpretation through their aesthetic quality, and as acts that generate reality. Above all, however, *Visual History* examines the types and effects of the creation and use of images (Paul 2012).

Second, the visual analyses in this chapter refer to the approach in *New Film History* by Robert C. Allen and Douglas Gomery (1985), which highlights various influences on film made by economics, technology and sociology. In this sense, it is not only the newsreels that need to be studied, but also various contextual materials – for example, reports from cinematographers, film reviews, letters from viewers, and magazine articles, which conveyed the visual sources into a cultural discourse.

Third, my understanding of film is based on neo-formalism, one of the most widespread film theoretical approaches. Introduced by David Bordwell and Kristin Thompson in the late 1970s (important work *Film Art: An Introduction*, 1997), neo-formalism locates the viewers as rational actors who follow the 'cues' in the film in order to understand the story being told (Kirsten 2016: 2).[6] In addition, Kristin Thompson proposes an analysis of film production processes in terms of their functions and the motivation for their application (Kirsten 2016: 5). As a method, neo-formalist film analysis allows the commentary text, pictures, music, and the connections between the newsreel reports to be investigated as intentionally applied, supporting cognitive factors ('cues')[7] for the viewers' understanding of the fashion reports. However, the overall methodology of film analysis I have pursued with the German fashion report newsreels is mainly *hermeneutic*,[8] whereby for interpretation, the filmic elements and their interaction in narrative strategies must among others be considered in the context of the history of film and newsreels (Hickethier 2012: 32–5).

Post-war newsreels in West and East Germany

After the Second World War, the Allies introduced their own newsreels in Germany. In particular, the British-American production *Welt im Film* was used for re-education matters. But in 1949, after the establishment of the two German states, the West German federal government sought to inform people with a new newsreel which was directed solely by Germans, in order to show incidents in Germany without any foreign influence from the Allies. So, at the end of the year, the *Neue Deutsche Wochenschau* (NDW) was founded, supported by the federal government and the press office. In the 1950s, several newsreels existed in West Germany. The *Welt im Bild* was the successor of *Welt im Film* and became the *Ufa-Wochenschau* in 1956.[9] Additionally, the private American production *Fox tönende Wochenschau* and the French-influenced *Blick in die Welt* were competitors on the West German newsreel market.

Whereas four newsreel productions existed at the same time in West Germany, in East Germany there was only *Der Augenzeuge*, which was produced by the state-owned production company Deutsche Film AG (DEFA).[10] Thus, it was the mouthpiece of the East German government and the central socialist party, the SED. The producers wanted the newsreel to educate the people ('echter Volkserzieher') (Maetzig, cited in Jordan 1990: 102). One of the specialities of *Der Augenzeuge* was its well-designed political reports ('gestaltete politische Sujets') (Jordan 1990: 93), aimed at showing political relations in everyday life and influencing people's political thinking. DEFA offered two editions per week (version A and version B) between 1957 and 1960 but then reduced production to one edition per week, probably for economic reasons.

In essence, each newsreel edition was an edited and compiled film. The weekly edition contained between eight and fifteen reports, which was in total 300 metres in length and offered approximately ten minutes of viewing time. The topics were entertaining and informative, such as politics, economics, technology, inventions, foreign countries, animal stories, disasters, state visits, sports and fashion shows.[11] Sometimes the reports were separated by intertitles, which carried the name of the city where the incident took place, or covered the topic of the event, incident or season, for example 'Alles für die Schönheit' ('Everything for beauty') in NDW no. 555 from 16 September 1960, which was a report on the latest autumn and winter shoe collection. The communication strategy implied that the reports were underscored by music, sound and commentary text. The tonality of the commentary differed; for example, it could be either factual or ironic and address the viewers both directly and indirectly. A special feature of these reports is the fact that the order of the reports was deliberate. The order of the report within a newsreel edition was important, and the transitions between the reports guided the viewers' understanding. The producers thought of 'their' newsreel as an audio-visual supplement to press and radio news. For governments all over the world, newsreels were useful for presenting economic and political progress or achievements. Their aim was to convey the good reputation of the state. Most newsreels were part of a worldwide exchange network,[12] and from the beginning of 1953/54 an exchange agreement existed even between East and West German newsreels. Pictures and films were exchanged and then newly underscored by sound and commentary text so they could be used for propaganda purposes.

Fashion – an important subject for newsreels

Many fashion reports can be found in the West German newsreels. Six years were chosen for the sample: 1950, 1951, 1954, 1958, 1962 and 1965, from which I have chosen interesting reports by way of example. Both 1950 and 1951 were essential years of economic resurgence; in 1954 reconstruction was nearly completed, while the backlog demand (*Nachholbedarf*) was covered in West Germany; in 1957 and 1958 there were strikes in the textile industry, and further steps in the economy, until 1965, took it close to recession. A study of the online film archives[13] indicates that each newsreel production – *Neue Deutsche Wochenschau, Welt im Film, Welt im Bild, Ufa-Wochenschau* – presented approximately ten reports per year. However, in the East German newsreel *Der Augenzeuge*, only two or three reports per year were presented – with the exception of the ten reports produced in 1959, which represent something of an anomaly.[14] It thus seems likely that the fashion industry and designing clothing were of greater importance in West than in East Germany. But this assumption might be misleading. Newsreels contributed to the 'agenda' of topics,[15] which was conveyed by all media, telling people what was important in Germany and in the world. Unsurprisingly, fashion reports could hardly be reflective of everyday life. What people wore in everyday contexts, however, can be seen in other reports, such as street scenes with passers-by.

Due to competition between the different newsreel companies in West Germany, the feedback from the cinema owners as well as the audience on an edition or single report was of great importance. From the (very rare) letters – written by viewers and sent to the newsreel production company of *Neue Deutsche Wochenschau*, and a survey from 1957 – it is known that fashion reports were very popular.[16] The viewers expected funny comments in fashion stories and good pictures, for example. According to one of the writers, women should be addressed in the fashion reports, in order to increase their interest in the newsreels and to prevent them from arriving late at the cinema.[17] However, the presented garments were also criticised for being too exclusive and only affordable for members of the high bourgeoisie.[18]

The cinematographers of the newsreels were invited to fashion shows and were provided with detailed information about the fashion on show. Written correspondence from the editorial team of the West German *Neue Deutsche Wochenschau* shows that, on the one hand, fashion was a 'reliable' topic, which was relevant for each season, whilst, on the other hand, the newsreel was a dependable partner for the fashion houses.[19] Consequently, both sides profited from this win–win concept. The newsreel reporters of *Neue Deutsche Wochenschau* were sometimes asked to mention the specific fashion designers or fashion houses[20] – thus, newsreel reports were a good means of advertising, which also shows how important fashion was in terms of its economic value. For each film recording, the cinematographers had to write a work report.[21] These reports reveal that filming the models was not always easy – some of them had a kind of 'star' status and behaved as such.[22] Other problems also occurred; depending on the venue, it was sometimes necessary to provide additional lighting. The big and heavy film equipment of the 1950s also needed more space than the lightweight, portable cameras introduced in the 1960s.

Unique characteristics of the fashion reports

Fashion reports were rarely main features and were placed instead in the middle or close to the end of each newsreel. The middle position was used to provide a mix of entertaining and serious topics, and the ending was used to put viewers in a good mood, ready for the main film that followed. The intertitles of fashion reports were often written in a beautiful curving font for themes like 'Modefrühling' ('Spring fashion'), for example. The voice-over comments were presented through both male and female voices. Very often, the male voice delivered a stereotypical 'male' perspective (making comments such as 'we like woman in such dresses') and the female voice would take on a stereotypical 'female' perspective (for example, 'with this dress, attracting men will be easy'). The commentary text often included wordplays, rhymes, and political associations as well. The models' names, the 'names' of the dresses – for example, 'Traumwölkchen' ('Dream cloud') – and the prices were sometimes mentioned. As the films are black and white, the commentary needed to describe the colours and the material of the fabric. The names of the designers, producers and trademark of clothing or accessories were mentioned in West German newsreels as a kind of advertising, whereas in the East German newsreel the performance of the state fashion industry was highlighted. Moreover, some famous designers also worked for the film industry that the newsreel was connected to, for example the West German Heinz Schulze-Varell.

The underscored music varied from film music, dance music (for example, South American rhythms of the cha-cha), to swing and jazz, traditional songs, and classical orchestra. In cases where two fashion reports had been placed in sequence, the music often bridged the stories. The cinematographers often used 'on-the-ground' or bird's-eye view to show special details. The cinematographers made sure that the modelled garments were well depicted through the use of pan shots from the head to the toe of the model, and vice versa.

The audience was indicated through inserted footage. The film editor would often use some extraordinary shots of facial expressions and the participants' reactions to comment on the fashion being modelled. The inserted footage was also used to indicate when celebrities from the film industry or other famous people had attended the event. First, this ensured the viewer could feel as if they too were amongst those interesting and famous people, and second, it shows that the label was 'in fashion', even for film stars.[23] Of course, the German cinematographers could not cover all fashion events abroad themselves, so the international exchange of the newsreels was very important for acquiring images of the latest fashion from Paris and other fashion hubs.

The fashion reports are not only unique because of their film design; the order of the reports and the positioning of them in the newsreel editions was carefully devised. Fashion reports were sometimes followed by reports on the textile industry. A report might also have focused on the fabric or clothes production and showed the outcome of the production, presented in a fashion show (especially in *Der Augenzeuge*). Fashion was an important part of trade fairs and was dealt with in this context. Furthermore, it was presented in combination with tourism. It is very interesting that in fashion reports stories were told – for example, a city tour with staged scenes at different places and landmarks.

The variety of fashion topics was huge, especially in West German newsreels, which contained fashion for all kinds of target groups – mostly separated into shows for women, men, teenagers and young adults, children – as well as fashion for dogs and dolls. We are not only presented with special clothing for each season – spring, summer, autumn, winter – but also for Easter, Carnival and Christmas. There were also special shows for swimsuits, coats, après-ski and ski fashions and for a variety of different social occasions: evening, afternoon and cocktail time as well as leisure time. The materials obviously played an important role when it came to dresses made from wool, silk or various new synthetic fibres. The commentary mentioned different styles, for example A-line, 'sack' fashion (always commented on as being abnormal and not acceptable), trapeze line, empire line, or more generally a boyish or feminine line. Additionally, the newsreels reported about shows for all kinds of accessories: shoes, bags, hats and caps, jewellery, wristwatches, stockings, glasses. The shows very often took place at hotels, in parks, at spa houses, on roof terraces, in front of or in castles, in factories, at horse races, trade fairs, museums, art exhibitions, gambling casinos, even on airplanes and at airports. Furthermore, well-known places and landmarks provided good scenery (providing a kind of tourism advertising) and the fashion was also directly presented at the designer's and photographic studios. As the commentary sometimes revealed, the West German fashion shows employed professional models from famous Parisian fashion houses, beauty queens or film stars,[24] whereas in East Germany, *Der Augenzeuge* highlighted the fact that normal workers presented the clothes on the catwalk, for example at fashion shows in industrial work halls.

It also obviously follows from the ideological divide that only West German fashion and Western European fashion (mostly from France) was displayed in West German newsreels,[25] countered by East German fashion and fashion from socialist countries in the East German newsreels. This shows how much the fashion of the other German state was ignored due to the differences in the political systems. The newsreel films from abroad show that East German fashion was presented in socialist and communist countries, and West German fashion was presented in West European countries and the USA. The following examples distinguish between reports on German fashion presented abroad and vice versa.

East German fashion in *Der Augenzeuge*

In *Der Augenzeuge* no. 5 from 1951, a report of improved performance in the textile machine industry was shown, followed by a report on a fashion show at a steel production plant. The commentary mentions that female workers were allowed to vote on the dresses, which should all be suitable for everyday wear. The dresses that had received the most approval were to go forward into production, since in the socialist system the workers were to have a say. The commentary tried to make the difference from capitalist systems clear: it was not the taste of 'Kaffeehaus-Damen' (coffee shop ladies) – which is a 'cue' for the viewers and was to be interpreted as the 'lazy and rich' women of 'high society' under capitalism – but that of the working people which should decide which clothes should be produced in the socialist East Germany in the future. It is mentioned that the cloth was from Czechoslovakia, thus drawing attention to the trade connections to other socialist countries. It is also promised that the coats being presented will be made available soon, in spring, by the state trade organisation (Handelsorganisation, HO). The comment reveals that this was not self-evident, because the planned economy on the Soviet model had only been introduced in 1951 (with the first five-year plan) and the governance of the economy was still causing problems (Steiner 2007: 71).

On the one hand, workers should be able to decide on the fashion of state production, and on the other hand, fashion designers, like Heinz Bormann, created their own lines. Heinz Bormann was the most important fashion designer in East Germany. His fashion house became a semi-state company in 1956, but he claimed that the government would not influence his work.[26] In *Der Augenzeuge* no. A79 from 1959, a model presented Bormann fashion in a daily routine story: what to wear from the morning to the evening (titled 'Eine Frau von 8 bis Mitternacht' ['A woman from 8 a.m. to midnight']). The commentary text was built in rhymes, spoken alternately by a female and a male voice, and the blonde model 'Evelyn' (see Figure 3.1) must have been well known by the viewers, because she was often seen in reports on Bormann fashion. Morning gowns, hats and coats, dresses for afternoon and evening were shown at stores, private rooms and in a bar. In every depicted situation, the commentary alludes to the fact that the clothes should be pleasing to men. The previous report, however, was on a successful female team leader in the textile industry in Zwickau, Saxony. According to the commentary, she was the prototype of the socialist 'new people' – as she committed herself selflessly, foregoing a higher salary, in order to lead a female work brigade to success in fulfilling the plan. Through the order of the reports, the newsreel

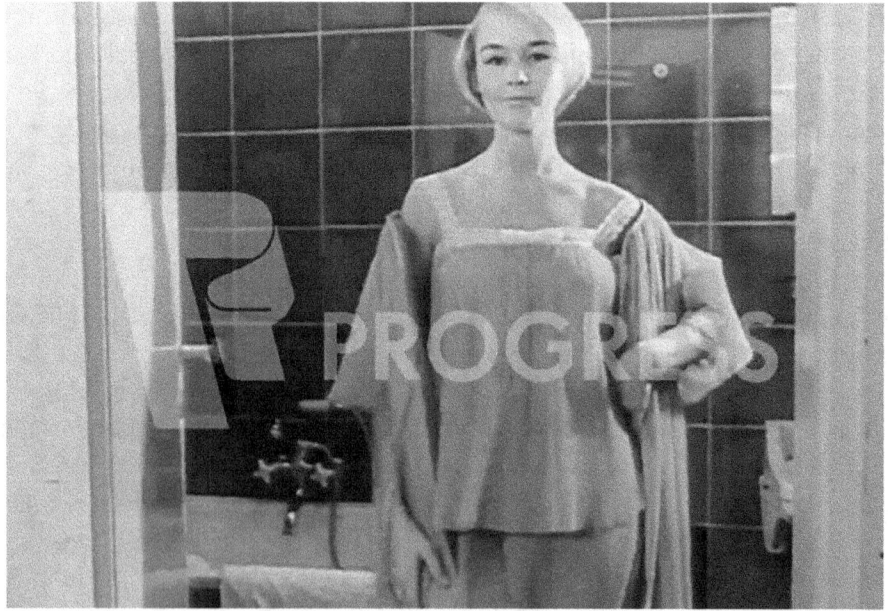

Figure 3.1 Bormann model in a morning gown, *Der Augenzeuge* no. A79, 1959

supported a 'cue' for the understanding of the viewers, as it gave a clear message: women work for women's fashion themselves – they not only wore the clothes but were also responsible for the production process and needed as workers in the socialist economy. But it also shows the contradiction that, on the one hand, fashion was made to attract men, but on the other hand, women should show self-esteem by leading work teams.

In *Der Augenzeuge* no. B64 of 1960, the Bormann company was portrayed again. The film team visited his studio, and the newsreel shows the full process of fashion production from initial sketch to the tailoring process. The commentary highlights the fact that Bormann is half-owned by the East German state and, with the support of the state, has been able to develop into one of East Germany's leading fashion houses. The influence of the state was indirectly made clear. It was also reported that Bormann produces ready-to-wear fashion, which indirectly conveys that he is not only a well-known fashion designer, but also creates useful fashion for the mass supply of the state's working community.

In no. 13 from 1963, the newsreel shows a sequence of reports: first, on one of the most modern textile machines of the world from the 'volkseigener Textilmaschinenbau' (East Germany's nationally owned textile machinery), as the commentator says, and introducing a new weaving procedure. Second, a report launches a new fabric made by those machines, branded 'Welvara', including the winter coats made from it. Having thus displayed the full production process and its result in the form of attractive, useful and cheap clothes produced with the support of the socialist state community, selected pieces from Bormann's new summer collection were presented to give a preview of the new fashion season. It can be assumed that if the order of these two fashion reports had been reversed, the audience's attention or even interest in the new fabric 'Welvara' probably would have been much lower.

East and West German fashion in *Der Augenzeuge*

In the East German reports, fashion contests from socialist countries were presented, such as those in Czechoslovakia, Romania and very often Poland.[27] One example highlights the international fashion show of six socialist countries in Warsaw in 1956, where the dresses from East Germany won the contest for the first time. The commentary expresses the hope that the clothes will soon be available in stores, which could be read as a subtle criticism, as this was still not always the case due to the planned economy.[28]

Another example is a report from 1959 about a knitwear fashion show from the state 'Modeinstitut' (fashion institute) in Prague, Czechoslovakia.[29] The female voice mentions the new line of knitted cocktail dresses, which modern women wear for the purpose of attracting men. A fashion show for teenagers in 1964 in a Warsaw textile factory reveals that the needs of young persons had been noted[30] – and they could now vote on the clothes too. The male commentary voice mentions that the ready-made dresses were well liked, and he used western expressions like 'Texas-Skirt' (in A-line, trapeze line). The message is probably that the youth fashion in socialist countries is not inferior to the fashion in western countries.

In contrast to the West German newsreels, *Der Augenzeuge* depicted the difference between the two political and economic systems. The East German newsreels also showed western fashion, but, for example, Parisian hats were presented with ironic commentary.[31] Absurd-looking pieces were chosen, and the comment implied that the models were simple-minded, as were the women who wore them (the commentary says, 'It has been proven that the straw in the head can also be shown on the head'). The pictures stem from a French newsreel and some of the models were also shown in *Neue Deutsche Wochenschau* no. 213 from 24 February 1954, but in a different way, of course – funny but not sarcastic. This is an excellent example of how the filmed footage was edited differently through the use of commentary and music in East and West German newsreels at the time. But only three years later, French fashion seems to have been accepted in East Germany too, when the state fashion industry showed the 'Line 57', which focuses on Paris, as the commentary said ('tonangebend auch für 1957 die Modeschöpfer in Paris'; 'setting the tone also for 1957 the fashion designers in Paris') at the Leipzig trade fair (see Figure 3.2). The presentation took place in front of new car models accompanied by pleasing tango music to emphasise the international touch.[32]

West German fashion in West German newsreels

The West German fashion reports show not only the beautiful dresses themselves but also how they were presented in or by other media. In *Welt im Bild*[33] no. 121 from 20 October 1954, the pure luxury of fur fashion was presented in tandem with beautiful fashion illustrations. Viewers were shown sketches of the coats by the fashion illustrator Eric Godall. The supplier, the famous fur fashion house Berger in Hamburg and Berlin, is mentioned – and

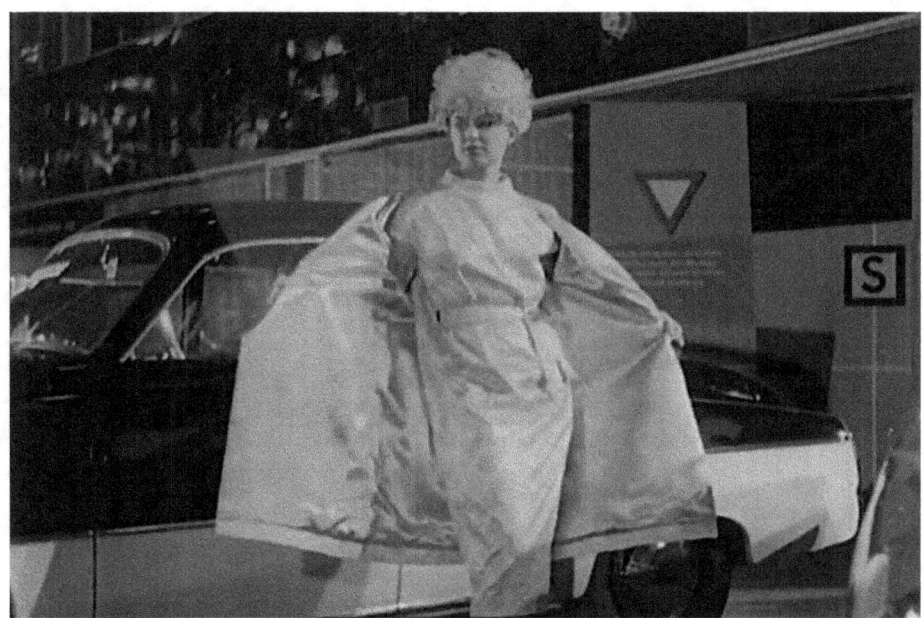

Figure 3.2 Parisian chic at Leipzig trade fair in GDR, *Der Augenzeuge* no. B14, 1957

the images convey the high quality of the products. The different species of fur animals were explained, for example Canadian mink, ocelot, Southwest African Persian, seal, and Russian iltis, the latter in playing with metaphors – should be a "warm bastion against the Polar front from the far North' – and the report was underscored with elegant South American dance music. Finally, it was indicated, husbands and gentlemen were expected to pay for the expensive coats. The West German Fashion reports did not just combine fashion shows with illustration, but also with fashion photography, music and dancing. The report from *Ufa-Wochenschau* no. 334 from 21 December 1962 shows how a photographer encourages the models to dance in the special 'Madison' way (a contemporary dance) in order to move naturally and in a modern way. In this way, the viewer is shown how the pictures for fashion magazines were produced. This report was accompanied by Schlager music, instead of the usual instrumental music. Modern music, dance and fashion were thus presented in the newsreels as features of the modern West German consumer society.

At the beginning of the 1960s, professional camera equipment became lighter and sound recording became easier with smaller devices, offering new work routines and reporting techniques. Filmed interviews and directly addressing the audience became elements of West German fashion reports.

In *Neue Deutsche Wochenschau* no. 423 from 7 March 1958, the designer Heinz Schulze-Varell[34] speaks directly to the audience (see Figure 3.3). He said that he had received telephone calls from women who were concerned about unwearable fashion. He now wanted to calm these women by reassuring them that his fashion would always be very wearable. In this way he expressed the idea that normal women could be dressed exclusively and acceptably that season.

Wearability depended not only on the design, but also on the material, which needed to be easy to care for in everyday life. The *Ufa-Wochenschau* from 7 May 1958 presents models from Heinz Oestergaard and Bessi Becker in outfits made from the well-known synthetic fibre 'Dralon'. The material had some very convenient characteristics as it was easy to wash, it dried quickly, and it was very durable. The larger the range of available fashion became, the more consumer groups were targeted. Whereas young people in East Germany had to wait until the end of the 1960s for their own fashion (Pelka 2014),[35] the new generation in West Germany was considered a powerful consumer group. The fashion industry gave them their own fashion style. In June 1962, *Neue Deutsche Wochenschau* no. 646 reported on a hat testing

Figure 3.3 Designer Heinz Schulze-Varell at his studio, *Neue Deutsche Wochenschau* no. 423, 7 March 1958

for young people. It was not just a hat testing; the teenagers and young adults were also invited to dance and listen to music. During the event, the young men were interviewed by a reporter who asked if they liked the hats, seemingly because this particular consumer group was of great importance to the headwear industry.

Western fashion in West German newsreels

In fact, no reports on fashion from eastern countries seem to have been shown in West German newsreels between 1950 and 1965. Undoubtedly, West German newsreels mainly referred to western fashion – for example, the report in *Welt im Film* no. 280 from 16 October 1950, which shows Austrian clothes being presented in a hotel. Like a cliché, the show ends with a nostalgic dress – reminiscent of the Austrian Empress Sissi – which was also a reference to the popular feature films about Sissi. In May 1954, it is reported that the French designer Jacques Fath had accepted an invitation to design for the stockings manufacturer Opal. The newsreel commentary thus promoted the stocking manufacturer too. The report shows Fath and his models enjoying a warm welcome in the Hotel Atlantic in Hamburg.[36] Only two weeks later, the *Welt im Bild* no. 100 from 26 May 1954 reported on the 'visit' of Emilio Schuberth and his models for a fashion show at the border of the British Sector in Berlin, whereupon German-born Schuberth was invited by another manufacturer of stockings, ARWA. The camera shows the ARWA label on a poster and then turns to the models getting off a bus in front of the Brandenburg Gate (Brandenburger Tor) in Berlin (see Figure 3.4). The pictures and wordplays of the commentary indicate the border between East and West Berlin, where the fashion show took place – especially as one of the models shows a 'reversible' coat. The report provided a variety of 'cues' for the viewers. The commentary reveals the Cold War through ironic plays on words and images. He says, for example, that the clothes became 'tangible reality' ('greifbare Wirklichkeit') – to allude to the economy of scarcity in East Germany. In the end, the commentary describes the fashion show as an 'unusual demonstration' on the otherwise hot pavement in front of the Brandenburg Gate – a 'parade of the king of fashion' – to allude to the mass parades before the socialist leaders that were customary in East Germany.

The most important country which represented the 'free world' to audiences was the United States of America. Although West Germany counted itself amongst that community of states, obviously West German fashion was

Figure 3.4 Emilio Schuberth's model at the Brandenburg Gate, *Welt im Bild* no. 100, 26 May 1954

very late in getting noticed by the USA. The *Neue Deutsche Wochenschau* no. 461 from 28 November 1958 reports on the first German fashion show in the USA for twenty-four years, which was clearly sponsored by Lufthansa, as the labels are visible on a wall in the background. The report in NDW no. 637 from 13 April 1962 is very special: 'Monsieur Heim' (aka Jacques Heim), a French designer, who spoke excellent German, is sitting in a bar with the bar keeper (in a very clichéd way) whilst his own spring collection and models of other French colleagues are shown. Obviously, in an effort to be personal and to make contact, he speaks directly to the audience through the camera. It seems likely that this new visual approach, and dedication to viewer proximity, was due to the competition from the new medium of television.

Differences and similarities of East and West Germany

The East German newsreel *Der Augenzeuge* presented mostly appropriate clothes at affordable prices (the prices were often mentioned). Consumers, the working people, should be able to make decisions about the production and to vote on the models. Since there was no competition in the planned economy, distribution in East Germany was clearly regulated by the central Trade Organisation (Handelsorganisation, HO) and the state-owned shops, called 'Konsum'. Both were mentioned by the newsreel commentary, not for advertising matters but for presenting the state trade system as a reliable system for providing people with all the goods they needed for their everyday lives. The presentation of fashion, technology and the textile industry were often connected in order to demonstrate the full production process, and the improvement in quality – especially when it came to new synthetic fibres. The collaboration between fashion houses and the textile industry in socialist countries was highlighted. Until 1956, French fashion was depicted as unsuitable, and the models were indirectly described as dubious. In contrast, the fashions from East Germany were depicted as wearable and stereotypically feminine at the same time. Only one important fashion designer was mentioned: Heinz Bormann in Magdeburg. He was called 'the Red Dior' ('der Rote Dior'), as he liked the French style. His preference for French fashion was accepted by the state since his work was important for the export of fashion goods. In 1957 the fashion reports started to highlight the Parisian style in a more positive manner – the reason being that it was probably better for East Germany's political relations with France,[37] the improvement of the economy in general, and also the high numbers of dissatisfied refugees moving from East to West.[38] *Der Augenzeuge*, which sometimes acted as an advocate for the viewers, criticised the fact that the fashion shown at the fairs was hardly ever available in the stores.[39]

In contrast to East Germany, West German newsreels presented fashion from many fashion designers and the names of their fashion houses[40] were mentioned on a regular basis. In 1960, the style of reporting changed: designers commented on their fashion themselves and they spoke directly to the viewers as potential consumers. Fashion was often combined with art, for example pictures or drawings in a gallery or at a studio – but not with industry (as it is in *Der Augenzeuge*). The inclination towards Parisian fashion is very obvious – but at the same time, the wearability in everyday life was also highlighted. It seems that West German women needed to be convinced that the dresses were not too extravagant. On the one hand, modern young women were targeted, while on the other hand, the length of the skirts was often commented upon in an old-fashioned and clichéd manner. The fashion designers and their models were ambassadors for their country, but it is still a fact that East German fashion is missing in West German newsreels. Instead, *Welt im Film* (the British-American newsreel) used fashion for political or even ideological messages, emphasising the advantages of the 'free Western World'.

Although it seems that eastern and western fashion was coined by two different political systems, the cultural meaning of fashion and the technical development of the textile industry resulted in some common experiences. The new synthetic fibres were named differently in the East and the West,[41] but the growing industry needed reports about fashion, made from the new cloth. NDW no. 536 from 6 May 1960 reported on a Europe-wide contest for designers, sponsored by the chemical industry, called 'Goldene Bayer Schere'[42] – and the results were presented in Milan. *Der Augenzeuge* no. A21 from 1959 reported on fashion made from synthetic fibres, presented at the Leipzig trade fair under the motto 'Chemistry makes [it] beautiful and happy' ('Chemie macht schön und froh'). Although the 'fashion world' was divided, Parisian fashion seems to unite both parts – all styles met in the French style. Another similarity worthy of mention is that prior fashion trends (even from former centuries) came back into style and were expressed in current fashion trends. In general, hats and caps were used for humorous, ironic or sarcastic commentary through the entire period covered in this study (1950–65).

The study also indicates that the current gender roles were continuously commented upon: women were seductresses, wanting to attract men, and the men (the husbands) were presumed to have the money to buy all the dresses and accessories women want. The set-up was slightly different in East Germany, from the point of view that if the husband did not contribute to the purchase, the wife would make it herself[43] – all in order to highlight the alleged gender equality guiding working East German women.[44]

Conclusion

What can be learnt from the analysis of the newsreel films? First of all, it is all about how fashion was presented in the West and the East and what means were used to promote the viewers' understanding and encourage them to draw conclusions. The insight comes from comparing West and East German newsreels. Fashion could not be perceived solely as a cultural, non-political topic; on the contrary, newsreel research reveals that it was highly political, especially in the 1950s. The competition between East and West is visible and audible through the selection of pictures and films (which stem partly from newsreels abroad) and through the wordplays of the commentary. The newsreels are characterised by one-sided reporting, bar the fact that audiences in East Germany were sometimes presented with selected fashion reports from western countries (what the viewers in East Germany saw were obviously mostly silly examples of western fashion). It seems that viewers in West Germany weren't aware of East German fashion at all. General attitudes seem to emerge: the West ignored the East, and the East compared itself with the West, denigrating the West by emphasising its own achievements and those of its socialist brother states.

The topic of fashion reveals that newsreel films should not only be read as documentary text, but in the sense of the *Visual History* approach, should also be regarded as research objects – to understand them as media, which conditions ways of seeing, shapes patterns of perception, transports modes of interpretation, and organises the relationship of historical subjects to their social and political reality (Paul 2012). For example, the usual catwalk performances of the 1950s, which kept audiences at a distance, were replaced in the 1960s by reports that created a proximity to the audience, by talking to them directly.

The reports' editing was not standardised, which resulted in unique reports in terms of the arrangement of the visual and acoustic elements. The editing expressed the attitude of the producers in East and West – whether controlled by the state in East Germany or protected by a constitution with freedom of the press and freedom of reporting in West Germany. On the one hand, a wide range of different cinematic designs are perceptible, while on the other, the cinematic means for directing the attention of the audiences were used in a similar manner in both German states. The German newsreel producers in West and East Germany were obviously well aware of how the attention of the audience could be directed by visual and textual 'cues'. According to an assessment by the writer and journalist Bernt Engelmann, dating from the 1960s, the commentary text was of secondary importance for a newsreel's impact. Engelmann furthermore postulated that any tendentious reporting emerges through the selection and montage of images, the sequence of cuts and the background music (Engelmann 1966: 39). In my view, the professionalism of the cinematographers is striking in the reports, as well as the tremendous skills of the film editors and text editors, always dedicated to presenting fashion at its best. Furthermore, written documents, for example work reports and letters from viewers, support the analyses of the footage, and the conclusions presented in this study. Without doubt, however, the reports not only served the humorous intent or extravagant amusement sought by the producers, as the audience letters prove; they also served as orientation and positioning in a world which was divided by the Iron Curtain.

Why should newsreels of the 1950s and 1960s still be of interest today? Cultural memory is shaped by media and these films are still used today in film and television, but the contexts are often missing. So, it is important to make comparisons when looking at history – particularly for producers of today's history formats, but also for interdisciplinary working academics.

Notes

1. Cinema visitors in West Germany and West Berlin: Increase in visitors up to 1956: 817.5 million; 1957: 801 million; 1958: 750 million; decrease in visitors beginning 1959: 671 million; 1960: 605 million; until 1965: 294 million (Roeber and Jacoby 1973: 206) (according to SPIO-Statistics). In 1957, 30 per cent of people visited a cinema twice a month; 20 per cent once a month, 16 per cent once per week (Hagemann 1959: 11). The older the cinema goer, the less he or she visited a cinema in 1956 (Noelle and Neumann 1957: 60).
2. The shadows from the stage show a string orchestra. Thus, for the viewers, it was obvious that the orchestra was not playing the music they were hearing.
3. Some empirical studies and surveys were conducted in the 1950s. They focused on the attitude towards newsreels in general and the topics preferred by the viewers (Hagemann 1959), but they didn't look at the effect on people's opinions.
4. For example, the two-part television biopic *Aenne Burda – Die Wirtschaftswunderfrau* (ARD, 2019) and the documentary on her life, *Ku'Damm 56*, as a three-part German television film on youth in 1950s (and continued in *Ku'Damm 58* and *Ku'Damm 63*) (ZDF, 2016, 2019); the trilogy *Heimat – Eine deutsche Chronik* (Edgar Reitz, 1981–2012) on a family in the period from the 1920s to the 1980s, a hybrid format with real existing places but a fictionalised story, produced for cinema.
5. I follow on from my contributions about, for example, German–German trade (Lehnert 2018a) and newsreels as an agent of history (Lehnert 2018b).
6. One of the central words of neo-formalism is 'Verfahren' (Russian 'priëm', English 'device'). For the Russian Formalists (movement of literary critics from 1915 to 1930), art – or film – is understood as the sum of its procedures. According to Thompson, the term refers to 'any single element or structure that plays a role in a work of art – a camera movement, a frame story, a repeated word, a costume, a theme, etc.' (Thompson 1995: 35, cited in Kirsten 2016: 4). Furthermore, the difference between syuzhet and fabula is important: 'In the [fiction] film, narration is the process whereby the film's syuzhet and style interact in the course of cueing and channeling the spectator's construction of the fabula' (Bordwell 1985: S. 53). The sequence of events in the film may differ from reality. The Russian formalist Viktor Sklovskij introduced the dichotomy of 'fabula' and 'syuzhet', which became significant for narratology. The fabula is the chronological sequence of events – as a cause–effect chain – in a certain time and space. Stories can be told in different ways. The syuzhet, usually translated as 'plot', is the actual presentation of the fabula in the film. Bordwell assumes that, in contrast to the syuzhet, style is not independent of the medium, but encompasses the means of representation (devices) of the respective medium. The syuzhet encompasses the film in the dramaturgical sense, the style – determined by the medium – in the technical sense.

7. The viewer actively searches for 'cues' (both at the level of sensory stimuli and at the level of narrative cues) and assembles them into expectations ('anticipations') and conclusions ('inferences') about what is audio-visually presented and the actions meant. The mediating element between 'cues' and 'inferences' are 'schemata' (Thompson 1995).
8. An attempt is made to make the ambiguity of the filmic works recognisable: not a linear approach, but a circular procedure in which the text of the film is confronted with individual findings and results of interpretation.
9. *Welt im Bild/Ufa-Wochenschau* and NDW were produced by the same company, the Deutsche Wochenschau GmbH, in Hamburg.
10. The production was started in 1946 by a special section at the DEFA; in 1952 the DEFA-Studio für Wochenschau und Dokumentarfilme was founded.
11. Due to the weekly production, the topicality was low, moreover the objectivity was low as well. Attraction and exclusiveness were sometimes needed instead.
12. This was the International Newsreel Association (INA), and single reports or whole editions were delivered abroad. But the pictures were edited and newly underscored by text, music and sound. So, it was likely that some pictures were used for propagandistic matters.
13. West German newsreels are available at Filmothek of Bundesarchiv: www.filmothek.bundesarchiv.de; the editions of *Der Augenzeuge* are available at the portal of Progress-Film in Berlin: https://progress.film/.
14. The strong attention to fashion might have been caused by the state involvement of the most important fashion house, Bormann, in the GDR and by the important Leipzig trade fair.
15. *Agenda setting approach* by Bernard Cohen and his main result: Media has no major impact on what people think but what they think about (Cohen 1963). The research on the effect of agenda-setting compares the salience of issues in news content with the public perceptions of the most important issue, and then analyses the extent of influence by guidance of the media.
16. Most-preferred topics by viewers in general: 1. politics, 2. sports, 3. art and culture, 4. disasters, 5. technology and science, 6. fashion. However, women preferred 1. politics, 2. sports, 3. fashion, 4. art and culture, 5. disasters, 6. technology and science (Hagemann 1959: 15).
17. The women should be interested in new inventions for the household, fashion shows and so forth. One hears 'rarely, that a woman is interested in the newsreel therefore also the late coming whereby punctual visitors are annoyed only', Letter of viewer Otto Klinkenberg, Niederau, to Bavaria-Filmverleih, Düsseldorf, 13.2.1959, Folder Korrespondenz, Film- und Fernsehmuseum Hamburg (FFMH). In fact, due to the losses of men in the war, cinemas had more female than male visitors at that time. Population in 1955: 45.5 per cent male, 54.5 per cent female (Noelle and Neumann 1957: 3).
18. The fashion shows shown are for the top 10,000, Letter of viewer Otto Klinkenberg, Niederau, to Bavaria-Filmverleih, Düsseldorf, 13.2.1959, Folder Korrespondenz, Film- und Fernsehmuseum Hamburg (FFMH).
19. Note in the cinematographer's work report for NDW no. 198, 11.11.1953: 'Please name: Sports fashions by Unnützer [underlined] München Maximilianstr.', BArch (Bundesarchiv Berlin), B 319/ (Deutsche Wochenschau GmbH).

20. See work report of Hans Egon Koch for NDW no. 198, 11 November 1953: Report on Winter fashions on the Zugspitze: Remarks: 'Please name: Sportmoden von Unnützer [underlined] Munich Maximilianstr'.
21. Work reports, which cinematographers were required to fill in, give further information about the circumstances of the production: for example, stating the amount of raw film material used, lighting conditions, place, time and topic, description of the motifs, and name of other newsreels or even television teams that had also filmed at the spot. In the work reports, sometimes the cinematographer also suggested the story title or text passages, adding brochures or newspaper articles for the editorial team's further information.
22. Elfi Wildfeuer was a popular model for Christian Dior and Jacques Fath (see Anonymous, Fotographie/Wildfeuer: Gut im Bilde, *Der Spiegel*, no. 16, 20 April 1950, pp. 32–4). See work report for NDW no. 198, 11 November 1953: 'Leider hatte das beste Mannequin Elfi Wildfeuer in letzter Minute abgesagt. Leider, die Anderen waren teilweise dof' [*sic!*] 'Unfortunately, the best mannequin Elfi Wildfeuer had cancelled at the last minute. Unfortunately, the others were partly stupid', BArch B 319/(Deutsche Wochenschau GmbH).
23. Additionally, the newsreel might have mentioned those people for maintaining good relationships to the film industry.
24. For example, Miss Germany 1950 Susanne Erichsen (NDW no. 192, 30. September 1953), actress Hildegard Knef (NDW no. 43, 21 November 1950).
25. In West Germany mostly French fashion in NDW and Italian fashion in *Welt im Bild* and *Ufa-Wochenschau*.
26. The state changed the company to a limited partnership (Kommanditgesellschaft) and took 60 per cent of the shares. Original quote: 'Der Staat redet mir nicht herein. Ich bin mein eigener Herr'. (Anonymous, 'Sowjet Zone: Roter Dior', *Der Spiegel*, 43 [1965], p. 59).
27. A German–Polish friendship was established on 6 July 1950 (Behrends 2006: 265–6).
28. *Der Augenzeuge* no. 28, 1956, original quote: 'Hoffentlich ist der Weg vom Laufsteg in den Handel nicht allzu weit.'
29. *Der Augenzeuge* no. A1, 1959.
30. *Der Augenzeuge* no. 20, 1964.
31. *Der Augenzeuge* no. 5, 1954.
32. *Der Augenzeuge*n no. B14, 1957.
33. *Welt im Bild* was the successor newsreel of the British-American newsreel *Welt im Film*.
34. He designed dresses and costumes for, among others, Zarah Leander and Lilian Harvey.
35. Fashion requires the admission of individuality, which, however, was initially not possible due to the state's efforts to make young people uniform.
36. NDW no. 224, 12 May 1954.
37. From February 1956 to June 1957, the socialist Guy Mollet was the prime minister.
38. In 1957 the number of refugees increased dramatically. Reasons for flight included dissatisfaction with the supply of upscale goods and restrictions on freedom to travel.
39. *Der Augenzeuge* no. A45, A55, A73 and B52 from 1958.
40. Like Jacques Fath, Christian Dior, Marie-Louise Carven, Jean Dessès, Jacques Heim (France), Elsa Schiaparelli, Emilio Schuberth (Italy, born in Germany), Heinz Schulze-Varell, Heinz Oestergaard, Helle Brüns, Bessi Becker (Germany).

41. For example, in West Germany Perlon was presented in *Welt im Bild* no. 102, 26 May 1954 in the presence of the 'inventors' (Hermann Staudinger, Paul Schlack).
42. Contest of eleven West German fashion schools and seven professional designers. Bayer is a great chemical corporation, and the prize was of course a tool for public relations.
43. *Der Augenzeuge* no. A77, 1959.
44. In the GDR, women had to work and were therefore more autonomous, but not completely equal, although this was claimed by the SED and presented in the newsreel (Würz 2016).

References

Allen, Robert C. and Douglas Gomery. 1985. *Film History: Theory and Practice.* New York: McGraw-Hill.
Assmann, Jan. 1988. *Kultur und Gedächtnis.* Frankfurt a. M.: Suhrkamp.
Behrends, Jan C. 2006. *Die erfundene Freundschaft. Propaganda für die Sowjetunion in Polen und in der DDR.* Cologne: Böhlau.
Bordwell, David. 1985. *Narration in the Fiction Film.* Madison: University of Wisconsin Press.
Bordwell, David and Kristin Thompson. 1997. *Film Art: An Introduction.* New York: McGraw-Hill.
Chion, Michel. 1994. *Audio Vision: Sound on Screen.* New York: Columbia University Press.
Cohen, Bernard C. 1963. *The Press and Foreign Policy.* Princeton, NJ: Princeton University Press.
Engelmann, Bernt. 1966. 'Vorhang auf für Bonns tönende Wochenschau'. *Deutsches Panorama*, 4, 35–9.
Ganeva, Mila. 2018. *Film and Fashion amidst the Ruins of Berlin.* Rochester, NY: Camden House.
Hagemann, Walter. 1959. *Filmbesucher und Wochenschau.* Emsdetten: Lechte.
Hickethier, Knut. 2012. *Film- und Fernsehanalyse*, 5th edn. Stuttgart: J. B. Metzler.
Jordan, Günter. 1990. 'DEFA-Wochenschau und Dokumentarfilm 1946–1949', unpublished dissertation, Humboldt-Universität, Berlin.
Jordan, Günter. 1996. 'Der Augenzeuge'. In *Schwarzweiß und Farbe: DEFA-Dokumentarfilme 1946–92*, edited by Günter Jordan and Ralf Schenk, 271–93. Berlin: Filmmuseum Potsdam and Jovis Verlagsbüro.
Kirsten, Guido. 2016. 'Neoformalismus und Kognitive Filmtheorie'. In *Handbuch Filmtheorie*, edited by Bernhard Groß and Thomas Morsch, 1–15. Wiesbaden: Springer VS.
Kleinhans, Bernd. 2013. *'Der schärfste Einsatz für die Wirklichkeit'. Die Geschichte der Kinowochenschau.* St. Ingbert: Röhrig Universitätsverlag.
Kraftwerk. 1978. *Das Model* [video]. Available at https://www.youtube.com/watch?v=2meuYmtjzdc (accessed 31 May 2022).
Lehnert, Sigrun. 2018a. 'Innerdeutscher Handel in Messeberichten der Kino-Wochenschau Ost-West (1950–1965)'. *Archiv und Wirtschaft*, vol. 51, no. 1, 14–29.
Lehnert, Sigrun. 2018b. 'The German Newsreels as Agents of History'. *Media History*, vol. 26, no. 3, 263–79. DOI: 10.1080/13688804.2018.1544886.

Noelle, Elisabeth and Peter Neumann. 1957. *Jahrbuch der öffentlichen Meinung 1957*. Allensbach: Verlag für Demoskopie.

Paul, Gerhard. 2012. 'Visual History, Version 2.0'. *Docupedia-Zeitgeschichte*, 29 October 2012 [online]. Available at http://docupedia.de/zg/paul_visual_history_v2_de_2012 (accessed 31 May 2022).

Pelka, Anna. 'Zum Verhältnis von Mode, Ideologie und Nachfrage in kommunistischen Diktaturen'. *Aus Politik und Zeitgeschichte*, 23 December 2014. Available at http://www.bpb.de/apuz/198382/zum-verhaeltnis-von-mode-ideologie-und-nachfrage-in-kommunistischen-diktaturen (accessed 31 May 2022).

Roeber, Georg and Gerhard Jacoby. 1973. *Handbuch der filmwirtschaftlichen Medienbereiche: die wirtschaftlichen Erscheinungsformen des Films auf den Gebieten der Unterhaltung, der Werbung, der Bildung und des Fernsehens*. Munich: De Gruyter.

Schwarz, Uta. 2002. *Wochenschau, westdeutsche Identität und Geschlecht in den fünfziger Jahren*. Frankfurt: Campus.

Steiner, André. 2007. *Von Plan zu Plan. Eine Wirtschaftsgeschichte der DDR*. Bonn: Bundeszentrale für politische Bildung.

Thompson, Kristen. 1995. 'Neoformalistische Filmanalyse: Ein Ansatz – Viele Methoden'. *montage/av*, vol. 4, no. 1, 23–63.

Würz, Markus. 2016. 'Frauen im Sozialismus'. *Lebendiges Museum Online*, Stiftung Haus der Geschichte der Bundesrepublik Deutschland [online]. Available at http://www.hdg.de/lemo/kapitel/geteiltes-deutschland-gruenderjahre/wirtschaft-und-gesellschaft-im-osten/frauen-im-sozialismus.html (accessed 31 May 222).

Chapter 4

'Third way' teenage fashion: housewives' films documenting ideals of middle-class youth culture in 1950s Sweden

Mats Björkin

In 1954, the short film *Tonårsmodet* (Teenage Fashion), produced by a new advertising agency, Husmors Filmer AB, was screened in Swedish cinemas as part of a free programme of information and advertising films. These so-called 'housewives' films', which had begun production two years earlier, would be a biannual itinerant event for over twenty years.[1] This chapter will discuss what made teenage fashion a subject suitable for an informational and advertising endeavour aimed at housewives (and their younger children) and how these films document a particular period in Swedish media and fashion history.

The housewives' films were not ordinary commercial films for cinema theatres. They were especially and carefully composed film programmes, about sixty to ninety minutes long, made up of seven to ten information and advertising films, each five to fifteen minutes long. A celebrity, well known either from women's magazines, entertainment, cinema, or later from television, would act as host for the show within the film programme. Stage events, showcases and quizzes often accompanied the screenings. Between 1952 and 1976 these programmes toured Sweden and were shown free at cinemas in the afternoons (Jansson 1996: 7–12). The company, Husmors Filmer AB, whose name came to be synonymous with the phenomenon, was founded by ad-man Bengt Davidsson, with the aim of making 'sober, fact-based advertising films'. Experts made sure the films were both informative and likely to aid sales. No reliable audience statistics are available, but at their ten-year anniversary celebration in 1962, the company claimed that they had had 'about four million visitors' attending the programmes (Berner 2002: 156).

The company started in 1952, just before the first public debate about commercial television, and two years before the first Swedish experiment with commercial television, the Sandrew-Week (Olsson 2004). Davidsson and his company were also pioneering advertisements themselves and were part of a fast-growing and innovative advertising environment with close links to Western European and US advertising and marketing trends. Print advertising was obviously the main inspiration. To accompany the films, they published a magazine called *Husmors-Journalen* (Housewife's Magazine). In the very first issue, the editor described the need for 'sober advertising', which ought to be both informative and at the same time able to market products. In the magazine, good advertising was seen as a way of making a housewife's day more efficient (Englund 1954: 1). Their definition of a 'housewife' was a married woman with children and a part-time job outside the home (even if only 25–30 per cent of all Swedish married women worked outside the home in the 1950s). Because of her life outside the home, she needed to run her home efficiently and to be as well organised as possible. Above all, she had little time to gather information about different products, which is why the company Housewife Films AB saw a need for an improved form of advertising.

The few Swedish scholars who have studied these films have seen the housewives' films as both an outcome of the post-war diffusion of American capitalist ideology, and as the product of three decades of social engineering (Berner 2002). Both interpretations tend to disregard the ways in which the housewives' films became embedded in contemporary media production and use. Perhaps a more useful way into the context of *Tonårsmodet* is through two conclusions made by the fashion historian Ulrika Kyaga in her account of the Swedish post-war fashion industry (Kyaga 2017). First, she noted how fashion designer, illustrator and educator Göta Trägårdh became a key actor within a changing fashion industry, and how that played out in an actual film. Second, she argued that this same film can be seen as documenting the specific ideology of a good-quality but affordable, ready-to-wear Swedish fashion line, Modellkonfektion, positioned between haute couture and mass-market clothing, in the very particular cultural, political and economic context of the 1950s Swedish welfare state. Kyaga compares Modellkonfektion to the Italian boutique style; however, in contrast to the Italian boutique style, Swedish Modellkonfektion was aimed at the domestic market, and was not for export. Thus, a national style identity was 'implicitly embedded in these garments' (Kyaga 2017: 230). This 'third way' of fashion thus became yet another instance of the Swedish post-war third-way exceptionalism created by Social Democrat politics.

To understand the housewives' films, we need to understand the aims of the Social Democrat government. Swedish neutrality during the Second World War was followed by continued attempts to create a 'third' position between socialism and capitalism. The business sector argued that they were a natural part of the western capitalist system (and with a similar legal framework to other western democracies), while the social democratic government was determined to strengthen an exceptional Swedish *third way*, by way of a strong state, an extended welfare system, and an internationally competitive privately owned industrial sector. One of the outcomes of this 'third way' was an option to 'neutralise' both public citizenship and capitalist consumerism by merging them into one well-informed individual, aware of his or her social and national attachment. This fundamentally nationalist agenda, with Sweden as the exception, also meant that industry, state and the growing cooperative sector were all well aware of and very responsive to what happened elsewhere in the world. Consequently, despite its deep engagement with the United Nations and the European Union in later years, Sweden has never been as international in its cultural, media and business approaches as it was during the 1950s.

I have elsewhere employed the technological historian Mikael Hård's concept of 'a development triad', a concept he used in an analysis of the development of Swedish housing standards (Björkin 2021): '[A] development triad consisting of private, public, and cooperative actors [that] fostered the formation and diffusion of new technical standards and solutions' (Hård 2010: 130). The *development triad* seems to have been particularly suitable for issues related to the human use of technologies, but also for the political and business interests of social change. Considering the widespread understanding of the foundational role of science and technology at the time, the concept of the development triad can help us understand many aspects of 1950s Swedish society. State and private actors advertised and marketed domestic products in new ways, often by cooperating with consumer organisations and women's organisations (Rosén 2010). The ideology of a harmony within the triad, of course, echoes Sweden's third way policy, but it also resembles a more general trend in Western Europe and the United States towards a 'new centre', as described by Fred Turner (2013: 175).

The most striking feature of many of the housewives' films concerns not just household design and efficiency, but the financing of any refurbishment, and ways of affording consumption in general. The household development ideology would not have been so successful were it not for a general growth in incomes, and the development of the credit market. Since the early years of the twentieth century, private savings had been a major concern of public policy and public information, often in cooperation with savings and commercial banks. The development of the cooperative savings and housing company HSB (*Hyresgästernas sparkasse- och byggnadsförening*) in the late 1920s further emphasised the joint activities of private, public and cooperative actors. After the Second World War the market for home or household loans increased, which boosted the buying of private houses and apartments, as well as funding the refurbishment of old houses and apartments and the purchase of household appliances, furniture, textiles and utensils. The rapid increase in private loans for housing and renovation thus helped construction companies (for example HSB), household appliance companies (Electrolux) and furniture companies (IKEA, which was founded at this same time). It was also important for the car industry (Volvo and the recently started Saab). Most new housing projects were located outside city centres and were therefore dependent upon both public transportation (Scania and Volvo buses), and privately owned cars (Saabs and Volvos). These new suburbs and peripheral urban areas also helped change the dominant modes of food purchasing. With more and more food not being bought on the day of consumption, housewives had to rely on private and public transportation (cars and buses) as well as on efficient and healthy food storage (Electrolux refrigerators). Consequently, there was a slow political and economic reorganisation from local or regional small-scale producers to large-scale national brands (Björkin 2021).

It is in this context that we should see the prospering Swedish textile industries in general and the post-1930s growth of the Swedish fashion industry in particular. It is in this context too that we ought to understand the establishment and success of Husmors Filmer AB. They managed during their first few years of operation to make use of the links within the development triad: networks of public, private and cooperative housing and other forms of consumer investments; changes in laws and regulations of domestic and professional activities; the marketing and sales of consumer goods; the changing media landscape; and the political goals of social change.

Tonårsmodet can also be seen as a – perhaps ephemeral and marginal – source of material for fashion history. In an article on fashion journalism as fashion history, art historian and fashion scholar Patrik Steorn argues that fashion history is methodologically a hybrid 'in-between the practises of journalistic writing and academic research, as well as curating, teaching, and so on' (Steorn 2021: 216):

> This multifaceted field where the meanings and narratives of fashion history are negotiated contains many types of texts, very often illustrated, that are frequently aimed at a general audience with a fashion interest:

exhibition catalogues and other museum publications, etiquette books and consumer advising, corporate publications, debate books and pamphlets, and above all the illustrated fashion history overviews. (Steorn 2021: 216)

And of course, films, in particular housewives' films. I would also suggest that, from a fashion history perspective, housewives' films are interesting to look at because of the way that their topics, for example fashion, are inscribed in contemporary media practices of blurred boundaries between consumer journalism and marketing and thereby document their media and cultural function. Even if housewives' films were internationally rather unique, they were inscribed in post-war advertising, public, private and cooperative interests in communication, the media landscape of printed press (and advertising), cinemas, exhibitions and other live events, public service radio, and the question of what would become of the new medium of television.

Göta Trägårdh and the community of fashion experts (introduction of film)

With so much focus on household issues, what does a film about teenage fashion do in this context? Through an analysis of the film, I will show that *Tonårsmodet* through the various details (objects, brands, gestures, speech and so on) not only documents a view on fashion trends for teenage girls in 1954. It also tells a story about how their mothers were supposed to prepare their daughters to be modern, functionalist, Swedish middle-class young women in the media context of the welfare society.

The opening credits introduce the spectators to the fashion, film and communication networks that made the discourse of the film possible. The opening credits also introduce the stylistic concept of the film and the fashion to be promoted in the form of fashion drawings. We learn that the film is 'edited' ('programledning'); in this case we should understand that as being produced and written by Brita Svenonius, with Göta Trägårdh as contributing expert. The joint efforts of Svenonius and Trägårdh are important for what makes this film interesting as a cinematic document.

Brita Svenonius (1903–91) wrote, directed or produced a handful of housewives' films in 1953–4. In 1952 she had written, with Anna-Lisa Lyberg, a book for Aktiv Hushållning about making beds, and the purchasing, care and production of bed linen (1952). Aktiv Hushållning was a state information agency founded during the Second World War to help households adapt to the wartime situation. In 1954, Aktiv Hushållning merged with Hemmens forskningsinstitut (Household Research Institute). Hemmens forskningsinstitut (HFI) was created in 1944, in close collaboration with housewives' and household teachers' organisations, to conduct household-related research. A governmental investigation in 1949 (SOU 1949: 18) on household research and information proposed an information unit within HFI to promote modern household improvement by way of publications, lectures, exhibitions, photography, radio and film.

Svenonius worked for the Malmö-based advertising agency Antoni & Gehlin in the 1950s; these partners had marketed themselves as a modern agency by writing a book about (their own) modern advertising (Antoni and Gehlin 1953). She then went on to design catalogues for Bra Bohag and later IKEA. The journey from a public information agency, through an up-and-coming advertising firm, to developing the concept of the IKEA catalogue shows that Brita Svenonius was a leading communications expert well acquainted with state initiatives, cooperative movements and advertising – a manifestation of Mikael Hård's concept of a development triad.

Göta Trägårdh (1904–84), by contrast, was educated at Tekniska skolan, now the University of Arts, Crafts and Design in Stockholm, during the early 1920s. After a short stay in Paris in 1925 she studied decorative arts at Konsthögskolan, the Royal Institute of Art in Stockholm. One of her first assignments after graduation was designing the garments of the staff at the 1930 Stockholm Exhibition, the breakthrough event of Functionalism and the International Style. During the 1930s she became a fashion journalist at the major newspaper *Svenska Dagbladet* and one of Sweden's leading fashion illustrators. In 1939 she started the Beckmans College of Design together with advertising executive Anders Beckman. She was responsible for their fashion education for a long time, and many of her former students went into the Swedish and international fashion business after the war. She was for a period the fashion editor and illustrator of leading monthly magazine *Bonniers Månadstidning*.

After the film's credits, we see the hands of Göta Trägårdh and hear her voice, recording a written text about Swedish teenage fashion. She argues that the contemporary Swedish fashion industry has created fashionable, sober, affordable and sustainable clothes for teenagers, thanks to listening to teenagers themselves through organised teenage councils. Trägårdh thereby presents herself as the typical 'expert', so frequent in housewives' films (Berner 2002). At the same time, she encourages (other) mothers of teenagers to listen to what teenagers actually want. Trägårdh thus becomes a less distant expert, combining her strong professional reputation with being herself the mother of a teenage girl and having an office in her modern, fashionably furnished home.

In the film, her daughter, Lena, is seen approaching her in a respectful and formal way (typical of middle- and upper-class behaviour at the time). Lena says that her friend Torun is with her and she wants to go shopping for a new coat, but she wants Lena's mother, Göta Trägårdh, to accompany them. Trägårdh says she does not have the time but trusts them to select a coat by themselves. Even if she remains in her office she will, as the film's real narrator, accompany them and the audience, too, throughout the film. In many housewives' films the experts are men and therefore more distanced from those seeking their help. In *Tonårsmodet* the expert is thus integrated into both the fictional story and the making of the film.

Before leaving her mother's office, Lena asks if she can show a new fabric to her friend. They admire the new textile, but soon turn off their gramophone music and leave for the shop. In the room they are sitting in, which most likely is the living room – a feature in modern functionalist homes – we find modern furniture, a new radio-gramophone and light-coloured wallpaper. The girls are stylishly dressed, and the music sounds like standard big band jazz dance music. Together with how they talk, everything signals an upper-middle-class context.

At the store, the female sales assistant approaches the girls in a very formal manner. Torun says she has seen a new model in an advertisement – a straight design, almost a tube. The salesperson presents an example to Torun, while Lena is looking around on her own. Torun appreciates the coat, so the salesperson guides her to a mirror to try it on. We get the modern advertisement process in one short scene, from seeing an advertisement, talking to friends, to visiting a store to make the purchase. A plausible interpretation of the scene is that the film tries to create trust in both advertising and the expert professionals, at least in certain situations. The coat Torun wants is also a step away from the marked waistlines, New Look-style, which had been popular for some time (and which in modified forms are present in the film). As I will argue later, the legacy of the New Look in *Tonårsmodet* is multifaceted.

The director of photography, Ragnar Frisk, was quite new to be given responsibility for the cinematography of a film. Most of the film is shot in a straightforward documentary style, but his interest in using reframing through doors and his use of clever mirror shots indicates his inspiration from the many feature films where he had been an assistant camera operator.

One example is when Torun tries on the coat, assisted by the salesperson, and a mirror opens up the room to include not only Lena, but also a younger salesperson entering to say that they are ready for a film screening upstairs.

The film-within-the-film is emphasised by the older saleswoman explaining they are arranging a screening of a film about the spring teenage fashions. To further emphasise that the girls are looking and behaving like the kind of teenagers that are interested in educating themselves as consumers, they ask if they can attend. The older saleswoman continues this mix of traditional upper-middle-class formality with the expression of modern sales methods by replying that she was just about to ask 'the ladies' if they were interested in doing so. Through the way of speaking and addressing each other, we learn that the store not only seems to be directed towards upper-middle-class customers, but also that it is an ambitious store that arranges film screenings for their young customers. They all walk upstairs, and the camera passes by the younger salesperson behind the 16 mm projector, a fairly modern and popular model, a Bell & Howell 621 from 1950, frequently used for informational and advertising purposes. The meta-reference promotes a normality around using films to inform and promote products. It also promotes itself as an informational and advertising tool. Most importantly, it clearly signals the separation of the advertising segment from the rest of the film. A group of teenage girls are already sitting in front of the screen, and the camera pans behind them before zooming into the screen. They are all dressed in a similar style, so as to emphasise trends rather than individual personal taste. The advertising/informational film within the film begins.

Advertising (the film within the film)

The film that the girls are watching is a rather conventional advertising film where models are presenting garments in different places and situations while a voice-over presents the brands and the particular features of the different garments. The voice-over is directly speaking to teenage girls, and to their mothers.

The film opens with the female voice-over, echoing Göta Trägårdh earlier, saying that it is always good to buy high-quality clothes, and then take good care of these clothes. The opening title, *Det unga modet* (Young Fashion), is shown over a woven fabric then cut diagonally from upper right to lower left by a pair of scissors. Three of the main brands of the film, Sahlins, Young Lady Larella and Zober, are shown, while the voice-over promotes the value of choosing well-known brands when buying coats, dresses and shoes. Then there is a cut to a spinning wheel with shoes, with the voice-over saying that they all come from major Swedish shoe brand Gyllene Gripen. Again, she argues, they are all fit for young women and are suitable contemporary garments for young women (high-quality leather, low heels, comfortable and straight lines). The name of the shoe models such as 'Yankers' and 'Idaho' refer to American popular culture phenomena, following up on Lena's 'alright' after her mother declined to join her and friend to go shopping, and Torun's 'yeah' before leaving the apartment. References to French fashion are almost entirely absent in the film. As we will see, even if the Swedish contemporary ready-to-wear interpretation of fashion trends was heavily influenced by French haute couture, its marketing rather referred to American or British fashion.

Then there is a cut to water in front of a large building from which a young model, a 'school girl' in a tweed ensemble from Larella, is seen to exit and to approach another girl in a wool dress from Tonnie-modeller and a camel-hair coat from Zobel. Already in the first shot, the film is presenting its three major brands (and thus sponsors). The second sequence begins at a golf course. Two girls, one carrying a golf bag, are in the foreground, with two boys approaching the green (just behind the girls) at the rear. The voice-over does not comment upon the boys' clothes, but they seem to be correct but casual in a modern sporty way, rather than traditional golf garments. The voice-over starts by saying that this is the right context for a velvet corduroy coat from Zober and a camel-hair, ulster coat from Larella, a brand from Upsala Kappfabrik. Both coats are said to be well suited for teenagers' walks and other outdoor activities, as the scene changes to two girls walking in a park area by the water, with the Nordic Museum, an easily recognised building on the Stockholm skyline, as a distant backdrop. This time the girls are dressed in two different ulster coats, one red wool from Zobel and one grey baize wool from Sahlins, the later with a separate shawl. They meet a third girl, dressed in a corduroy coat from Zober. The camera then tilts down to the girls' feet to show their shoes from Gyllene Gripen. We see and hear the details, in a clear and recognisable Stockholm setting. At the same time, it is far from most teenage girls' everyday experiences. The exclusive building, the golf course and the fashionable eastern part of Stockholm signifies a traditional upper-middle-class ideal.

After a transition from the shoes to the dark red of the back of one of the girls' Larella wool coats, the next scene opens up when she slowly walks away from the camera. This time we are at the quay in front of the

Royal Castle (behind the camera), close to the prow of a ship, in another well-known Stockholm location, Skeppsholmen island, with the characteristic neo-medieval styled former Admiralty Building. The camera pans to the left to another girl entering in a marine-blue skirt suit. The voice-over remarks how useful it is for different purposes by just changing accessories. While the camera closes into a medium shot of the girls, the voice-over comments that a pleated skirt (just below the frame) is elegant and dressy on a young slim girl. The camera then tilts, passing down the pleated skirt and the wool coat to the 'teeners' shoes from Gyllene Gripen. The camera cuts back to a position just left of the opening shot, with the ship at the right, Skeppsholmen at the back, as the girls exit to the left. A swipe from right to left ends the film screening.

This naval scenery, and the uniform-style garments, may be seen as a move to a professional life. We have thus gone from students, via leisure activities, to (possibilities of future) work. On the other hand, the models are not presented as actually working (or studying). The advertising film, as with the entire *Tonårsmodet*, does not promote any particular future at all. It just presents different alternatives, if within a quite narrow range. If anything, teenagers are presented as just existing in their own right, not as in a transition to something else. They walk around the city observing each other, while the film's spectators look at them. The teenage girl in the advertising segment becomes an apparition, 'la passante', for the competent consumer girls in the audience to imagine not only how the garments might look on them, but how they themselves might move and be present in the city (Rocamora 2009: 136–7), very much in contrast to the more active teenagers in the film. The 'film within the film' moves the housewives, as the mothers of teenage girls, one step away from the desiring 'look' at the garments. *Tonårsmodet* thus documents the potential of two different female gazes: the girls' gaze of 'la passante', and the mothers of the teenagers as competent consumers.

Teenage fashion, class and gender in the welfare society (the party in the country house)

Back in the shop, the music changes back to contemporary big band dance music. When Lena and her friend return to the ground floor they comment on two garments not shown in the film we saw, a red coat shown outside the Dramatic Theatre and a blue tweed skirt suit. Lena's friend returns to looking at coats while Lena looks at shoes. She takes one she likes to show her friend.

The camera then closes in to the shelf showing shoes and some accessories, followed by a transition to the girls being back home at Lena's home. Again, objects are used for transition between settings.

A third girl is sitting in a modern lounge chair reading a magazine when Lena and her friend enter. She has come to ask if Lena has some black shoes she could borrow for a dinner party. Lena confirms she has some new ones for her while Lena's mother, out of frame, says there is a phone call for her. Lena and Torun exit. There follows a close-up of a black (LM Ericson) Bakelite telephone and a tilt upwards to a close-up of Lena smiling while answering the phone. She looks happy and we hear her approving something by saying that it really sounds fun. There is a cut back to Lena's room where Torun has picked up Lena's black shoes for their friend. She tries them on and asks if she can borrow them. Lena enters and says that of course she can, but then adds that they are invited by their male friend Sigge to Tyresö (south of Stockholm) over the weekend. The three of them are invited, as are Buster and Pelle (obviously two male friends of theirs), and some boys from an advertising school and some girls from Märthaskolan, a couture-oriented school and fashion house. They do not say which advertising school, but given Trägårdh's engagement in Beckmans, they may come from there. In any case, the advertising business was at the time seen as modern and in many respects representative of the growing post-war prosperity, patterns of consumption and the modernisation of Swedish society. On the other hand, Märthaskolan represented both French haute couture and solid, upper-class society. What we thus can expect is modern boys and traditional girls, with Lena (and her mother as narrator) in between.

Lena's friends are also happy with the invitation. Lena ends by saying they will be picked up by car, as the scene changes to outside the house, to a first-floor balcony above the entrance. Lena and Torun exit the building and the camera backs to the other side of the street, to show that it is a modern functionalist building. This is a completely different environment from that of the advertising film. It is still a fashionable area of Stockholm, but this time representing the international style, functionalism, in architecture and city planning. This style was introduced in Sweden and internationally recognised and acclaimed at the 1930 Stockholm Exhibition. Göta Trägårdh was invested in functionalism in many ways. As already mentioned, she designed clothes for the exhibition staff. Even Beckmans design school was an outcome of functionalism. Likewise, the film's producer, Brita Svenonius, was also invested in functionalism through her background in wartime efficiency and post-war housing development issues.

A red convertible (MG TD-style) comes to pick up the girls. They jump in and the car drives away. Then there is a cut to a medium close-up of the legs of a girl in trousers and comfortable shoes, trying to start a white scooter (with central Stockholm licence plates) in a similar neighbourhood. The camera tilts up and pans slightly to the left to show the red convertible with Lena and Torun waving to the girl with the scooter. She starts the scooter and drives away while the camera tilts to the sky, cuts to the sky above trees and tilts down to a narrow road in the woods where the girl on the scooter arrives with a boy sitting behind her. This sequence is a startling contrast to the setting and the mood of the advertising film. Functionalist residence areas and young women who are actually doing things, such as driving scooters, are far from the strolling and posing in the advertising segment. Combined, though, it may be interpreted as an argument that even well-dressed (upper) middle-class teenagers drive scooters and sports cars, not just 'Americanised' working-class youth. The music turns into a more Latin American inspired big band dance music, fashionable at the time. The camera follows them to a red-brick late nineteenth-/early twentieth-century country house surrounded by oak trees. The red convertible and some bicycles are parked in front of the house. This sequence ends with a romantic close-up of the scooter girl smiling by a rowanberry branch, before the scene moves on to an image of a similar branch in a vase indoors.

Behind the rowanberries a girl and a boy sit on a sofa talking. The camera backs up to show Lena sitting beside them. They laugh while the music becomes more distinct, and two dancing couples turn up between them and the camera. The camera pans to the right where two other girls sit in front of a 1950s-style brick fireplace. A short tilt down shows a portable gramophone by their feet. Then there is a cut to the sofa from the perspective of the girls in front of the fireplace. Lena comments on the skirt of one of the dancing girls. The boy turns towards her and ask if 'you girls can talk about anything else than clothes', in a very contemporary vernacular Stockholm dialect (far from the radio and film way of talking we have heard previously in the film). The girl besides her replies, in a slightly more formal Stockholm dialect, that 'you boys can't talk about anything but "hojar och vrålåk"' (slang for motorcycles and fancy cars), and suggests they can talk about shoes instead. One of the dancing couples, Torun and a boy, sits down on cushions on the floor between the sofa and the camera and put their feet on the fireplace bricks. Lena looks out of frame to the right and comments on the yellow moccasins of the girl by the gramophone. Lena says she saw those in a film the other day, and she acknowledges that the girls also appeared in the film. The girl by the gramophone, obviously one of the girls from Märthaskolan, was one of the models from the film Lena and Torun watched at the store. The boy in the sofa sounds surprised by this, while the girl on the sofa remarks that the boy and girl who stopped dancing have the same kind of shoes.

The camera changes position to high above the rowanberries, with the sofa on the left and the boy and girl with the same kind of shoes to the right. An off-screen female voice (the girl on the floor) says she had not noticed it while a similar off-screen male voice (the boy on the floor) says that he too could be fashionable. The girl comments, first with an informal 'tycker du', that is, 'you think so', then correcting 'du' to 'ni' which was a more formal way of addressing someone. The camera tilts upwards to another young man, probably the host, Sigge, who expresses his surprise and dislike that they say 'ni' to each other. Carrying two carafes containing a red drink (which looks like wine but is probably non-alcoholic), he then walks towards a table at the rear of the room.

'Du' in Swedish was at the time rarely used outside family or close friends, and sometimes not even within families, when addressing older people. Lena, for example, did not use 'du' when she spoke to her mother earlier in the film. She did not say 'ni', either, but addressed her as 'mother'.[2] So Sigge, although his formal Stockholm dialect, fashionable suit, fancy car and obviously modern-style country house indicate that he comes from a rather wealthy family, thus signals here a more modern, even functionalist, informality.

Sigge asks a boy sitting by the table, Pelle, to go to the kitchen and get some sodas ('sockerdricka'). The girl next to the fireplace asks Sigge if she can help. The camera returns to the view of the sofa, Lena and the couple with the same shoes on the floor, and the fireplace to the right. Sigge hands plates to everyone and a girl says, in a vernacular Stockholm style, that they are getting food. A boy asks who is overseeing the gramophone and another girl says that she is. A third girl asks her to play some nice music ('något tjusigt'). The music changes again into a Latin American music with a louder volume. The girl on the sofa asks Sigge if they could have the music on lower so they can talk more easily. Sigge then suggests, to the others' happy dismay, that he will tell a fairy tale. The volume of the music increases and the camera pans to and zooms in on the fireplace.

This final scene puts Lena at the centre in two ways – first physically, since she sits between three groups: the boy and the girl on the sofa, the two girls by the gramophone, and the two dancing couples. Second, she also makes sure that the discussion of fashion focuses on the garments presented earlier in the film, by combining the three groups. In this sense, she is an independent character at the centre of the film (Figure 4.1). On the other hand, she was subject to her mother, as both mother and expert, at the beginning of the film, and to Sigge, as host (and man) at the end of the film. Lena, throughout the film, is positioned as a semi-independent character. She is both the main character, and a character who is guided by others. The earlier close-up of Lena on the phone talking to Sigge may look like a typical 1950s 'girl on the phone shot' (Kearney 2006). However, Lena is neither fully contained in the family, like the girls in the discourses on US teenage girls, nor is she fully liberated. The 1950s was more complicated than those frequently repeated dichotomies suggest, which is often easier to see when looking at other parts of the world (Minton 2017). Again, the housewives' film version of the 'girl on the phone shot' is followed up with her continued role in the film as a semi-independent girl, following in the footsteps of her fashion expert mother, but also as a girl free to do what she wants.

The film ends with piano-based dance music, similar to the beginning of the film, and a close-up of fashion drawings of the garments shown in the film, with sample textiles, and the brand names written on the drawings: Tonnie-modeller, Zober, Ripsa, Sahlins, Larella Young Lady, and Gyllene

Figure 4.1 *Tonårsmodet*, Husmors Filmer 1954, © Petter Davidson. Composite of images by author

Gripen. The drawings make us understand Göta Trägårdh's presence and thus her role as the one who is really narrating the story.

Göta Trägårdh as curator and marketer

Göta Trägårdh's narration and argument within the film is also a form of 'curation' and, by doing so, she is a marketer of particular brands. The selection of brands documents her network rather than being just a reflection of what was available for teenagers at the time.

Tonnie-modeller became a trendy fashion company in the 1960s. The fashionable department store Nordiska Kompaniet (NK) in Stockholm became one of their main buyers.[3] Margareta Westberg and Tore Marklund started Tonnie-modeller in 1952 and it became famous after a celebrated show at the restaurant Riche in Stockholm 1953. Westberg studied at Yrkesskolan för sömnad och tillskärning (a vocational school of sewing and cutting) from 1946 to 1948 and at Anders Beckmans skola from 1946 to 1950, probably with Göta Trägårdh as teacher. It was perhaps the first teenage fashion company in Sweden. Westberg ran the company in different forms until the 1980s. She received many awards (*Femina*'s Oscarina for design in 1965 and 1966 and *Damernas Värld*'s Guldspaden in 1988), and she had shows and 'personal appearances' at Lord & Taylor, Bergdorf Goodman, Macy's New York, MayCo Denver, NK Sthlm, Gbg, Malmö and elsewhere.[4] Konfektions AB Zober started in Kristdala, Småland (southeast Sweden) in 1936, and then in Tranås from 1936 onwards. They seemed to have specialised in sports wear for both men and women. They were also established in Malmö. Ebba von Eckermanns Textilier started in Ripsa, southwest of Stockholm, in 1949 and became famous for hand-woven textiles, particularly pleated skirts. The company closed around 1980. Ebba von Eckermann was the daughter of Marg Schwerin, the founder of the Märthaskolan, a sewing and tailoring school in Stockholm, and a luxury fashion brand, AB Märthakonfektion. In the film, the girls at the party who were also modelling in the advertising film came from Märthaskolan. Sahlins konfektionsfabrik began in Eslöv, southern Sweden, in 1894 and specialised in children's clothes. Larella Young Lady was a brand of AB Upsala Kappfabrik, which began in Uppsala in 1904. The founder's daughter-in-law ran the company between 1943 and 1959, directing it towards more modern fashion. Under the name Young Lady, it went through some mergers in the 1960s and closed down in 1970. Larella and Young Lady were two brands of ladies' coats of the 1950s and 1960s.

Gyllene Gripen was the result of a merger of three old Swedish shoe factories (Malmö Skofabrik, Eslövs Skofabrik and Malmö Läderfabrik). From 1957 Katja Geiger, later world famous as Katja of Sweden, designed shoes for Gyllene Gripen. During the 1940s Gyllene Gripen became a leading shoe manufacturer with innovative advertising, including a special advertising issue of the then-new photo magazine *Se* in 1942 in which they emphasised not only quality and design but their social responsibility in taking good care of their workers.

Trägårdh's network was not only built up by Beckmans and her fashion journalism. Between 15 September and 14 October 1945, Göta Trägårdh (fashion) and Anders Beckman (design) organised a major fashion exhibition at Liljevalchs art gallery in Stockholm, celebrating the hundredth anniversary of Svenska Slöjdföreningen (Swedish Society of Crafts and Design). The exhibitors represented both old and new textile and fashion actors in Sweden at the time: Algot Johanssons Kläder, AB Béve and C:nis Kappfabrik, Erling Richard AB, AB Fasilko, AB Jersey-Modeller, Jolantakonfektion, AB Kaplans Konfektionsfabrik, AB Märthakonfektion, Sahlins Konfektions AB, Konfektions AB Salén, AB J. A. Wettergren & Co and AB Zober (Kyaga 2017: 212).

Of these, Sahlins and Zober contributed garments to the film, while Märthakonfektion contributed through models and actors. What happened between 1945 and 1953 was, on the one hand, that Upsala Kappfabrik obviously became more oriented towards a younger female audience, and most notably, through the establishment of Tonnie-modeller, by one of Trägårdh's former students at Beckmans. *Tonårsmodet* thus combined brands related either to Beckmans or to modernised Swedish textile industries. In such a way, Trägårdh and *Tonårsmodet* not only promotes the affordable high-quality clothes she talks about at the beginning of the film, but at the same time promotes a key feature of Swedish functionalism, people's ideology of a middle-class ideal grounded in domestic industrial traditions, combined with modern technology and modern design. Rather than a simplified 'trickle-down' model of fashion, the kind of fashion Trägårdh promotes in the film could be described as a functionalist appropriation of both haute couture and mass-market fashion. In *Tonårsmodet*, many dresses and coats can be seen as 'functional' interpretations of New Look design. In line with Angela Partington's analysis of fashion and working-class affluence in Britain around 1950, I would argue that *Tonårsmodet* documents a curating role of the expert which transforms any potential conflicts between haute couture and mass-market fashion. The curator as fellow mother of teenage girls thus both 'trains' consumers to appreciate fashion and invites Swedish mothers of teenage girls (and boys) into 'a complete redefinition of the values of the clothes, an insistence on the prerogative to use clothes in meaning-making practices which are dependent on class-specific skills' (Partington 1992: 159–60).

It may seem paradoxical that the frequent references to class-based consumption is employed in a teenage fashion context which, a few years later, in a Danish context, has been interpreted as a vehicle for a transition into a more consumer-based fashion (Riegels Melchior 2010: 15). In a Swedish context, it was not at all surprising because the political aims of transforming class-oriented behaviour (deliberately including affluent workers of the middle class) went hand in hand with industrial aims of reaching new, and more, consumers. It is worth reminding ourselves of Swedish social democracy's somewhat paradoxical view of social mobility and class. On the one hand, there were its old goals of aiming for a classless society, with reduced differences in income, wealth and social status. On the other hand, there was a political practice which slowly seemed to make as many as possible into members of the middle class, economically, socially and culturally. *Tonårsmodet* is in this respect a perfect example of how the goals of sober advertising and informed consumers had moved away from wartime scarcity and restrictions to post-war affluence and an expansive consumption-driven, middle-class social democracy, based on the standards of established, educated, middle-class ideals.

Conclusion

There are four ways of understanding *Tonårsmodet*. First, with *Tonårsmodet* as an entry point into Swedish 1950s housewives' films, it becomes evident that Husmors Filmer AB should be seen as an advertising agency, not an extension of the Home Research Institute (HFI) or any other consumer-oriented organisation. Even if Brita Svenonius had a background at the wartime information agency Aktiv Hushållning, she was primarily an innovative graphic designer and communications expert. With this perspective, her future work for IKEA says more about Husmors Filmer AB's position in the Swedish media landscape than the frequent references to consumer information and social engineering. HFI was an applied research institute working with and for state, private and cooperative actors, all with their own information and marketing agendas. Given HFI's late 1940s extended mission on communication, their information material became ubiquitous, not only in the marketing of consumer goods, but in public campaigns on housing, food and nutrition, and the political aims of educating responsible citizens and competent consumers. Husmors Filmer AB's mission to provide sober advertising fits well in this context, but their film programmes could not have existed without the international diffusion of new marketing and advertising methods, or the rapidly increasing marketing budgets of Swedish companies.

Second, Husmors Filmer AB was not an odd exception in Swedish 1950s society. Its reputation in later years as an old-fashioned oddity was definitely not representative of its activities in the 1950s and into the 1960s. They identified a market niche at a time of increasing demand for advertising, without radio or television as vehicles. They also identified a way to combine the marketing and information demands of state, cooperative and private actors in a novel format for a well-identified audience. Rationalisation by way of new technologies and new practices was a ubiquitous discourse at all levels of Swedish post-war society. The strong emphasis on efficient household life was not driven by a direct concern for women as housewives. Household rationalisation was the outcome of a political agenda of encouraging women to work part-time outside the home, while still doing domestic work. It was also the result of state, private and cooperative endeavours in improving housing (kitchen standards, new textiles suited for communal laundry rooms and so on) and society infrastructure (private cars, public transportation, new credit systems and so forth). Most of all, it was a time when innovation (not only technological) had become a sales argument.

Third, *Tonårsmodet* is an example of the strong impact of social networks between education, media and industry here manifested by the centrality of Göta Trägårdh as the film's both real and implied narrator. She embodied the transformation of Swedish fashion from the old textile industries to modern, functionalist, ideals of elegant, practical, affordable and sustainable design – not avant-garde, not mass market, but, in a very Swedish way, something in between. Trägårdh, as mother and expert, also embodied a collaborative attitude towards teenagers, their mothers, women's magazines, and the old and new fashion and textile companies. This same collaborative approach made Göta Trägårdh into a pre-television professional. With commercial television, she could have become a completely different media celebrity, but with the public service monopoly, her strong connection to women's magazines, the fashion industry and the private design school Beckmans became a disadvantage. Public service media found their fashion experts among journalists. Interestingly, the commercial neutrality of public service media would lead away from the middle way of Modellkonfektion in favour of haute couture (as spectacle) and mass-market clothing (as consumer and business news).

Finally, films like *Tonårsmodet* may provide new perspectives to popular narratives of who introduced teenage fashion in Sweden. Obviously, the popularity of Gunilla Pontén and Kerstin Lokrantz through photos of them in their own garments in magazines and newspapers created an interest in new design. Nordiska Kompaniet's teenage fashion presentations that started around 1950, on the other hand, required actual manufactured clothes to exist. Even if media images of other, maybe more avant-garde, clothes for teenagers existed, it seems difficult to not regard Tonnie-modeller as much a creator of Swedish teenage fashion as Pontén and Lokrantz, through the actual marketing and selling of clothes to teenagers (and their mothers) in Sweden. Even if Göta Trägårdh had personal connections to Margareta Westberg, it is not surprising that her company Tonnie-modeller is the main provider of teenage fashion in the film. As a middle stance between haute couture and mass-market fashion, Tonnie-modeller was perfectly positioned to prosper in the Swedish 1950s market. It is probably also the reason why it has not received much attention in Swedish fashion history. *Tonårsmodet* could thus be a good starting point to continue the growing field of research in Swedish post-war fashion history (Kyaga 2017), by looking not only at the most (in retrospect) fashionable fashion, but at what actually worked in the market at the time.

There seems to be a difference in how the popular press and housewives' films thus represented fashion. Even if both were advertising driven, the documentary style of many housewives' films included so much more than the actual garments. Setting, actors' and models' movement, and speech, situate fashion in specific social and cultural contexts. Housewives' films later included many newsreels from the catwalk presentation of haute couture, but *Tonårsmodet*, by following the standard mix of showing, telling and situating products, in this case fashion, makes them into useful documents of imagined and promoted ideals of well-informed consumption. The fact that a brand was featured in a housewives' film should be proof of historical importance, not a reason for neglect.

Notes

1. I will use Husmors Filmer AB (literally Housewife's Films Ltd) for the company, but follow previous use of the term 'housewives' films' for the concept.

2. 'Du' is comparable to 'Du' in German or 'toi' in French, while 'ni' is comparable to 'Sie' in German and 'vous' in French.
3. From the obituary of Margareta Westberg, born 1931, in *Dagens Nyheter*, 8 June 2003.
4. From description of dress at photo library DigitaltMuseum: https://digitaltmuseum.se/011023834901/klanning, based on an article in *Damernas Värld* 1988 no. 7, a Guldknappen questionnaire from 2008, and information from her daughter Gabriella Westberg; and biography from *Vem är hon*, pp. 490–1.

References

Antoni, Frode and Hans Gehlin. 1953. *Reklamens medel: En orientering för dem som använder reklam*. Stockholm: Forum.

Berner, Boel. 2002. 'Housewives' Films and the Modern Housewife: Experts, Users and Household Modernization: Sweden in the 1950s and 1960s'. *History and Technology*, vol. 18, no. 3, 155–79.

Björkin, Mats. 2021. *Postwar Industrial Media Culture in Sweden 1945–1960: New Faces, New Values*. Amsterdam: Amsterdam University Press.

Englund, Ingegerd. 1954. 'Ge konsumenterna saklig reklam'. *Husmors-Journalen*, Spring 1954, 1.

Hård, Mikael. 2010. 'The Good Apartment: The Social (Democratic) Construction of Swedish Homes'. *Home Cultures*, vol. 7, no. 2, 117–33.

Jansson, Puck. 1996. 'Om produktionen av husmorsfilmerna och lite historik'. In *Husmors filmer: dokumentation från forskarsymposium på Arkivet för ljud och bild, 8 maj 1996*, 117–33. Stockholm: Arkivet för ljud och bild.

Kearney, Mary Celeste. 2006. 'Birds on the Wire: Troping Teenage Girlhood through Telephony in Mid-twentieth-century US Media Culture'. *Cultural Studies*, vol. 19, no. 5, 568–601. DOI: 10.1080/09502380500365499.

Kyaga, Ulrika. 2017. 'Swedish Fashion: Rethinking the Swedish Textile and Clothing Industry', dissertation, Department of Media Studies, Stockholm University.

Minton, Kirra. 2017. 'How to be a Girl: Consumerism Meets Guidance in the *Australian Women's Weekly*'s Teen Segments, 1952–1959'. *Journal of Australian Studies*, vol. 41, no. 1, 3–17. DOI: 10.1080/14443058.2016.1252936.

Olsson, Jan. 2004. 'One Commercial Week: Television in Sweden Prior to Public Service'. In *Television After TV: Essays on a Medium in Transition*, edited by Lynn Spigel and Jan Olsson, 249–69. Durham, NC: Duke University Press.

Partington, Angela. 1992. 'Popular Fashion and Working-Class Affluence'. In *Chic Thrills: A Fashion Reader*, edited by Juliet Ash and Elizabeth Wilson, 145–61. London: Pandora Press.

Riegels Melchior, Marie. 2010. '"Doing" Danish Fashion: On National Identity and Design Practices of a Small Danish Fashion Company'. *Fashion Practice: The Journal of Design, Creative Process & the Fashion Industry*, vol. 2, no. 1, 13–40. DOI: 10.2752/175693810X12640026716357.

Rocamora, Agnès. 2009. *Fashioning the City: Paris, Fashion and the Media*. New York: I. B. Tauris.

Rosén, Ulla. 2010. '"A Rational Solution to the Laundry Issue": Policy and Research for Day-to-Day Life in the Wellfare State'. In: *Science for Wellfare and Warfare: Technology and State Initiative in Cold War Sweden*, edited by Per Lundin, Niklas Stenlås and Johan Gribbe, 213–32. Sagamore Beach, MA: Watson Publishing.

SOU. 1949. Kvalitetsforskning och konsumentupplysning. Betänkande avgivet av 1946 års utredning angående kvalitetsforskning och konsumentupplysning. Stockholm: Handelsdepartmentet, Statens offentliga utredningar.

Steorn, Patrik. 2021. 'Fashion History As Hybrid: A Transnational Perspective on the Distribution of Fashion History in Sweden, 1950–1980'. *Fashion Theory*, vol. 25, no. 2, 215–41. DOI: 10.1080/1362704X.2019.1594630.

Svenonius, Brita and Anna-Lisa Lyberg. 1952. *Bädda rätt och sova gott: en broschyr från Aktiv hushållning om bäddar och bäddmöbler, om inköp, vård och tillverkning av sängkläder.* Stockholm: Aktiv hushållning.

Turner, Fred. 2013. *The Democratic Surround: Multimedia & American Liberalism from World War II to the Psychedelic Sixties.* Chicago, IL: University of Chicago Press.

Filmography

Tonårsmodet [Teenage Fashion], Husmorsfilmer AB, 1954.

Chapter 5

A maverick on the streets: Bill Cunningham and the documentary process

Karen A. Ritzenhoff

Bill Cunningham, the legendary *New York Times* photographer, who died in 2016 at the age of eighty-seven, knew intuitively that it is not only stars, celebrities and the affluent American elite such as the Vanderbilts and Rockefellers who rule fashion, but the regular folk on the street too. He also embraced gender fluidity and transgender individuals long before his employer was ready to print their imaginative looks, ultimately succeeding in granting them a legitimate print platform of acceptance. This chapter studies Cunningham's legacy, based on two popular documentaries that have depicted his life and work: Mark Bozek's documentary *The Times of Bill Cunningham* (released posthumously in 2018) and the earlier *Bill Cunningham New York*, directed by Richard Press in conjunction with the *New York Times* in 2010. Two different topics of enquiry will be pursued: first, how does Cunningham himself document fashion and why does he perceive himself as a 'fashion historian', not photographer? Second, what differentiates these two full-length documentaries about Bill Cunningham?

There are several paradoxes that seemingly emerge when thinking about fashion and the process of documenting trends and styles through still photography, as Cunningham did. The fashion world provides fantasies and make-believe, together with a display of exclusive consumerism. The documentary mode in film generally prides itself on wanting to detect 'truth', especially aspects of realities that may provoke discussion and shed light on social injustices (Ellis and McLane 2005; Grant and Sloniowski 2014; Nichols 2017). Fashion, by contrast, is a world of looks and facades and is inherently somewhat deceiving. First, there can hardly be a bigger economic gap than that between those who wear haute couture and the general population. Second, fashion models who appear on the runway are usually very young, extraordinarily slim, tall, agile, and trained to strut rather than walk – all pure artifice to display photogenic clothes to best advantage. Third, there is a tremendous contrast between the exclusive and the mundane; couture fashion is prohibitively expensive and only a handful of women (and men) in the entire world can afford to buy the clothes seen on the runway (see commentary about 'These are the Real "Crazy Rich Asians"' in *Harper's Bazaar*).[1] It is only a small number of extremely wealthy women who can afford haute couture exclusive clothes, either by being married to a rich partner, through inherited wealth or through success in their professions, and of course this often precludes youth. By contrast, the majority of women who buy fashion do not wear it as they see it on the runway, but make it their own, copying looks and styles, and translating those observations into 'fashion on the street'. Cunningham addressed all these paradoxes in his body of work, attending fashion shows and documenting runways all over the world. He spent most of his time on the street in order to watch emerging styles in fashion, but he also devoted much time circling (and cycling to) the parties of the rich and famous in New York.

Fashion photography as cultural anthropology: Bill Cunningham at the *New York Times*

Born into a lower-middle-class family with strict Catholic morals in Boston, close to Fenway Park, Cunningham was forced to go to church every Sunday and marvelled at the women's elaborate hats. He recalls that he assembled his first own creation for his mother as a ten-year-old but that she refused to wear it. There is even a picture of his high school yearbook in Mark Bozek's 2018 documentary, where the dapper young man noted his interest in politics and the air force. As a nineteen-year-old, Cunningham went to New York and lodged with an aunt and uncle who wanted him to go into advertising. His interest in fashion blossomed and he learnt the trade of hat making on weekends while being employed in the advertising branch of a major department store, Bonwits. An early discovery for the young Cunningham was the experience that rich New York socialites would come to Bonwits and later to Chez Ninon, to get dressed. He was asked to supply fantasy hats. Cunningham only used his first name and called himself 'William J', working odd jobs to be able to eventually start his own business as a milliner on 52nd Street, while being employed as a janitor and so granted a free room in the attic. Since the relatives were still not satisfied with his career choice, Cunningham moved in with a tribe of fellow bohemians and lived for fifty years in a loft in Carnegie Hall (until he and his fellow bohemians were evicted shortly before his death), alongside – at different times – Editta Sherman, Bernadine Morris, Leonard Bernstein, Marilyn Monroe, Katharine Hepburn, Norman Mailer and Marlon Brando. In the 1950s, Cunningham spent a short time in the American military and was sent to France instead of to Korea like some of his peers. It was in Paris that he was introduced not only to street photography but to fashion houses and shows.

Bill Cunningham wanted to become invisible through the process of working. As sensitive as Cunningham was to every detail he observed, he was negligent when it came to his own comfort. He saw himself as a *documentarian* of clothes, accessories, colours and styles. 'It's not photography, I'm just documenting what I see. I let the street speak to me', he would explain in the few interviews he granted. Many of the people who Cunningham had worked with while being in the business of fashion had no idea about his background or personal life (Figure 5.1).

His stand-up shower and toilet were communal and on the same corridor as other lofts. Cunningham slept on a makeshift mattress, mounted on top of boxes with negatives. Until he discovered his own signature uniform, the blue work clothes of those who worked for the sewage company in Paris, he actually wore hand-me-downs from rich widows who gave him their deceased

Figure 5.1 Bill Cunningham amongst his filing cabinets in his tiny artist's loft on the top floor of Carnegie Hall. Screen capture from *Bill Cunningham, New York* by Richard Press (2010)

husbands' clothes. He also bought striped shirts on sale and at thrift shops. This attitude towards his own body and his needs went even further. While on fashion shoots at galas and fundraisers all over Manhattan, Cunningham would refuse to accept even a glass of water. As he stated with a smile, he wanted to be 'bird-like', free to explore, not bound by fiscal commitments. Both documentaries focus on this aspect of his personality. Cunningham was not anti-fashion, but he did not embrace any of the vanities of clothes for himself.

The uniqueness of Cunningham's legacy was in plain sight while he was still alive. There is no other photographer in the world of fashion who has taken such joy in being always on the street, each day of the week, grabbing images of trends and new fashion sensibilities. Anna Wintour, who was one of Cunningham's longest-serving subjects in front of his lens, since he had snapped pictures of the *Vogue* magazine editor from the time when she was in her twenties, stated that he was most interested in moments of originality, like her jumping across a water puddle in a rainstorm. She also muses that Cunningham would be at the same runway shows and the same social events she had attended as the *Vogue* figurehead, but would pick up on nuances and details that neither she nor her elaborate team would have noticed. 'Six months later those would be actual trends,' she explains. Cunningham saw details, delighted in nuance, picked up fashion by looking at hats, shoes, handbags, jewellery, colours, patterns, cuts, sizes and length of pants, skirts, caftans. He noticed beauty even in the mundane, for example in the homeless. In a particularly gripping statement, one of the few that appear in both documentaries, Cunningham compares the clothes and faces of homeless women in New York with those of women in medieval Europe. He even states that some of the Japanese designers were inspired in their high fashion collections by the look of the 'bag women'.

Cunningham furthered his knowledge of gender equality in fashion his entire life and has left behind an extensive oeuvre of photo negatives in boxes, not only portraying cultural history by mirroring the rich and infamous, but also chronicling the New York Gay Pride parade and the movements of stylistic street trends and looks over decades. He paid attention to people from different economic and ethnic backgrounds if they wore accessories like hats, handbags, socks, shoes, gloves, jewellery, scarves (even leashes with little dogs attached) and clothes that he found to be stylish. He valued the display of attire in higher social class events and on the runway of exclusive fashion shows in Paris, Milan and New York as much as the everyday style of the people on the sidewalks. As his obituary in the *New York Times* states, he 'turned fashion photography into his own branch of cultural anthropology on the streets of New York' (Bernstein 2016).

The self-proclaimed 'fashion historian' was using only a cheap bike to cycle through the American metropolis. He was understated, yet powerful – for Cunningham had access as a staff photographer to the *New York Times* and his own editorial playground, having ultimately full control over the style section's fashion segment each Sunday, where he was responsible for filling his own two columns. One was called 'On the Street' (later in his career this was also retrievable as a podcast with voice-over narration). The other, titled 'Evening Hours', was a crafted page with pictures he took at galas and fundraisers, documenting the rich and important players of the New York high society scene.

The idea that Cunningham was not only a trendsetter but also part of celebrity culture and a star photographer of fashion is illustrated by these two non-fiction films about his life, explaining his enigmatic personality and his rise to status in the elitist fashion world as a democratic, non-elitist force. However, similar to his preferred low-budget form of transportation and his frugal attire, Cunningham used a defunct technology, analogue photography, in the twenty-first century to capture reality. As revolutionary as Cunningham was in his original approach to fashion and his sense of democratising style, his mode of representation in a leading print newspaper may seem outdated now. Street photography has taken on a life of its own with the proliferation of smartphones, quick snapshots of attire on the streets, and the subsequent proliferation of fashion on social media platforms. Now, fashion trends do not need the backdrop of a prestigious mainstream newspaper and the *New York Times* 'Sunday Style' section to become popular – they are formed by young people and their smartphones on social media.

Who was the man behind the lens? The two documentaries use different approaches to try to capture Cunningham's personality while also focusing on the process of picture-making.

Bill Cunningham New York (Richard Press, 2010)

In the documentary by Richard Press, *Bill Cunningham New York*, we hear Cunningham calling a photo shop from his office at the *New York Times* (NYT) and telling them that he is 'the guy on the bike'. He continued to work with analogue film even when the world had transferred to digital. Cunningham sent his graphic designer to pick up the developed negatives and told the store owner, 'The guy who is coming is a friend of mine with long hair.' The NYT employee patiently takes leave to pick up the work, helping Cunningham to not only make his publishing deadline but continue to work within the framework that he had developed over the decades of screening, selecting and then designing the page.

When Cunningham took to the streets of New York he captured what was trending, documenting 'fashion history' by snapping pictures with his analogue camera, while using the bicycle to get around so that he could jump off his saddle quickly when he spotted something new and exciting. Cunningham democratised style. His process of reproducing trends was laborious but comparatively fast: he would snap the picture, have it developed in a photo lab, look at the stills on a lighting table, and then have the chosen frames digitised and assembled by a graphic designer into the weekly 'Style' section page in the *New York Times* (Figure 5.2).

Adam Szymanski explained in his 2012 article '*Bill Cunningham New York* and the Political Potentiality of the Fashion Documentary' that Cunningham's picture-taking bridged the gap between exclusivity and access. Based on Walter Benjamin's classic analysis of mass media and mechanical reproduction, Szymanski contests that there is 'a real distance created through illusion' in the

Figure 5.2 Bill Cunningham worked with analogue technology, shooting pictures on film rolls that needed to be developed for him to process. Here he is looking at a film roll that would then be digitised so he could work on his layout for the *New York Times* Style section. *Bill Cunningham, New York* (2010). Screen capture by author

haute couture fashion industry, where regular mortals do not gain entrance when the latest trends are being showcased on the exclusive runways, making fashion 'constantly out of reach for the masses who have access only to the photograph but not to "fashion" itself' (2012: 291).

In this way, Szymanski looks at *Bill Cunningham New York* not as a celebration of the photographer himself and the historical archive of negatives he left behind, but as a specific mode of film-making that used to complement the street photography of fashion but has gone out of style. He even debunks the myth that Cunningham was unique, despite having been a trailblazer for 'street style fashion photography'. Szymanski contests that this can hardly be seen as a 'revelation today':

> In fact, 'on the street' and DIY fashion photography have become commonplace, as the internet is filled with websites, blogs and social media sites that specialize in this highly accessible genre of photography. For example, see sites such as Pinterest.com, Lookbook.nu and Streetpepper.com. (2012: 295, fn. 6)

'The kids are here,' Cunningham would lovingly call out (*Bill Cunningham New York*, 2010, hereafter *BCNY*, 0:50:18). The 'kids' kept him in high respect because he allowed the marginalised and flamboyant to shine on his pages. Transgender advocate 'Kenny Kenny', 'visual poet and [New York] nightlife icon' (Nichols 2014), is featured in Press's documentary and recalls when they were first photographed by Cunningham:

> 1986... and *The Times* said... he came to me the next week and he said, I am so disappointed. *The Times* said, 'we can't put you in because you are wearing a dress.' And he said, 'but I'm gonna keep trying to get you in.' And I was like, 'what the hell,' I said, 'I am wearing a pair of workmen's boots with that dress.' And he said, 'I know Kenny, but they won't put you in. But I am trying.' And now... he can put anything in. He is such a maverick. Really a maverick. He means so much to people like us. He is an artist. (*BCNY*, 0:51:26 to 0:52:02)

Harold Koda, curator of the Costume Institute of the Metropolitan Museum of Art, describes Cunningham as a 'true egalitarian': 'However, that does not mean that he is not aware of the nuances of cultural division and hierarchies. He just treats it all the same' (*BCNY*, 0:50:18).

BCNY celebrates Cunningham as a producer of images who works for a larger news corporation. Although we also see that he selects images on the lighting table and makes choices when assembling the weekend columns with his graphic designer, he is working as part of a service industry, the media corporation. Press has edited a fast-paced, flamboyant ode to Cunningham, closely linked with the working environment in the *New York Times* building. The photographer is seen in his office, collaborating closely with his editor, interacting with colleagues. As with Dziga Vertov's wife Yelizaveta Svilova in *Man with a Movie Camera* (1929), we see Cunningham screen and select single images, either by holding up the developed analogue negatives towards the light or by using an outmoded analogue light projector, made defunct by digital technology. Cunningham looks like a dinosaur with an outmoded craft, kept on staff to add colour and curiosity to the NYT 'Style' section. He comes across as moody, quirky and obsessed, neglecting to eat while trying to meet his deadlines, being demanding towards his editor while also being charming with people like the owners of the photo development lab on the phone. The *New York Times* co-sponsored the making of the documentary, thereby using this mode of film-making as a form of extensive commercial, almost a promotional video for a corporate product.

Cunningham explains in *BCNY* that 'when it rains, things happen'. He is seen in his NYT office, taping inexpensive duct tape on dollar store ponchos that rip easily when he follows his subjects on the street. He calls New Yorkers 'extravagant and wasteful' as he tapes a black plastic poncho together in his cubicle before heading back into the streets. In contrast to the 2018 documentary where the *Vogue* editor Anna Wintour, one of Cunningham's trusted subjects, is only introduced with a brief quote at the very end of the movie, in this 2010 documentary Wintour is prominently introduced at the very outset. This is another indication that the earlier film is more interested in the fashion world and the process of Cunningham's work than in his personal and private philosophies as a 'fashion historian'.

For Press, the street plays a significant role, as if it were an additional actor in Cunningham's life. The film starts with images of the photographer rushing through the streets of Manhattan, bending down, sizing up women's shoes (and the tattoos on their calves), taking snapshots. Not only do we see the published image that he took but also cut-ins with the sound of a quick shutter movement, replicating the hurried feel of street life. 'I let the street speak to me,' Cunningham exclaims. Then we see him looking at analogue negatives on a lighting table, a direct visual reference to *Man with a Movie Camera* (1929), the experimental silent film by Russian documentary film-maker Dziga Vertov (who changed his given name from David/Daniel Kaufman to his artistic pseudonym). Vertov is the Russian word for 'truth', the French version of 'la vérité'. The French writer and film-maker Chris Marker reappropriated the Vertovian concept of cinematic truth in the 1960s when coining the term *cinéma vérité* in the tradition of Russian pioneers.² Bill Cunningham's work can be seen in this visual legacy of trying to capture reality as it unfolds in the everyday occurrences on the street.

One of the key scenes in Dziga Vertov's *Man with a Movie Camera* is when the cameraman – actually Kaufman's brother Mikhail who did the cinematography – is shooting a short episode of fashionably dressed Russian people in a horse-drawn open carriage. They are seen mounting the mode of transportation, and then a carriage parallel to theirs depicts the 'man with a movie camera' who is cranking the silent camera by hand. There needs to have been a third carriage, parallel to the other two, with yet another cinematographer, who remains unseen, filming this segment. To the surprise of the viewer, the movement unexpectedly stops and Vertov cuts to a darkroom where his wife, the Ukrainian editor Yelizaveta Svilova, is looking at the raw film stock. She is sitting at a cutting table, selecting the negatives of the carriage scene as well as other street scenes of children and adults. We see single images in close-up stills, filling the frame, suggesting that she is making choices as to what to include, and what to delete, where to cut and how to edit images together so they are creating a continuous story of life in the city. The German film-maker Walter Ruttman had produced a similar oeuvre with *Berlin: Symphony of a Metropolis* in 1927, where he captured the cyclical rhythms of the big city, finding a certain beauty and music in the serenity of the morning, the acceleration of men and machines at midday, followed by the intermission of lunch, the hustle and bustle of the afternoon, and the leisure time of the everyday people in the evening, congregating in parks and by rivers in Berlin. Similar to Ruttman, Dziga Vertov documents a process of image-making and highlights the selections of raw footage needed to be made up. This creative mechanism is made obvious by Dziga Vertov in order to demystify the process of image production, documenting to the viewer that what they are seeing is indeed a constructed event. In addition, Vertov called the camera lens a 'mechanical eye', emphasising that the technology is directed by humans but also has a built-in industrial aspect to it. The camera lens is an extension of the human perception, an idea that would resonate with Bill Cunningham who saw himself as a 'historian' rather than an artist, in a rather self-effacing mode.

There could be different interpretations as to why Vertov shows the process of editing in such detail. First, he may have wanted to enforce the point that images were actually taken on the street, lifted from reality and then cut together so as to represent a form of reality to the viewer that can be traced (and replicated). Second, it could also illustrate the actual process of image-making, a form of taking away the myth that documentary is 'reality', because it is always selected by an individual (or several), starting with the director, then the cinematographer, then the editor. This tradition of street photography and film-making can be followed when looking at other photographers, such as Vivian Maier, who has also been immortalised by a recent feature-length documentary that describes the found footage left behind by this American woman pioneer in *Finding Vivian Maier* (John Maloof and Charlie Siskel, 2013). She was a street photographer like Cunningham, Ruttman and Vertov, and by extension even director Stanley Kubrick, who began his career as an amateur photographer for *Look* magazine in New York, without any formal training. Vivian Maier never had a platform to display the more than 100,000 pictures that she had secretly taken during her lifetime. Her legacy was discovered when the documentary film director and historian John Maloof bought her negatives at an auction by chance. Maier's images had never before been seen, contrary to Cunningham's historical documentation of street life that was given a celebrated and distinguished outlet in the *New York Times*.

The Times of Bill Cunningham (Mark Bozek, 2018)

Mark Bozek follows Cunningham's biography in a mostly linear trajectory, interspersing specific memories every now and then. The audience learns where the photographer was born, where he lived, how he entered the field of fashion despite his family's reluctance and lack of moral support. This documentary was featured prominently in the September 2021 'immersive exhibit' of Bill Cunningham's work at the Seaport Gallery in New York. Bozek was also interviewed extensively by the media in 2020, explaining his unique access to Cunningham's private sphere.[3] As journalist Aria Darcella explains in her 'Chic Report' in February 2020, 'In 1994 Mark Bozek landed the interview of a lifetime: a three-hour chat with Bill Cunningham. For the first – and only – time, the legendary photographer opened up and got personal on-camera.'

Bozek's documentary starts with a black screen and a soundscape only. The audio-montage builds through a cacophony of sounds like an orchestra that is trying to warm up: horns, street sounds, subway screeches, police sirens, cars braking, indistinct chatter, soundbites of people walking, the buzzer of a building, doors opening and closing, and footsteps heard going up stairs. This is the music of the big city, immediately recognisable as the soundtrack of Manhattan. Even though Cunningham's full-time job in the Style section of the *New York Times* was to capture the performative aspect of everyday attire on the streets, his thousands of colourful newspaper pictures do not yet drive the story. So, rather than depicting the process of picture-taking and editing those found images into narratives for the *New York Times*, this documentary is instead listening to the man behind the camera. Throughout the same continuous interview sequence, we see Bill Cunningham in a bright room, sitting on a chair, looking at the director next to the camera. This is clearly one long take with a single camera. Hardly any close-ups are used, there is no crossing the line. As intimate as the medium shot of Cunningham seems to be, it is still not exploitative of his emotions. The representation of the photographer in standardised film conventions shows little creativity in the actual taping of the interview. Here, the interviewer keeps a respectful distance that does not exploit Cunningham's emotions. Only in the second half of the film does Cunningham break into tears when remembering the AIDS epidemic and the loss of many of his artist friends. The camera stops rolling, rather than zooming into his face or capturing his tears on camera.

American film scholar Bill Nichols coined the term 'documentary modes of representation' in his classic text *Representing Reality* (1991). He explains the differences between the four modes in documentary film-making: expository, observational, interactive and reflexive (Nichols 1991: 32). The observational mode limits 'the filmmaker to the present moment and required a disciplined detachment from the events themselves' (Nichols 1991: 33). Nichols elaborates that 'interactive documentary rose from the availability of the same more mobile equipment and a desire to make the filmmaker's perspective more evident. Interactive documentaries wanted to engage with individuals more directly while not reverting to classic exposition' (Nichols 1991: 33). In the context of Bozek's film, these two modes intersect and overlap. On the one hand, the director observes his subject with deliberate respectful distance, not exploiting emotions, a style typical of the observational mode; on the other hand, the adherence to the conventions of standardised and conventionalised framing and lighting techniques, while still allowing the voice of the interviewer to be heard, helps to anchor the documentary in the interactive mode.

Nichols elaborates, stating that 'observational documentaries are what Erik Barnouw refers to as direct cinema and what others like Stephen Mamber describe as cinema verité' (1991: 38), insisting that the director has little interventional power. In the case of Bozek's film, he structures the entire documentary around the recorded one-time interview with Cunningham.

He lets the fashion icon talk on his own terms and amplifies the statements with B-roll. This is a less constructed mode of representation than that of the earlier *Bill Cunningham New York* documentary of 2010. By the same token, it connects Cunningham's story of his life journey with the tradition of *cinéma vérité* and Dziga Vertov's work in *Man with a Movie Camera*. Paul Ward (2005) has reflected on the role of documentary film-making and what defines this genre in the context of authenticity and truth:

> these notions of objectivity and transparency resonate through the history of documentary and other forms of nonfictional/factual programming. Certainly, with regard to television documentary output, with strong links to broadcast journalism and current affairs, there seems to be a distrust of anything that deviates from a 'fair and balanced' position. (Ward 2005: 10)

The camera movements of the interview in Bozek's film are controlled and few. The framing adheres to documentary tradition of placing the subject slightly off centre and providing a bust shot with enough head room. Cunningham looks off screen right, suggesting that Bozek is sitting right next to the single camera, so that his interviewee can always have eye contact with him. In the epilogue, the shot is framed wider and shows the background of Cunningham's apartment. He sits in front of a nondescript white background, maybe a closet, and to his left are a few plants. They are cut off from the frame, so there is very little context to this generic shot. Bozek asks him from the off whether he wants to add anything to the interview: 'Anything else you want to say?' In this instance, Bozek diverges from the observational mode. This is a key moment in the documentary because the director intervenes directly. He elicits the most emotional response from his subject that differentiates the documentary from the earlier, more corporate and polished version, that highlighted the corporate look of the *New York Times* instead of Cunningham's personal views.

After being asked by Bozek whether he wants to add anything to the recording, Cunningham waves his arms and exclaims that he thought this would all have been shorter. The camera zooms in and settles again in the comfortable medium bust shot. Cunningham has a striped shirt on and explains that he only tends to wear thrift shop garb, cheap sales items and hand-me-downs from friends and acquaintances who are widowed; he can list the original male owners of his shoes, jackets, pants, ties. In an anecdote in which he recalls having been asked by a friend to join the British Duke of Windsor and his American wife Wallis Simpson, Cunningham recounts that he had to assemble his own wardrobe from these second-hand items. He raves about the charm and natural elegance of the duke but is rather critical of Simpson's assumed lack of style. A black-and-white shot of the royal couple is used as B-roll to enhance Cunningham's memories. The audience is never introduced to the other man behind the camera, director Mark Bozek, but we hear him, and his female assistant, laughing at Cunningham's jokes or listen to him as he offers his interviewee a glass of water or a break from taping. 'This was only supposed to be ten minutes, and we have been going on for hours,' jokes Cunningham at the end of the one hour and fifteen-minute edited session.

The documentary ends with black-and-white footage of Cunningham's head shot which is rewinding as if playing on an analogue VHS recorder. A title card states 'the tape ran out', and the documentary fades to black before the credits roll. This style indicates two important aspects of the documentary: first, none of the footage is staged, in line with Cunningham's vivid description of why he prefers moments of spontaneity on the streets to orchestrated fashion shoots. Second, this is a posthumous homage to Cunningham, based on analogue footage that had never been used. Once the footage runs out, there cannot be any more material. Bozek taped the three-hour interview in 1994, over twenty years before the subject of the interview passed away from old age. Little is known about the gestation of this project. It may be comparable to Jonathan Demme's interviews with Jean Dominique – an outspoken radio host and political commentator in Haiti – which had been recorded in the 1990s while Dominique lived in exile in the United States but were to be assembled into a documentary when Dominique was assassinated in 2000, leading to the making of *The Agronomist* (2003).

Rather than showing Cunningham as an eccentric old bird, as the 2010 documentary does, where we see the protagonist throwing himself onto the streets, clicking away before we hear one word out of his mouth, Bozek is more fascinated by the spoken word. He documents the close relationship he developed with Cunningham, using his subject as the witness of a particular cultural period in the United States. Cunningham explains that he is in temperament more like his mother, a homemaker in Boston, who was rather shy. He reveals that it is sometimes hard for him to engage with people and that he has had anxieties about this aspect of his profession as a documentarian. 'It is hard for me to go out in the streets,' says Cunningham and suddenly bows his head. He looks as if he is about to cry and Bozek offers him a glass of water. 'I am basically very shy,' he states. Cunningham's father worked at the post office and was outgoing, but also religious and conservative.

Neither parent approved of Bill's early interest in hat making or fashion. The undercurrent of this issue is homosexuality. This is never addressed but Bozek gives hints that Cunningham might have been discouraged by his family and relatives from entering the fashion world because the men there were frequently labelled as gay.

One hour into the film, the director chooses to allude to Cunningham's fascination with taking pictures of New York's Gay Pride parades and opens a little window into the protagonist's own potential sexual affinities. Cunningham had documented all the parades since their beginning, but never shared the negatives, until a historical society asked him for access. Cunningham muses out loud that they would have possibly wanted to find two men kissing but 'these are pictures I don't take'. He does not want to 'steal' people's joy, he explains. Cunningham does admit that he feels as if he is taking people's 'shadows' at times. He makes it very clear that he is not interested in sensationalising or capturing people's intimate moments. 'If somebody is not dressed with style, they are of no interest to me,' he tells the camera.

In a related anecdote, he recounts taking pictures in Paris in front of the Galeries Lafayette. One of the owners of a perfume store called the police because she claimed that Cunningham was using the camera as a prop to steal people's handbags. He had to explain to the police that taking photos was his profession and that he was not a thief. However, his concern for people's privacy is similar. He knows that he takes something from them when he snaps a picture and then publishes it in the 'Style' section of the *New York Times* for everybody to see. It is fascinating that he does not seem to ever refer to the publication as a form of self-accreditation.

'We all get dressed for Bill,' is a famous statement by Anna Wintour, one of Cunningham's muses and the long-time editor of *Vogue*, the diva of fashion. At the end of Bozek's documentary, a female voice-over states nostalgically: 'Many now wonder if there will ever be anyone like Bill Cunningham to dress for again?' Cunningham claimed that everyday women who had style were always his preference to photograph and 'work' with, not actresses and people in show business. Cunningham flippantly remarked in an interview with Mark Bozek that he thought Hollywood actresses had very different looks in private from their glamorous personas on the screen. He reasons that the illustrious Hollywood star Joan Crawford 'did not have style' – not even Elizabeth Taylor, who once visited the dress room Chez Ninon, run by two of Cunningham's early allies and employers.

Several times in Cunningham's interview with Bozek he recalls people who introduced him to photography and has astute memories of how he started his passion as a fashion historian. He insists that he has 'to stay in the background', be invisible, and follow his instinct when 'looking at the streets'. 'I enjoy myself every day,' he claims. Cunningham enthusiastically describes that he senses freedom when being able to go out with 'the whole world to discover', free like a bird (Figure 5.3). Antonio Lopez gave him a used camera, 'an idiot box', and wished him good luck. Pierre Houlès, a French photographer, as well as the street photographer Harold Chapman, taught him the techniques of a documentarian in the tradition of Cartier-Bresson. 'It was a revelation,' Cunningham recalls, 'suddenly I could photograph anything, inside and out.' He insists that he has worked as a 'fashion historian' rather than a professional photographer and does not dare compare himself to somebody like Weegee: 'I am light-weight stuff.'

Cunningham explains that the streets of Manhattan can be looked at as a stage that records politics and social upheaval in the country like a seismograph. He argues that there are three intersecting levels of fashion:

Figure 5.3 Bill Cunningham wanted to be 'bird-like', free to explore, not bound by fiscal commitments when he took photographs at fancy galas as well as on the street. Here he is at the end of Bozek's 2018 documentary, *The Times of Bill Cunningham*, spreading his arms like wings. Screen capture by author

what is shown; what is written about, and finally, what is actually worn – on the streets. 'We are out to capture the story,' he states, 'you cannot disturb the story.' If you get involved in setting up a scene, Cunningham learnt, it turns into something 'fake' and 'not real'. Within this same argument, he describes how rain and snow are the perfect conditions for taking candid and serendipitous snapshots, rather than orchestrated polished frames (Figure 5.4). This is also why Cunningham liked to cycle everywhere – he used about fifty bikes throughout his long career. 'You can jump off,' he states, and can get around. The quality of his bikes? 'The cheaper, the better.' Cunningham did fly coach class to fashion shows in Europe and stayed in mundane hotels, similar to his cave-like existence in the Carnegie Hall loft where he slept on a mattress on top of negative boxes most of his adult life.

Bozek points out that the photographer sponsored charities and donated to AIDS foundations, also supporting fellow artists by buying their work. He had a 'quiet generosity'.

Figure 5.4 Fashion on the street: Bill Cunningham captures the latest fashion trends in Manhattan while photographing two young African American men who smile at his lens. Screen capture by author. *The Times of Bill Cunningham* (Mark Bozek, 2018)

Conclusion

When comparing the two documentaries about Bill Cunningham, one can easily detect that Mark Bozek is fascinated by revisiting the 1994 raw footage, reassembling the soundbites into providing a chronological account of Cunningham's life. Towards the end of the film, a voice-over by the actress Sarah Jessica Parker explains that Cunningham might even have regretted his participation in the earlier 2010 version. Supposedly, he never saw the *BCNY* movie and left his house on the night of its premiere to photograph on the street. Bozek thereby sets Cunningham's work deliberately apart from *The Times of Bill Cunningham*, insinuating that the subject of his own film might have been more satisfied with the less structured and simplistic posthumous film.

It is in the spirit of being more of an outlier or odd outsider that Mark Bozek wants to depict Bill Cunningham. In his documentary, Cunningham tears up, falls silent, shows his vulnerabilities. It is more the 'man behind the camera' than the products themselves that are of interest to Bozek. As the female voice-over states at the end of Bozek's movie, the death of Cunningham in June 2016 was similar to the 'loss of a good friend'. She explains that Cunningham 'celebrated beauty' wherever he found it and made consumers see Manhattan street life (and fashion) in a 'new way', counteracting the 'hurried pace of city life'. Cunningham loved serendipity, and the unexpected, that occurs on the street but not on the runway.

While Bozek pointed out that the *New York Times* did not initially allow Cunningham to showcase the fashion of 'the kids', transgender icons of Manhattan nightlife, *BCNY* makes it look as if the photographer has a free hand in his storytelling choices, seemingly uninhibited by newsroom politics. In this way, *BCNY* is as deceiving as the world of fashion, building an illusion of beauty and excess while idealising consumerism. The 2010 documentary uses the mechanism of factual storytelling as part of an effort to build the heritage of the newspaper and thereby adds to the authoritative institution of the press. The motivation of Bozek's documentary is to gain exclusive access, a 'once-in-a-lifetime chance' to hear from the reclusive photographer, thereby idealising Bill Cunningham as a LGBTQ New York icon. The fact that Bozek uses the edited version of his three- hour original interview from 1994 as the main building block and only adds B-roll as additional visual proof is presented as an 'observational' documentary. Supposedly it is less crafted and constructed than the 2010 documentary that Bill Cunningham claimed not to have wanted to watch. Even though Bozek's representation of Cunningham's life is equally as manufactured as Press's promotional film, he insinuates that it is more authentic. Bozek is the one who got chosen to be added to the prestigious retrospective of Bill Cunningham in September 2021 in New York and has had much more visibility in the fashion scene and press than the earlier film.

One of the positive aspects of documentary film-making as a medium to inform is described by Paul Ward in the conclusion of his 2005 monograph, *Documentary: The Margins of Reality*. Ward writes, 'One of the other more encouraging recent developments has been the ability of people to make documentaries very cheaply and, perhaps more crucially, find ways of getting them to a reasonably large audience' (2005: 101). This can certainly be said about Mark Bozek's documentary, which had a production budget of $300,000 (according to IMDb). Bozek's documentary ends with an analogue video tape of Cunningham's recorded interview footage from 1994 rewinding; it looks as if the image of Cunningham's familiar face is split into stripes like window blinds. The rewinding footage is in black and white, in contrast to the previous interview in colour. Bozek achieves two effects with this choice of ending the film. First, there is no more tape left to tell Cunningham's story and he is kept alive only through this constructed memory, captured during his lifetime on tape, an analogue medium, similar to the photographer's technique of working with analogue photography. Second, in this way, the technology of the later documentary is seemingly 'truer' to Cunningham's mode of producing and documenting reality because it works in a bygone visual format. Similar to Dziga Vertov, who showed his wife at the lighting table in *Man with a Movie Camera*, and who lets us peek behind the illusion of cinematography and visual storytelling, Bozek lets viewers glimpse behind the facade of the screen, laying bare his own technology. By rewinding the footage that distorts the original image of the interview subject, the viewer can feel slightly alienated and thrown off the illusion of 'film truth'. This was a technique, already used by Russian directors, of the *cinéma vérité* and *Kino Pravda*, the 'film-truth-movement'. They wanted to demonstrate through montage techniques that reality and film illusion were highly manufactured.

Why have there been two documentaries about Bill Cunningham and an eight-week exhibition in New York in autumn 2021, featuring excerpts from Bozek's documentary? One could argue that Cunningham is an outmoded model himself, working in a defunct technology in a mode of fashion documentation that has been overtaken by smartphones, consumer websites and social media platforms. Cunningham is a vestige of a bygone era where people dressed up, even when going to work, not frolicking around in sweatpants, sitting all day behind a computer screen, only visible in bust shots. As the Covid-19 pandemic loosens its grip in spring 2022, new forms of fashion vlogging and blogging have emerged and become acceptable, even enticing the *New York Times* to embrace new modes of depicting the fashion world online, with an entire rubric on 'Designer DIY' and a parallel style section rubric on 'self care'. Elizabeth Wissinger has labelled this form of self-styling and self-branding 'glamour labor' in her book *This Year's Model: Fashion, Media, and the Making of Glamour* (2015). Maybe this is one of Bill Cunningham's most enduring legacies: he allowed the people on the street to be glamorous rather than the elite models, irrespective of their access to the mainstream fashion industry, paving the way for democratising fashion and its visual representation in social media.

You could go a step further and say that depicting Cunningham's life in two feature-length documentaries by male directors is itself an older model of fashion in film. The future is written with super-short, animated fashion TikTok videos and possible YouTube visits to the clothing closets of the rich and famous, in Asia and elsewhere in the world, filmed with hand-held smartphones – and by women, even by teenagers, rather than by men with bulky movie cameras.

Notes

1. 'These Are the Real "Crazy Rich Asians"'. YouTube, 15 August 2018. Available at https://www.youtube.com/watch?v=g01YnqH-2ek (accessed 28 June 2022).
2. Patricia Aufderheide explains, in her *Documentary Film: A Very Short Introduction* (2007), that Eric Barnouw wrote an authoritative history of documentary film-making in 1971. She sees Barnouw as promoting a linear trajectory from Vertov to Grierson to American direct cinema. 'Unsentimentally and with a wealth of specifics, Barnouw portrayed documentary makers overall as voices of freedom, conviction, and engagement with the world. He showed them exploring the medium to tell stories neglected by the ever-more-powerful mainstream media' (2007: 131).
3. In 2020, Mark Bozek was interviewed by fashion giant the late André Leon Talley. The thirty-minute dialogue is available on YouTube at https://www.youtube.com/watch?v=sPcYEI2pbsk (accessed 28 June 2022).

References

Aufderheide, Patricia. 2007. *Documentary Film: A Very Short Introduction*. London: Oxford University Press.
Bernstein, Jacob. 2016. 'Bill Cunningham, Legendary *Times* Fashion Photographer, Dies at 87'. *New York Times*, 25 June 2016. Available at https://www.nytimes.com/2016/06/26/

style/bill-cunningham-legendary-times-fashion-photographer-dies-at-87.html (accessed 28 June 2022).
Darcella, Aria. 2020. 'The Untold Story Behind the New Bill Cunningham Documentary'. *The Daily Frontrow*, 20 February 2020. Available at https://fashionweekdaily.com/bill-cunningham-documentary-mark-bozek/ (accessed 28 June 2022).
Ellis, Jack C. and Betsy A. McLane. 2005. *A New History of Documentary Film*. New York: Continuum.
Grant, Barry Keith and Jeannette Sloniowski, eds. 2014. *Documenting the Documentary: Close Readings of Documentary Film and Video*. Detroit, MI: Wayne State University Press.
Nichols, Bill. 1991. *Representing Reality: Issues and Concepts in Documentary*. Bloomington: Indiana University Press.
Nichols, Bill. 2017. *Introduction to Documentary*. Bloomington: Indiana University Press.
Nichols, James Michael. 2014. 'After Dark: Meet Kenny Kenny, Visual Poet and Nightlife Icon'. *Huffington Post: Queer Voices*, 31 August 2014. Available at https://www.huffpost.com/entry/kenny-kenny-after-dark_n_5742624 (accessed 28 June 2022).
Szymanski, Adam. 2012. '*Bill Cunningham New York* and the Political Potentiality of the Fashion Documentary'. *Film, Fashion and Consumption*, vol. 1, no. 3, 289–304.
Ward, Paul. 2005. *Documentary: The Margins of Reality*. Short Cuts. London: Wallflower.
Wissinger, Elizabeth. A. 2015. *This Year's Model: Fashion, Media, and the Making of Glamour*. New York: New York University Press.

Audio-visual sources

Berlin: Symphony of a Metropolis. Directed by Walter Ruttman, 1927. Germany.
Bill Cunningham New York. Directed by Richard Press, 2010. First Thought Films.
Finding Vivian Maier. Directed by John Maloof and Charlie Siskel, 2013. Ravine Pictures.
Man with a Movie Camera. Directed by Dziga Vertov, 1929.
The Agronomist. Directed by Jonathan Demme, 2003. USA.
The Times of Bill Cunningham. Directed by Mark Bozek, 2018. Live Rocket.

Chapter 6

Extending the exhibition narrative: making sense of non-fiction fashion footage

Boel Ulfsdotter

Introduction

Over the past twenty-odd years, fashion exhibitions have increasingly become subject to significant academic criticism and research. During the same period, fashion curation has gained extensive academic and museological kudos and become a sought-after professional occupation. In concert with these developments, the spatial organisation and narrative of dress exhibits has received increasingly serious and careful consideration in museology.

Alexandra Palmer, in a much-cited article in *Fashion Theory* in 2008, called for museums to 'mount clearly curated, researched exhibitions that are educational and do seriously attempt to add to a larger body of cultural intellectual knowledge' (Palmer 2008: 57). At about the same time, Valerie Steele stated: 'I believe that a significant percentage of museum visitors really want to learn something when they see an exhibition. There is no reason why exhibitions cannot be both beautiful *and* intelligent, entertaining *and* educational' (Steele 2008: 14, emphasis in original). For the purpose of this essay, I argue that these two cues represent the first outright calls for the museification of fashion, and thus encouraged the development I outline above.

To begin with, both Palmer's and Steele's statements aired a deeply set affinity and agreement with the twofold remits of the 'new museology' idiom that exhibitions should provide both entertainment and education (see Hooper-Greenhill 1992, 2000). 'New museology' emerged in Great Britain in the 1970s and 1980s and 'investigates the functions, mission, need, and development of the museum, with a particular focus on its relations with visitors' (Mandelli 2019: 7). Having gleaned the most cited academic texts on fashion curation and fashion-related museology published over the past twenty years, it is my contention that the historiography of fashion display increasingly reflects a museum discourse underlining the fashion display's cultural worth in direct relation to audience reception. Fashion curation today (2022) seems to effortlessly respond to the above scholars' call for an educational and intellectual exchange between the exhibited material and the visitor in accordance with the new museology idiom. However, bar the occasional mention of catwalk footage, the overall discursive implications related to moving images have never been discussed in detail by scholars or academic critics involved with visual culture or the museification of fashion.

This chapter thus considers the museological practice of using non-fiction moving images to further contextualise a fashion exhibition narrative, either in the form of documentary footage, or a directed and edited film production for public relations (PR) purposes. To be more precise, it endeavours to outline the discursive remits of how documentary footage currently animates the fashion exhibition narrative. What documentary modes are used to assist or expand a fashion exhibition narrative today, to pacify the battle between objectified aestheticisation and narrative contextualisation? Which unique documentary formats of the traditional 'museum film' have been developed for use in fashion exhibits, and how do they expand the discursive remits of fashion curation? I shall be looking into these matters from the point of view of the ongoing museification of fashion, beginning with the discursive relation between film and museology.

Museology and moving images

In her study of the museum as a *cinematic* space, Elisa Mandelli has suggested that museums were aware of the epistemological as well as entertainment value of moving images very early on:

> [During the first decades of the twentieth century] cinema was increasingly recognized as an effective tool for museums to attract visitors. It thus became one of the solutions adopted by museums to reach a broader and more popular public, to achieve a wider dissemination of ideas, concepts, and meanings ... (Mandelli 2019: 23)

The earliest type of museum film was ethnographic in form, preserved in the museum's archives, and screened in museum auditoriums. This documentary film genre is today assisted by different modern formats with the same museological purpose. From a discursive point of view, Mandelli's historical exposé thus suggests that while the museological outlook on moving imagery in the museum context remained firm during the twentieth century, 'the emergence of immersion and interactivity [in compliance with the emergence of "new museology", are now] crucial concerns of contemporary museums; [including] the increasing importance attributed to audio-visuals and moving images' (Mandelli 2019: 7). Focusing on present-day museum practice, Mandelli makes the general observation that all 'films and audio-visual displays serve as tools for contextualization, explanation, or visitor engagement' (Mandelli 2019: 2). 'Films, photographs, text, graphics, and audio recordings have the same value as objects in the transmission of historical knowledge and are combined to create a coherent narrative" (Mandelli 2019: 83).

Haidee Wasson has studied the discursive treatment of the museum films' epistemology in relation to visitor reception (Wasson 2011). According to her, this documentary footage has merely been referred to as 'archival footage' in written museology or media theory today. Wasson, however, identified a particular documentary film format referred to as the 'museum film', based on the Metropolitan Museum of Art's practice of making in-house film productions to help the visitors 'order the proliferating assemblage of things [by] directing the eye to one particular object, for a predetermined amount of time' (Wasson 2011: 197). As early examples of didactic cinema, she concludes that '[t]he small screen, short length, and slowness of these films allowed cinema to become more useful to the spaces and temporalities of the museum' (Wasson 2011: 197). Because it assisted the visitors in finding pleasure and making sense of their museum visits, Wasson consequently categorised the museum film as 'useful cinema', adding that this cinema in turn can include 'a variety of didactic films that are fictional as well as non-fictional, narrative as well as non-narrative' (Acland and Wasson 2011: 4).

While acknowledging Wasson's notion of 'useful cinema', Mandelli focuses on its screening space by underlining the 'need to consider [these] films in the framework of the practices, discourses, and [display rhetoric] that are intertwined with the specific activities and goals of various institutions' (Mandelli 2019: 9). Because the Metropolitan Museum of Art's films were mainly in-house media productions at the time, both scholars agree that this particular body of cultural materials reflected a unique 'disposition, an outlook, and an approach' to the documentary film medium by the museum at the time (Acland and Wasson 2011: 4). The films' direct didactic purpose was clearly limited, to facilitate visitors' engagement with the museum's displayed artefacts and overall visual fabric.

Immersing the visitors in the exhibition narrative through film has indeed become a leading aspect of 'new museology'. Despite this rise in popularity and recognition, there is still, however, a profound lack of informed knowledge about the actual discursive contribution provided by moving images in twenty-first-century fashion exhibitions. Fiona Anderson's observations regarding visual media's intervention with modern fashion curation at the turn of the millennium reflects its initial, clearly hesitating approach to visitor reception (Anderson 2000). Her exposé revolves around the use of moving imagery in three fashion displays in London in the late 1990s. Based on empirical data from these exhibitions, Anderson concluded that new museology in tandem with the museological approach to fashion history at this time had resulted in the use of promotional fashion videos to produce 'increased emphasis on contextualization' (Anderson 2000: 379). Anderson explained the appearance of this new content by claiming that curating fashion exhibitions demanded an 'increased focus on representation and the body and a shift of emphasis from production to consumption', influenced by 'cultural studies approaches which focus on representation and linguistic texts' (Anderson 2000: 374, 375).

This shift in emphasis from production to consumption resulted in pivotal changes to the fashion curation practice at, for instance, the Victoria and Albert Museum (V&A) in London. As one of the world's leading exhibitors of fashion, the museum now allowed its 'purist', object-based exhibition narratives to include the screening of promotional fashion videos for additional contextualisation (Anderson 2000: 379). This attempt at an extended visual narrative, however, negated two customary museological aspects of fashion curation, first of all by muffling the demand that the museum *animate* the exhibited garments. Screening promotional footage also revoked the need for an exhibition hypothesis set to balance the entertainment versus education dichotomy, by 'providing entertaining and increasingly non-didactic educational experiences about fashion' (Anderson 2000: 388).

In retrospect, it seems plausible that these attempts at increased entertainment value, or 'edutainment' (entertainment designed to be educational), were meant to make fashion exhibitions more attractive and accessible to a larger audience.[1] On the other hand, it appears to have made both fashion curators and scholars realise that such an imbalance between entertainment and education within the exhibition narrative actually represented a risk of permanently devaluing the institutional, didactic agenda for fashion displays. Hence the above-mentioned outright scholarly calls for more balanced exhibition content by Alexandra Palmer and Valerie Steele ten years later.

Fashion exhibitions and moving images

The general relevance of the film medium to fashion and dress practice was realised more than a century ago. Paul Poiret was seemingly the first couturier to use a film of a mannequin parade to promote his fashions in 1911 (Evans 2001). Cinematography's ability to reflect reality was quickly picked up by other fashion designers as well, such as Charles Worth and Jeanne Paquin. They all used the new medium for PR purposes as early as the 1910s because it gave the onlooker the opportunity to see how their creations flattered the moving woman's body. From 1910 British newsreel companies such as Pathé and Gaumont included footage of Paris fashions in their newsreels, and in 1911 Pathé produced a series of short films on forthcoming fashions. In 1911 Liberty in London participated in the making of a film showing mannequins parading. Throughout Europe and the United States, film thus rapidly became a medium through which knowledge of elite fashion was disseminated to a mass audience (Evans 2001: 285). We can therefore safely determine that the practice of producing documentary footage representing dress culture was established early on in film history, as was the dissemination of couture fashion in edited film formats, for promotional or other purposes. It also explains why Elisa Mandelli generally grants filmed footage a higher epistemological value than photography, in that 'film, being able to capture the "flux of time", is more effective than photography in preserving the memory of the past' (Mandelli 2019: 18).

According to Valerie Steele, '[t]he first popular fashion exhibition was held at the International Exhibition in Paris in 1900. Housed in the Palais du Costume, it consisted of thirty tableaux containing waxwork figures arranged in both historical and contemporary scenes' (Steele 2008: 9). In terms of the *modern fashion* exhibition (as opposed to such displays of costume and dress), Diana Vreeland's exhibitions for the Fashion Institute in the 1970s represent an important milestone, despite their outright collision with historical fact (Steele 2008; Palmer 2008). In view of the broadly painted cultural concepts characterising some of Vreeland's exhibitions, I therefore assume that screening any form of archival footage would have imposed unwanted veracity on her chosen exhibition narrative.

As contemporary museology is geared towards reception and visitor engagement, fashion curators today seem increasingly to embrace the use of moving images as an active organising principle when designing an exhibition. The professionally curated museum exhibition today is based on at least three central concepts: a curatorial hypothesis, an exhibition narrative, and an aesthetic approach to this narrative (Horsley 2015: 49). I thus suggest that any filmed or animated footage displayed in connection with a fashion exhibition today must be read also as an attempt to expand the object-based exhibition narrative from both a didactic and entertaining point of view, in compliance with new museology.

The first explicit statement related to the use of documentary footage in a fashion exhibition remains uncertain, possibly because this type of media material has seldom been subject to academic reflection when screened in an exhibition space. With regard to the time span of my study (1990s–), I can only say for certain that one of the first exhibitions to have employed moving images as an explicit *didactic* tool was mounted at the Royal Ontario Museum, Canada in 2002. Curated and later discussed by Alexandra Palmer in an academic article, Palmer recounts how, in *Elite Elegance: Couture Fashion in the 1950s*, she used archival film footage to emphasise the socio-cultural milieu in which dress was worn, rather than foregrounding the work of its designer (Palmer 2008). It means that Palmer departed from the traditional museological idea that 'art museums tend to present objects in isolation to be viewed primarily through the lens of connoisseurship' (Steele 2008: 24), thus replacing a merely object-based principle of study for one that also embraces contextualisation.

Fashion displays as a museological topic now seem to have established a framework of genres, varying between three different narratives: '[Fashion] exhibitions tend to focus either on an individual designer or fashion house…, on a historical movement…, or on the theory and conceptual underpinnings of fashion' (Corner 2016: 126). This outright imitation of the display genres established for art and design exhibitions is hardly surprising, given the hard work devoted to raising fashion from being just an aspect of popular culture to an art form worthy of museological attention. This confirmation also appears to be crucial for the overall museification of fashion.

By and large, the monographic exhibition is most often dedicated to one particular designer or fashion house. It is normally based on the designer's alleged pivotal contribution to fashion history, encouraging the museum to employ an object-based organising principle. The visual style of the display is generally conceived according to one of two different exhibition narratives and is therefore either chronological or thematic. The implementation of documentary footage is, however, more diverse, as we shall see from my study of some different exhibition narratives below.

Designer monograph exhibition

Balençiaga: Shaping Fashion

The Spanish master couturier Cristóbal Balençiaga (1895–1972) has been the subject of several monographic exhibitions in recent years. The Victoria and Albert Museum in London exhibited more than a hundred of his designs in 2017–18 to great public acclaim. As per the exhibition title, the thematic exhibition narrative and displayed garments were clearly geared towards the architectural look of his craft. The cabinet texts, however, also celebrated his bold choice of colours along with the creations' abstract architectural shapes, as well as his innovative ways of cutting and folding difficult fabrics to achieve a certain shape. There was an opulence of photography, sketches and other print matter.

Given the curatorial hypothesis which focused on the connection between architecture and Balençiaga's art, the moving imagery included in this exhibition represented a vital component within the overall narrative. It also managed to cover both the requirement for entertainment and information in line with the tenets of new museology. Under the vignette *Inspired by Balençiaga*, the entertainment angle was secured through a short series of in-house filmed interviews with contemporary designers, such as London-based Molly Goddard. The series, and fashion history's unstoppable continuum with it, was further reinforced in a video titled *Shaping Fashion: Balençiaga's Legacy*, which is technically based on animation technique, showing how a certain creation by the couturier has morphed into a new shape in another designer's hands over the years. Three didactic shorts provide information on how Balençiaga solved difficult design issues such as the cutting of a particular fabric, or the handling and folding of a certain fabric, and how he achieved a historically inspired draping for a particular evening gown. All three shorts share the same editing: first, the morphing of animations, indicating how the different dress panels were designed and meant to come together, followed by video footage documenting a contemporary dressmaker repeating the actual execution of the design work with a similar material, and, at the end, an archival photo of the original creation worn by a model at Balençiaga's establishment. The most important example for the purpose of this study, however, is the museum film in the V&A's longstanding series *How Was It Made?* (Figure 6.1). The long perspective characterising these in-house productions entails a meta-perspective making their entire museum collection eligible for the visitor's closer inspection.

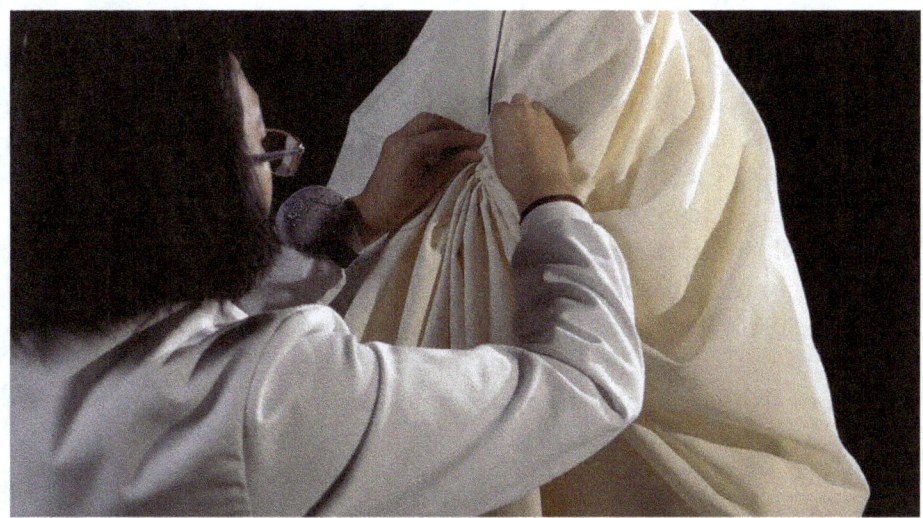

Figure 6.1 Screenshot from *How Was It Made? Constructing Balençiaga's Historically Inspired Evening Dress*. Exhibition video featuring Ying Wang, 2017. © Victoria and Albert Museum, London

These video productions are very informative (especially if you have some knowledge of the craft) because the cinematography is overall pedagogical and non-glamorous. In my view, this type of media production generically corresponds to Haidee Wasson's above-cited discussion regarding the application of 'useful cinema' in the museum space. From a museological point of view, it also indicates the museum's awareness of its role as educator, which in this case takes the form of sharing its newly obtained knowledge on matters pertaining to a particular designer's craft with the museum audience.

To this end, the archival footage screened in *Balençiaga: Shaping Fashion* was apparently selected to reflect the exhibition's focus on the craft mechanisms involved in haute couture practice. One instalment subsequently features the fitting of a female customer's suit by one of the head seamstresses at the fashion house. Originally screened as part of a newsreel, the footage represents a good example of Balençiaga's preferred form of PR, as it not only points to his own craft, but also to his celebrity clientele. By inserting it into the exhibition narrative of *Balençiaga: Shaping Fashion* the curatorial team indicates that this documentary footage has now taken on a completely new meaning. It has transcended its original documentary PR genre to become an item of visible evidence.

Mary Quant

By the early 1960s, British popular culture, including fashion, was evolving in giant steps and was subject to wide interest from professional branches like television, PR agencies, media entrepreneurs and journalists. One of the foremost representatives of the new generation was Mary Quant (1934–), which explains the enormous amounts of footage featuring both her persona and her fashion business currently provided through the V&A's YouTube channel (summer 2022). The moving imagery used in the 2019–20 exhibition on Mary Quant, one of the most important female entrepreneurs in modern fashion history, therefore contributes a very important piece to the discourse laid out in this chapter.

Amongst its many films, three instalments seem especially pertinent for my argument here, but also as to why they were included in the exhibition. First, the interview with Mary Quant from 1985 in a talking-heads format is informative in that she talks about her fashion business in retrospect. This perspective allows her to pinpoint more precisely what she wanted her clothes to express in terms of youth culture, female emancipation and the great expectations for the future held by her generation. Interestingly, her account in this interview fully matches the narrative played out in *The London Look: 1960s British Fashion Youth Quake*, presented by Puritan Fashions Corporation, UK (no date). Originally made for international PR purposes for the benefit of the Mary Quant and Tuffin & Foale trademarks, this 12-minute production presents itself as a perfect documentary proto-feminist time capsule today. It means that the young women driving the narrative were not just filmed modelling Mary Quant's designs outdoors using a style resembling direct cinema. The editing of the women's entire performance and the urban *mise en scène* reflect a desire to propel female activity from the periphery into the centre of a male-dominated society. Dressed mainly in minidresses and low heels, the young women incessantly propagate equality by trespassing into different male spaces, such as appearing in charge of – for example – building sites. Moving easily in their comfortable clothes, these women also invade the spaces given to statues of important men in the city space, and they go clubbing together without male escorts. Their understated political activism is interlaced with visits to female spheres like the hairdresser and the fashion boutique (Bazaar). Looking back, the entire narrative is played out in a manner that comes across as representing the liberated female agency that always underpinned Mary Quant's fashion philosophy, as confirmed in the interview with her from 1985.

Extending the fashion exhibition narrative **131**

Figure 6.2 Screenshot from *Fashion Unpicked: The 'Wet Collection' by Mary Quant*. Exhibition video featuring curator Stephanie Wood, 2019. © Victoria and Albert Museum, London

The third entry of special interest to this study is *Fashion Unpicked: The 'Wet Collection' by Mary Quant* which is an in-house museum film production produced for the exhibition. In this four-minute information film, the exhibition's co-curator Stephanie Wood expertly details Quant's pioneering use of PVC plastics for several collections of women's rainwear, first launched in 1963 (Figure 6.2). She carefully lays out and demonstrates the different design and manufacturing strategies used by Quant, based on different models of raincoats donated to the museum. The instructive atmosphere and privilege of this mini-tour is emphasised by the fact that the film is edited with several informative close-ups of the garments. The investigative and didactic *mise en scène* of this video footage is further emphasised by the fact that it was filmed backstage at the museum, in one of the workshops. It has all the qualities of 'useful' cinema.

Gianni Versace Retrospective

The Textile Museum in Borås, Sweden, mounted an homage to Gianni Versace in 2019–20. The items on loan belong in private collections and were especially selected to allow a thematic presentation of his work. The garments and accessories were subsequently grouped under headings like

'Roots', 'Italiana', 'Pop Art' and 'Miami' with the intention of giving the visitor an impression of how these themes were reflected in Versace's creative practice, and how they resonated with his own biography.

The catwalk footage accompanying *Gianni Versace Retrospective* was presented as a 32- minute film loop, with the sequences chronologically edited. Gianni Versace only appears once, in the last instalment showing the AW/97–98 collection. The earliest and longest instalment was shot at Atelier Versace, during the launch of his SS/91 collection. Filmed on the premises in Paris, the models come down the staircase, hence copying a classical form of entrance once devised by Lucile of London (Evans 2001: 274). The lighting used for the show was golden, soft and warm, as if set by the Mediterranean sea. Classical music was mixed with disco, especially featuring Madonna's 'Vogue'. The song line 'strike a pose' is repeated again and again as a command to the models, during the presentation of Versace's line of evening wear. Christy Turlington opens the show, followed by Helena Christensen, Claudia Schiffer, Linda Evangelista, Tatjana Patitz and Cindy Crawford – all very beautiful-looking, although the camera mainly embraces Versace's creations in medium long close-ups. At the same time, some models flirt with the camera by looking seductively straight into it, performing for it, and clearly 'selling the goods'.

One year later, these so-called supermodels of the 1990s present Versace's AW/92–93 collection, seemingly in the same space. They show the creations in small groups or solo. Some models dance on the catwalk and seem to be very aware of their allure. It is obvious to the onlooker that the creations are now custom-made for each model. Unlike the year before, the camera also tends to cinematographically embrace each supermodel in close-ups, whereas the creations are conveyed in full format only from a distance. Alternatively, if the model is less famous, the camera takes a close-up of the creation. I also note that the supermodels are given celebrity entrances: Claudia Schiffer enters in the dark, walks to the centre of the runway and strikes a pose before the light is turned on. She then smiles and slowly takes off her jacket while the audience applauds.

The above-mentioned aesthetic factors and visual tropes make this documentary catwalk footage unusual, maybe even unique. I suggest that the main reason for its inimitable look is that it was shot on video by the German fashion photographer Peter Lindbergh (1944–2019) (see Loriot 2016). Because the footage seemingly lacks post-production work, these images have all the intimate markings of an 'observatory' documentary, a notebook, 'because of the progressive, accumulative way in which it came into being, as notes taken by the director on a day-to-day basis, without a clear overall strategy at the onset of the film' (Rascaroli 2009: 149). I suggest this footage was initially intended mainly for private rather than promotional consumption. However, like some of the above-mentioned exhibition footage, it too has transcended its original purpose when screened as part of an exhibition narrative.

My third observation is that, as a result of its genre, this footage offers a very private view of the supermodels, once they had been launched by Lindbergh, and Gianni Versace's 'house' models. It is my contention that these three components – Lindbergh's cinematography, Versace's creative genius, and the supermodels' subjective approach to the modelling of Versace's collections – make it impossible to fold this exhibition film into the genre of the mechanical and objective set-up of traditional catwalk footage. However, it works perfectly as a time capsule, not only demonstrating Versace's creative practice, but also providing an intimate glimpse of the fashion shows staged by one of the most celebrated designers and his team of models in the 1990s. It therefore comes across as a cinematic notebook of important documentary footage turned into 'useful cinema'.

Exhibiting a certain historical movement

Themed fashion exhibitions tend to draw a wide audience because of their distinct effort to pivot on visual pleasure through a variety of couture highlights. Alexandra Palmer, as one of a very few curators, has offered a detailed account of the rationale behind her inclusion of archival film of fashion shows in *Elite Elegance: Couture Fashion in the 1950s*, in 2002. 'Unlike traditional exhibitions on haute couture that focus on the couturiers' names and artistry, this exhibit set out to interpret the museum's 1950s couture collection within the socio-cultural framework of the postwar years in Toronto' (Palmer 2008: 52). In concert with the locally collected creations, Palmer thus accentuated the local history further by selecting footage that emphasised the socio-cultural milieu in which the dresses were once worn. Instead of screening the excerpts separately, she installed moving imagery from newsreels, fashion shows and publicity documentaries *inside* the exhibition cases, behind the garments on display, to ensure maximum immersion (Figure 6.3). As a result, this is a case where the documentary footage very clearly becomes an integral part of the display, from both a didactic and an entertainment point of view. It becomes an exhibit in its own right by offering the visitor a wider scope of information, including local history, in relation to the garments on display.

Figure 6.3 *Christian Dior* exhibition with historical film projection inside the case. Royal Ontario Museum (ROM), Toronto, 2017. Photo: Alexandra Palmer. Courtesy of the Royal Ontario Museum, Toronto. © ROM, Toronto

Much like the fashion curators at the Victoria and Albert Museum in London, Palmer has continued to develop the Royal Ontario Museum's use of moving imagery for didactic purposes over the years. Her use of documentary footage to further instruct museum visitors on unexpected topics, such as fashion design for people sitting in wheelchairs, seems to be most helpful. Palmer was also able to secure the copyright to produce a documentary of the entire chain of production of a couture Dior dress now in the museum's collection (Palmer 2020). Yet another of her documentary modes is the decision to record on video all meetings with donors of textiles and fashion to the museum (Palmer, personal correspondence with author, 2020).

Exhibiting theory and the conceptual underpinnings of fashion

The British curator Judith Clark's exhibitions represent clear cases of distinct theoretical and conceptual approaches to the entire fashion system. *The Vulgar: Fashion Redefined* at the Barbican Art Gallery in London in 2016–17 is a case in point. Clark described it as a project 'about taste, but it is also about the relationship between psychoanalysis and fashion, and about psychoanalysis and curatorial practice, in this case fashion exhibition-making' (Clark 2017: 16). As for 'the vulgar' being the leading concept of the exhibition narrative, Clark stated that it is

> just as much about hierarchies of value within the museum as within the fashion system. ... The certainty of interpretation is as much a risk within curatorial practice, if we acknowledge that each visitor is bringing their own individual history to what they see, and this might be more powerfu than captions. (Clark 2017: 16)

Looking into the history of the 'vulgar' as a concept, this exhibition screened a very limited amount of moving imagery on a specially designated wall securely separated from the rest of the exhibition. Unlike other fashion exhibition genres, but completely in line with the conceptual exhibition of artefacts in art museums, this type of display narrative invites the screening of recorded dialogues (or monologues) between people in the know. It thus demonstrated how a theoretically informed display encouraged a discussion of fashion as an art form, rather than screenings of contextualising non-fiction footage. To make this clear, Judith Clark had opted for a talking-heads documentary format where she was in conversation with different fashion designers about how the idea of the vulgar has historically infused the visual image of dress, and the designer's own appreciation of it. Transcribed for the catalogue, I offer one example of how a filmed discussion might evolve, in an effort to frame the theoretical exhibition hypothesis leading to this type of exhibition:

> *Judith Clark*: We have etiquette books in the exhibition, and they warn us not to put clashing colours together. In the etiquette books of the 1880s, it warns us not to put red with yellow: what's your answer?
>
> *Christian Lacroix*: My mother said not orange with violet, not green with blue, and, of course, for me, it was the most beautiful mixing and matching of colours ... the best, no rules. (Alison and McCarthy, 2016, 231)

Ballerina: Fashion's Modern Muse

The Museum at Fashion Institute of Technology in New York in 2020 mounted *Ballerina: Fashion's Modern Muse* to explore how the fashion world has appropriated the visual and material aesthetics of the classical ballet costume during the twentieth century. The theoretical underpinnings of this exhibition hypothesis were presented in an introductory video containing both still and moving images that outlined the historiography of ballet dancing, the ballerina and her costumes throughout dance history. The moving imagery includes excerpts of world-famous ballerinas like Anna Pavlova dancing in the early twentieth century, Maria Tallchief, America's first really famous prima ballerina, and the legendary Dame Margot Fonteyn. There is also a lavish array of live recordings from dance performances around the world, in tandem with excerpts from celebrated Hollywood film productions like *The Red Shoes* (Michael Powell, 1948). This footage has been mixed with still images of selected fashion garments and media images in order to further illustrate the transition of – especially – the tutu from the dance stage to fashion collections, as explained in the curator's (Patricia Mears') voice-over. The list of images very interestingly shows that most of the video clips already exist on YouTube or in other public domains, which means that the museum's introductory video represents a compilation of documentary footage which offers the theoretical underpinnings of the exhibition narrative.

Contrary to fashion curation's recurring predicament with the animation of displayed garments, an additional effect of the exhibition hypothesis for *Ballerina – dance costume into fashion –* is that this introductory video footage inadvertently mollifies this particular conundrum as well. The topic's inherent idea is, after all, that of designing for a moving body, which makes the remediation of this particular fashionable look so much easier.

Discussion

It seems that the question of how fashion curators have solved the issue of animating the garments displayed in a particular exhibition have been the centre of attention in most texts on fashion curation published over the past twenty years, including those thematically framed within fashion journalism (see for example Evans 2001; Palmer 2008; Horsley 2015; Mida 2015; du Mortier 2018). And yes, any collected item of clothing going on display is in itself an innate object, offering raw data including certain aspects to do with the designer's artistry and/or specific craft traditions, or material, or historical provenance. Therefore, museological remediation of fashion has traditionally been twofold: concerned both with the wearer's embodiment of the garment, *and* the onlooker's visual and haptic appreciation of the same piece of clothing (see for example Entwistle 2015). The question is whether the only way to make it meaningful again is to mount it on a human form, preferably complete with correct hair, makeup and stance (Horsley 2014: 79). And whether, in its absence, Jeffrey Horsley is right when he suggested that contemporary art-derived strategies could stand in for the mannequin convention through the implementation of runway presentations, photo and/or digital imagery, art film and the fashion film short, as already mentioned (Horsley 2014: 89–90).

The formats Horsley mentions obviously align with 'the increasing importance attributed to audio-visuals and moving images' (Mandelli 2019: 7), according to new museology. However, the audio-visual solutions he suggests seamlessly ratify the ingrained idea that fashion curation is primarily about artistic display and subsequently can only be animated by beautiful but anonymous models or actors. It is my contention that having documentary footage with, for example, a socio-cultural content screened in the exhibition space is doubtless more informative, if less glamorous.

With this hypothesis in mind, I wish to direct the reader's attention back to Haidee Wasson's study and the fact that it widens the concept of 'useful' cinema to include other types of in-house film formats than the museum film. She mentions documentary formats such as 'inventory film', or a film format that is more of a 'utilitarian record' (Wasson 2011: 194). These formats were originally meant to be consumed primarily by the museum's personnel, but I suggest that revisiting certain neighbouring backstage modes of 'useful' cinema represents a gratifying route of exploration in relation to how fashion ought to be documented to suit the purposes of *both* new museology and contemporary fashion curation.

Elisa Mandelli's historiography of the screening history of moving images in museums shows that modern media literacy has worked to the benefit of the cinematic experience in the museum's overall visual fabric. Based on her statement that 'visitors enjoy direct access to a large quantity of images that document historical events [. . . and] that are seamlessly placed alongside objects or artworks' (2019: 82), it also seems that the screening of moving imagery is no longer primarily an audience catcher. It has become an effective didactic tool within the framework of new museology. My analysis of the display of moving imagery in the above exhibitions suggests that, taken as a whole, these exhibitions demonstrate a new and much broader approach to moving imagery in fashion curation today. If applied as an outright didactic tool, the auteur exhibition, however, seems to offer the most varied and innovative diversity of imagery. It would seem that certain northern European and North American museums have led the way here. The Royal Ontario Museum has documented the artistic process behind their exhibited textiles on many occasions. Alexandra Palmer has also combined the purposes of donors' oral witness statements about a garment's history with local fashion historiography and the museum's collection by continuously video-filming her meetings with them.

The Victoria and Albert Museum has provided different types of backstage films on the designer process that forego the official launch of, for instance, a collection of raincoats. Short documentaries demonstrating designers' expert cutting and construction of a certain garment, or skilful draping of a piece of cloth, is another instance of 'useful cinema' in relation to the didactic side of fashion curation and display.

On the other hand, the epistemological value of Peter Lindbergh's catwalk footage of the supermodels modelling Gianni Versace's collections is obscured by its intimacy, from a museological point of view. Lindbergh's semi-private documentation is admittedly an important deviation from customary catwalk footage, and thus unique. Using it as part of an exhibition narrative, however, makes higher didactic demands on its museological setting, since it reflects a type of visual culture that fans out from the designer monograph exhibition per se to indicate a historical movement in the history of fashion modelling and fashion photography (the supermodels). I suggest that the same rationale can be applied to *The London Look: 1960s British Fashion Youth Quake* in the Mary Quant exhibition discussed above. The didactic value of this particular film also begs a different setting in order to communicate its entire value. Suffice to say that, in the eyes of a twenty-first-century onlooker, the visual content of both productions has transcended their original media formats. This is especially clear when watching the British production whose initial PR narrative has now transcended into communicating a socio-cultural, even feminist, discourse.

From an epistemological point of view, it is hardly surprising that exhibitions aspiring to make visible the theoretical and conceptual underpinnings of fashion through a comparative analysis of historical objects in situ do not primarily depend on moving images as a didactic tool. A dialogue or discussion among 'talking heads' is a lot more likely to sustain and expand the fashion curator's exhibition narrative in these cases. A talking-heads documentation of these intellectual discussions is therefore helpful in that they may clear up and illuminate the avalanche of new information the visitor meets in the display. Another way to get prepared for such an exhibition is of course to read the catalogue before visiting the show. Consequently, moving images do not seem to be the correct didactic tool for these advanced, theoretical types of fashion displays.

Conclusion

Elisa Mandelli's above exposé and her assertion that 'Moving images … are showcased as if they were concrete exhibits, as witnesses to the past' (2019: 82) confirm the medium's initial transformation into a valid cultural form within the concept of new museology over the past thirty years. This development has resulted in an increasing production of museum films by the most prominent producers of fashion exhibitions. It therefore seems particularly appropriate to apply the concept of 'useful cinema' to this documentary side of fashion curation since it represents the need for a particular 'outlook, an approach toward a medium on the part of institutions and institutional agents' (Acland and Wasson 2011: 4).

Visible evidence from exhibitions at the forefront of fashion curation indicates that the screening of moving images in these exhibitions works along two major strains of new museology: that of extending the fashion narrative through the animation of clothing through, for instance, newsreel excerpts (entertainment); and that of informing the visitor (education). Modern technology has subsequently initiated a change in the screening of traditional museum film (ethnologically geared, non-intellectual film footage screened in a specially designated auditorium) to the benefit of new museology's didactic demands on the film's seamless proximity to the topic in case, from both an intellectual and a physical point of view.

Another observation relates to the obvious and apparently uncontroversial inclusion of dress in the V&A's long-standing series of formative exhibition videos titled *How Was It Made?* On a conceptual level, these productions empathically declare dress history a natural segment of the museum's collection, and thus encourage the museification of fashion. Narratively, they also reflect how a pertinent museological aspect of a museum's inner workings (such as internal research of particular items in its collection) can be shared with the visitors.

Consequently, the most compelling conclusion of my study is that fashion curators at the forefront of museum work today seem to increasingly apply documentary formats in the vein of the traditional museum film, in an attempt to direct the visitors' attention to, for example, the conservation or the actual crafting of the garment on display. A pertinent example is the

Figure 6.4 Screenshot from *Christian Dior: Behind the Scenes at Royal Ontario Museum*, 2017. Karla Livingston, technician, mounting Saadi by Christian Dior for the exhibition. Exhibition video. Courtesy of the Royal Ontario Museum, Toronto. © ROM, Toronto

compiled documentary short *Christian Dior: Behind the Scenes at ROM* (2017). Each segment of this film short points to an individual topic suitable for documentation: catalogue production, conservation regimes, preparation of display mannequins, the preparation and mounting of a couture dress from the museum's collection, and so on (Figure 6.4).

I thus suggest that the contemporary application of moving images to expand a fashion exhibition narrative has encouraged the development of unique types of 'backstage' film formats such as 'inventory films', or films that seem to be forms of 'utilitarian records' (Wasson 2011: 197). A rather unexpected instance of the latter would be, I suggest, Peter Lindbergh's observational footage of the supermodels modelling Gianni Versace's collection in the 1990s. The increasing ambition to expand the screening of this type of moving imagery from the private regions of the fashion industry or the backstage of the museum to its frontstage, official fashion displays – to make these types of installations public, in short – is to my mind the most discursively important visual development of documentary footage in fashion exhibitions. When, in the next step, the most ambitious museums go on to upload some of these documentary productions on their official YouTube channels, it means that the museum permanently expands the discursive remits of its fashion curation and museum space. It is my contention that museums like the Royal

Ontario Museum and Victoria and Albert Museum have both already taken these non-glamorous formats on board and that these 'fluid' film formats are key when it comes to the museification of fashion.

Note

1. This goal has been easily reached, given the blockbuster success of exhibitions like *Heavenly Bodies* at the Metropolitan Museum of Art in New York which attracted in excess of 1.6 million visitors in 2018, or *Christian Dior: Designer of Dreams* at the V&A in London in 2019, which attracted almost 600,000 visitors, or *Thierry Muegler: Couturissime* in Montreal 2019 which attracted almost 300,000 visitors.

References

Acland, Charles H. and Haidee Wasson. 2011. 'Introduction: Utility and Cinema'. In *Useful Cinema*, edited by Charles R. Acland and Haidee Wasson, 1–14. Durham, NC and London: Duke University Press.

Alison, Jane and Sinéad McCarthy, eds. 2016. *The Vulgar: Fashion Redefined*. London: Koenig Books and Barbican Art Gallery. Exhibition catalogue.

Anderson, Fiona. 2000. 'Museums as Fashion Media'. In *Fashion Cultures: Theories, Explorations and Analysis*, edited by Stella Bruzzi and Pamela Church Gibson. 371–89. London and New York: Routledge.

Corner, Frances. 2016. *Why Fashion Matters*. London: Thames & Hudson.

Entwistle, Joanne. 2015. *The Fashioned Body: Fashion, Dress and Modern Social Theory*. Cambridge: Polity Press.

Evans, Caroline. 2001. 'The Enchanted Spectacle'. *Fashion Theory*, vol. 5, no. 3, 271–310. DOI: 10.2752/136270401778960865.

Hooper-Greenhill, Eilean. 1992. *Museums and the Shaping of Knowledge*. London and New York: Routledge.

Hooper-Greenhill, Eilean. 2000. *Museums and the Interpretation of Visual Culture*. London and New York: Routledge.

Horsley, Jeffrey. 2014. 'Re-presenting the Body in Fashion Exhibitions'. *International Journal of Fashion Studies*, vol. 1, no. 1, 75–96. DOI: 10.1386/infs.1.1.75_1.

Horsley, Jeffrey. 2015. 'A Fashion "*Muséographie*": The Delineation of Innovative Presentation Modes at ModeMuseum, Antwerp'. *Fashion Theory*, vol. 19, no. 1, 43–66. DOI: 10.2752/175174115X14113933306789.

Loriot, Thierry-Maxime. 2016. *Peter Lindbergh: A Different Vision on Fashion Photography*. Berlin: Taschen. Exhibition catalogue.

Mandelli, Elisa. 2019. *The Museum as a Cinematic Space: The Display of Moving Images in Exhibitions*. Edinburgh: Edinburgh University Press.

Mida, Ingrid. 2015. 'Animating the Body in Museum Exhibitions of Fashion and Dress'. *Dress*, vol. 41, no. 1, 37–51. DOI: 10.1179/0361211215Z.00000000038.

du Mortier, Bianca M. 2018. 'Introducing Movement into the Motionless: Fashion in the Rijksmuseum'. *Film, Fashion & Consumption*, vol. 7, no. 1, 73–8. DOI: 10.1386/ffc.7.1.73_1.

Palmer, Alexandra. 2008. 'Untouchable: Creating Desire and Knowledge in Museum Costume and Textile Exhibitions'. *Fashion Theory*, vol. 12, no. 1, 31–63.

Palmer, Alexandra. 2020. Personal e-mail exchange with author.

Rascaroli, Laura. 2009. *The Personal Camera: Subjective Cinema and the Essay Film*. London and New York: Wallflower.

Steele, Valerie. 2008. 'Museum Quality: The Rise of the Fashion Exhibition'. *Fashion Theory*, vol. 12, no. 1, 7–30. DOI: 10.2752/17514108X268127.

Wasson, Haidee. 2011. 'Big, Fast Museums / Small, Slow Movies'. In *Useful Cinema*, edited by Charles R. Acland and Haidee Wasson, 178–204. Durham, NC and London: Duke University Press.

List of exhibitions

Balençiaga: Shaping Fashion. Victoria and Albert Museum, London. 7 May 2017 to 18 February 2018.

Ballerina: Fashion's Modern Muse. The Museum at Fashion Institute of Technology (FIT), New York. 11 February to 18 April 2020.

Elite Elegance: Couture Fashion in the 1950s. Royal Ontario Museum, Toronto. November 2002 to May 2003.

Gianni Versace Retrospective. Borås Textilmuseum, Borås, Sweden. 30 November 2019 to 16 August 2020.

Mary Quant. Victoria and Albert Museum, London. 6 April 2019 to 16 February 2020.

The Vulgar: Fashion Redefined. Barbican Art Gallery, London. 13 October 2016 to 5 February 2017.

List of exhibition videos

Ballerina: Fashion's Modern Muse. New York: Museum at Fashion Institute of Technology (FIT), 2020. Exhibition video.

Christian Dior: Behind the Scenes at ROM. Toronto: Royal Ontario Museum, Canada, 2017. Exhibition video.

Fashion Unpicked: The 'Wet Collection' by Mary Quant. London: V&A Media, 2019. Exhibition video.

Gianni Versace Retrospective. Catwalk footage shot by Peter Lindbergh. Borås Textilmuseum, Borås, Sweden, 2019. Exhibition video.

Inspired by Balençiaga. London: V&A Media, 2017. Exhibition video.

Mary Quant, Fashion Designer, Talking Personally. London: Thames TV, 1985. Exhibition video.

Shaping Fashion: Balençiaga's Legacy. London: V&A Media, 2017. Exhibition video.

The London Look: 1960s British Fashion Youth Quake. Puritan Fashions Corporation, UK (no date). Exhibition video.

Digital references

Exhibition videos, YouTube: https://www.youtube.com/playlist?list=PLq7I3h28zSMib-GjG1K2IiedvzCit133oM (accessed 29 June 2022).

Victoria and Albert Museum: https://www.youtube.com/user/vamuseum (accessed 29 June 2022).

Expanding interview 2
Boel Ulfsdotter in conversation with Alexandra Palmer at Royal Ontario Museum, Canada

Boel Ulfsdotter [BU]: Hello Alexandra Palmer! You are the Nora E. Vaughan Senior Curator, Global Fashion and Textiles and Chair of the Veronika Gervers Research Fellowship at the Royal Ontario Museum (ROM) in Toronto, Canada. Our conversation will revolve around your method of using documentary footage in your fashion exhibitions. You introduced this film format in your very first exhibition, *Elite Elegance: Couture Fashion in the 1950s*, at ROM in 2002, when it was still a mainly pre-digital practice.

Alexandra Palmer [AP]: Yes, when I was writing my dissertation about 1950s couture in Canada, I became curious and wanted to find out what happened to these dresses when they left the design houses, and arrived in Canada, and who were the buyers, et cetera. I was desperate for information about the local documentation of fashion, so I went to the National Archives in Ottawa where they have a vast film collection. It was really interesting because the CBC, the Canadian Broadcasting Company, which started in the 1950s, have saved a lot of the early material. Posey Boxer was the first fashion reporter for television in our country and she reported from the fashion shows in Italy, commenting on the wonderful dresses coming down the Spanish Steps. CBC also interviewed Norman Hartnell when he came to Canada to introduce his clothes, sitting smoking in the studio and answering the male interviewer's questions about how it was to design clothes for women, including the Queen. This black-and-white footage caught my attention, especially the astonishing material in Eaton's archives, because this chain of department stores also had its own film and photography studio, since they were in operation well before television started. They made films for in-store fashion training and for their own public fashion shows. All in all, it was this fantastic material that got me interested in documentary footage of fashion because it gives you a visual record of fashion at the time. My interest in this type of transmission of fashion information made me watch a lot of archival footage, since I realised it was so different to more contemporary footage which brings you inside fashion shows and designer studios in a completely different way. Years later, because I knew this material existed, I wanted to screen some of it in the *Elite Elegance* exhibition (2002–3). I wanted the exhibition to be about the women and their dresses, not so much about the designers.

BU: *What type of documentary material did you screen?*

AP: An Eaton's fashion show segment shot in rich Technicolor like a fiction film, for instance. Those shows were very thorough and showed what to wear during the different times of day, and what you should wear to look fashionable that season. All the footage had live commentary that was in scripts in the archives too. Apart from being straightforward documentations of the bi-annual fashion shows, some of the films [were] made to train Eaton's staff on how to sell clothes, the look of the season with all accessories like hats, gloves and umbrellas for instance. I also screened black-and-white TV interviews from the 1950s, featuring some of the designers, on a separate wall in the exhibition space. Hearing these famous male designers, and how they talked about ladies' fashion in these early talk shows, is quite extraordinary.

BU: *And you then compiled these documentary excerpts to be screened in the exhibition, I suppose?*

AP: Yes, after all the copyright issues had been cleared … The CBC was also very happy to help with the technical side of things. They were excited because no one had ever asked to use the material before. Among their footage I found a short excerpt of a lady wearing a Dior dress in a Holt Renfrew fashion show held in the new Toronto shop. This was on a monitor near the displayed dress from the ROM collection [*Elite Elegance*]. So, I was really pleased that they were so forthcoming. Other material I had already seen was just ordered from the National Archives in Ottawa and prepared for the exhibition by our audio technicians.

BU: *And you then custom fit each video-loop to the relevant display cabinet?*

AP: Yes, with ROM exhibit designers, we set them up like exhibition objects, either to function as live 'wallpapers', or else, they were set up to screen excerpts on separate monitors, which was the case with the Eaton's material, for instance. Some screening stations were provided with headphones so that the visitor could listen to the commentary provided at the time, others were silent and the visuals self-explanatory. I also usually work with an ambient soundtrack in my exhibitions, as well as being very conscious of how any information texts are parceled out. The visual set-up is important because if visitors walk up to a cabinet that is just full of text panels, they just leave it and continue to the next cabinet. But there is after all some information you really want the visitor to read, and we know that they want to share the information, so curation practice actually involves a constant negotiation of the fine line between museology and visual planning.

BU: *Please tell me a little about how you came to realise the importance of using documentary video footage in your exhibition work. Did you already have an interest in film when you started out as a fashion curator?*

AP: Part of it is a way of animating the static objects and making them come alive. Documentary archival footage takes you immediately into the period, regardless of the fact that it was filmed in black and white. It conjures up visual evidence of what you are trying to show in the exhibition and helps the visitor to break up the presentation of object after object and make sense of them. Not having each with its own sound is a good thing, because you want to focus on the visual aspect of fashion, and in the exhibition space it becomes noisy and distracting. Most recently, in the Dior exhibition [*Christian Dior*, ROM 2017–18], I really wanted the visitors to experience the dressmaking practice in the atelier, so I had documentary footage of Monsieur Dior draping directly on a person, that was shown within the exhibition's introductory display case. It set the tone for the entire show. In terms of research, finding this particular footage was no problem now that there is a proper Dior Archive, which tends to Dior's legacy. It meant that now this type of footage on Dior was already prepared and available for the asking, which is excellent. I didn't have to search out the copyright for material in different archives myself. That is very time-consuming and expensive. They know about the rights use now, which is fantastically useful.

In this exhibition, we also projected graphics as film to explain the technical side of dressmaking in the form of film stills. In other instances, I wanted pico-projectors screening short excerpts of women modelling Dior dresses related to that display. These were screened directly onto the platform floor near relevant dresses to create an atmosphere of dressmaking and fashion show practice. It animated the static mannequins. We also provided a section where visitors could sit down and watch newsreels of Dior and the designs (Figure E2.1). The exhibition really focused on how the clothes were made, which is to say how a fashion house operates on a practical and design level.

Figure E2.1 *Christian Dior* exhibition with archival film seating area. Royal Ontario Museum (ROM), 2017. Photo: Alexandra Palmer. Courtesy of the Royal Ontario Museum, Toronto. © ROM, Toronto

BU: *Do you mean to say that you provided most of that practical information on the side, so to speak, instead of presenting it in the immediate vicinity of the visual set-up of the exhibition?*

AP: Yes, because I wanted the visual experience of the exhibition to look like a jewellery box, without the text and graphics interrupting that particular atmosphere of luxury and glamour. But the main theme of the exhibition is about how the clothes are made. There were embroidery samples that explained the embroidered dresses. There were iPads that the visitor scrolled through with four to five screens of information on each dress – who made it, images of the inside construction, Dior's sketches and swatches, and society photos of the woman wearing it, if possible. Again, the process of making fashion. So, the information was rich, but not all print.

BU: *I think that is an unusual theme for a fashion exhibition. Normally the focus is on the outright visual glamour of the garments, especially with themed exhibitions, of course.*

AP: Yes, the films add atmosphere. I had used the same idea in the exhibition *Fashion Follows Form* show [2014–15], which featured the work by Canadian designer Izzy Camilleri. She designs fashion for people who are seated and use wheelchairs, so it is probably the most difficult exhibition I have ever produced. It's all about her redesign of basic clothes – a white shirt, or a pair of jeans – and how Izzy has redesigned these specifically for a person seated in a wheelchair. At one stage I actually wanted to call the show 'This is not Alexander McQueen' because it was so demanding to make a visually alluring show about plain Gap-like clothes and such a difficult subject. How do you get the audience to understand that these clothes are really amazing and interact with them? How do you actually display and explain pattern-making, design research, artistic originality, cut and technique processes that such clothes demand? The clothes are cleverly engineered, and if are not correctly designed they can cause serious illness and even death from sores made by abrasion from folds or thick seams that they can't feel. So the topic of this exhibition has a really serious side to it, which made it exceptionally museologically and visually demanding.

Izzy's designs are actually amazing from a technical point of view, so the films that she had already made to accompany and present her specialised practice were captioned and included in the exhibition. They are all focused on the specific technical requirements for clothes worn by a person continuously sitting in an L-position, which meant that we had to, for instance, specially order and design museum mannequins for the visual demonstration of them in the exhibition. We showed the garment seated and it looked fine. We showed the same design on a standing mannequin to show that the design did not work that way – well it could be cool but did not hang like the conventional garments that are made for standing, not sitting. The introduction to the exhibit was a short video made by Scott Loane [Senior Video Producer, ROM]. It explained fully the idea of fashion designed for standing people and that this exhibit was about fashion for seated people. We also added new films of Izzy sketching designs and working in her studio on a rather big screen to immerse the viewer in her practice.

BU: *Do you mean to say that Izzy Camilleri had already documented her practice when you started working on the exhibition project with her?*

AP: Yes. She was a pioneer and had to explain what she was doing, so she documented her clothes on a variety of seated clients on video. We got permission to use them for the show. The practice of making clothes is really a central concept in our fashion curation here at the museum. It has resulted in my making videos – going underneath an embroidery frame for the purpose of the *Viva Mexico!* exhibition [2015–16], at one point. But it is always worth the effort. Explaining how you make items of clothing in text is really boring, whereas if you visualise it, the onlooker gets engaged and starts looking at the displayed items in a different way.

BU: *But it must be very difficult to know which phase of a creative process to document...*

AP: Yes, but I know what I want and generally when I come back from these excursions I go through the filmed material and make a master script for the ROM AV staff to work from. It means that I have become a sort of editor-producer, which is very time-consuming, but I think it is the only way to do it. I am currently working on a museum film project called *Object Lessons*, about Dorothy K. Burnham, our former curator of fashion and textiles. They will be an amazing asset to our educational visual material (videothèque) once they are up and running.

BU: *That sounds like a project well within the frame of new museology.*

AP: Yes, I know, and part of my research is revolving around these issues. I also have hours and hours of filmed interviews with donors where we talk about how and when they used to wear the garment they are donating (Figure E2.2). It's a hugely time-consuming practice but also very moving and represents a very important piece of social history.

I recently showed an excerpt from an interview I did with a ninety-six-year-old Hungarian physician who came to Canada after the war, to some students. In Canada today, the young generation has little understanding about war, or displacement, or being a refugee. They don't learn enough about World War II, even, so it's important that they get to know the history of this anonymous-looking, seemingly uninteresting, seventy-five-year-old man's black wool coat, made by a tailor in Budapest before the war, worn during the difficult times during the war, and repurposed a number of times

Figure E2.2 *A Chanel Tie Embroidered by Joseph Wong*, ROM, 2020. Composite of screenshots from video with donor conversation. Courtesy of the Royal Ontario Museum, Toronto. © ROM, Toronto

after the war, before it was donated to our museum. It is such an amazing story, and so moving when he tells it, and that is really why clothes matter. It is really my way of animating an otherwise dead object, and making people care about it. I spoke with him years ago and took notes when I took his clothes into the museum. But now with the ease and cheapness of video, I went back to ask if I could interview him on film. He is charming and so informative about his clothes – he's wonderful.

BU: *You have a more or less ethnological approach to the museum objects, then.*

AP: Yes, I think so. I use oral history in order to get at the information I need. This information is not normally written down, so I really have no choice. Video is now my way of documenting these meetings and interviews that before I only did on tape, or took notes by hand.

BU: *I am very curious as to how you received permission to document the production process of a Dior dress for the museum in 2011. Please tell me a little about that.*

AP: Yes, I really wanted a Christian Dior couture dress designed by John Galliano, a contemporary piece, in other words. It was to be his last collection for the Dior label, and I had received a grant for the purchase of a dress, which also included a video of its making. The two were inextricable for me, although museum management thought the dress was the most important thing about the project. But the video was really important to me. I had to find out who they would let in to make the video, their requirements on its editing, and whether the people at Dior would be able to manage the interruption it would entail on their working process. What I wanted was of course to capture the Dior secrets, how they make things and to show what makes haute couture haute couture. It is not just because it is expensive – it is time, it is knowledge, it is skill. I knew it was the first time anything like that had been done, although it has now become customary to include snippets from the design process in different types of promotional luxury material.

It was a very difficult process with Galliano leaving the house, and it also took some time before we had all the logistics and mechanics in place to actually shoot the film. We were of course completely in their hands as they have a business to run. In the end, we had two different local film photographers on the job, and when they finally finished the film, it was a wonderful documentation of the entire creative process, including the transportation of different dress panels to different locations in Paris during the making of it. Very precisely, I wanted the footage to show an overview of the unique system needed to make these creations, and the film photographers really succeeded in documenting exactly that.

The most astonishing thing was, that when the finished film was screened at the fashion house, the team that had made the dress was very moved, because they had never seen the entire process behind the making of the creations. They only ever saw the item when it was in front of them on the table, you see. They were really astonished to see how it developed before it entered the fashion show.

This particular dress was the lead garment for a fashion exhibition entitled *BIG* (2012–14) here at the museum, so it was on the posters, and all other promotional material. It was also the very first item you saw when you entered the show, and it really is a truly remarkable piece. The visitors would spend quite some time looking at it before they moved on. It was also quite clear that the two-minute version of the video really amazed them, and they went back to really look at the dress more closely. Especially since the labels also conveyed information of how much material was needed, how many hours of work it had taken, et cetera. I like this manner of unpacking fashion down to the basic levels of detail.

BU: *Could the visitor see the entire video somewhere else in the exhibition?*

AP: No, we made a special event of screening the entire 45 minutes at one point, but that was all. I have screened it on other occasions as well, though.

I however again explored this particular manner of documentation when we did the exhibition *Iris van Herpen: Transforming Fashion* and *Philip Beesley: Transforming Space* [2018]. Again, it was hard to get funds for the video to be part of the purchase of the dress, but the museum did it and it is great. I very much wanted to show the collaboration of design with Philip Beesley, a Canadian architect, who has frequently worked with van Herpen in making the 'textile'. I worked with Iris's studio to arrange the film about the dress. Stylianos Pangalos produced a wonderful documentary of the creative process behind a dress, which was also acquired by the museum. For him too, it was nice to start the project from the beginning – before the dress was made and to understand my point of view, as well as that of Iris of course. He captured its making in Toronto and Amsterdam and presentation in Paris. As the museum commissioned a dress that had not been designed, I wanted to document the entire process and Iris and Philip's interactions. Again, I wanted the ROM dress to be documented from its inception to creation and its presentation in the fashion show. The dress itself is rather impossible. It does not look like a dress, but that is also what is so special about van Herpen's fashion design. It is difficult for the museum visitor to understand how the creations are actually made because the techniques are very high-tech. The 'textile' used for our creation is zinc consisting of over 300 metal domes, which requires many, many hours of work to create and assemble. I don't think one can quite understand how Iris van Herpen made the dress without watching the footage documenting the process.

BU: *Exhibition narratives tend to be either traditionally based on a classical museological, textual approach or an overarching use of visuals and new technology. You, however, seem to prefer a combination of new museology and documentary narratives. Not one or the other, but both?*

AP: Yes! But you know, fashion exhibitions are really very limited formats. If the visitor leaves with even one piece of new information, you have done a great job.

BU: Aha. *Do you mean to say that you don't really believe in the textual exhibition format from a didactic point of view?*

AP: Oh, I do, but I think one always has to aspire to the reaction we had on the *Fashion Follows Form* show. People really got into it, just like me, you know. When I first saw Izzy's clothes and realised these were people for whom fashion design as we know it in the west did not function well, it was like a revelation. I never thought cutting techniques and decisions on material could be so vital to life. It was a really emotionally challenging exhibition thinking about and working with so many interesting disabled people. This was a new experience for me and made me rethink the importance of fashion – physically and emotionally. The visitors came out and were profoundly moved because they were engaged, and their point of view challenged. For me, that was the best gratification because it is the most difficult exhibition I have ever curated, but also one of the most important.

BU: *The visuals are essential when it comes to catching the extent of the topic, then?*

AP: Yes, in order for the visitor to become immersed in the material, it is really important. They add new information in a different way. The visuals flesh out the exhibited material and bring further understanding to it.

BU: *From your experience, how does the screening of moving images help to make an object relevant for the overall exhibition narrative?*

AP: Moving imagery screened big can really immerse the spectator in a particular aspect of the overall topic.

BU: *How is your gallery organised in order to allow documentary video screenings in tandem with your exhibitions? Your colleagues seem to be working with a similar approach as well.*

AP: Well, yes, we do use them frequently depending on the exhibition project. They are not always an appropriate auxiliary material, but often enough. I find that when you are talking about textile techniques, people nowadays cannot always follow due to lack of knowledge of sewing. It's surprising since there is such a resurgence of DIY projects, and especially craft-making. I have therefore found that explaining about the demands of particular skills, the working hours spent, and the technical complexity of creating any ravishing textile, is most elegantly and most effectively presented through film. Showing visitors how things are made helps them to understand, and they see it is complicated and have a deeper appreciation for what they see. It's therefore the most obvious thing to do, although it is also very time consuming to record and edit these videotapes.

BU: *Do you have a permanent videothèque where the visitors can sit down and watch the films?*

AP: No, unfortunately not. I wish we had a website dedicated to our textile collection where visitors could see all the documentary films that have come from it. It would be so good, especially for students, since I think the hands-on information about the handling of textiles is really missing from most fashion programmes.

BU: *Is the Toronto audience generally passionate about fashion?*

AP: Yes, I must say it is. I feel especially honoured when men who have been dragged along by their female companions actually take an interest in what we are showing. Who knew that fashion could be so interesting beyond the dress itself, they seem to be thinking when they watch the video documentation? They suddenly understand why a dress is really expensive, and worth two cars, and so on. Also, they suddenly start thinking back on how their mother or sisters were dressed, and that is somehow moving them to think beyond the exhibited garment itself. And this is really what it is all about; to make fashion interesting beyond the hangers in the clothes shop.

BU: *Would you say that your exhibitions are a forerunner when it comes to the use of documentary imagery? I mean, when you visit a fashion exhibition, they would normally screen catwalk footage which does little to expand the fashion narrative in the end.*

AP: Since our collection comprises both fashion *and* textiles, in addition to being global and moving across time, I find it frustrating that people today see fashion as merely a question of aesthetics. But you cannot create fashion without a skilled knowledge of textiles, and this is the message we try to get across with our exhibitions here. We therefore present a more holistic approach, bordering on the ethnographical, and socio-cultural studies in our exhibitions. For me, it's all about people, why do we collect and painstakingly preserve certain textile items, what is the history behind them, what do they represent across time and different cultures? This is important to me in my work, and it is in the tradition of this particular museum. Working here means that you inherit the collection and serve mainly as a stepping-stone for its continuation. In terms of fashion and clothes, the interest in textile techniques has always been dominant at the ROM.

BU: *Yes, and you seem to have so much interesting material to work with.*

AP: Absolutely, and it is all thanks to the outstanding curators we have had in the Textile Department over the years. The items they collected have proven to be extremely important for fashion history. For example, they knew to collect the paper dresses of the 1960s. They were on to these less conventional garments very early, and I am very grateful for that. In short, it allows me to make the connection between a Coptic shirt and an Issey Miyake creation today. I personally very much like to collaborate with ROM scientist curators in order to learn more about, for instance, floral patterns, or furs, et cetera, and there is nothing stopping me from bringing in this perspective in an exhibition.

BU: *Yes, it seems to me you have a lot of professional and practical freedom at the museum. Is that why you also felt at liberty to include documentary imagery to the extent that you do, in your exhibitions?*

AP: Yes, I suppose so. I really want to make people look and truly understand what they are seeing so it's a really helpful tool in the toolbox, I think. It has become so handy now, too, with all the digital development that has taken place.

BU: *Still, it seems to me that you are readily working with documentary footage to do more than just animate the objects on display. It seems to play an important role in your exhibition narrative, after all.*

AP: Yes, it shows the item from another perspective and so expands the storytelling aspects of the object, if you see what I mean.

BU: *Do you think your visitors have come to appreciate your exhibition mode? Do they understand what you are after with your use of documentary footage?*

AP: Yes, I think they do. More and more, and I think this image literacy is very connected to the development of the film and camera technique in our mobile phones. On the other hand, this particular technical development has made people stop and simply document the material with their phones, instead of staying for some time to take in the item on display. From that point of view, it has generally become harder to retain the visitors in the exhibition halls.

BU: *The media scholar Haidee Wasson has suggested that the in-house production of documentary film is a form of archival record for museum purposes. Does that resonate a little with what you do?*

AP: Interesting, because particularly my donor interviews feel like a very important addition to the average fashion narrative. I make them because I am interested in documenting how ordinary people shop, make decisions and wear their clothes. For instance, the museum has a fantastic private collection of Martin Margiela creations, which were donated by a woman who was a lawyer's administrative person. She wore these clothes to work. The clothes themselves of course represent fantastic pieces of fashion design, but I think it's even more fascinating to hear about how this woman wore them in the workplace, or on special occasions. I make these donor interviews because I want to document the social history of a particular clothes item before it was donated to our museum, simply. I have decided that this documentation is my main contribution to fashion history. It's another point of view.

References

Acland, Charles R. and Haidee Wasson, eds. 2011. *Useful Cinema*. Durham, NC and London: Duke University Press.

Palmer, Alexandra. 2008. 'Untouchable: Creating Desire and Knowledge in Museum Costume and Textile Exhibitions'. *Fashion Theory*, vol. 12, no. 1, 31–63.

Wasson, Haidee. 2011. 'Big, Fast Museums / Small, Slow Movies'. In *Useful Cinema*, edited by Charles R. Acland and Haidee Wasson. 178–204. Durham, NC and London: Duke University Press.

Audio-visual references

Izzy Camilleri exhibition: https://www.rom.on.ca/en/exhibitions-galleries/exhibitions/fashion-follows-form-designs-for-sitting

Iris van Herpen exhibition: https://www.rom.on.ca/en/exhibitions-galleries/exhibitions/iris-van-herpen-transforming-fashion; https://youtu.be/VixjmKe6rX8

Part II
Television

Chapter 7

Documenting fashion history: television and the temporalities of cultural remembrance

Jihane Dyer

> One day perhaps someone will put on a play in which we shall see a resurrection of those costumes in which our fathers found themselves every bit as fascinating as we do ourselves in our poor garments ... And then, if they are worn and given life by intelligent actors and actresses, we shall be astonished at ever having been able to mock them so stupidly. Without losing anything of its ghostly attraction, the past will recover the light and movement of life and will become present. (Baudelaire 2004 [1863]: 38)

It has been some 150 years since Charles Baudelaire, contemplating a set of fashion plates from decades past, mused about the time-crossing potential of a skilfully animated presentation of fashion history. Such a production would, perhaps, conjure the 'flowing movement' that '[l]iving flesh imparted ... to what to us seems so stiff'; 'It is still possible today,' the poet and critic claimed, 'for the spectator's imagination to give a stir and a rustle to this "tunique" or that "schall"' (Baudelaire 2004 [1863]: 38).

By the 1930s, costume parades of the kind envisioned by Baudelaire had become a popular mode of presenting dress history within a number of European museums, borrowing from the mannequin parades that had become an integral feature of fashion's retail sphere (Hjemdahl 2016). But in 1937, their locus shifted to the television screen in the pioneering six-part programme *Clothes-Line*. Airing on the BBC's (British Broadcasting Corporation) nascent television service just a year after it had been launched, the series staged live-model parades of (largely) authentic fashions from the 1750s to the 1930s across a vaguely defined period setting. The Victoria and Albert Museum's James Laver – co-creator of the programmes alongside BBC producer Mary Adams and the artist-cum-dress-historian Pearl Binder – provided an eccentric commentary, while Binder produced on-the-spot illustrations at an easel. As a reviewer of the series' opening episode was eager to point out, *Clothes-Line* demonstrated an unfamiliar and experimental format for newly inaugurated viewers more accustomed to radio broadcasts, films and pre-recorded newsreels:

> When it was over, we were left wondering quite what it was we had just seen and heard – a poetry-reading, a lightning-artist display, a mannequin parade, or what? Actually, it was of course no one of those things but a new sort of television feature borrowing in part from the technique of all three. (The Listener 1937: 733)

Eighty years later, this composite approach to presenting fashion history on television has evolved enormously. While the costume parade has all but disappeared amidst changing attitudes to the modelling of extant historical dress, the survey approach covering a span of multiple decades remains a popular format for what has become a distinct, albeit modest, subgenre of factual television (on British screens, at least) which I refer to as the 'fashion history documentary'. Taking the BBC's output as an indication – it being the UK's principal public broadcaster – the last three decades in particular have seen a marked rise in major, multi-part series that have each required significant resources and prime-time slots in the viewing schedule. In line with programmes dealing with the history of art, music and architecture, such documentaries now regularly incorporate archive footage, popular music, interviews, voice-overs and many other now-familiar documentary conventions.

Yet they have also developed a diverse set of techniques for the presentation of clothing and the conveying of sartorial experience. As I argue in this chapter, these techniques have lost little of the trans-temporal effect that Baudelaire believed could be evoked through wearing and witnessing. Indeed, I suggest that modern fashion history documentaries continue to enact compelling resurrections of the past in the present. Through their specific configurations of documentary 'aesthetics' – the organisation or crafting of their visual, material, temporal and affective codes and the experiences they produce – fashion history documentaries are powerful technologies of cultural remembrance: the ongoing renegotiation and reproduction of a collective past and the processes of engaging with it in the present.

In this chapter, I propose a provisional enquiry into the framing and functions of fashion's past in television history documentaries. I suggest that fashion history programmes offer a unique potential for cultural remembrance:

their supplementation of conventional documentary aesthetics with various representations of clothing and the sartorial experience promote remarkably intimate engagements with (supposedly) shared heritages of style and social imaginaries. The chapter begins with a brief examination of the relationship between history-on-television and the concept of cultural memory. Taking as an initial foundation a broad definition of cultural memory proposed by Astrid Erll in her introduction to the interdisciplinary handbook, *Cultural Memory Studies* – 'the interplay of present and past in socio-cultural contexts' (Erll 2008: 2) – I explore the ways in which documentaries and their established codes and conventions enact trans-temporal narratives. The concepts of 'archival aesthetics' as developed by media theorists are then built on using the insights gained by fashion scholars regarding the multi-temporalities of fashion and dress, particularly within the museum context.

Finally, I draw examples of trans-temporal cultural remembrance in action from three multi-part series broadcast by the BBC: *Ready to Wear*, a six-part series shown on BBC Two in 1999; *British Style Genius*, shown in five parts on BBC Two in 2008; and *Oh! You Pretty Things: The Story of Music and Fashion*, broadcast in three episodes on BBC Four in 2014. While these three series by no means offer an exhaustive representation of fashion history documentaries in the UK, they are equally illustrative of both a shared language of documentary conventions as well as a more nuanced diversity of approaches to narration and presentation. They share a predominant focus on British fashion history, prioritising the twentieth century and life within living memory. Viewed together, it also becomes clear that they prioritise certain canons of the nation's social and popular past. The different series frequently highlight the same prominent British designers and labels (Biba, Burton and Vivienne Westwood, for example), and successions of subcultures and style tribes (Teddy boys, Mods, punks, new romantics).

It should be noted, as James Thompson has pointed out in his investigation into the BBC's representations of the Victorian age, that the 'BBC has never been a monolithic organisation pursuing a consistent historiographical line' (Thompson 2004: 151). Yet each of these series – major, multi-part programmes requiring considerable investment in time, resources and viewing slots, and which have since had repeated broadcasts – have inevitably contributed to shaping collective imaginaries of British style- and social-heritage for widespread audiences nationally and beyond. The central concern guiding this chapter, then, is not which versions of the past such programmes have communicated, but how they have used and developed specific documentary techniques in order to renegotiate the past within the present.

Television and/as cultural remembrance

Compared with two decades of now-flourishing scholarship addressing the display of fashion within physical exhibition environments, the salient lack of research into the ways in which fashion history has been mediated through television programming is striking.[1] And yet it is less so when recalling that television histories in general were for a long time regarded as 'dumbing down' the academic discipline of history – a charge that fashion history itself is all too familiar with.[2] Whether or not deemed too 'popular', however, television programmes remain a chief source of public historical knowledge and are undoubtedly more accessible for geographically widespread audiences than museums.

As Ann Gray and Erin Bell point out, European and North American television networks have experienced a 'history boom' since the 1990s, a trend also reflected beyond the screen in other sites of public discourse including the British national curriculum (Gray and Bell 2013: 1). As a result, scholarship investigating the content, conventions, authenticity, wider production contexts and politics of factual history programming has since multiplied, often within collections addressing public history more broadly. Examinations of the broadcast historiography of major wars and other widely commemorated events have been at the forefront of this turn. However, those dealing with televisual histories of social and popular culture are gaining ground: for example, Paul Long and Tim Wall's (2013) study of the construction of histories of popular music in the BBC's *Britannia* franchise, and various accounts of the presentation of everyday history through the lens of celebrity genealogies in another BBC flagship, *Who Do You Think You Are?* (for examples, see Holdsworth 2011; de Groot 2016).

This broad turn has also involved an interdisciplinary shift towards the critical contemplation of television less as a conveyor of history as such, more as a dynamic technology of memory. As Sam Edwards explains in an essay identifying the analysis of moving-image-as-memory as a 'third way' (beyond more customary analysis as an audio-visual primary source or as a secondary interpretation of the past), 'some films and television programmes can be viewed as "sights" of memory; audio-visual *memorials* designed to communicate a particular image and idea of the past' (Edwards 2018: 46, emphasis in original). Similarly recognising this divergence from traditional television research, Finnish media theorist Anu Koivunen (2016) has marked the late historian Raphael Samuel's writings on the heritage capacity of television as a critical turning point in how the medium has been understood;

his view in *Theatres of Memory* (1994) of 'television as a medium that was constantly looking toward the past, eagerly seizing every occasion – an anniversary, a commemoration, an obituary – to travel down memory lane, revisiting and recycling old film footage' stood in contrast to earlier theorists who 'tended to discuss television as an amnesiac medium, caught in the perpetual present of liveness and now-time' (Koivunen 2016: 5270).

The field of cultural memory studies has influenced the theoretical foundations of a significant strand of such 'third way' work on the analysis of history programming on television. Yet the notion of cultural memory itself has proved notoriously difficult to define. A frequent observation, and often a source of puzzlement, is the diversity of terms with which it is often used interchangeably – collective/social/public/popular memory – as well as the plethora of related concepts that have emerged from its transdisciplinary richness; Erll lists some of these as: '*cadres sociaux*/social frameworks of memory, ... *mnemosyne, ars memoriae, loci et imagines, lieux de mémoire*/ sites of memory, invented traditions, myth, *memoria*, heritage, commemoration, *kulturelles Gedächtnis*, communicative memory, generationality, postmemory. The list could go on' (Erll 2008: 2–3). Erll instead suggests that cultural memory is best conceived of as a wide-ranging umbrella term that takes in all of these nuances and more (tradition, historiography, archive, canon) and that this umbrella quality enables us to see it as 'sometimes functional, sometimes analogical, sometimes metaphorical' (Erll 2011: 99). This, and Sharon Macdonald's assertion that cultural memory more specifically 'indicate[s] memory whose primary form of transmission is through cultural media, such as texts, film and television, and museums and exhibitions, rather than through direct person-to-person transmission' (Macdonald 2013: 15) has informed my own preference for the term in this context.

Nevertheless, Maurice Halbwachs's notion of collective memory (*la mémoire collective*), developed during the 1920s, has proved the most frequent springboard for contemporary cultural memory studies and offers some foundational characteristics for the concept (see Halbwachs 1992). His adoption of a Durkheimian perspective to assert that memory, even that of an individual, always carries a social dimension is critical to addressing memory's cultural framework. So too is Halbwachs's attendant theory of collective memory as the transmission of cultural knowledge, of shared versions of the past within groups and communities, that implicates it in the processes of identity formation, whether on the levels of family or nation. At the root of his thinking lies a distinction between history and memory;

as Erll summarises: 'For Halbwachs, history deals with the past. Collective memory, in contrast, is oriented towards the present, and thus proceeds in an extremely selective and reconstructive manner' (Erll 2011: 17).

Halbwachs's collective memory has influenced much cultural memory work since, returning during the resurgence of memory studies in the 1980s, typified by Pierre Nora's writings on *lieux de mémoire* (1989). For Nora, too, the distinction between memory and history is key: 'Memory', he writes, 'is a perpetually actual phenomenon, a bond tying us to the eternal present; history is a representation of the past' (Nora 1989: 8). Nora locates memory in the spatial, the material and the symbolic: it 'takes root in the concrete, in spaces, gestures, images, and objects; history binds itself strictly to temporal continuities, to progressions and to relations between things' (Nora 1989: 9). Conceptualised around the same time, the paradigm of cultural memory (that term being coined as a result) developed by German scholars Aleida Assmann and Jan Assmann is also underpinned by Halbwachs's collective memory. Their many respective works have detailed the links, distinctions and transference between 'communicative memory' – the memory of lived experience passed on through direct communication – and cultural memory as institutionalised and objectified (see for example Assmann and Assmann 2008). More detailed accounts of the multi-nodal conceptual trajectory of cultural memory studies have been assembled by Erll (2008, 2011) and others. Here, I wish to focus instead on the ways in which the specific temporal dynamics of cultural memory that have tended to unite its thinkers have been theorised and how they are enacted by the television documentary.

The recent history of the notion of cultural memory, Alon Confino argues, developed out of a wider interpretive shift in scholarship from emphasis on 'society' (in social history, for example) to 'culture' and 'memory' (cultural studies/memory studies). The difference in the temporal discursive structures underscoring these camps is important, as Confino (2008: 82) points out:

> The notion of society, broadly speaking, was based on a linear concept of history developing forward along one temporal timeline and privileging social and economical topics interpreted in terms of their function and structure. The notion of 'culture', in contrast, is based on a multi-temporal concept of history where past and present commingle and coalesce, capturing simultaneously different and opposing narratives and privileging topics of representation and memory interpreted in terms of experience, negotiation, agency, and shifting relationship.

This understanding of the temporalities integral to cultural memory is echoed by Erll, who suggests that the term refers broadly to the 'interplay of present and past in socio-cultural contexts' (Erll 2008: 2), adding that 'much of what is done to reconstruct a shared past bears some resemblance to the processes of individual memory, such as the selectivity and perspectivity inherent in the creation of versions of the past according to present knowledge and needs' (Erll 2008: 5). Mediated as cultural memory, the past is never simply *of the past*, but 'forms a part of meaning-making in and of the present' (Jenss 2015: 7).

Considering this position, cultural memory is thus better understood as a process rather than a static entity – as remembrance. For Ann Rigney, in her challenge to the risk of implied stasis in earlier memory work, particularly Nora's memory-sites metaphor, the performative dimension of the term 'remembrance' connotes that collective memory is constantly '"in the works" and, like a swimmer, has to keep moving even just to stay afloat' (Rigney 2008: 345). This performative aspect, as Rigney's description suggests, also hints at the necessity of cultural memory's doing/being done, enacting/being enacted. It is this notion of interplaying past and present timescapes being operational and operated that is also indicated by Sharon Macdonald's use of the phrase 'past presencing' (Macdonald 2013) and Vanessa Agnew's 'collapsing temporalities' (Agnew 2007). Here I use these, as well as comparative notions of trans- and multi-temporality, interchangeably.

Archive aesthetics and the times of television

Media scholar William Uricchio has characterised television as a 'time machine'. In a 2010 essay examining what he terms the medium's 'production of history', he claims that, like Michel Foucault's conceptualisation of the library or museum, television is a heterochronic medium: '"a place of all times that is itself out of time", television is a temporal aggregate, an accumulation of visions, tastes, forms, and ideas gathered into one place' (Uricchio 2010: 30). Despite its material and temporal presence, the television contains and enables other time-scapes or -zones made manifest through the medium's myriad (re)combinatory strategies. This, Uricchio asserts, is key to its 'distinctive engagement with history' – understood here as the enactment of cultural remembrance – that unlike the library or museum, however, 'plays out as a linear sequence *over time*, not outside it' (Uricchio 2010: 30). How, then, do Uricchio's notions of television as 'a temporal aggregate' and 'a space of endlessly recombinatory artefacts' (Uricchio 2010: 30) operate in the context of the history documentary?

Within discussions of what he terms the 'aesthetics' of documentary, another prominent media scholar, John Corner, has directly addressed the specific temporalities of the documentary form. In his view, three broad dimensions of time are expressed in the programming of the genre. First, 'there is time as historical time, the specific times at which the images and sounds were recorded, whether or not these times are made explicit to the viewer, perhaps as part of a strategy of historical exposition' (Corner 2012: 69). Historical time in documentary is often fundamental to narrative structures; as Corner adds: 'In documentaries which have a marked interest in development over time, which many do, historical time becomes a feature of what we can call narrative time or expositional time, the organisation of the viewing experience as, self-consciously, one of recognising the *passage* of time' (Corner 2012: 70, emphasis in original). The second dimension of documentary time highlighted by Corner is 'durational design' – 'a crucial factor in documentary planning and practice', that is expressed through such considerations as the length of shots or durational value of specific sequences within the overall shape of the programme. Finally, and a feature of audio-visual media more generally, the third dimension is described as 'phenomenological time':

> it derives from the alignment of the 'time' of what is happening on the screen with the 'time' of watching. It follows from the inherent 'immediacy' of watching cinema and television ... Essentially, it is a (temporary) modifier of historical time, introducing a co-temporality of viewing relations which does not in most cases significantly displace knowledge about the specific temporality of what is shown. Nevertheless, the sense of temporal co-presence is a powerful dimension of getting and sustaining viewing engagement, providing a form of relationship to the screen across which a range of different historical times and of durational values can be organised and projected. (Corner 2012: 70)

It is the elicitation of this sense of multi-temporality in and through the marking of historical time and durational value that serves a crucial function within history programming's performance of cultural remembrance – its interplay of past and present, its collapsing temporalities.

Corner's more specific notion of 'archive aesthetics' in the context of history programming is important, in that it addresses the ways in which commonly used documentary artefacts – such as archive footage, purpose-filmed oral history interviews, voice-over narration, soundtracks and photographic montages – as they are organised within a programme enable complex temporal arrangements. The effectiveness of this in producing an affective 'experience' of reception, according to Jaimie Baron's formulation of the 'archive effect' (Baron 2014), is dependent, whether consciously or not, on the perceived temporal disparity between such documentary materials: the now-time of purpose-created footage and testimonial interviews, and the historical-times of photographs and other archival artefacts, both read within a single sequence or segment. Temporal disparity, Baron suggests, may be indicated not only by an archival artefact's content but by its aesthetic qualities (the differences in black-and-white and colour footage, for example) and appropriation within and by the documentary itself.

Although concerned with the mass circulation of memories of traumatic pasts and not interested solely in documentaries, Alison Landsberg has also considered large-scale cultural remembrance as an affective experiential event. Following her conception of 'prosthetic memory', cultural remembrance holds the potential to engage groups across lines of difference within the same mass-memory project – 'people are invited to take on memories of a past through which they did not live' (Landsberg 2004: 8). Understood as affective, cultural remembrance through the television history documentary may engender deeply felt, embodied connections within individuals that serve not simply as 'an individual psychological state, but a social and cultural force' (Koivunen 2016: 5271). Indeed, Koivunen has suggested in her analysis of Finnish history documentaries that affective historiography – here, cultural remembrance – that exploits the indexical temporalities of archival material has the power to render collectives as broad as the nation as an 'intimate public', a shared 'community of feeling' (Koivunen 2016: 5280). As phenomena that are closely connected to notions of temporality and memory, as well as embodying an uncanny relationship with the most intimate sphere of all – the body – fashion and clothing add a uniquely potent dimension to cultural remembrance enacted through the television documentary.

Fashion, memory and time

Fashion is an inherently temporal phenomenon. It is ephemeral, punctuated by the seasons, 'of the now' or, heaven forbid, 'out of date'. Fashion scholar Christopher Breward has described its role as that of the 'cultural clock' (Breward 1995: 185). Expanding this metaphor, Heike Jenss writes that it 'ticks in the economic and industrialized rhythm of production, distribution, promotion, and proposal of the new, which produces the obsolescence of its own immediacy' (Jenss 2015: 22). Indeed, fashion has been conceptualised as perhaps the most powerful symbol of modernity, and Agnès Rocamora (2014), pointing to the growth of fast fashion and digital mediascapes, has highlighted the temporal acceleration of fashion which has accompanied the 'intensification of speed and the valuing of immediacy and real time' characterising late modernity. Fashion – like television – has thus been conceptualised as a highly amnesiac medium, where the production of the new banishes the old or, at least, makes it 'so last season' (Rocamora 2014: 61). However, fashion's being of-the-now is also highly co-dependent on its past: constantly quoting itself and materially tying together distant points in time, fashion frequently *is* a process of remembrance.

Walter Benjamin's writings on fashion during the 1930s, despite his otherwise general dismissal of the phenomenon, have proved fundamental to the historical materialist view of fashion revitalised shortly into the new millennium in texts by Ulrich Lehmann (2000, 2018) and Caroline Evans (2003). In Konvolut B of *The Arcades Project* – a section dedicated to fashion – Benjamin claims: 'This spectacle, the unique self-construction of the newest in the medium of what has been, makes for the true dialectical theatre of fashion' (Benjamin 1999: 64). This mode of quotation in fashion is, argues Lehmann, 'sartorial remembrance – as much able to create an intricate temporal relation as chart a metaphysical experience' (Lehmann 2000: 164). As with the process of cultural memory enacted in history programming, fashion's '"tiger's leap" into the past isolates diachronically a figure or idea from history, yet activates it for the present and thereby underscores the notion of repeated configurations and patterns in the historical process' (Lehmann 2018: ch. 2, para. 10.61). In this way, brands harness and rework the symbols of their heritage within new collections, for example, and cultural memory itself – of nations, subcultures, architecture and more – finds its continual reimagining in the process of fashion design. Fashion itself thus performs trans-temporally as a medium of cultural remembrance, making it a prime subject for the televisual performance of cultural memory.

Indeed, cultural sartorial remembrance is not limited to newly produced fashions; it does not cease when fashion quickly reaches its obsolescence. In 1993, in a moving lecture in memory of a friend, Peter Stallybrass discussed the garments that people leave behind after they pass away and identified such clothing and the wrinkles, stains and scents they carry as material sites of memory. For Stallybrass (2012), it was his own wearing of his late friend's jacket that enmeshed its material memories – traces of its previous owner – with his own. Wearing as a mode of remembrance is similarly fundamental to Heike Jenss's exploration of fashion and cultural memory in the context of youth culture's adoption of vintage style. Examining contemporary 1960s-style enthusiasts in Germany from an ethnographic perspective, Jenss also accounts, however, for the visual transmission of memory in fashion culture effected through the circulation of 'image worlds' across time and space: 'It is the mediation of the past in images, in addition to the material-sartorial presence of the past in surviving objects, that enables the fashioning of memory – or what could be called "past presencing" – through modes of clothing and embodiment' (Jenss 2015: 128).

Re-wearing is also, of course, simply not an option in certain engagements with the fashions of the past. At the beginning of this chapter, I called attention to early fashion history series' preference for the presentation of historic garments on live models in the form of mannequin parades. This strategy is rarely employed in more recent documentaries on the subject, even in the case of contemporary clothing not subject to conservation and preservation concerns (it is principally only in the case of reconstructed historic garments that their wearing and consequent demonstration of 'natural' movement remains relatively commonplace within documentaries; it was deployed successfully and reflexively as a central component of the 2018 series *A Stitch in Time* presented by Amber Butchart). Nevertheless, television viewing primarily activates visual perception and involves documentary makers' attempts to heighten that perception. The multi- or trans-temporal effect must, therefore, be imparted by other means. The same goes for engagement with dress in the museum environment; thus, attempts to conceptualise the transmission of memory through the mediation of surviving garments there offer fruitful insights for an assessment of fashion's potency within televisual cultural remembrance. Indeed, in the words of Andreas Huyssen, the museum is 'a primary site of social interaction with objects embedded in other times and other spaces' (Huyssen 2016: 108).

Bethan Bide has explored the capacity for clothing objects in museum collections to transmit second-hand memories in a manner that resonates with Landsberg's idea of prosthetic memory. Rooted in her assertion that '[o]bjects evoke memories: they connect the past and the present', she argues that historical garments in museum collections 'are imbued with details of individual lives in their marks of wear. Moreover, these marks have the power to evoke memories – both first- and second-hand – and reveal how the experiences of past individuals continue to resonate and shape societies today' (Bide 2017: 451). Bide's method of extracting clothing's memory capacity involves two key research practices: 'close looking', drawing on material culture readings of objects, and 'experimental archivism', involving the juxtaposition of austerity-era museum objects with her family's own stories and images of the period. The latter assemblage-like approach raises parallels with the presentation of clothing in fashion history documentaries. While Bide draws links between 'anomalous' museum objects (objects that do not fit established cultural narratives about austerity clothing) and 1940s photographs of her grandmother, documentaries perform montage sequences involving clothing – either filmed garments, archived visual and textual representations or the recall of sartorial experience through memory-work – overlaid or juxtaposed with any combination of other documentary artefacts.

For Bide, her use of these two methods together highlighted how, '[t]hrough the non-linear temporality of memory, in which the past gets reconstituted within the present, the uncanny materiality of the museum objects brought distant memories of [her] grandmother's past into the present' (Bide 2017: 472). Fashion possesses a unique and dialectical relationship with the body which augments its affective capacity to facilitate cultural remembrance in the manner of the prosthetic. In her important research on the development of historical dress display in western European and North American museums, Julia Petrov has developed this line further through a conception of the museum as a 'prosthetic device, and artifacts external storage for cultural significance' (Petrov 2012: 227). For Petrov, fashion takes on a ghostly quality on entering the museum; stripped of its economic value as a commodity, it becomes closer to a second skin, empty of a body yet full of the *expectation* of a body and, as we have seen, still bearing the traces of past corporeality. At its most powerful, Petrov suggests, fashion viewed in the museum can instil a sense of deathliness; she calls on the evocative words opening Elizabeth Wilson's seminal book, *Adorned in Dreams*, to illustrate this notion:

> There is something eerie about a museum of costume. A dusty silence holds still the old gowns in glass cabinets. In the aquatic half light (to preserve the fragile stuffs) the deserted gallery seems haunted. The living observer moves, with a sense of mounting panic, through a world of the dead. (Wilson 2005, quoted in Petrov 2019: 168)

Curators have indeed been preoccupied with substituting and revivifying the absent body through the use of mannequins and performative scenographies, yet as this quotation suggests, it remains in a limbo between past and present. Fashion and clothing thus contain and enable multiple temporalities. Like Uricchio's descriptions of television, they are heterochronias or temporal aggregates. As a result of mediation, whether through the museum or the fashion history documentary, they become entangled with the temporalities contained within the archive as well as the now-time of the mediation itself.

Documenting fashion history on the BBC

As three fashion history documentaries broadcast by the BBC that share a focus on the British context, reworking the sartorial and social past as cultural remembrance for a diverse national (and even international) audience, *Ready to Wear* (*RTW*), *British Style Genius* (*BSG*) and *Oh! You Pretty Things* (*OYPT*) offer a fertile set of case studies to analyse how such programming enacts trans-temporal dynamics. Importantly, they share a language of aesthetic conventions, but equally evidence other varied presentational techniques primed to benefit from the powerful remembrance-potential offered by clothing and the sartorial experience.

Ready to Wear

RTW was clearly billed as showing British social history *through* the lens of fashion. In the *Radio Times* magazine listings it was described as the 'series that takes a look at social change over the last 50 years as reflected by the clothes people wear' (Radio Times 1999b: 82). Broadcast between April and June 1999, it was produced by Emma Willis (later Head of Documentary Commissioning at the BBC) with fashion historian and curator Christopher Breward consulting.[3] Each of the six episodes adopted a thematic view across the period's span, covering the 1940s into the 1980s. They examined, respectively, suits and tailoring; youth fashions and subcultures; leisurewear and the impacts of greater access to transport, travel and migration; wartime rationing, subsequent austerity and Dior's New Look; home dressmaking, from necessity to hobby; and finally, women's workwear.

Guided by an overheard narrator, *RTW* focused primarily on the lived experiences of Britain's working and middle classes and utilised the voices of 'real people' to achieve this. It made extensive use of testimonial talking-heads segments with individuals from across the British spectrum, who were frequently filmed in their own homes and who brought their own archives of photographs, home videos and clothing into play, enabling highly personal memories to enter into a much broader sphere of cultural remembrance. It also found ways to incorporate the voices of those no longer alive; readers' letters to magazines, for example, were voiced-over by actors. Other types of archival footage, primarily newsreels, served as the series' other principal resource in a manner typical of recent-history documentaries; selecting *RTW* as the factual 'choice' of the week (and indeed several weeks during its run), a *Radio Times* reviewer commented: 'From the opening credits, you know that this is going to be one of those fabulous documentary series that's crammed wall-to-wall with archive footage' (Radio Times 1999a: 86).

British Style Genius

Nine years later, *BSG* similarly featured overheard narration, extensive archive footage and a wealth of oral testimonial interviews. However, this time the focus was weighted towards figures involved within the fashion industry – designers, tailors, retailers, models, journalists – and celebrities. Shifting the emphasis to fashion talent, dissemination and visibility in this way aligned with the series' strikingly exceptionalist message; it was described in the *Radio Times* listings as an 'entertaining exploration of what makes British fashion and style so distinctive and influential' (Radio Times 2008: 80).

Each of *BSG*'s five episodes was themed according to a supposedly enduring characteristic of British style: first, its democratic spirit as traced through the development of high street fashion and retailing; second, its excellence in tailoring, from Savile Row to the Kings Road to the foreign markets 'buying in' to the British suit; third, its rebellious nature, typified by designers including Vivienne Westwood and Alexander McQueen as well as institutions such as Central Saint Martins College; fourth, its royal and aristocratic associations, with a heavy focus on royally appointed brands and country style; and finally, its street-derived edge, recalling a familiar canon of subcultures from Teds to contemporary style tribes influenced by hip-hop. The series – produced by William Naylor with fashion scholar Alistair O'Neill consulting – was positioned in the October–November 2008 viewing schedule to create a string of fashion-focused Tuesday nights on BBC Two, following the rather less well-received *Twiggy's Frock Exchange*. As with its companion show, which saw the Swinging Sixties model leverage the concurrent trend for 'swopshopping' and refashioning second-hand clothing, *BSG* was equally primed to take advantage of the vintage boom of the early 2000s, offering a televisual counterpart to the material-driven climate of sartorial remembrance.

The sense that *BSG* was conspicuously harnessing the past through the prism and purposes of the present is furthered by its anchoring within the present day; rather than following a chronological narrative, each episode used the 'unfolding' current events of the contemporary fashion industry – the creation of a collection by Kate Moss for fashion retailer Topshop or an exhibition of English tailoring held at the British Embassy in Tokyo in March 2008 – as a springboard to leap back and forth across time through 'flashbacks'. These reached as far back as the early nineteenth century, drawing connections between Beau Brummel and 1960s Mods, for instance. Clearly mobilising the multi-temporal materiality of the documentary potential, they recall the metaphor of the 'crumpled handkerchief of time' evoked by Michel Serres (and harnessed in Caroline Evans's writing on fashion's historicity), bringing distant points on the linear plane of time into contact:

> If you take a handkerchief and spread it out in order to iron it, you can see in it certain fixed distances and proximities. If you sketch a circle in one area, you can mark out nearby points and measure far-off distances. Then take the same handkerchief and crumple it ... Two distant points suddenly are close, even superimposed. If, further, you tear it in certain places, two points that were close can become very distant. (Serres and Latour 1995: 60)

Oh! You Pretty Things

A similar time-hopping effect was achieved in the final series to be raised here, BBC Four's *OYPT*, which examined the relationship between British fashion and music, concentrating chronologically on just three decades: the 1960s through to the cusp of the 1990s. Like *BSG*, its three episodes each began in an unfolding present – a 2011 Burberry menswear show, or the streets of central London whose population, according to the overheard narration by presenter Lauren Laverne, bore traces of the subcultures of the past – which then looped back to the decade in question. This is just one of the ways in which the documentary deployed its multi-temporal potential to mediate a shared yet pluralistic sense of heritage which was further indicated by Laverne's overheard narration: 'Through the love affair between our music and our fashion we've expressed ourselves. ... It's allowed us to believe in something … and belong to something … At some time in our lives, we've all delved into this fabulous dressing-up box.'

Stressing subcultural ebbs and flows, *OYPT* looked at the trendsetting relationships between musicians, designers and stylists on one hand, and fans and style tribes on the other. Oral testimonies were prioritised, as with the previous two series, but here the interviewees' personal archives of clothing, images and videos (partly a reflection of the programme's emphasis on fandom) took on an even greater role as documentary artefacts, as did their now-time reflections on old music videos. Watched on mobile phone screens and tablets, this technique was particularly effective in highlighting the notion of collapsed temporality – the active reassessment of pasts quite literally framed by the technologies of the present. Combining these highly personal outlooks on the past with archival footage and the use of a 'curated' soundtrack, the broader, collective narratives of social history were again brought to the fore. Episode 1, 'Tribes', underscored its story of music and fashion in the 1960s and 1970s with Biba-era freedoms for women, psychedelic drug culture, and discourses around Commonwealth immigration and fascism framed by reggae and skinheads. Episode 2, 'Idols', devoted much of its attention to issues of gender, sexuality, class and subversion in the 1970s and 1980s, spanning the leather look of Suzi Quatro to the goth-punk of Pam Hogg and Siouxsie Sioux. Finally, episode 3, 'Image', traced a route from ska and two-tone, via new romantics, to 1980s glamour and Soul II Soul's Funki Dred, zeroing in on Britain's economic climate, Thatcherism and multiculturalism along the way.

Affective trans-temporal remembrance

Beyond the more general types of past-presencing techniques employed in these series, their uses of clothing and the sartorial experience introduce further, compelling dimensions of cultural remembrance. Clothing is presented within them in several ways and for a variety of purposes. Like archival materials, garments are sometimes used as memory aids for the testimonials given in talking-head interviews. They are also presented as museum objects, as signifiers of evidence and authenticity, as part of the *mise en scène* or as costumes and props in scenes of reconstruction. Clothing also features within the presented archival materials themselves, appearing in photographs, footage, magazine spreads and advertisements. Drawing together different combinations of these presentational devices, three sequences demonstrate the various ways in which affective, trans-temporal remembrance is engendered within the selected series.

The first example is a reconstruction sequence that formed part of *RTW*'s fifth episode, 'Fashioned at Home', which focused on home dressmaking. In a segment on the dissemination of paper patterns with women's magazines, the sequence begins with a close-up shot of a readers' letters page. Panning down towards the text – a letter exclaiming a woman's delight at having completed her first home-made dress – an actor expressively voices the words in a northern English accent. As the voice-over continues, we see a 1950s issue of *Women's Weekly* as it rests on an open sewing box. The camera pans upwards, slowly revealing the length of a floral day dress hung on a typically mid-century coat stand, a Singer sewing machine in the background. A sudden widening of the shot places the scene within a dim room with light streaming through the gap in a pair of half-closed, unquestionably 1950s curtains. We return finally to the letter's text as the reader signs off. A relatively simple sequence at first sight, a closer reading extracts some of its more ghostly and affective attributes.

Layering the visualised archival document – the magazine page – with the present-day voice of the actor creates an immediate archive effect, revitalising evidence of the past with a sense of immediacy and liveness. This combination creates an engaging lead-in to the view of the stylised room, positioning the viewer as if they are there, in the sewing room of a 1950s suburban home at the moment that the reader's letter describes, eyeing the very dress she has just completed. As if she has only just disappeared, the traces of her that remain – the open sewing-box, the half-drawn curtains and the silhouette and subtle sheerness of the dress hit by the daylight – create a sense of emptiness, a body missing. The scene is thus mapped with another uncanny feeling that the viewer has almost become the reader; her experience strives to become ours. This entangled moment gathers multiple layers of signified pasts and presents, giving a highly constructed yet intimate glimpse onto a heritage – a 'national obsession' for home dressmaking, as the programme soon states – that is irretrievably lost at the same time.

Another pair of sequences – one in *BSG*'s tailoring episode and the other in *OYPT*'s first instalment – utilise the same garment as a referent for testimony, but in two different ways. The protagonist is a 1960s blazer in William Morris Golden Lily patterned fabric by the Swinging London boutique, Granny Takes a Trip. Owned by the C20 vintage fashion collection which loaned it to the two productions, the blazer is shown in *BSG* as a referent in a segment with

Granny Takes a Trip co-founder John Pearse. First shown in a photograph being worn by The Beatles' George Harrison, it is then seen mounted on a tailor's dummy with Pearse standing alongside, his arm around the dummy's shoulders as if reunited with an old friend. Donovan's 'Hurdy Gurdy Man' provides the soundtrack and Pearse is next seen seated opposite the dummy exclaiming, 'Well, it takes me back a long time, it's like saying "Daddy, what did you do in the war?" Well this is what I did, son! I was wandering through Liberty's, possibly after being out all night, seeing this cloth, saying, "Yeah!"' The presence of the blazer thus triggers Pearse's own shuttling back and forth between the past and present, and the active, even reflexive construction of his memory through imagined speech. Meanwhile, a sombre black coat positioned in the background emphasises the rupture from what came before – the Savile Row tradition (Pearse was famously a Savile Row dropout) – to the psychedelic palette of the 1960s, while close-up shots of the blazer give a highly detailed view of its extant materiality, right down to the fabric's weave. The sequence ends with Pearse opening the jacket to reveal the Granny Takes a Trip label inside: 'Rumour had it that if you licked it, you would go on a trip yourself!' With this, the label's mushroom hallmark begins to pulse as animated vines and florals inspired by those on the coat take over the screen.

The extant garment thus performs in multiple ways in this sequence: as a memory prompt, but also as a material memory in and of itself. The sense of a ghostly body is heightened by the mannequin, Pearse's gestures towards it and the conversational positioning of the pair. Opening the jacket, taking a close reading of its interior, the garment and its past become quite literally animated through the conspicuous intervention of the documentary makers. These effects, layered together in a not-so-subtle sensory onslaught, build into an affective assemblage of archive aesthetics. Folding Pearse's personal memory and creativity into those of the nation, the sequence stages a vivid moment of cultural remembrance.

The blazer's memory-jogging potential similarly opened up a segment on the psychedelic culture of the 1960s in *OYPT*. This time both producer (another co-founder of Granny Takes a Trip, Nigel Waymouth) and consumer deliver the testimony; here, I focus on the latter. Nigel Lesmoir-Gordon had owned the blazer during the late 1960s, and the segment opens with present-day shots of the country town in which he (at the time of filming) appears to live. Now in his living room, sitting beside his wife, Jenny, the pair are faced with a large box which he opens in anticipation to reveal the blazer folded inside. Again, the sense of reunification in this encounter between wearer and jacket, as if friends were meeting again after many years, is clear ('Oh, there it is!'). Smiling, the couple inspect the garment inside and out, recognising its details once more. Moreover, the encounter serves to firmly and intimately link the jacket with the counterculture in which its former owner engaged; as Lesmoir-Gordon explains, 'I mean, this jacket kind of expressed what we felt like inside', the camera pans across the blazer, pausing for just a moment longer above the distinct signs of wear – its heavily worn-down collar – which *BSG* had overlooked. The couple present black-and-white photographs of Lesmoir-Gordon wearing the jacket, while Laverne's narration explains that they were 'part of a curious generation, seeking new ways to understand the world'. The subsequent focus on the bohemian climate of LSD use in 1960s London is simultaneously accompanied by hazy home-video footage taken by Lesmoir-Gordon during their 'trips', with shots reverting back to the present day and the very camera that recorded the footage almost fifty years earlier. In the nexus of material, visual and personal memory assembled within this sequence, the shifting and shuttling temporalities they bring forth, and Laverne's appeal to the broader social context, Lesmoir-Gordon's experiences and the psychedelic subculture he was involved in are again, but in a different way to *BSG*, affectively transmitted to become part of the BBC's cultural remembrance of 1960s Britain.

Considering the futures of the fashion history documentary

The limited selection of examples discussed demonstrate Anneke Smelik and Liedeke Plate's contention that cultural memory is 'continually subject to negotiation and renegotiation, at the crossing point between the personal and the collective, and between the past and future' (Smelik and Plate 2009: 1). The subject of fashion history, and the codes and conventions that have been developed by the fashion history documentary genre – particularly the use of garments and their representation within other documentary artefacts – add a further powerful dimension to the history documentary's capacity to enact affective forms of cultural remembrance. While the archival aesthetics common to history documentaries are already understood to implicitly engender transtemporal effects, bringing past and present into contact where each becomes viewed through the lens of the other, fashion and clothing enable and contain multiple memoryscapes in themselves: layered together in montages and further renegotiated through the direct interventions of the documentary programme-makers – from close-up camera work to sourcing garments to aid testimony – the archival aesthetics of fashion history documentaries produce complex entanglements of time.

In view of the affective nature of this process, it follows that Landsberg's concept of prosthetic memory, where cultural remembrance can engage audiences with experiences that are not their own, becomes uniquely potent in the fashion history documentary. Fashion and clothing's dialectical relationships with time, memory and the ghostly body activate cultural remembrance in highly intimate ways. For the BBC, this potential has been harnessed in attempts to engage viewers across Britain (and even internationally) with shared cultural imaginaries of the nation: its social past, its cultural characteristics and exceptionalism, and its plurality.

One can only hope that this preliminary theorisation of fashion history documentaries may offer food for thought for future onscreen programming, as well as for subsequent analyses of this important and wide-reaching mode of fashion historiography that has for too long been a neglected object of study. Indeed, if the clear rise in popularity of big-budget fashion biopics and podcasts such as *Dressed: The History of Fashion* and *Bande à part* is anything to go by, the mass consumption of fashion history is certainly in vogue. Viewing the television fashion history documentary as a deeply affective technology of cultural remembrance may productively pave the way for increasing representations of cultural diversity within such programming, as well as turns towards more global discourses. If it is indeed possible to profoundly embrace memories across borderlines through this type of programming, the fashion history genre poses a compelling potential for more radical trans- and inter-cultural remembrance. On the flipside, the academy must continue, as it slowly has done in the context of other mediations of fashion history, to probe and problematise the versions of the past and the scope of cultural representation that existing programmes have so far achieved.

Notes

1. Only *Clothes-Line* has received notable academic attention; Lou Taylor, whose mother Pearl Binder kept a personal archive relating to the production of the series, included *Clothes-Line* within her seminal account of the development of dress history. See Taylor (2004: 54–8).
2. It should be noted that fashion history in the museum has also been subjected to similar claims of a 'dumbing down' of academic enquiry, hence its own delay in receiving sustained academic attention.

3. The involvement of academic fashion scholars and other notable authorities on fashion history within the production of documentaries of the genre is prevalent across the BBC's output of multi-part series and resonates with the early programming conceived by key figures such as Laver, Binder and Doris Langley-Moore. Consequently, such programming has also been aligned to contemporary fashion scholarship as well as the broader collective conscious.

References

Agnew, Vanessa. 2007. 'History's Affective Turn: Historical Reenactment and Its Work in the Present'. *Rethinking History*, vol. 11, no. 3, 299–312. DOI: 10.1080/13642520701353108.
Assmann, Jan and Aleida Assmann. 2008. 'Communicative and Cultural Memory'. In *Cultural Memory Studies: An International and Interdisciplinary Handbook*, edited by Astrid Erll and Ansgar Nünning, 109–18. Berlin: De Gruyter.
Baron, Jaimie. 2014. *The Archive Effect: Found Footage and the Audiovisual Experience of History*. London: Routledge.
Baudelaire, Charles. 2004 [1863]. 'The Painter of Modern Life'. In *The Nineteenth-century Visual Culture Reader*, edited by Vanessa R. Schwartz and Jeannene M. Przyblyski, 37–42. New York: Routledge.
Benjamin, Walter. 1999. *The Arcades Project*. Cambridge, MA: Harvard University Press.
Bide, Bethan. 2017. 'Signs of Wear: Encountering Memory in the Worn Materiality of a Museum Fashion Collection'. *Fashion Theory*, vol. 21, no. 4, 449–76. DOI: 10.1080/1362704X.2017.1290204.
Breward, Christopher. 1995. *The Culture of Fashion*. Manchester: Manchester University Press.
Confino, Alon. 2008. 'Memory and the History of Mentalities'. In *Cultural Memory Studies: An International and Interdisciplinary Handbook*, edited by Astrid Erll and Ansgar Nünning, 77–84. Berlin: De Gruyter.
Corner, John. 2012. 'Temporality and Documentary'. In *Time, Media and Modernity*, edited by Emily Keightley, 69–84. Basingstoke: Palgrave Macmillan.
Edwards, Sam. 2018. 'The Moving Image as Memory: Past and Present on Screen'. In *Histories on Screen: The Past and Present in Anglo-American Cinema and Television*, edited by Sam Edwards, Michael Dolski and Faye Sayer, 45–62. London: Bloomsbury.
Erll, Astrid. 2008. 'Cultural Memory Studies: An Introduction'. In *Cultural Memory Studies: An International and Interdisciplinary Handbook*, edited by Astrid Erll and Ansgar Nünning, 1–15. Berlin: Dde Gruyter.
Erll, Astrid. 2011. *Memory in Culture*. Basingstoke: Palgrave Macmillan.
Evans, Caroline. 2003. *Fashion at the Edge: Spectacle, Modernity and Deathliness*. New Haven, CT: Yale University Press.
Gray, Ann and Erin Bell. 2013. *History on Television*. Abingdon: Routledge.
de Groot, Jerome. 2016. *Consuming History: Historians and Heritage in Contemporary Popular Culture*. London: Routledge.
Halbwachs, Maurice. 1992. *On Collective Memory*. Chicago, IL: University of Chicago Press.

Hjemdahl, Ann-Sofie. 2016. 'Fashion Time: Enacting Fashion as Cultural Heritage and as an Industry at the Museum of Decorative Arts and Design in Oslo'. *Fashion Practice*, vol. 8, no. 1, 98–116. DOI: 10.1080/17569370.2016.1147695.

Holdsworth, Amy. 2011. *Television, Memory and Nostalgia*. Basingstoke: Palgrave Macmillan.

Huyssen, Andreas. 2016. 'Memory Things and Their Temporality'. *Memory Studies*, vol. 9, no. 1, 107–10. DOI: 10.1177/1750698015613977.

Jenss, Heike. 2015. *Fashioning Memory: Vintage Style and Youth Culture*. London: Bloomsbury.

Koivunen, Anu. 2016. 'Affective Historiography: Archival Aesthetics and the Temporalities of Televisual Nation-Building'. *International Journal of Communication*, vol. 10, 5270–5283.

Landsberg, Alison. 2004. *Prosthetic Memory: The Transformation of American Remembrance in the Age of Mass Culture*. Columbia, NY: Columbia University Press.

Lehmann, Ulrich. 2000. *Tigersprung: Fashion in Modernity*. Cambridge, MA: MIT Press.

Lehmann, Ulrich. 2018. *Fashion and Materialism*. Edinburgh: Edinburgh University Press.

Long, Paul and Tim Wall. 2013. 'Constructing the Histories of Popular Music: The Britannia Series'. In *Popular Music and Television in Britain*, edited by Ian D. Inglis, 11–26. Farnham: Ashgate.

Macdonald, Sharon. 2013. *Memorylands: Heritage and Identity in Europe Today*. Abingdon: Routledge.

Nora, Pierre. 1989. 'Between Memory and History: Les Lieux de Mémoire'. *Representations*, vol. 26, 7–24. DOI: 10.2307/2928520.

Petrov, Julia. 2012. 'Cross-Purposes: Museum Display and Material Culture'. *CrossCurrents*, vol. 62, no. 2, 219–34. DOI: 10.1111/j.1939-3881.2012.00231.x.

Petrov, Julia. 2019. *Fashion, History, Museums: Inventing the Display of Dress*. London: Bloomsbury.

Radio Times. 1999a. 'TV Choices for Tuesday 27th April'. *Radio Times*, 22 April.

Radio Times. 1999b. 'Ready to Wear'. *Radio Times*, 6 May.

Radio Times. 2008. 'British Style Genius'. *Radio Times*, 2 October.

Rigney, Ann. 2008. 'The Dynamics of Remembrance: Texts Between Monumentality and Morphing'. In *Cultural Memory Studies: An International and Interdisciplinary Handbook*, edited by Astrid Erll and Ansgar Nünning, 345–53. Berlin: De Gruyter.

Rocamora, Agnès. 2014. 'New Fashion Times: Fashion and Digital Media'. In *The Handbook of Fashion Studies*, edited by Sandy Black et al., 61–77. London: Bloomsbury.

Samuel, Raphael. 1994. *Theatres of Memory: Past and Present in Contemporary Culture*. London: Verso.

Serres, Michael and Bruno Latour. 1995. *Conversations on Science, Culture, and Time*. Ann Arbor: University of Michigan Press.

Smelik, Anneke and Liedeke Plate. 2009. 'Technologies of Memory in the Arts: An Introduction'. In *Technologies of Memory in the Arts*, edited by Anneke Smelik and Liedeke Plate, 1–12. Basingstoke: Palgrave Macmillan.

Stallybrass, Peter. 2012. 'Worn Worlds: Clothes, Mourning and the Life of Things'. In *The Textile Reader*, edited by Jessica Hemmings, 68–77. London: Berg.

Taylor, Lou. 2004. *Establishing Dress History*. Manchester: Manchester University Press.

The Listener. 1937. 'Clothes-Line'. *The Listener*, 6 October.

Thompson, James. 2004. 'The BBC and the Victorians'. In *The Victorians Since 1901: Histories, Representations and Revisions*, edited by Miles Taylor and Michael Wolff, 150–66. Manchester: Manchester University Press.
Uricchio, William. 2010. 'TV as Time Machine: Television's Changing Heterochronic Regimes and the Production of History'. In *Relocating Television: Television in the Digital Context*, edited by Jostein Gripsrud, 27–40. Abingdon: Routledge.
Wilson, Elizabeth. 2005. *Adorned in Dreams: Fashion and Modernity*. London: I. B. Tauris.

Audio-visual references

British Style Genius, five episodes, BBC Two, 7 October to 4 November 2008.
Clothes-Line, six episodes, BBC, 30 September to 9 December 1937.
Oh! You Pretty Things: The Story of Music and Fashion, three episodes, BBC Four, 17 September to 1 October 2014.
Ready to Wear, six episodes, BBC Two, 27 April to 2 June 1999.
Twiggy's Frock Exchange, three episodes, BBC Two, 7 to 28 October 2008.

Chapter 8

Italian ready-to-wear fashion through Cori-carousels

Giulia Caffaro

Introduction

While Italy was experiencing the consistent spread of ready-to-wear fashion at the beginning of the 1960s (Merlo 2012: 8), a network of manufacturers started constructing a vision through which to pilot the expressive choices of their consumers by testing new forms of product communication. This process was linked to the necessity to act systematically in order to offer a versatile and attractive product for the mass of possible buyers, who still had to be pushed to purchase standard clothes on the market. Therefore, the function of ready-to-wear fashion, together with other expressions of the cultural industry, including television, became that of renewing and modernising the imagery of consumption (Fava 2018: 14).

Up to the beginning of the 1960s, the industry's ability to dress everybody and to maintain a competitive price range were advantageous features, because they allowed the widespread distribution of the product, but then, in the middle of the decade, these things began to have negative connotations because they were seen to be synonymous with low quality and homogeneity. As a matter of fact, moving towards a democratisation of luxury, as Ivan Paris states, 'consumerism of the novelties of the 1950s was replaced by the distinction of social competition through consumption, and by the affirmation of status expenses' (Paris 2006: 358).

Thus, for the clothing industry, the situation began to get complicated: how was it possible to satisfy the population's clothing needs and, at the same time, to provide ready-to-wear garments capable of expressing a set of strong and specific values to be embodied by iconic profiles? Assuming this question as the main influencer of the communication strategy of many Italian manufacturing companies, I attempt to shed light on an important case study that provided some interesting solutions among the huge range of possible answers. Considering the case of the Gruppo Finanziario Tessile, one of the main ready-to-wear fashion industries in Italy, I am going to look at Cori's female brand market improvement through the lens of a new medium for the mass consumption era. This medium is *Carosello*, the first Italian television broadcast dedicated to the advertising of consumer goods (Calabrese 2019). During the post-Second World War period, the Turin-based company known by the acronym GFT played a decisive role in the massification of ready-to-wear clothing, going down in history thanks to the famous 'size revolution' that began in 1954 (Paris 2006: 104–13; Caffaro 2018). However, during the 1960s the GFT proved to be a pioneer not only in the standardisation of the production system but also in the experimentation with mass media as vehicles for transferring brand values to a wide audience.

In particular, this essay deals with the production of female carousels promoted by the GFT between 1964, when the first 'Cori-carousel' was broadcast, and 1973, when the format became decidedly evocative and distant from the original 'sketch' (Giusti 1995: 268–9), proving that the communication market was changing together with the clothing one. As for the sources, this analysis uses the original films preserved by the GFT Archive in Turin that have been digitised by the Archivio Nazionale Cinema d'Impresa. They are now available on the Archive's YouTube channel (Archivio Nazionale Cinema d'Impresa, 2016) among other important digitisation projects, such as the Marzotto one (Archivio Nazionale Cinema d'Impresa, 2015), allowing scholars to consider the importance and the specificity of these media supports for the historical heritage of the Italian fashion industry. Hence, crossing visual data with archival documents, correspondence and press reviews of the period, I aim to demonstrate, through the example of the women's clothing line of GFT, the extent of the connection at that time between the fashion industry and the media industry in Italy.

In this regard, the literature now discovered (mostly in Italian) about *Carosello* helps to contextualise the topic within the period in which the massification of clothing consumption came together with the advertising channels (Dorfles 1998; Calabrese 1975). In fact, the stylistic and content evolution of the Cori-carousels clearly reflects the transformation that the Italian industry was about to face, both in terms of production and communication, confirming also that television (during the analysed chronological period) 'became the leading mass medium of social self-reflection in Europe' (Hickethier 2008: 76).

Carosello: advertisement and 'edutainment'

In order to include *Carosello* among the tools of the Italian ready-to-wear fashion documenting process, it is important to consider the design features that made it a unique format in the history of television and product advertising. *Carosello* was born on 3 February 1957, three years after the first television broadcasts (Auteliano 2011: 101). It first aired on the National Programme and then on the RAI channel for twenty years, a period in which 'Italy was the only Western European country to broadcast advertisements for networks that reached the entire national territory, but it was also the country where the users' interest in the television advertising medium was deliberately stimulated by a shrewd commercial strategy' (Ambrosino, Cimorelli and Giusti 1996: 24).

In fact, when SIPRA, the advertising agency for RAI, decided to start broadcasting advertising messages to subscribers, it developed a special television format which would be entrusted to experts whom Vance Packard (1958) defined as the 'hidden persuaders', because they were capable of triggering purchase desires disguised as entertainment and education (SIPRA 1974). The new TV format had to respect the minimum percentage of commercial advertising allowed into the National Programme, but, at the same time, it should represent the fabulous world of consumption and a new way of living. According to this reasoning, the rigid structure of *Carosello* involved the juxtaposition of autonomous narrative segments: a part of the show called '*pezzo*', made of 1 minute and 45 seconds of narration, and the '*codino*', lasting 30 seconds and given over to the advertising products. The passage from the 'piece' to the 'coda' always took place through a key phrase pronounced by the protagonist or by the narrative voice out of sight. Only at the end did the narrator's voice-over reveal the claim of the company promoted together with the product brand.

The real audience engagement was thus confined to the final part of the carousel because it was there that jingles and product slogans, words and music, which now belong to the collective memory, were revealed. In fact, as Calabrese noted, each carousel had a fairy-tale 'happy ending' (Calabrese 1975: 20), which also coincided with the epiphany of the product and even more with that of the brand. In this positive mood, a large audience of future consumers was addressed through repeated messages that easily crept into the public's mind, becoming purchase wishes (Eco 1965: 169). So, bearing in mind the historical context, the key to *Carosello*'s success was definitively the connection between the narrative and the commercial vein, together with other specific features that helped the industrial saturation in the television's time and space.

First, *Carosello* was broadcast on the RAI channel every evening, after the newscast, at 8.50 p.m. with four sketches advertising four different products and producers. Each sketch was introduced by the opening of the curtain with musical accompaniment, an immediate reference to the world of theatre and with affinities also to the variety and the musical comedy genre (Arcagni 2006: 84). Considering this entertainment legacy, its placement in the show schedule after a national information programme such as the newscast was a winning strategy. In that precise moment, in fact, Italian families found themselves at home, in front of the TV, with the latent desire for a short entertainment before the end of the day. During that last peaking of the consumer's attention, *Carosello* amused and, in a friendly way, educated the audience in the world of modern consumption.

Furthermore, reflecting on this educative and explicative peculiarity of carousels, some typical elements of the industrial documentary genre emerge. For example, as Hediger and Vonderau remark (2009: 10), industrial films have to be considered, regardless of their content, as deeply linked to their purpose and context. In this regard, we can see the GFT carousels – such as those of the many industries in Italy – as representing and reflecting the dominant discourse in relation to the industrial complex and the society in which they operated, for they were doing on a small scale what many other industrial documentaries were doing in Europe in the same period (Sørenssen 2009: 382–8).

This fusion of industrial and television media provided a narrative for the industrial reality of the 1960s and the early 1970s by introducing garments into the daily life of every 'modern' woman in Italy, through the use of the most popular channel of the moment. In this sense, entering into the Italian historical television contest, these carousels become one of the many attempts of that period to embed the new media in a democratic discourse (Bignell and Fickers 2008: 24), representing a specific industrial reality and its products. As Grasso argues, together with the pedagogy of consumption, *Carosello* introduced the pleasure of purchase via a funny moment in the Italian routine (Grasso 2004: 98). This combination is the reason why we use the word 'edutainment' in this section's heading to describe an innovation that led to a less sacred use of television as a welcome channel for the diffusion of modernity.

At the end of the financial year 1963, SIPRA noted that advertising 'by video' had contributed to influencing the Italians' social behaviour and

Carosello had become a reference point for the audience's daily routine. Moreover, *Carosello* appeared to be a true catalyst for radical transformations in the country's marketplace thanks to the acquisition of new products and new purchasing habits (Ambrosino, Cimorelli and Giusti 1996: 23). In this regard, despite the use of an aesthetic imbued with clichés (Grasso 1989: 56), Abruzzese underlines that *Carosello* was used precisely to emancipate the population, offering new and attainable lifestyles through a perfect language (Abruzzese 1988: 19). By including the work of GFT in this scenario, we observe also that women were the preferred target of the carousels – because they were managing the house, but above all because they were more susceptible to a change in their lifestyle, abandoning finally the role of 'Snow White' (Dorfles 1998: 37–8). In 1964, riding the wave of this consumer revolution, GFT relied on communication agencies such as Agel, Seller and Masius (GFT 1965–71),[1] who designed this audio-visual format for the Cori brand and adapted it to the content to be communicated, through specific strategic studies and market surveys that allowed the creation of series and scripts consistent with the company aims (GFT 1964; LCM Graman 1971).

Industrial fashion shorts on TV

Looking at the overall production of Cori-carousels, the narrative format follows the *Carosello*'s structure, which as mentioned before involved the juxtaposition of autonomous segments, but in addition to this, 'it recalls the structure of the film in episodes' (Auteliano 2011: 101). In fact, its advertising vocation refers to its industrial origin, but its location within the television show schedule makes it also dutiful to its heterogeneity and seriality rules. Therefore, it becomes unsuitable for the pure definition of industrial film, although produced by an industrial manufacturer to promote its products and defined in the relationship between industry and society as product of the one for the other (Pellizzi et al. 1972: 17).

The Cori-carousel can be included within this general and macroscopic category only because it develops a theme of general interest and explores the features of an industrial product, like standardised clothing, and its production processes 'in relation to the impact on the development of a social context' (Pellizzi et al. 1972: 29–31). In other words, the Cori-carousel is above all an advertising short film created to encourage the consumption of the industrial fashion products of the period, highlighting their qualities and potential for the new way of living. So, it is important to remember that the effectiveness of carousels lies precisely in emphasising the ability of advertised products to satisfy a hidden need inherent in the social context, generically called a 'consumer target'.

Considering the economic and social environment in which the spread of models of mass consumption developed, this target had been overwhelmed by a repetition of 'call to mind-images' (Eco 1973: 254), which illuminated the deep repercussions that the televisual communication of clothing had in society. In this regard, compared to the first carousels, where if clothes were observed it was only to promote sewing machines (Dorfles 1998: 8), in the mid-1960s clothing had started to carve out an important role among consumer goods and therefore also within television broadcasts. As Dorfles writes (1998: 49–53), the growing presence of clothes, spirits and cars within the television proto-advertising of those years revealed a desire for a new 'social status' associated with new opportunities to take advantage of free time. However, ready-to-wear fashion had still to be accepted as an expressive asset capable of meeting the needs of feminine elegance, one of the most eloquent concepts associated with clothing of this period, as Paris notes (2006: 360). Some of the best-known couturiers of the time, such as Biki, the sisters Fontana and Jole Veneziani, also noticed the same issue in a television episode dedicated to the 'problems of Italian Fashion', broadcast by RAI on December 1961 (ArchiviModaSAN, 2011). In this broadcast style creators, together with the invited columnists, namely Emiliana Granzotto and Noemi Lucarelli, denounced the distrust of consumers towards Italian manufactured clothing, which was clearly underestimated compared to French fashion. It emerged from this meeting that the Italian 'gentle woman' had to be educated in the choice of style, and then encouraged to trust the industry in its production of affordable dresses that were very similar to the tailored ones.

We can, then, understand both the relevance and the evolution of choice in terms of medium, language, format and characters during the communication phase of ready-to-wear fashion. Consequently, we can also understand the GFT's purpose in enticing the female audience into new clothing consumption patterns through a television communication performed by well-known icons of elegance and modernity. Among the many national companies that dealt with the production of 'comedy shorts' to advertise their products on the TV screen, the work of GFT deserves special attention. For the female brand Cori, GFT created five *Carosello* series, starting in 1964, to promote new female identities suited to their clothing lines and to retain new consumers. GFT chose as testimonials three famous actresses within both the Italian and international cinema, Eleonora Rossi Drago, Capucine and Catherine Spaak, in order to convince the brand-new consumers that Cori dresses could make them suitable for every occasion and make them as fascinating as these celebrities. Moreover, to achieve this result in a minimum predefined time and through a form of television entertainment, GFT relied, in addition to the aforementioned communication agencies, on marketing experts and film directors, who structured compelling copy messages and narrative–advertising combinations that had not existed previously.

The outcome looks like a sort of forerunner of the 'industrial fashion short', a particular media through which Cori was trying to influence Italian women, stimulating their imagination and, as *Carosello* ruled, 'favouring their unconscious rather than their rationality' (Abruzzese 1988: 18). Therefore, the Cori-carousel was more properly an unusual form of industrial communication, conveyed and regulated by television, at a particular historical moment of consumption, exactly when 'the mass communication system fed the mass consumption market and vice versa' (Ambrosino, Cerimorelli and Giusti 1996: 23). In this sense, the Cori-carousel may be included among Elsaesser's notion of industrial film 'as an event', whose characteristics are to be strongly conditioned by the context, by the coexistence of planning and accident, by temporal and spatial limits and by heterogeneous consistency of contents. This research approach appears to be very useful for analysing the media production of GFT during the 1960s, because it entails extending 'the traditional categories around non-fiction, documentary, industrial film, advertising films' and also around those industrial media productions that lie on the boundaries (Elsaesser 2009: 32).

Cori-carousels and icons of elegance

As Auteliano remarks (2011: 102), *Carosello* seemed to design an artificial 'time-place' in which an ideal dimension of everyday life took shape, a dimension made concrete and tangible thanks to the presence of real characters and products. As mentioned before, in order to insert garments into this kind of media environment GFT involved directors and actresses from the cinema and television fields, who worked not only to create compelling stories that lasted a few minutes but also to find the most amusing connections between the scene and the *coda*, exploiting moralism and the fairy-tale structure to disguise the advertising (Ambrosino, Cimorelli and Giusti 1996: 110).

Italian ready-to-wear fashion through Cori-carousels **189**

The evocative narrative, dominant with respect to the descriptive one, gave a magical and mysterious nature to the Cori-carousel, which guaranteed the interest of spectators regardless of their purchasing preferences. But that interest was definitely due to the presence of famous and reliable icons of style that Cori employed for the success of the operation. For example, from 1964 to 1967, Eleonora Rossi Drago – an icon of Italian cinema in this decade – lent herself to wear Cori clothes and played the leading role in the television comedy shorts to publicise the Cori Lady line. The first one was the Cori series *Eleonora Rossi Drago*, directed by Anton Giulio Majano, expert in television drama; the second was the series *Una scelta sicura* by Antonio Moretti; and the last was *Agente Segreto* in 1967, directed by Lionello Massobrio (Giusti 1995: 268–9). The presence of Eleonora Rossi Drago in these series of carousels increased the prestige of the clothes she wore and therefore the fame of the clothing brand. Considering, for example, the episode titled 'Smeraldo' in the series *Agente Segreto*, the Italian actress plays a casual secret agent called Elisabetta Schapper who wears different (not detailed) Cori outfits according to the occasion. She is a classy woman, dedicated to good manners, who manages to solve every enigma with elegance (Giusti 1995: 269).

The script, set in many locations around Rome, is linked to the advertising *coda* with a revelatory phrase by one of the lead actors, which contains the narrative solution: 'Congratulations Eleonora, as always you have solved everything with great elegance.' It was followed by the narrative voice outside the field that introduces the advertised product: 'A natural and refined elegance, the elegance of those who wear Cori' (Archivio Nazionale Cinema d'Impresa, 2018a). At that exact moment, the actress transforms herself into a model walking on the runway and takes the Cori clothes from the Autumn/Winter 1967 collection (Figure 8.1), underlining the motivation for her choice: 'Cori, a sure choice for my elegance. Cori, a sure choice for your elegance. A light elegance refined like the wing of a butterfly, the symbol of Cori.'[2] The carousel closes with the Cori logo, a butterfly, and with the brand's payoff. Everything seems clear: the Cori logo began to be conveyed through the concept of 'refined elegance', exploiting the image of a famous actress and the power of the associated claim, again as *Carosello* suggested (Veltroni 1992).

The use of television celebrities as testimonials for the brand in order to convey this message specifically began with the collaboration between GFT and the designer Biki (Fava 2018: 16; Segre Reinach 2019), who in 1962 was portrayed next to the face of Cori of the moment, 'the most elegant

Figure 8.1 Eleonora Rossi Drago posing during the shooting of the Cori-carousel series *Agente Segreto*, 1967, GFT Archive (folder 2892, vol. 4), Turin/AsTo

woman in Italy', Sophia Loren, who strongly represented the brand's motto, 'Elegance on a butterfly's wings' (GFT 1962; Caffaro 2017: 62). Therefore, this slogan, mentioned again in the carousel series *Agente Segreto* broadcast in 1967, had already been used for the advertising campaign which featured Sophia Loren and, thanks to that winning move, the company opened the way to the stylistic qualities of the product and of the brand at the same time (Paris 2006: 198).

In the 1960s Sophia Loren and Eleonora Rossi Drago were synonymous with 'Italianness' and truthfulness, but also with femininity and elegance (Carrano 1985: 168–95). They were the women of the 1960s, who perfectly embodied the brand target of Cori, reassuring consumers through their strong personalities. From 1964 to 1967, just as with Sophia Loren, the image of Eleonora Rossi Drago was conveyed on all the copy used in the closing of the carousels: 'Cori, the elegance on a butterfly's wings' or 'Cori, a safe choice for your elegance' (Seller Agency 1964: 142). Therefore, the Cori advertising message provided expressive traits that were supposed to create sales, together with the clothes themselves. GFT was trying to sell a status, that of the 'elegant woman', and did so through the sale of ready-to-wear clothing worn by the most elegant celebrities of the moment. The company's purpose was thus to create a close connection between the undoubted style of Eleonora Rossi Drago and that of the items chosen for her wardrobe, in order to build customers' loyalty to the lifestyle of the brand and not only to the garment itself (GFT 1967).

For this reason, the narrative and linguistic choices adopted for the Cori-carousels during this period highlighted the necessity of shifting the focus from the values of the product to the values of the brand. This change allowed the operation of a sort of conceptual transfer in favour of the Turin manufacturing industry, whose female labels had begun to guarantee reliability regardless of the type of product supplied as tailoring creations. Towards the end of the decade, the narrative forms adopted for its advertising increasingly put the accent on the imagery connected to the dress and more generally to the brand, enclosing all the technical and commercial characteristics of the product specifically through the company logo. Consequently, the 'fashion-carousel' gradually assumed an aesthetic and narrative value for GFT, as well as a commercial one.

Carosello in the ready-to-wear fashion system

Carosello became a 'detonator of the economic miracle' and, contrary to what was initially thought, product advertising did not disturb the audience (Ambrosino, Cimorelli and Giusti 1996: 110). Quite the opposite, it seduced them and stimulated a general change in their life and their purchasing habits, including clothing. Even for ready-to-wear fashion, in fact, the inluence exerted by *Carosello* was not limited to the economic sphere alone; rather, it generated changes in the broader social and cultural context of the country, giving rise to new forms of communication and behaviours (Ambrosino, Cimorelli and Giusti 1996: 21).

As a matter of fact, with the growing affirmation of television as a medium, the attention of industries shifted from the film to the variety format. At the same time, the great directors of art cinema or theatre, like Luciano Emmer, Dino Risi, Sergio Leone, Ermanno Olmi (Auteliano 2011: 103), and many actors, started coming together in 'the small screen', demonstrating 'through' *Carosello* the existence of the dialogue between the various media (Auteliano 2011: 103; Grossi 2019: 193–202). Thanks to the episodic and animated narration, these characters then became reliable and recognisable for general users, popular icons of style and value, real guarantors for the purchase. For example, looking at the carousels commissioned by GFT we can observe that these TV shorts contributed to the building of 'femininity' through the use of clothes and their expressive potential, but above all through the representation of new identity standards by which to identify new consumers. So, the Cori garments were worn by female characters who identified the desire of Italian women for both emancipation and a change of social status, in its various evolutionary phases within the context.

The Cori-carousel presented clothes with the charm of a cinematographic language but, of course, being the advertising of an industrial product, it emphasised values and virtues that any buyer could inherit with that particular line of clothing. First of all, the protagonist of the carousel had to become an icon whose speech and behaviour were loved by the audience. Then, the use of stereotypes and models of mass culture favoured the association and overlapping of the concepts represented, creating a magical aura around products. Clothes were only shown at the end of the short, but what really mattered was to gain more and more space among the essential purchases for a modern lifestyle.

For GFT, *Carosello* was only a pretext into which to launch the product of its ready-to-wear fashion industry, which at the end of the 1960s was shaken by new identity needs, greater expressive freedoms that exalted the character of a new woman. This target was made up of attentive and savvy consumers, with not only national but also European reference models. As Dorfles observes (1998: 38–40), in this period television consumers were shown images of big cities, foreign cultures and imaginaries, referring to the possibility of travelling and breaking down national and usual borders to be affected by exciting new experiences. In 1968 the Cori brand therefore chose an advertising plan that included an exceptional effort of both investment and creative renewal. A Cori release reported:

> Advertising planning is, basically, like a military plan, with tactical and strategic problems, with objectives to be achieved, with positions to be conquered. This year Cori's advertising will be enhanced on television and radio; it will appear in the biggest press campaign ever made to date ... There is news to underline among other things: the presence of Capucine, a wonderful actress and one of the most elegant women in the world, in the TV Cori commercials. The results of this great advertising campaign will not be lacking. And to you all: good sales![3] (GFT 1968a)

For that year, GFT chose to associate a prestigious figure with a prestigious product and to go on television with a carousel performed by Germaine

Lefebvre, known by the pseudonym Capucine. The actress embodied all the adjectives that a woman would like to hear applied to herself, such as elegant, refined, classy, but above all, modern and unconventional. She was chosen for the new series of *Carosello*, titled *Parigi è sempre Parigi* (Paris Is Always Paris), directed by Luciano Emmer in 1968 (GFT 1968b), with an immediate cinematographic reference to the namesake film directed by him in 1951 (Emmer 1951). Capucine is seen in picturesque Parisian streets and squares, pursued by the camera which observes her in all her charm as a diva of the international cinema: a European woman who plays with luxury in the French capital, in the Louvre, in cafes, with painters in Montmartre, in restaurants or department stores, places that become the titles of the various episodes (Archivio Nazionale Cinema d'Impresa 2018b).

Looking, for example, at the episode titled 'Pittore', we note that Capucine wears suit separates, made up of an eight-button coat and a knee-length skirt with a white turtleneck, but no details on garments are given as the diva wanders among painters of all nationalities in Montmartre. Respecting the rules of the format, the attention falls, in fact, on Cori clothes only in the last 30 seconds of the spot, when the atelier where Capucine has a portrait created is turned suddenly into a catwalk where five models showcase the outfits of the following Cori season (Archivio Nazionale Cinema d'Impresa, 2018c). However, compared to other consumer goods, the ready-to-wear garments are present from the beginning of the carousel and remain under the eyes of the spectator for the entire duration of the advertising film. They are presented in different shots of Capucine, and the viewer is able to appreciate their wearability, their details and their powers of expression. In the first two minutes, Emmer prefers wide shots which frame the actress front and back as she walks, with some zooms on the details of clothes, such as buttoning at the back, seams and collars. Close-ups prevail in the carousel's *coda*, when the painter focuses his attention on the actress's face and on her proud gaze. At this moment the slogan and the short parade of clothes starts and then the finale opens: the director fixes the front camera on the whole subject, while she is moving away, widening the frame more and more to include the background, in which the Eiffel Tower stands out.

Capucine's body language and the style of clothes she wore were reminiscent of the elegance proposed, for example, by Jole Veneziani during the 1960s, with her sober, lightly decorated and close-fitting garments, her models looking proud to wear them (Gnoli 2013: 172). The only difference to highlight here was the wide accessibility of that type of elegance, made possible now by the industrial production of fashion, as exemplified by *Vogue Italia* with an article titled 'Obiettivo Moda Pronta' (Vogue Italia 1966: 128–35) that showed some examples of refined garments designed by Misses Veneziani and Marucelli, but produced by industrial manufacturers. Therefore, the transfer of prestige and expressiveness from the testimonial to the Cori clothes she wears is evident in the narrator's final message: 'This woman is Capucine, one of the most elegant actresses of today. Do we want to discover the secret of this sober and refined elegance?' The answer is given by the voice-over during the parade of clothes in the *coda*: 'This woman wears Cori.'[4]

Metaphorically speaking, the Cori clothes, the Parisian lifestyle and the personality of Capucine became desirable for the Italian consumer because they were both symbols and vehicles of a more cosmopolitan idea of 'Italianness'. Consequently, the use of icons and stereotypes belonging to popular culture, as well as the implicit parallelism between these elements, were aimed at increasing the appeal of Cori clothing for the mass market, through the triggering of a spontaneous desire for belonging and recognition, as shown by the associated Cori advertising of this season (Vogue Italia 1968b: 28).

Young celebrities for new change

With the change of decade, the clothing industry had to be capable of interpreting through the industrial product the signs of change that came from within society: 'the search for alternatives to serial manufacturing, the birth of an international fashion that followed "imponderable" dictates, the segmentation of the market from which new categories of consumers were born, including young people'. They all became signals of a new fashion system (Merlo 2012: 11). As expressed by the title in *Vogue Italia*'s issue of April 1968: 'Young Fashion Waits for You!' (Vogue Italia 1968a: 116). The young person became an icon of freedom and innovation, the bearer of revolutionary and progressive ideals. He or she became an indicator of new trends and styles of clothing (Paris 2006: 385–8).

Cori's advertising also transmitted the message that Italian feminism was beginning to claim freedom of female expression and a different perception of the body (Gundle 2007: 286–9). In fact, GFT adapted to this revolutionary wave and changed the communication strategy of its ready-to-wear fashion lines, focusing more and more on the deconstruction of a static and outdated idea of the 'elegant woman'. Following the revolution demanded by young consumers (Calabrese 1988), from 1971 to 1973 Catherine Spaak, a young French film actress also known as a singer, a dancer and a television presenter, and a perfect icon of this historical moment (Gundle 2007: 288), became the celebrity diva of the Cori-carousels and the chief testimonial for the seasonal collections of those years (GFT 1972).

Catherine Spaak wore Cori clothes for every occasion; she acted in different contexts within the communication campaigns, and always with the same ease: as a gardener, a spy, an international tourist, an actress, a woman, the young and famous Mrs. Dorelli,[5] she embodied the perfect testimonial for the new collections of clothes, and she was able to satisfy the young, varied consumer audience. There were many reasons for the choice of Catherine Spaak as a testimonial for Cori: first, she was the daughter of an actress and of an important screenwriter,[6] and so she could afford to attend high society occasions without necessarily inheriting their rigid and obsolete conventions. She was modern, informal but at the same time elegant, like the clothes she wore, so we think about the revealing function of Cori female advertising, in relation to a kind of fashion that reflected the social femininity expression of modern women (Paris 2006: 358). In fact, the young actress perfectly exemplified the ideals of beauty and feminine elegance of that decade of change: a young, sporty, casual woman, who made her freshness a key strength through which women could rebel against an oppressive system of values imposed by previous fashion. She was a woman of the 1970s, characterised by 'a seductive temperament and open mind' (Gundle 2007: 310). In 1973 Catherine Spaak was already a famous Cori testimonial and she participated in a series of carousels titled *La Casa dei Vip*, directed by Luciano Emmer (GFT 1972–7), who managed to amuse the audience by creating a close connection between celebrity and everyday life, and between cinema and popular language (Figure 8.2). In these screenplays the advertising proclaimed the gap between consumers and industry, guiding consumers during the purchase. Moreover, it created an audience of the brand's fans that were no longer moved by the simple need for products, but more by the desire for the expressive nature of clothing represented in these television campaigns. In particular, we cite the episode 'Sylva Koscina' in which Spaak, in a domestic-guide version, is an accomplice of the voyeuristic game of guessing who lives in that house (Archivio Nazionale Cinema d'Impresa 2018d) (Figure 8.3). The game demands that Spaak discover, room by room, clues about the owner's personality that the audience can guess 'from the elegant and refined hand'. The title of the game, which is played by the actress

Figure 8.2 Advertising Cori A/W 1973/74: Catherine Spaak performing in the Cori-carousel series *La Casa dei Vip*, 1973, GFT Archive (folder 2894, vol. 6), Turin/AsTo

Figure 8.3 One of the pictures selected for the Cori advertising campaign A/W 1973/74: Catherine Spaak performing in the Cori-carousel titled 'Sylva Koscina', *La Casa dei Vip*, 1973, GFT Archive (folder 2894, vol. 6), Turin/AsTo

and presented by Cori, is 'Let's see your home and I'll tell you who you are'.[7] In every carousel of this series the brand appears only at the end, along with the sanction of the omniscient narrator who embodies the values of the brand. The final slogan is: 'Did you like this woman, who amiably juggles her way into a VIP's home, but at the same time jokes and winks at the viewer to draw attention to her gestures? She dresses in Cori.'[8]

The Cori dress therefore expressed the character of its model. Thus, operating a kind of a conceptual transfer, the same dress could be worn by different personalities, so becoming a unique style despite the use of mass-produced goods. It was a corporate video for consumers in which the product takes second place to enhance other values connected and promoted by the company. The whole series was real storytelling in episodes, which made the consumer understand who the Cori woman could be.

Conclusion

From research into the GFT communication strategies, it emerges that the availability of documents kept in industrial archives in Italy and the growing digitisation of audio-visual material make the reconstruction of the phenomenology of fashion more stimulating and needing more insight.

In fact, by observing particular sources that adapt more frequent media formats to specific uses, such as Cori-carousels did, we are able to derive interesting details of the ways in which the Italian fashion industry communicated and thus influenced the social behaviours of consumers. Therefore, in my view 'documenting fashion' becomes an ongoing process of 'documenting sources', which during the early 1960s and 1970s includes garments, of course, but also a heterogeneous bunch of media representations that speak of the social and economic features of a precise historical context.

In particular, this study aims at contributing to this process by exploiting an engaging television storytelling that talks about garments' inclusion among consumer goods. In this sense, the GFT fashion carousels enter into a more general discourse assuming an important role in the formation of purchase desires for Italian consumers, and, in the meantime, becoming video evidence of a precise evolutionary phase of the society in which garments started to become powerful catalysts for the improvement of life quality. In short, even if Cori-carousels cannot be affiliated to the documentary genre, they demonstrate that GFT can provide informative material about the society in which it operates through the narration of its products, purposes and values. Moreover, this particular case study could respond to the more inclusive category of media 'at work in social and industrial organization' that help us better understand the emergence of a certain type of social practice (Hediger and Vonderau 2009: 11–12), such as large-scale industrial production of clothing.

The Cori-carousels ended in 1973, with five broadcasting cycles, a few years before the final disappearance of *Carosello* in January 1977 (Auteliano 2011: 103). This fact allows us to link the functionality of this particular media format to a certain historical moment, in which the communication of products and styles of consumption still had to carve out its space within national mass communication. As a matter of fact, from that moment on, advertising became a central element in the organisation of television schedules, and it was no longer proposed as a narrative form of edutainment but as a pleasant commercial content (Auteliano 2011: 103). The 35 mm black-and-white films were now a legacy of the past, surpassed by the more compelling colour commercials that GFT also began to commission through new strategies, new testimonials and new cultural combinations, more suited to designers' creations, and that embodied more complex social desires through a fashion that aimed to stand out from the crowd (Merlo 2012: 73–81). The Veneziani dress gave way to those of Albini, Krizia and Schön, to name just a few, and GFT would also start producing women's prêt-à-porter with important brands like Ungaro (GFT 1971) and Armani (GFT 1978). Therefore, *Carosello* was no longer suitable for documenting fashion, because clothes needed another kind of communication and representation now that consumers no longer needed to be educated in clothes purchasing. It was the beginning of the end of pedagogical and single-channel television, soon surpassed by the private channel, which sought instead to entertain the public rather than offer itself as a source of learning (Dorfles 1998: 110).

However, it is beyond doubt that in the period of the greatest activity of *Carosello* the ready-to-wear fashion industry – represented here by GFT – used the media industry 'to sew a reality on clothing' and to transfer it to the consumer as expressive power. By observing the Cori-carousels like forerunner forms of fashion television communication, we can follow the evolution of Italian purchasing attitudes and, specifically, understand how the clothing industry managed to approach and retain loyalty to a target that until a few years before was only trusted in tailoring fashion. Within this rising system, the role that *Carosello* played in the development of an 'Italian image culture' has been investigated by the exhibition *Carosello. Pubblicità e televisione 1957–1977*, held at the Magnani Rocca Foundation in Parma in 2019 (Cimorelli and Roffi 2019) and realised thanks to the archival sources preserved by the CSAC Archive of the University of Parma, the General Audiovisual Archive of Italian Advertising, the Galleria Campari Archive, and many other private collections. This exhibition, curated by Dario Cimorelli and Stefano Roffi, displayed a large number of posters and sketches together with critical texts and with the main carousels that have 'accompanied the transformation of the Nation from the country of the bell towers ... to that of the cities' (Cimorelli and Roffi 2019: 11).

As Roberto Lacarbona (2019: 297) writes in the exhibition catalogue, *Carosello* had revealed a make-believe world, made up of incentives to 'dress better, eat better, drink more, change the car – and the underwear – have some fun, coffee, bitter, cigarettes: in short, a large dose of illusion and collective metamorphosis made of accelerations, hopes, models of emancipation'. Considering the historical moment and the enormous influence of the television medium, this primitive advertising format had therefore allowed the construction of a territory of symbolic values around products, including clothes, expanding the expressive scope of goods and thus bringing them closer to new customers. By documenting Italy's evolution, *Carosello* had also captured the essence of the Italian fashion of those years and had enhanced its continuous changes and its symbolic and utilitarian power, bringing out problems and aspiring solutions. Returning thus to the mentioned exhibition, the Cori-carousels could enter by right into this 'memo album', with the purpose of including garments within this fabulous story of consumption that, albeit short, had changed the Italian way of living.

Notes

1. In 1964 the Cori-corousels were curated by Agel Agency, in 1966–7 by the Seller Agency, and from 1968 to 1972 female carousels were designed by Masius.
2. Voice-over translated by the author.
3. Translated by the author.
4. Voice-over translated by the author.
5. She had recently married the singer and actor Johnny Dorelli.
6. Claudie Clèves and Charles Spaak.
7. Sentence translated by the author.
8. Voice-over translated by the author.

References

Abruzzese, Alberto. 1988. *Metafore della pubblicità*. Genoa: Costa & Nolan.
Ambrosino, Paola, Cimorelli, Dario and Giusti, Marco, eds. 1996. *Carosello: non è vero che tutto fa brodo: 1957–1977*. Cinisello Balsamo: Silvana editoriale.
Arcagni, Simone. 2006. *Dopo Carosello: il musical cinematografico italiano*. Alessandria: Falsopiano.
Auteliano, Alice. 2011. *Il cinema infranto*. Udine: Forum.
Bignell, Jonathan and Andreas Fickers, eds. 2008. *A European Television History*. Oxford: Blackwell.
Caffaro, Giulia. 2017. 'Standard Celebrities: Evolution of Communication Strategy in the Ready-to-wear Fashion Industry'. *ZoneModa Journal*, 7 [online]. DOI: 10.6092/issn.2611-0563/7534.
Caffaro, Giulia. 2018. 'The Revolution of Sizes: The Pioneering Work of the Gruppo Finanziario Tessile (GFT) through Archival Sources'. In *The Size Effect: A Journal into Design, Fashion and Media*, edited by Antonella Mascio, Roy Menarini, Simona Segre and Ines Tolic, Reinach, 39–52. Milan: Mimesis International.
Calabrese, Omar. 1975. *Carosello o dell'educazione serale*. Florence: Clusf.
Calabrese, Omar. 1988. 'Appunti per una storia dei giovani in Italia'. In *La vita privata. Il Novecento*, edited by Philippe Ariès and Georges Duby, 79–106. Rome-Bari: Laterza.
Calabrese, Omar. 2019. 'Armando Testa e la pubblicità italiana'. In *Carosello. Pubblicità e televisione 1957–1977*, edited Dario Cimorelli and Stefano Roffi, 55–65. Cinisello Balsamo: Silvana Editoriale.
Carrano, Patrizia. 1985. 'Sophia Loren'. In *Le Dive*, edited by Aldo Bernardini et al. 168–95. Rome-Bari: Laterza.
Cimorelli, Dario and Stefano Roffi, eds. 2019. *Carosello. Pubblicità e televisione 1957–1977*. Cinisello Balsamo: Silvana Editoriale.
Dorfles, Piero. 1998. *Carosello*. Bologna: Il Mulino.
Eco, Umberto. 1965. *Apocalittici e integrati*. Milan: Bompiani.
Eco, Umberto. 1973. *Il costume di casa*. Milan: Bompiani.
Elsaesser, Thomas. 2009. 'The Place of Non-Fiction Film in Contemporary Media'. In *Films that Work: Industrial Film and the Productivity of Media*, edited by Vinzenz Hediger and Patrick Vonderau, 19–34. Amsterdam: Amsterdam University Press.
Fava, Elena. 2018. *Vestire Contro*. Milan: Bruno Mondadori.
GFT. 1964. *Corrispondenza e analisi relative a campagne pubblicitarie curate da Masius Omnia* (folder 2243). GFT Archive. Turin/AsTo.
GFT. 1968a. *Comunicato ai venditori-dettaglianti, Campagna comunicazione CORI – autunno/inverno* (folder 2229). GFT Archive. Turin/AsTo.
GFT. 1971. *Corrispondenza con la maison Ungaro* (folder 947). GFT Archive. Turin/AsTo.
GFT. 1972. 'Visto Cori? Anche Catherine Spaak veste Cori' – cartelli Cori con calendario dei passaggi pubblicitari sui mezzi di comunicazione – A/I 1972/1973 (folder 2808). GFT Archive. Turin/AsTo.
GFT. 1978. *Registri degli acquisti Giorgio Armani* (folder 712). GFT Archive. Turin/AsTo.
Giusti, Marco. 1995. *Il grande libro di Carosello: e adesso tutti a nanna…* Milan: Sperling & Kupfe.

Gnoli, Sofia. 2013. 'Fashion Pioneer'. *Vogue Italia*, vol. 758 (October), 172.
Grasso, Aldo. 1989. *Linea allo studio*. Milan: Bompiani.
Grasso, Aldo. 2004. *Storia della televisione italiana*. Milan: Garzanti.
Grossi, Emmanuel. 2019. 'Carosello e il Cinema'. In *Carosello. Pubblicità e televisione 1957–1977*, edited by Dario Cimorelli and Stefano Roffi, 191–221. Cinisello Balsamo: Silvana Editoriale.
Gundle, Stephen. 2007. *Bellissima: Feminine Beauty and the Idea of Italy*. London: Yale University Press.
Hickethier, Knut. 2008. 'Early TV: Imagining and Realising Television'. In *A European Television History*, edited by Jonathan Bignell and Andreas Fickers, 55–78. Oxford: Blackwell Publishing.
Hediger, Vinzenz and Patrick Vonderau. 2009. 'Introduction'. In *Films That Work: Industrial Film and the Productivity of Media*, edited by Vinzenz Hediger and Patrick Vonderau, 9–16. Amsterdam: Amsterdam University Press.
Lacarbona, Roberto. 2019. 'Un mondo che non esiste. Pino Pascali e Carosello'. In *Carosello. Pubblicità e televisione 1957–1977*, edited Dario Cimorelli and Stefano Roffi, 297–307. Cinisello Balsamo: Silvana Editoriale.
LCM Graman. 1971. *Analisi di validità messaggio pubblicitario televisivo Carosello Cori* (folder 2109). GFT Archive. Turin/AsTo.
Merlo, Elisabetta. 2012. *Moda e Industria. 1960–1980*. Milan: Egea.
Packard, Vance. 1958. *The Hidden Persuaders*. New York: Pocket Books.
Paris, Ivan. 2006. *Oggetti cuciti. L'abbigliamento pronto in Italia dal primo dopoguerra agli anni Settanta*. Milan: Franco Angeli.
Pellizzi, Carlo et al. 1972. *Cinema Industriale e società italiana*. Milan: Franco Angeli.
Segre Reinach, Simona. 2019. *Biki. Visioni francesi per una moda italiana*. Milan: Rizzoli.
Seller Agency. 1964. 'Cori advertising'. *Vogue Italia*, vol. 165 (December), 142.
SIPRA. 1974. *Cento anni di pubblicità nello sviluppo economico e nel costume italiano*. Turin: SIPRA.
Sørenssen, Bjørn. 2009. 'A Modern Medium for a Modern Message'. In *Films That Work: Industrial Film and the Productivity of Media*, edited by Vinzenz Hediger and Patrick Vonderau, 377–90. Amsterdam: Amsterdam University Press.
Veltroni, Walter. 1992. *I programmi che hanno cambiato l'Italia: quarant'anni di televisione*. Milan: Feltrinelli.
Vogue Italia. 1966. 'Obiettivo Moda Pronta'. *Vogue Italia*, vol. 185 (October), 128–35.
Vogue Italia. 1968a. 'Una moda giovane vi aspetta'. *Vogue Italia*, vol. 202 (April), 116–25.
Vogue Italia. 1968b. 'Advertisement Cori'. *Vogue Italia*, vol. 204 (June), 28.

Audio-visual sources

Archivio Nazionale Cinema d'Impresa. 2016. *GFT-Gruppo Finanziario Tessile* [Online series]. Available at https://youtube.com/playlist?list=PL15B-32H5GlIQzvvvGN-epeUdnys5XLvzk (accessed 30 June 2022).
Archivio Nazionale Cinema d'Impresa. 2015. *Marzotto* [Online series]. Available at https://youtube.com/playlist?list=PL15B-32H5GlJ3U3G8zKtP4F54q92lds5G (accessed 30 June 2022).

Archivio Nazionale Cinema d'Impresa. 2018a. *Carosello – Cori – Agente Segreto - Smeraldo, Agente Segreto* [Online video]. Available at https://www.youtube.com/watch?v=5FEzemwe-_A (accessed 30 June 2022).

Archivio Nazionale Cinema d'Impresa. 2018b. *Carosello - Cori – Parigi è sempre Parigi - 5 caffè, Parigi è sempre Parigi* [Online video]. Available at https://www.youtube.com/watch?v=-A-QmrUuds0 (accessed 30 June 2022).

Archivio Nazionale Cinema d'Impresa. 2018c. *Carosello - Cori – Parigi è sempre Parigi - Pittore, Parigi è sempre Parigi* [Online video]. Available at https://www.youtube.com/watch?v=xp2l6-PnFIU (accessed 30 June 2022).

Archivio Nazionale Cinema d'Impresa. 2018d. *Carosello - Cori – La casa dei Vip - Sylva Koscina, La casa dei Vip* [Online video]. Available at https://www.youtube.com/watch?v=f1NYG1Qje8s&list=PL15B-32H5GlIQzvvvGNepeUdnys5XLvzk&index=98 (accessed 30 June 2022).

ArchiviModaSAN. 2011. *I problemi della moda italiana - Rai Teche, Rai Teche* [Online video]. Available at https://www.youtube.com/watch?v=dN4w7YXIMgE (accessed 30 June 2022).

Emmer, Luciano. 1951. *Parigi è sempre Parigi* [film]. Rome: Minerva Film.

GFT. 1962. *Fotografie della stilista Biki e di Sophia Loren, vincitrice del Concorso-referendum Cori-Amica "Prima donna elegante d'Italia"* (folder 2882). GFT Archive. Turin/AsTo.

GFT. 1965–71. *Cortometraggi pubblicitari Cori* (folders 3013–3018). GFT Archive. Turin/AsTo.

GFT. 1967. *Fotografie di Caroselli Cori con protagonista Eleonora Rossi Drago – A/I 1967/1968* (folder 2892). GFT Archive. Turin/AsTo.

GFT. 1968b. *Cortometraggi pubblicitari Cori* (folders 3015). GFT Archive. Turin/AsTo.

GFT. 1972–7. *Cortometraggi pubblicitari Cori* (folders 3020). GFT Archive. Turin/AsTo.

Chapter 9

Fashioning self-care: *Queer Eye*, affect and makeover culture

Elizabeth Affuso

Premiering in February 2018, Netflix's *Queer Eye* provides an update of Bravo's earlier reality TV hit, *Queer Eye for the Straight Guy*. The reboot maintains the structure of the Fab Five – five experts who help makeover subjects in fashion, culture, food and wine, grooming and design – while updating the model to extend beyond straight men. The new *Queer Eye* tackles makeovers for subjects from a range of gender, sexuality, ability, class, race and national backgrounds. This chapter will focus on Tan France and Jonathan Van Ness, the fashion and grooming experts, respectively, on the 2018 reboot. France and Van Ness are arguably the breakout stars of the new series, with robust followings on social media, books, podcasts and YouTube series as part of their larger celebrity brands. This success points to the potency of fashion and beauty content within reality TV cultures and the branding potential for cast members in these areas.

Within the logic of the new *Queer Eye*, makeovers are positioned within the culture of self-care, and makeover subjects are encouraged to pursue grooming and fashion makeovers as a tool of caring for themselves and of projecting that care outward. In line with reality TV's history of providing experts for audiences, France and Van Ness provide instruction not only for the show's makeover subjects, but also for the home audience in how to pursue the best representation of self-care through fashion and grooming practices. This chapter will root this discourse on the show within larger trends in fashion and beauty branding towards self-care, to consider how reality television reverberates larger fashion and beauty ideologies to audiences. The kinder take on makeover TV represented in the *Queer Eye* reboot reflects larger conversations about inclusivity and body positivity within the fashion and beauty industries that seek to widen these spaces with inclusive sizing, diverse palettes and affordability.

Through the lens of Tan France and Jonathan Van Ness, this chapter will additionally examine the role of the expert in reality TV media and the affective relationship this role produces with audiences. Through close formal and textual analysis of the show and related social media content, it will be especially interested in the affective differences that occur in the spectatorial relationship to expert culture from reality TV to social media with its documentation of everyday life. It will also examine the historic function of gay men as arbiters of taste within fashion cultures and the larger implications of this for gender, sexuality and care work.

Makeover culture and reality TV

Makeover shows have been one of the most popular areas of reality TV content since the genre's rise to prominence in the early 2000s. Within reality TV cultures, makeover shows are part of the 'challenge and transformation' vein of shows that came to popularity during reality TV's second generation from 2001 to 2005 (Kavka 2012: 110–44). Challenge shows that began airing in this period, including *The Amazing Race*, *The Bachelor*, *The Biggest Loser* and *Queer Eye for the Straight Guy*, are amongst the longest running and most durable concepts in reality TV. According to Kavka (2012: 113), makeover shows fit within the logics of challenge via 'the self-improvement challenge of transforming property and personal appearance in makeover formats' and the 'conflicting ideologies of self-realisation' that these transformations ask subjects to overcome. Within the subgenre, makeover shows fall into several different categories, depending on the extremity of the transformation on display. Plastic surgery shows like *Extreme Makeover*, *The Swan*, *Dr. 90210* or *Skin Decision*, among others, fall into the extreme category with their narratives of permanent body transformation through medical procedures. Other popular makeover shows such as *What Not to Wear*, *100% Hotter* and *Queer Eye* utilise fashion and beauty interventions rather than surgical ones to makeover their subjects. This second type of show will be the focus of this chapter. On these shows, the focus is on fashion and beauty success as reflective of inner self. As Sender (2012: 5) has written, 'makeover shows draw on already popular genres, including self-help literature, soap operas, and talk shows, that are attentive to intimacy, value emotional expression, and offer narrative frames within which audiences, especially women audiences, interpret experiences'. This framing within self-help genres is important, as the makeover shows utilise larger neoliberal, late capitalist discourses of perpetual self-improvement as the dramatic throughline playing on the audience's pre-existing relationships to these logics. This idea is what Gill (2007: 156) refers to as 'the makeover paradigm'. Of it she writes, 'This requires people . . . to believe, first, that they or their life are lacking or flawed in some way; second that it is amenable to reinvention or transformation by following the advice of relationship, design, or lifestyle experts and practicing appropriately modified consumption habits.' Shows like *Queer Eye* further perpetuate these cultural narratives by using regular people as their subjects, giving the audience the sense that they too should be able to achieve what is being represented onscreen. As Ouellette (2014: 108) has noted:

> On reality television as in life, the scope of intermediaries has expanded, as lifestyle experts of all kinds now provide consultation, skills, resources, and motivational strategies, drawn from market principles, for maximizing one's own health, success, income, relationships, and well-being. The paradox is that as intermediaries are stitched into more and more domains of social life, the imperative to monitor, incentivize, and manage oneself accelerates.

The central idea of makeover TV is that with access to experts and enough willpower anyone can improve themselves. These shows overcome whatever economic, temporal or social issues may be impeding the makeover subjects from achieving their best self by providing them as part of the show, but never deal with the larger systemic issues that are causing them. These systemic issues have to do with work/life balance, equity in the home, economic/social capital, and prejudice. *Queer Eye*, as a makeover programme set in the Trump era, often addresses these issues in a cursory way, but suggests that with confidence and improved aesthetics, systemic issues can be overcome.

Rooted in contemporary ideas of body positivity, *Queer Eye* provides a more inclusive model of makeover TV. Makeover subjects are encouraged to makeover the body and homes they already have rather than seeking out radical transformation. The show is less focused on a dramatic makeover reveal than a narrative of the process of transformation. This is emphasised by a de-emphasis on the makeover reveal, relegating it to a video-recorded portion at the end, where the Fab Five watch from afar, removed from the in-person affective experience of it. While many makeover shows are focused on women, *Queer Eye* features a range of makeover subjects who identify as male, female, non-binary, gay, straight, lesbian and trans among others. The range of identity positions for makeover subjects points to cultural shifts around gender, sexuality and identity that have occurred in the years between *Queer Eye for the Straight Guy* (2003–7) and the *Queer Eye* reboot (2018–), including the legalisation of same-sex marriage in the United States and the expansion of the trans rights movement. Though the show acknowledges these shifts, it still maintains a problematic position through its deployment of stereotypes around gay men and domesticity in the makeup of the Fab Five. Within reality TV cultures, these stereotypes have a long history within the lifestyle subgenre, with gay men often deployed as home design, renovation, beauty and style experts. As a result, reality TV has played a key role in perpetuating these stereotypes, as Gorman-Murray (2011: 436) has noted: 'the normalized correlation between gay men, homemaking, and domestic style is not pre-given ... Rather, gay domesticity is a discursive construct, produced through a confluence of social mores, cultural associations, and media representations'. Of course, in *Queer Eye*'s selection of makeover subjects from a range of sexual identities, the show ends up depicting gay men who don't – within the terms of the show – exist as domestic style and beauty experts, but it doesn't explicitly explore this nuance, likely because it would undermine the show's entire conceit that gay men are the experts on how to live well.

Instead, much of *Queer Eye*'s narrative is concerned with helping people manage the obligations of neoliberal late capitalism and its relentless demands. This model is a convention of makeover TV as described by Weber (2009: 51):

> In makeovers we see a dramatization of Wendy Brown's contention that neoliberalism 'figures individuals as rational, calculating creatures whose moral autonomy is measured by their capacity for "self-care" – the ability to provide for their own needs and service their own ambitions,' thus removing this obligation from the state. The makeover enforces this need for self-care in After-bodies, while stressing that Before-bodies are incapable of such salutary management ... The logic goes something like this: if you are unhappy, it is because you have not made good choices. The makeover intervention enables better self-care, thereby posing less of a burden on others. If you resist self-care, your 'mismanagement' merits your unhappiness, cellulite, and sagging skin ... All told, this neoliberal stance favors the abdication of state obligations that might address obesity, poor nutrition, or bad self-esteem, in favor of individual solutions, obligations, and decisions.

This dynamic plays out over and over again on *Queer Eye* where the show expresses compassion for the difficulties of living in late capitalism, such as in the episode 'Camp Rules', where makeover subject Bobby holds two jobs to support his family of eight, which only leaves him time for two hours of sleep a night. As a result, Bobby is 'strug to func' (struggling to function), as Van Ness explains. However, the show contends that all that's needed to resolve the issues are better habits and systems, rather than changes to the larger structures that make it impossible for people to support their family with a single job. *Queer Eye*'s tips often fall into categories that involve streamlining certain aspects of day-to-day life, such as organising your wardrobe in such a way that all the component elements go together and then organising your closest from light to dark or casual to fancy in order to make dressing 'grab and go', as France suggests to comedian Joe in the episode 'Below Average Joe'. It is as though these systemic issues can be resolved via better organisational practices – an idea rooted in neoliberal notions of productivity.

In recent decades, self-care and wellness discourses have proliferated in fashion and beauty spaces, so that participation in these practices is seen not just as a tool of aesthetic presentation, but also as symbolic of being well cared for. Thus, failure to appropriately participate is seen as a sign of lack of self-care. Much of *Queer Eye*'s narrative is dedicated to caring for those who have put care of others above caring for self in a martyr type of narrative. The vast majority of makeover subjects on *Queer Eye* are seen as culturally successful through romantic relationships, family, employment or home ownership, but as failing at presenting these successes to the world. The martyrdom is usually reflected in living spaces that don't reflect a focus on self, as in the decaying home of Pastor Noah in 'Preaching Out Loud'. The Fab Five tour the home noting the decaying walls, exposed pipes and collapsed ceilings of the rectory. Of the original *Queer Eye for the Straight Guy*, Weber (2009: 179) has written:

> the show followed a narrative formula much in keeping with the makeover format: begin with the spectatorial overview and critique; move on to quasi-secret ambushes, quickly followed by search and seizure (and mocking); bring in individual tutorials with the Fab Five in grooming, cooking, style, etiquette, and home decor; and conclude with amazing reveals, usually themed around heterosexual events (marriage proposals, weddings, romantic evenings, etc.).

The show continues to prioritise reveals centred around events that produce normative ideas of romance, family, friendship and other affective relationships. The structure of the show is designed to make sure that makeover subjects have the home decor, cooking and culture skills, and fashion and beauty looks to be good neoliberal subjects. It roots these new skills in notions of self-care and in the idea that taking care of home, food, fashion and beauty is a sign of good mental health and happiness.

Self-care discourses have been prevalent from the twentieth century with the rise of self-help movements, therapeutic culture, and the public airing of these in spaces like television talk shows. The period from 2005 onward has been characterised by Ahmed (2010: 3) as 'the happiness turn'. In this period, she notes, 'The demand for happiness is increasingly articulated as the demand for better social ideals, as if what explains the crisis of happiness is not the failure of these ideals, but our failure to follow them' (2010: 7). This idea that happiness can be achieved by the following of social ideals, however misguided, is at the core of how expert fashion and beauty makeovers operate. Subjects feel that they are unhappy because they have been unable to conform to particular social ideals about what bodies should look like. In the case of *Queer Eye*, the focus is on a slimming appearance and neatness of clothes, hair and house. The experts swoop in and provide instruction for how to make bodies conform to these ideals through better routines, better skin and better clothes. This move also positions good taste or tasteful objects as inherent to happiness. The rooting in consumer goods provides a positionality that allows for those who have been perceived to have good taste (in the case of *Queer Eye*, gay men) to be arbiters of happiness. As Ahmed (2010: 34) writes:

> To become oriented means to be directed toward specific objects that are already attributed as being tasteful, as enjoyable to those with good taste. I have suggested that the objects we encounter are not neutral: they enter our near sphere with an affective value already in place, which means they are already invested with positive and negative value. Bodies also do not arrive in neutral: the acquisition of tendencies is also the acquisition of orientations toward some things and not others as being good ... We acquire habits, as forms of good taste that differentiate between objects in terms of their affective as well as moral value. We have to work on the body such that the body's immediate reactions, how we sense the world and make sense of the world, take us in the 'right' direction.

The makeover experts, in this case the Fab Five, provide instruction on how to orient towards specific good objects in the production of happiness, the counterpoint being that if you are surrounded by bad objects, you can never be happy. The most maligned bad object on *Queer Eye* is clutter, which is depicted in close-up for the viewer to gawk at as if they've walked into *Hoarders* in nearly every episode. Viewers are invited to stare at the mountains of sippy cups in 'Camp Rules', the piles of clothes in 'To Gay or Not Too Gay' and the dust in 'On Golden Kenny'.

Privileging good objects is also the logic of clutter guru Marie Kondo (2014), who asks readers, viewers and organisational subjects to only keep objects that 'spark joy' for them, and of stores like The Container Store, which promise life improvement through organisation. In the episode 'Camp Rules', home guru Bobby Berk mimics Kondo's process by asking makeover subject Bobby if there is any item in the living room that needs to be kept. In this case, a table made from childhood church pews is identified. Berk refinishes the table and removes the tabletop clutter, replacing it with candles and stylish place settings. During the makeover reveal, the repositioning of this piece is emphasised to remind viewers to design their homes with respect for sentimental objects. Many of the makeover subjects positioned by the Fab Five are messy; clearing up this mess and streamlining fashion, beauty and home is shown to be the solution for all of life's problems. The concern seems to be that the makeover subjects are showing people their emotional burdens through bad spatial management. The focus is less on the emotional burdens and more on how to hide them through presentation. These notions of self-improvement are also linked to distinctly American ideas of mobility and positive thinking, ideas that have become especially entrenched within late capitalism. As Ehrenreich (2009: 8) notes, 'If early capitalism was inhospitable to positive thinking, "late" capitalism or consumer capitalism is far more congenial, depending as it does on the individual's hunger for *more* and the firm's imperative of *growth*.' It is only through the participation in consumer capitalism that the makeover subjects can be improved and the access to capital needed for transformation acquired through participation in the reality TV machine. Without Netflix's money, expertise and sponsorship deals none of this would be possible.

The relationship of happiness, mobility and dissemination of taste is part of a larger history of post-war consumer society that requires what Bourdieu (1984: 325) calls 'cultural intermediaries'. Writing of the relationship of 'cultural intermediaries' to subjects, Rizzo (2015: 65) asserts, 'These individuals served as guides to the postwar culture of consumption, helping people shift from society where thrift was a virtue to one where leisure consumption was paramount.' The lifestyle experts on makeover TV function as cultural intermediaries; as McRobbie (2009: 142) states, 'Bourdieu's concepts of cultural capital and cultural intermediaries also provide fine tools for understanding these programs as a genre. In front of the camera, the cultural intermediaries, flaunt, play up, often flamboyantly, their own middle, or upper middle-class backgrounds.' McRobbie is writing about British makeover programmes and while the stars of *Queer Eye* project middle- and upper-middle-class backgrounds through style, their personal celebrity narratives are that of upward mobility. This represents a distinctly American relationship to class mobility that the show plays out mostly in accordance to regionalism, with coastal style elites travelling to parts of the country that are perceived as less sophisticated to teach citizens about style. This points to the ways that fashion and beauty can be used as a tool to project class position to those around you. On *Queer Eye*, this can be seen in France's focus on fitted suits, blazers, dress shoes and fashion sneakers, which are all objects that are associated with the upper class, especially as everyday looks. Van Ness is focused on neatness of hair and skin, to reflect professionalism and order. This is seen in the episode 'Make Ted Great Again', where subject Ted's beard is declared by culture expert Karamo Brown to be 'out of order and out of date'. Van Ness shaves Ted's beard and trims his hair to make his look more befitting of a mayor, reflecting the ways that style integrates with political image-making. In the sequence of Van Ness trimming the hair away, the close-up is deployed to demonstrate how 'out of order' it is from a scalp-edge vantage point not available to the naked eye.

This dissemination of taste, status and position relates to how the self-care narrative on *Queer Eye* operates. The show is structured so that gay men with access to money, domestic help and wellness gurus go into communities where these resources are inaccessible and try to indoctrinate makeover subjects into finding the time to replicate their style. Usually this is positioned as self-care and fits into cultural discourses about taking time for yourself in an increasingly 24/7 world. Self-care discourse permeates social media with hashtags like #selfcaresundays and Instagram text posts quoting Audre Lorde and promoting rest. It is within this discursive moment that *Queer Eye* lives.

Fashion and beauty as self-care

This chapter places its primary focus on how Jonathan Van Ness and Tan France, the grooming and style experts respectively on *Queer Eye*, position fashion and beauty as tools of self-care and how these ideals disseminate beyond the show into celebrity branding and social media discourse. The show gives priority screen time to Van Ness and France's beauty and style makeovers, and these areas contain the largest number of tangible tips that can be taken away by the audience for their own self-care. Part of why the fashion and grooming makeovers are so compelling is that they reflect self-doubt around appearance that is relatable for the audience. The makeover discourse on *Queer Eye* is positioned within its larger 'More Than a Makeover' branding, which seeks to position the show as one of depth, linking makeovers to larger social problems. This idea hits best when dealing with issues around sexuality and fares worse when the show attempts to take on race and police brutality, as they tried to with a prank involving a cop pulling over the car which Karamo Brown, the only African American member of the Fab Five, was driving in the episode 'Dega Don't'.

Regardless of whether the audience can relate to the makeover subject, they can relate to the focus on aspects of appearance that they may not like or feel confident in. Unlike other makeover shows, France and Van Ness are never mean about subjects' appearance and instead position themselves as cheerleaders, there to show subjects that these issues do not matter. Radical transformation in the form of weight loss or plastic surgery is not the name of the game. Instead, the show focuses on smaller transformations such as learning what silhouettes flatter your body shape, what colors look best with your complexion, and how to best care for your skin and hair. To complete these transformations, the show pairs with national clothing retailers like Target, Old Navy, Destination XL, Theory and Bonobos. These locations are chosen because of style, price point, or to meet a particular need such as tall clothes at Old Navy in 'Groomer Has It' or fuller-figured at Destination XL in 'Unleash the Sexy Beast'.

Queer Eye is careful to make clothes shopping inclusive, to show that participation in these forms of consumer capital need not be limited to those whose bodies conform to broader cultural standards. In 'Unleash the Sexy Beast', France takes makeover subject Leo to Destination XL not to shame him for his body, but to instruct him on how clothes and shoes designed for his body will make him more comfortable. France gives Leo several tips on how to de-emphasise his middle through styling, including wearing T-shirts that are longer than his jackets and buying slim-fitting blazers but leaving them unbuttoned. The success of these styling tips is shown through close-ups of Leo's middle to show the viewer how France's tips work. After seeing himself in the fashion picks, Leo states that the clothes, 'don't show me like a big guy, more like a comfortable person' and France declares that he looks like a 'rad dad'.

The price point of the stores also points towards style being available at all ranges of budget. France is clear that the focus is on style rather than fashion and states, 'Style is not fashion. Fashion is not trendy after a season. I don't give a shit about fashion. Style is dressing the way you feel confident and what is appropriate for you, your age, your body type.' This distinction encourages the makeover subject and the home viewer alike to think about fashion and style as distinct ideas and to move away from the trend focus that has become so central to the fashion business with the emergence of fast fashion in the last thirty years.

The idea of style versus fashion is also designed to soothe the makeover subject, so they do not have to consider continual wardrobe updates, but instead focus on staples like a good pair of jeans, a versatile sneaker and a well-fitted jacket. It also allows for France's tips to be distilled down and made easily consumable because they don't really change from episode to episode. France's signature French tuck – a style where the front of the shirt is tucked in while the back remains untucked – is deployed as an all-purpose trick to provide a slimming, professional look in lieu of a normal tucked-in shirt. This look also allows for makeover subjects who are not comfortable with their waists to show off some, but not all of their middle. This style move is consistent with France's larger emphasis away from bodily slimming through diet; rather, he encourages subjects to employ visual tricks to achieve the illusion of a slimmer body.

These slimming tips are a regular feature of the #qehiptip segment at the end of each episode. Slimming #qehiptips include, 'Slim is In' on how to use tapered jeans to make your body look longer and leaner, and 'Jelly Belly', which suggests layering your shirts if you are self-conscious about your middle. The position of the hashtag here allows *Queer Eye* fans to document how they are employing the shows' tips and tricks into their real life via Instagram or Twitter shares (Figures 9.1 and 9.2).

Van Ness is in charge of 'grooming', which is what the show calls beauty. This language turn is a nod to the original show which used grooming instead of beauty to masculinise the category. As with style, the makeover subjects are pointed to drugstore brands, such as Neutrogena, to achieve better skincare routines. Van Ness alternates between doing hair makeovers himself and partnering with stylists at local salons in the shooting location to complete the hair looks. This focus on local beauty businesses shows the audience that one does not need access to nationally renowned experts to be expertly groomed as resources probably already exist in your own town.

The show is also invested in Americana, which is made explicit in the Season 5 opening which features the Fab Five in Colonial American garb. *Queer Eye* is dedicated to promoting ideas of inclusion within the Trump era, especially around institutions such as the family, religion and community. This focus on Americana can be seen in episodes like 'Make Ted Great Again', with its focus on a small-town Georgia mayor. In the episode, the Fab Five

Fashioning self-care: makeover culture 213

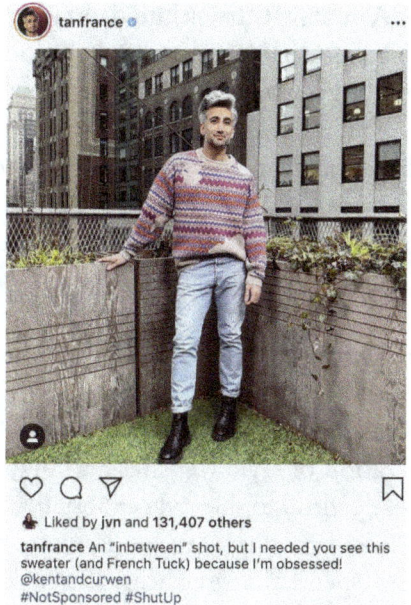

Figure 9.1 Post by @tanfrance featuring the French tuck. 2020. Accessed 16 October 2020

Figure 9.2 Selfie by fan @diarmuidferry featuring the French tuck and the #qehiptip. 2020. Accessed 18 October 2020

arrive in Clarkston, GA in a GMC truck kitted out with American flag bunting to makeover Mayor Ted for his Welcome Resolution meeting with leaders from refugee and immigrant communities. The show uses this makeover to present an ideology of an inclusive, welcoming America along with a vision for the American South that is in line with Georgia's contemporary position as a purple state (i.e., evenly divided between Republican and Democrat voters). The promotion of local brands, whether shops, beauty salons, restaurants or American automobiles roots the show within US capitalism and 'buy American' discourse. This focus on accessible shops points towards the democratisation of the makeover show and of makeover culture, which no longer fetishises the shopping trip to New York City as central to locating a stylish look, as seen on previous shows like *What Not to Wear*. This also speaks to the proliferation of style websites and digital shopping resources that make location less central to the style experience.

Meanwhile, Van Ness's pairing with local stylists for the hair makeover portion allows him to spend the time with the makeover subject chatting about his favourite topic: confidence. Van Ness's primary role is as confidence guru, with his array of catch phrases such as 'Yas queen', 'Love yourself, honey', 'Gorgeous', and 'Slay' that are deployed to boost the spirits of the makeover subjects. These catch phrases have become such signatures that they now appear on mugs, T-shirts, greeting cards and more, in retail spaces such as Etsy, RedBubble and Target. Of confidence, Banet-Weiser (2018: 94) has written, 'Confidence... is tied to *action*, an external quality that one works to achieve... confidence is about *mastery* – it takes practice, determination, and resilience.'

Since confidence can be mastered, the idea here is that confidence can be taught as part of the makeover process. Many of Van Ness's beauty tips also relate to the confidence game, helping subjects find confidence despite rosacea, hair loss or ageing. Ageing, in particular, is an area where Van Ness seeks to break down conventional ideas of beauty. He encourages makeover subjects to embrace their age, as seen in the episode 'DJs on Repeat' where Van Ness encourages subject Ryan to embrace his natural beard color, stop tanning, and trim his hair to make him look more confident. The repetition of these ideas serves to disrupt societal narratives about age. This discourse can be linked to others that have been popular in the social media age such as #menocore (for dressing like middle-aged women) and #grombre (for celebrating gray hair). This new inclusive push serves to make fashion and beauty cultures open to a wider number of consumers, but it also tends to reinforce the same norms, just for a wider audience, so shiny hair, moisturised skin and fashion looks can be sold to more people.

Affective experts

Queer Eye attempts to create makeovers that are doable and within the achievable scope of their subjects, with its focus on mass-market fashion retailers and drugstore beauty brands. This differentiates the show from many others in the makeover category like *Love, Lust or Run* and *Extreme Makeover*, which seek to provide beauty services and fashion looks that are unattainable beyond the scope of the show. Rather than shooting in coastal media centres like New York and Los Angeles, the show travels to Atlanta, Kansas City, Philadelphia and Texas to find its diverse array of subjects. By choosing these locations and pairing with local businesses, *Queer Eye* does attempt to create fashion and beauty looks that can continue to be replicated by both the makeover subjects and the home viewer.

This replication by the home viewer is key to the positioning of a show like *Queer Eye*, which is not just helping the makeover subjects onscreen, but also providing fashion and beauty tips and tricks to the audience at home. Within the #qehiptip segment, easily distilled tips such as the slimming ones already discussed are paired with ones that can easily be made from household items. In the homemade lip scrub #qehiptip from the episode 'Dega Don't', Van Ness tells the audience to 'Start off with half a cup of coconut oil, two tablespoons of brown sugar, a touch of honey, and any essential oil that tickles your fancy. I chose grapefruit because everyone knows that citrus has a touch more of exfoliating power.' This tip points towards cost consciousness with kitchen staples and notions of self-care with the addition of essential oils to 'tickle your fancy'. The idea that 'everyone knows that citrus has a touch more exfoliating power' centralises the type of knowledge that a viewer would gain from following beauty culture and from watching *Queer Eye*. This notion of finding the pleasure in beauty rituals and treating them as moments to pause and take care of oneself is central to Van Ness's beauty guru brand. As Ouellette (2016: 52) has noted:

> Consumer culture and popular media are technologies of individualization, to the extent that they circulate a 'repertoire of styles' that individuals are encouraged to 'monitor and adapt' for themselves (Chaney 2000, 81). Lifestyle television plays an especially visible role in the process of individualization by offering TV viewers an assortment of customizable templates, models and resources for 'choosing' and assembling their identities and lifestyles.

The fashion and beauty advice promoted by France and Van Ness falls clearly into this 'repertoire of styles' discourse. Makeover subjects are encouraged to have well-fitted jeans in a range of washes, slimming shirts or dresses in prints and solids, stylish sneakers and boots, and a good jacket. All are encouraged to pay attention to proportion and to wash their face and moisturise. These tips are specific to the makeover subjects, but also general enough to be adaptable to a wider audience. They become templates that continually reinforce that, in order to be good at caring for self, one must also be good at caring for body and image. Beyond the dedicated tips section, the entire show functions as a kind of advice column for the audience.

This access to experts is a hallmark of reality TV that has been exacerbated in the social media era. France and Van Ness's capacity to give fashion and beauty advice extends beyond the reality show, with the podcast *Getting Curious with Jonathan Van Ness*, the YouTube series *Dressing Funny*, and the books *Over the Top: A Raw Journey to Self Love* (2019) and *Naturally Tan: A Memoir* (2019) by Van Ness and France, respectively. Social media, notably Instagram, allows France and Van Ness to share tips and model style through branded tie-ins that provide much of the pay for influencer and lifestyle celebrity brands. These social media tie-ins provide instruction, but also provide audience members with a glimpse of France and Van Ness's 'real life' along with continuous streams of beauty, fashion and lifestyle advice. This continuous stream of advice makes the social media audience constant subjects for the *Queer Eye* lifestyle, one that is rooted in self-love and self-care. Jonathan Van Ness in particular (@jvn, 5.3 million followers) leans into the self-love vibe, with his affirmations and his referring to his audience as 'gorgeous' and 'honey', using pet names for the entire follower pool. He leans into the intimate spaces of his home life, so that followers feel as though he is speaking directly to them.

This is aided by the direct address to the camera on social media as seen in an Instagram video (Fig. 9.3) showcasing Biossance Elderberry Jelly Cleanser, which had 347,427 views at the time of this writing. In the video, Van Ness shows followers how to wash their face using the cleanser while providing a glimpse into his home bathroom and providing instruction on how to wash your face. The self-care aspects of face washing are emphasised when Van Ness says, 'I'm really giving myself a sensory journey, smells incredible.' He ends the video with 'Love you, sleep tight', pointing towards the day-to-day intimacy of this sort of posting. Biossance – a sustainable beauty brand – is one of several sponsored relationships that Van Ness has. Others that are regularly featured include Poopourri – a fragrant toilet spray – and FitOn – a home workout app. These brand partnerships speak to the relationship of conventional beauty culture to fitness and home perfume products for a complete lifestyle package.

Fashioning self-care: makeover culture   **217**

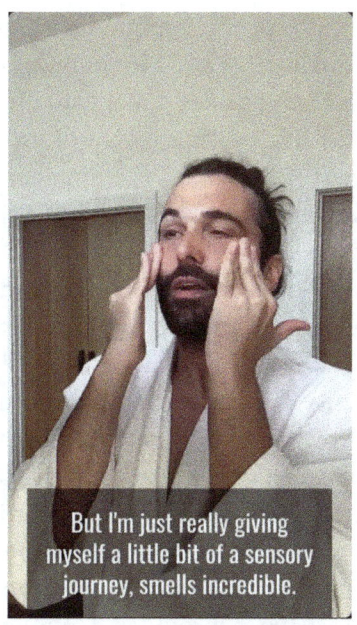

Figure 9.3 Still from an @jvn IGTV video showing how to cleanse your face with Biossance Elderberry Jelly Cleanser. 2020. Accessed 5 October 2020.

Tan France's Instagram (@tanfrance, 3.9 million followers), meanwhile, points towards opportunities for branding lifestyle beyond fashion. On Instagram, France features a cup and saucer designed by him for a contest with Pepperidge Farm Milano cookies, emphasising the importance of a tea break and showcasing a sleek kitchen. Travel content to glamorous destinations is also featured in hotel collaborations with the Times Square Edition, 1 Hotel West Hollywood, and Soho House. These forms of sponsored content present France as a lifestyle influencer beyond fashion, showing his audience how to live well through travel, food and home decor. Fashion is never far behind, and France is seen posing in clothes from brands such as Adidas and Michael Kors, among many others. Larger-scale partnerships, with Express and Etsy, allow France opportunity to collaborate and push his signature-style items. Instagram also provides near continuous opportunity for France to remind followers of his style signature, the French tuck. Posts either feature the French tuck or showcase how to wear the French tuck over and over again, pointing to the ease of the style. France also adds signature looks to his feed, notably the robe, which returns again and again to show followers a dishevelled, just-got-out-of-bed fashion look. France is focused on these #wokeuplikethis looks, which provoke hundreds of complimentary responses from followers and show how with good self-care (and a lot of money) style can be effortless (Figure 9.4). Instagram also enables France to normalise his glamorous lifestyle with 'stars are just like us' moments of him fanboying on the set of *Coronation Street* or *Great British Bake Off*, aligning him with his followers as a fan and also reinforcing his national identity as a Brit, while simultaneously promoting Netflix content with GBBO.

Instagram allows for the documentation of everyday life, and it is in these seeming quotidian practices that style and life lessons are disseminated over and over again to audiences. This day-to-day lifestyle documentation connects with that of reality TV and traditional documentary media formats such as the confessional or the autobiographical forms. Within film studies, the autobiographical mode has been well theorised (Russell 1999; Renov 2004; Arthur 2005) and social media documentation shares elements of what Renov (2004: 199) refers to as 'the preservational' aspects of autobiographical film-making and home movies. Whereas home movies were largely made for private use, Instagram provides a public archive of day-to-day experiences.

Figure 9.4 Post by @tanfrance in a robe promoting his Etsy collaboration. 2020. Accessed 19 October 2020

According to Kelly (2018: 211), 'Mobile and social media, including platforms such as Instagram, present a new stage in this documentary tradition – a widespread method of collecting and storing micro historical perspectives on both an individual and collective scale.' Instagram serves as a communal archive where followers can regram, screengrab and save others' images to their own personal archive. The interactive, communal aspects of social media and the intimacy of presentation make followers affectively connect to both Van Ness and France, but also to other account followers. Within digital culture, 'blogs, social networks, Twitter, YouTube: they produce and circulate affect as a binding technique', as Dean (2010: 95) has stated. This 'binding technique' creates the affective network of social media where likes, comments, recirculations and affirmations are the currency. This affective network produces cultures of care work that produce community via social media documentation.

Fashion and beauty experts have always provided these lifestyle models for wide audiences through magazine features in *Vogue* and *Architectural Digest*, coffee table books about the rich and stylish, and documentaries, but social media provides new spaces for the ongoing spread of these ideas. The difference between lifestyle celebrities like France and Van Ness and fans/followers is flattened by the logics of Instagram where stars imitate regular people and regular people imitate stars. As Marwick (2015: 142) has noted:

> Since both celebrities and 'regular people' have accounts on Instagram, it's perhaps not surprising that 'regular' selfies often emulate celebrity -related media, while celebrity selfies often closely resemble those of the nonfamous ... Instagram selfies allow the platform's users, whether celebrities or not, to show glimpses of their lives to others, connect with audiences, and receive instant feedback on their self-images. Van Ness and France, along with their followers, show images that follow similar logics with photos of baked goods, pets, travels, hikes, and stylish ensembles. Within social media spaces, everyone is performing, and the daily documentation of lifestyle occurs from professionals and amateurs alike. The repetition of the same tropes turns everyone into a lifestyle brand.

Of lifestyle television, Lewis (2008: 443) has written:

> The content of television [is] becoming increasingly concerned with ordinary, everyday life, a shift that is marked by the sheer numbers of ordinary people who now feature on television (Bonner 2003) ... this process has also seen an expansion of what kinds of knowledge get valued on television and who gets to present these modes of ordinary expertise.

It seems certain that there could be no Instagram influencers without reality TV and its radical reshifting of who can be a celebrity away from the conventional star system to 'ordinary' people. This structural change is what enables the everyday style advice given by France and Van Ness to exist. Beyond the scope of their reality television stardom, France and Van Ness are given the opportunity to showcase their everyday lives on a near-continual basis. In a sense, the reality TV cameras are turned back on them, and we are all potential makeover subjects. This life-sharing can create difficulties for celebrity brands and Van Ness and France are no exception, with audience members sometimes calling out political content in favour of the style or beauty advice they are expecting.

As Nathanson (2019: 10) asserts, this dynamic

> reflects larger shifts in the 'symbiotic relationship' (Warner 2010) between fashion and celebrity. While celebrity may increasingly be seen as a democratic space and fame as experiencing 'de-glamourisation,' Warner argued that these trends are 'managed' so as to maintain the economically and culturally beneficial relationship between celebrities and the fashion industry.

We can see these benefits over and over again on @jvn and @tanfrance. The feeds provide opportunity for fashion and beauty to be featured in ways that feel more personal than conventional fashion or beauty advertising. Having Van Ness directly address followers as 'gorgeous' allows them to be put in a mindset where they too are makeover subjects encouraged by their personal confidence guru. At a time where audiences are more narrowcasted than ever, social media allows fashion and beauty brands to target audiences across the widest range of platforms and doing it through lifestyle celebrities like Van Ness and France builds trust and intimacy with the audience.

We also must be mindful of the limitations of asking gay men and especially gay BIPOC (black, indigenous and people of colour) men to do care work for large swathes of people on both reality television and in social media spaces. As Sender (2006: 137) says, 'The show deploys gay men's longstanding reputation as affluent and as having great taste in order to court both gay consumers and heterosexuals who want to be associated with the positive attributes of the gay market.' The reliance on this stereotypical reputation can reinforce attitudes about gay men that are not inclusive, as we see again and again in episodes such as 'To Gay or Not Too Gay' and 'Preaching Out Loud' when gay makeover subjects express feelings of being less than, due to their lack of fashion, beauty or home knowledge.

Much of the discourse around the original *Queer Eye for the Straight Guy* (2003–7) concerned the relationship of homosexual men to heterosexual men with regard to the notion of the metrosexual (Clarkson 2005; Miller 2005; Sender 2006). By the launch of the reboot in 2018, metrosexuality had become entrenched, as seen in the proliferation of beauty products directed at men and the reorienting of the beauty aisles in stores like Target, CVS and Rite Aid to accommodate products from brands like Dove Men and Neutrogena Men. The reboot also positions the show not as gay versus straight, as makeover subjects come from a wide range of gender identities and sexual orientations. This reflects larger social changes that have occurred since the original series. The series still maintains one structure of marginalisation from the original series that was noted by Sender (2006: 143):

> The queer eye, however, has an ambiguous status in the narrative of the show. Because of the long association between gay men and the style trades, the queer eye is the expert eye, coolly assessing fashion violations and bad taste. But the queer eye is also the marginalized eye. Having done their work, the Fab Five are ejected from the reveal, the site of heterosexual rebonding, only to observe the fruits of their labor by video screen.

While the subjects of the show are no longer entirely heterosexual, the show still marginalises the Fab Five at the point of the reveal, relegated to their loft to watch on video. Additionally, while the show may no longer be about heterosexual makeover subjects exclusively, the transformations are usually designed to, in some way, improve the subjects towards heteronormatively coded experiences.

The position of Tan France and Jonathan Van Ness on *Queer Eye* and throughout the lifestyle celebrity sphere points to the multitude of ways that fashion and beauty advice can be disseminated from lifestyle experts to audiences. The tools of daily documentation on social media combine with reality TV celebrity to provide ongoing opportunity for fashion and beauty standards to be codified to audiences. The affective interaction of contemporary celebrity along with the proliferation of digital documentation due to smartphones and social networking sites has made style even more significant to day-to-day life as the constant threat of photography encourages a different relationship to presentation. This is a world where the quotidian and banal become stylised and the affective boost provided by likes and comments encourages further participation. The documentation of style is more present than ever before and when paired with neoliberal discourses of self-care, participation becomes more important than ever.

References

Ahmed, Sara. 2010. *The Promise of Happiness*. Durham, NC: Duke University Press.
Arthur, Paul. 2005. *A Line of Sight: American Avant-Garde Film since 1965*. Minneapolis: University of Minnesota Press.
Banet-Weiser, Sarah. 2018. *Empowered: Popular Feminism and Popular Misogyny*. Durham, NC: Duke University Press.
Bourdieu, Pierre. 1984. *Distinction: A Social Critique of the Judgement of Taste*. Cambridge, MA: Harvard University Press.
Clarkson, Jay. 2005. 'Contesting Masculinity's Makeover: Queer Eye, Consumer Masculinity, and "Straight-Acting" Gays'. *Journal of Communication Inquiry*, vol. 29, no. 3, 235–55.
Dean, Jodi. 2010. *Blog Theory: Feedback and Capture in the Circuits of Drive*. Malden, MA: Polity.
Ehrenreich, Barbara. 2009. *Bright-sided: How the Relentless Promotion of Positive Thinking Has Undermined America*. New York: Metropolitan Books.
France, Tan. 2019. *Naturally Tan: A Memoir*. New York: St. Martin's Press.
Gill, Rosalind. 2007. 'Postfeminist Media Culture: Elements of a Sensibility'. *European Journal of Cultural Studies*, vol. 10, no. 2, 147–66.
Gorman-Murray, Andrew. 2011. '"This Is Disco-Wonderland!" Gender, Sexuality and the Limits of Gay Domesticity on the Block'. *Social & Cultural Geography*, vol. 12, no. 5, 435–53.
Kavka, Misha. 2012. *Reality TV*. Edinburgh: Edinburgh University Press.
Kelly, Patrick. 2018. 'Instagram as Archive: Constructing Experimental Documentary Narratives from Everyday Moments'. In *Critical Distance in Documentary Media*, edited by Gerda Cammaer, Blake Fitzpatrick and Bruno Lessard, 209–29. Cham: Palgrave Macmillan.
Kondo, Marie. 2014. *The Life-Changing Magic of Tidying Up*. Berkeley, CA: Ten Speed Press.
Lewis, Tania. 2008. 'Revealing the Makeover Show: Introduction'. *Continuum*, vol. 22, no. 4, 441–6.
Marwick, Alice E. 2015. 'Instafame: Luxury Selfies in the Attention Economy'. *Public Culture*, vol. 27, no. 1, 137–60.
McRobbie, Angela. 2009. *The Aftermath of Feminism: Gender, Culture and Social Change*. Los Angeles, CA: SAGE.
Miller, Toby. 2005. 'A Metrosexual Eye on Queer Guy'. *GLQ: A Journal of Lesbian and Gay Studies*, vol. 11, no. 1, 112–17.
Nathanson, Elizabeth. 2019. 'Ageing On and Off the Red Carpet: Joan Rivers, Celebrity Culture and Postfeminist Television'. *Celebrity Studies*, vol. 12, no. 1, 1–16.
Ouellette, Laurie. 2014. 'Enterprising Selves: Reality Television and Human Capital'. In *Making Media Work: Cultures of Management in the Entertainment Industries*, edited by Derek Johnson, Derek Kompare and Avi Santo, 90–109. New York: New York University Press.
Ouellette, Laurie. 2016. *Lifestyle TV*. New York: Routledge.
Renov, Michael. 2004. *The Subject of Documentary*. Minneapolis: University of Minnesota Press.

Rizzo, Mary. 2015. *Class Acts: Young Men and the Rise of Lifestyle*. Reno: University of Nevada Press.
Russell, Catherine. 1999. *Experimental Ethnography*. Durham, NC: Duke University Press.
Sender, Katherine. 2006. 'Queens for a Day: *Queer Eye for the Straight Guy* and the Neoliberal Project'. *Critical Studies in Media Communication*, vol. 23, no. 2, 131–51.
Sender, Katherine. 2012. *The Makeover: Reality Television and Reflexive Audiences*. New York: New York University Press.
Van Ness, Jonathan. 2019. *Over the Top: A Raw Journey to Self Love*. New York: HarperOne.
Weber, Brenda R. 2009. *Makeover TV: Selfhood, Citizenship, and Celebrity*. Durham, NC: Duke University Press.

Audio-visual references

100% Hotter (2016–). Television programme. Channel 5.
The Amazing Race (2001–). Television programme. CBS.
The Bachelor (2002–). Television programme. ABC.
The Biggest Loser (2004–). Television programme. NBC.
Coronation Street (1960–). Television programme. ITV.
Dr. 90210 (2014–). Television programme. E!.
Dressing Funny (2019–). Web series. YouTube.
Extreme Makeover (2002–7). Television programme. ABC.
Getting Curious with Jonathan Van Ness (2015–). Podcast. Earwolf.
Great British Bake Off (2010–). Television programme. BBC/Channel 4.
Love, Lust or Run (2015–16). Television programme. TLC.
Queer Eye (2018–). Streaming television programme. Netflix.
Queer Eye for the Straight Guy (2003–7). Television programme. Bravo.
Skin Decision: Before and After (2020–). Streaming television programme. Netflix.
The Swan (2004). Television programme. FOX.
What Not to Wear (2001–7). Television programme (UK). BBC.
What Not to Wear (2003–13). Television programme (US). TLC.

Part III
Digital media

Chapter 10

From newsreel to 'see now, buy now': a genealogy of the fashion show live stream

Rebecca Halliday

Since the first dedicated efforts at 'real time' online transmission of fashion shows in 2010, the live stream has become a standard medium of fashion communication. Fashion shows on the ready-to-wear Fashion Month circuit in New York, London, Milan and Paris – in addition to those produced for lower-tier fashion weeks in other international cities – are now routinely live-streamed across a plethora of media platforms that include official brand websites, fashion press and fashion film websites, event producer websites, and dedicated streaming and archival websites.[1] Fashion scholars and the fashion press have touted the seismic impact of the live stream on industry timelines and on the speed and measure of visual (if not spatial or tactile) access to the latest collections (Rocamora 2012, 2013; Geczy and Karaminas 2016; Rees-Roberts 2018). Nick Rees-Roberts attributes the proliferation of non-fiction fashion footage, and the fashion documentary medium, to consumers' 'immediate access' to fashion show spaces and to 'fashion in motion' that the live stream facilitates, as well as a hunger for fashion content that the medium continues to fuel:

> The recent rise of the [non-fiction fashion footage] ... is partly indexed to the growth in online participatory cultures, fueled by the desire for vicarious backstage access to design studios and trade events, and immediate involvement in runway shows, which brands and designers have responded to through the increased use of live streaming. (2018: 75)

The production of fashion shows with attention to screen interfaces is but one phenomenon in an overall process of mediatisation in fashion, referring to the infusion of media practice into all facets of production, communication and consumption (Rocamora 2017). The live stream must, however, be historicised within prior fashion show footage disseminated to audiences since the invention of motion capture and the popularisation of cinema as mass medium.[2]

To contextualise contemporary consumer interactions with fashion show live streams, this chapter draws from media histories in fashion studies that outline uses of electronic media to disseminate runway footage. I describe the fashion show live stream using Bolter and Grusin's (2000) concept of *remediation*, here of film and television, illustrating techniques and aesthetics and demonstrating how these media have offered (or denied) a measure of consumer access to fashion. Bolter and Grusin coined the term *remediation* to outline how new media formats 'refashion' their predecessors, appropriating elements, interfaces and techniques of earlier media while facilitating new modes of inscription and reception (2000: 15). Recent work from Caroline Evans, Jussi Parikka and other scholars involved in the 'Archaeology of Fashion Film' (AFF) project advocates for a media archaeological approach that functions to 'unearth forgotten, suppressed and even unrealised media forms in order to recast the technological present in a new light' (Evans and Parikka 2020: 324). This 'methodological tool' permits researchers to scrutinise media content from multiple vantage points to discover potencies in and across moments or even movements (Evans and Parikka 2020: 324), and to conceive of the fashion film format as itself a 'heuristic that helps to look at the ways in which it is remediated' (Evans and Parikka 2020: 335). While the work of the AFF project brackets out fashion show live streams (Evans and Parikka 2020: 324), a media archaeology nonetheless contextualises aesthetic and technical resonances between records that might reveal themselves across decades and nuances the commercial imperatives of mediatised fashion show content at different historical or temporal points.

A focus on the mediatisation of fashion shows positions live streams as a representative example of the industry's multifarious uses of media in this decade. The live stream exemplifies a condition that Marketa Uhlirova describes as 'the new ubiquity of fashion as moving image' made possible thanks to digital media affordances (2013: 153). It offers consumers unprecedented temporal access to fashion shows and affords brands and intermediaries tools by which to transmit 'live' content across fixed and mobile devices, and, in certain well-reported social media initiatives, across screens installed in retail spaces or urban tourist centres (Uhlirova 2013: 152). However, the degree to which spectatorship can be deemed immediate depends on one's position in relation to the screen interface, and that of the camera(s) in relation to the runway.

This chapter first outlines media, film and performance-based theories of spectatorship and user positionalities to explore the manner in which electronic media invite interaction, and also to problematise the notion that 'real time' transmission can be described as such. Next, a genealogy of fashion shows' dissemination across film, television and online media reveals, first, that fashion show content explicated fashion trends to consumers one hundred years before online media's temporal democratisation of fashion, and, second, that scholars read fashion show footage in terms of its manipulation of the gaze, often harnessed in the service of consumer desire. The remainder interrogates the technical and aesthetic qualities of live streams with a focus on fashion shows that take inspiration from television spectacles to fulfil a commercial intent. A final section introduces as an example of this practice American athleisurewear impresario Tommy Hilfiger's TommyNow collaborations with models, influencers and celebrities, produced as 'see now, buy now' fashion events in which consumers can purchase items online while the show streams.

Internet spectatorship and 'real time'

Online media has transformed the economies of fashion communication and the materialities of consumer interaction with fashion content. Live streaming operates within a history of media formats that altered and resituated modes of spectatorship, access and embodied interaction across temporalities since the industrial modern period. The Internet combines textual and visual elements of print media as well as the electronic media of film and television (Bolter and Grusin 2000: 15). Agnès Rocamora reads fashion websites and blogs as a remediation of print, while print magazines 'have also remediated fashion blogs by incorporating the latter's visuals and take on fashion in their own pages' (2012: 101–3), lending credence to new media practice and enabling multi-media and multi-directional movements of fashion content.[3] The most fundamental transformation in fashion reportage arose, however, with the rampant adoption of the live stream, which, as stated, reduced the time frame of consumer access to looks from six months to instantaneousness (see also Rocamora 2012: 97). The transmission of the fashion show adheres to Philip Auslander's earlier definition of mediatisation as the infiltration of electronic media into live performance's spatialities: Auslander asserts that an 'authentic' condition of *liveness* is dependent upon mediatisation (2008b: 11). Rosie Findlay (2017), observing Australian Fashion Week, uses Auslander to expand

John J. MacAloon's concept of spectacle (1984), describing how mediatised fashion shows extend the spectacle of the brand to the consumer via virtual realms. Sarah Bay-Cheng further asserts that virtual environments can instil a sense of presence and even interaction with a performance: '[P]resence is defined not by physical touch but through avenues of participation. In a digitally connected and networked world, participation creates presence. In a digital context, people do not participate by being there; people are "there" by participating' (2010: 130). This approach expands our capacities to examine the interactive and material properties of mediatised content, or our experience of the live via media. The fashion industry capitalises on this same ideal of virtual presence, promoting consumer access to live streams in terms that indicate that users should feel an absence of interfaces and perceive the event as if seated in the front row.

Nonetheless, online fashion show content privileges attendees' spatial presence as a measure of influence while advertising a *virtual* sense of inclusion to consumers as a novel means of brand interaction. Auslander (2008a) makes a distinction between *spatial* and *temporal* co-presence of performer and audience, as a mediatised culture holds up the affective combination of both forms as the most *immediate*. Mediatised fashion show footage reveals the extent to which media companies and content producers purport to achieve the same experiential effect. For Bolter and Grusin, one's experience of *immediacy* in media use results from the collusion of interfaces, or rather users' perception of a virtual environment as real or seamless is the product of multiple, simultaneous processes that media technologies attempt to efface (2000: 9). *Hypermedia* aims to instil a sense of the 'real' through a confluence of visible media that, when combined, 'create a feeling of fullness, a satiety of experience, which can be taken as reality' (Bolter and Grusin 2000: 53). *Transparent media* attempt to negate users' awareness of technical processes (Bolter and Grusin 2000: 53). Despite companies' desire to replicate a sense of spatial presence, fashion shows, streamed across websites and social media with continuous tracking and multi-perspectival shots, operate under the condition of hypermediacy, which 'acknowledges multiple acts of representation and makes them visible . . . representation is conceived of not as a window onto the world, but rather as "windowed" itself' (Bolter and Grusin 2000: 34). Users can watch live streams via interfaces that place other representations within the frame or can comment on shows and/or collections through textual utterances or emojis, sometimes necessitating opening other windows or applications or activating a textbox which imposes other users' reactions onto the screen.

The basic intent behind the use of live streaming as a medium has remained somewhat static: a means to transmit content from the space to a spectatorship that watches it over a screen-based interface in as instantaneous a time frame as bandwidths will permit. Fashion companies have, however, profited from the creation of new (often portable) devices, applications and features to facilitate more innovative brand interactions. Rather than become more transparent, however, the fashion show live stream has evolved into a more cinematic viewing experience. Recent fashion show transmissions have used techniques, shots and aesthetics that cinema and television made possible, invoking the modes of spectatorship that these media established. Still, while each medium is derived from its predecessors, 'each demands a different way of attending to the event' (Wissinger 2013: 134) – just as each fashion show should be considered for its own production elements – and therefore the economies of the fashion show live stream must be dissected both as a product of electronic media and on their own terms.

Crucial to fashion's discourses of presence and liveness is the use of the term 'real time' to describe the speed of transmission and the overall sense that consumers can watch the fashion show *as it happens*. 'Real time' and its immediate sensation is sold as the latest (democratised) invention in content transmission. However, even within the venue, fashion's performance and broadcast schedules remain in flux. Media and performance scholars problematise notions of 'real time' transmission as, to cite Rebecca Schneider, a 'manufactured' construct that effects a 'denial' of mediatisation processes (2011: 93; see also Auslander 2008b). Numerous phenomena combine to undermine live streams' claims to 'real time' transmission. Fashion shows are notorious for starting late, due to packed schedules that require rapid travel within metropolises and to the late arrivals of important persons. Producers instruct users to tune in to live streams at a show's scheduled start time, but users have to calculate time zone differences and often watch attendees' arrivals for several minutes. User perception of 'real time' is further dependent on the reliability and speed of Internet connections as lags or crashed feeds interrupt processes of consumer identification (White 2006: 85). Human and technical deficiencies therefore reinforce discrepancies between the time of the *live* performance and its virtual reception.[4]

Fashion companies, media outlets and intermediaries also film the content with the intent that consumers can watch it over and over, access it at a time of their convenience and/or pause or take screenshots. It is common for an archived video to appear on a brand's website or YouTube channel within seconds of the end of the live stream; websites such as *Fashion Week Online* run looped footage of previous fashion shows if none are taking place. Streams from Facebook Live can also be archived in news feeds for users to access and share (as was also possible with Twitter's now-defunct Periscope). The Facebook app runs the video as users scroll past, so streams can be reanimated at the swipe of a finger. That live stream broadcasts or short videos can now be archived undermines the status of the fashion show as ephemeral event. It is no coincidence therefore that brands encourage consumers to watch live streams at the 'real time' moment of their transmission. While the above-mentioned phenomena concern the 'real time' condition of the fashion show live stream, this privileging of immediacy as experiential should be read as part of the industry's obsession, under late capitalism, with instant access and a resultant overhaul of production, communication and retail schedules, culminating in the creation of the 'see now, buy now' model.

Fashion shows on film

Film and television, the predecessors to the live stream, rendered fashion content more accessible to the mass market than ever before, and thus bore their own democratising influence, even as each of these forums emphasised fashion's exclusive social constructs for the purpose of instantiating aspiration. Film offers a recorded, edited document of the live fashion show. As a medium, it permitted an unprecedented number of consumers across all economic strata to witness collection presentations onscreen in a manner that emphasised clothing movement and detail. Film erased the theatre's cultural dominance and popularity – including as a showcase medium for fashion trends – due, first, to its technical capabilities, notably the close-up shot and slow-motion effects, and, second, its capacities to be duplicated for cinemas across nations and the comparative inexpensiveness of cinema attendance (Rappaport 2001; Auslander 2008b; Schweitzer 2009). Uhlirova demonstrates that fashion's communication in film reflects a societal fascination with 'temporal experience and greater mobility' that has existed since modern industrialism (2013: 138).[5] Film became an appropriate medium to 'promote fashion' as it could 'recast consumption as seductive visual entertainment' (Uhlirova 2013: 140). In the 1910s, audiences in 'Europe and the United States' watched newsreels of fashion presentations from Paris and later from New York (Evans 2001: 285). As numerous scholars have chronicled, these records allowed cinema goers a peek at the world of high fashion and stoked their desire for the looks, copies of which could be purchased at various price points (Berry 2000; Schweitzer 2009). Caroline Evans remarks that film reels 'brought the image of haute couture to a wider audience through the very process of promulgating its mystique and aura of exclusivity' (2001: 285). Newsreel producer Pathé-Frères later created *'Florence Rose Fashions,* a series of thirty-one short films produced between 1916 and 1917, which were tied into leading newspapers and stores with articles describing the clothes printed twelve days before the films appeared' (Berry 2000: 55). In 1911, Paul Poiret made films of his mannequin parades to use as a promotional tool for a US tour, while similar films were produced for a 1915 US tour for Charles Worth and Jeanne Paquin (Evans 2001: 285). Confluences between cinema and retail, or the 'commercial use of the cinematic fashion show', continued into the 1930s, when consumers could watch 'a series of short films sponsored by *Vogue* magazine that were released every two weeks' (Berry 2000: 55).

Fashion-themed cinema thus took the form first of informational (and aspirational) newsreels, followed over the next decades by more commercial films dedicated to fashion, in collaboration with department stores and print publications. A subset of 1930s films set in a fashion house or retail environment incorporated focal fashion show scenes into fictional narratives to showcase the latest trends (see Berry 2000). Charlotte Herzog describes the commercial function of this fashion show film as 'powder puff' or 'soft promotion', that couched 'subtle, illusive' advertisements in the feature (1990: 136). A distinctive series of 'long, lingering, scrutinizing' shots replicated the onscreen audience perspective: the cinema audience discerned clothing details and identified with the models and the attendees of a fictional event (Herzog 1990: 154–9). This filmic genre should be considered a cinematic precursor to the aesthetics and camera shots used in later forms of fashion reportage for the simultaneous aims of information and desire production. Film has remained a medium for the production of consumer fantasies and the revelation of fashion's behind-the-scenes environments, all of which contribute to a continued fascination with fashion as spectacle.

Fashion on television

While television has been considered a remediation of film, its earliest incarnations functioned as an audio-visual transmission of live in-studio enactments, presenting a novel format that was both recorded and experienced as 'immediate' in its temporality and placement in the home

(Auslander 2008b: 12–13, 60). It was not, however, until 1980 that informational broadcast television devoted to the international fashion scene became a distinct format which scholars have termed 'fashion-themed television' (Fulsang 2004) or 'fashion television' (Arrington 2017).[6] CNN's *Style with Elsa Klensch* (1980–2001), hosted by the late Elsa Klensch, is considered the pioneer in the format (Arrington 2017). Two Canadian-produced programmes debuted within the decade: CityTV's *FashionTelevision* (1985–2012), hosted by television personality Jeanne Beker, and CBC Newsworld's *Fashion File* (1989–2009), hosted by London-born columnist Tim Blanks. Runway footage, still edited after-the-fact, employed familiar, tracking shots, with the focus moving from the toe upward to the head, that could be found in cinematic fashion show depictions, intercut with closer shots of models from the waist or chest up. Commentaries were overdubbed, as was an up-tempo, electronic soundtrack. *FashionTelevision* and its contemporaries 'democratised fashion and broadened the appeal of fashion across genders as well as class and economic distinctions', offering viewers an insider's look at the environments of fashion weeks in New York, London, Milan and Paris (Fulsang 2004: 315). The hosts did not just report on fashion and design trends but interviewed designers in their workspaces (Fulsang 2004: 325), simultaneously demystifying fashion as a business and consecrating its practitioners as artists. The programmes also revealed intimate backstage environments, often filmed in the middle of the melée during chaotic, crowded moments, sparking a public interest in behind-the-scenes action that companies have continued to exploit in online content. Television's consumer reach and the shows' frenetic and stylised format combined to offer consumers an unprecedented exposure to stimulating and informational fashion footage (Fulsang 2004; Wissinger 2015).[7] Renowned fashion show producer Alexandre de Bétak cites the television broadcast of fashion shows as a shift in consumer access to fashion (from a reliance on print media) that necessitated new production set-ups and filming methods: '[Fashion shows] used to be mainly for journalists and photographers from monthlies that would come out a month later. Suddenly TV became more important and we started to cater more to that medium, which meant we had to create moments that, when isolated, would be great TV material' (as cited in Anaya 2013: n.p.). Fashion-themed television shows benefited from constant footage of the world's most stunning models, and indeed perpetuated the supermodel reign. Moreover, television as a domestic medium enhanced the public's familiarity with individual models (Wissinger 2014: 11; 2015: 62–3) as well as a sense of 'immediacy' to the hosts and trust in their expertise (Staples 1993 as cited in Arrington 2017: 160). Despite the trade-related content in fashion-themed television series, the hosts routinely endeavoured to obtain the requisite soundbites on the collections from celebrities, with the understanding that celebrities' appearances would maintain viewer interest.

The frenetic pace of fashion television reportage further influenced print fashion journalism practices that both remediated television reportage and led to its obsolescence. The format took inspiration from music videos, not just in the use of beautiful bodies and feature of skin but also in the brief duration of individual stories and use of shorter, more staccato camera shots (Fulsang 2004: 317–18). Fulsang suggests that the short-form pace of fashion television reportage ushered in a 'lite' form of print journalism: 'Sidebars, snippits of text, and often point-form notation represented the tendency of simplifying information for a public inundated with an ever-increasing volume of information presented at an increasing speed for those with an ever-decreasing amount of free time' (2004: 323). This format can also be considered a forerunner to online and social media in our oversaturated attention economies, for example, the 'real time' of live streams, the 'Insta' of Instagram, the disappearance of Snapchat posts, and the 280-character limit of tweets (see also Wissinger 2013). The press attributed *FashionTelevision*'s cancellation in 2012 to the live stream and other technologies that rendered content *more* perceptibly immediate: 'A changing media landscape has meant stiff competition from fashion websites that livestream runway shows, and bloggers who provide to-the-minute fashion coverage' (Chetty 2012: A3). In 2005, *FashionTelevision* released a cable-access offshoot series, *RAW*, which consisted of unedited runway footage using tracking camera mechanisms but without slow-motion shots or close-ups. The picture quality resembled that of a VHS home video, and there was no attempt to overdub the shows' bass-laden music, which lent the broadcast a tinned sound. The uncut *RAW* can be read as a *premediation* of the live stream, which occurs when an existing medium predicts the features of a subsequent medium and creates the conditions for its adoption and interface (Grusin 2010). Elizabeth Wissinger (2013: 134) observes that in a mediatised era the fashion show has become much more edited and frenetic as broadcast or depicted on television than it is *live*. The 'lite' format of fashion-themed television is a precursor to later *fashiontainment* series from music video network MTV as well as reality television series and fashion-themed dramatic series such as *Sex and the City* that have featured real and fictional fashion shows in or as climactic sequences.

Fashion shows and/as sporting events

The capability to broadcast fashion shows in real time has existed, it must be noted, since television itself was invented. Sporting events – that cater to a public fascination with idealised, linear and even extreme bodies – were televised as early as 1936 at the Berlin Olympics.[8] While haute couture and ready-to-wear fashion shows are not televised in their entireties, the lingerie brand Victoria's Secret, from 2001 to 2018, produced an annual, star-studded runway spectacle featuring the world's premiere models (hosted on the ABC network at the time of its cancellation in 2019). In the manner of a sporting event, the fashion show was produced *for* and coordinated around the technical requirements of a television broadcast. In this case, the fashion show assumed characteristics of more participatory *media rituals*, as Nick Couldry has identified, such as voter-based reality television series and championship tournaments (2012: 66–8). The last of the Victoria's Secret fashion show broadcasts were taped the week before their airdate and then aired to public fanfare and a host of accessible online content. The viewership of the Victoria's Secret fashion show, which dropped from 9.7 million in 2013 to 3.3 million in 2018 (Low 2019), does not approach that of televised media rituals such as the Superbowl, whose broadcast in 2020 reached 102 million viewers. Nonetheless its ratings were comparable to episodes of reality television competition series. The Victoria's Secret fashion show offers, for Wissinger, the most spectacular example of televised fashion shows' stylisation: 'shaped by a breathless pace of quick cuts and wild camera angles, [it] is paced so fast it is sometimes hard to know where to look. It organises bodies in space and time very differently than the fashion show's traditional form' (2013: 134). In 2009, the producers aired a reality competition, the Victoria's Secret Model Search, in which unknown beauties auditioned to become the next Victoria's Secret angel. In an *American Idol*-inspired process of audience participation, viewers across the United States phoned in to vote for the winner. The two finalists were dressed up for their runway debut, and the winner performed her walk seconds after the live announcement, while the runner-up had to turn around and walk to the dressing area in her costume. Consumers were thus invited not just to watch the 'live' broadcast but also to decide, to mix some metaphors, which angel received her wings, and which angel had to remain waiting in another set of wings.

The fact that television has not often broadcast fashion shows *live* can be attributed to their late start times and brief durations, which do not fit within a network schedule, or to the difficulties of tailoring technical elements to make the live presentation read across the screen – a concern still prevalent in live streams. Furthermore, the Victoria's Secret brand bears (or bares) more middle-class associations than the monied elitism of haute couture and ready-to-wear. Fashion companies' decision to live stream fashion shows permits companies to employ a consumerist rhetoric but also to protect lines' cultural status from the commercialism that surrounds the Victoria's Secret fashion show and similar televised media rituals. The Victoria's Secret fashion show could also be streamed on the brand website, where visitors could watch the archived video and access reams of behind-the-scenes photographs and clips.

Fashion in the live stream

Historical representations of fashion shows have mediated consumers' expectations and perceptions of live streams and provided precursors not just for present modes of fashion show interaction and reportage. All audiences regardless of position or location (in actual or virtual spaces) experience and read the condition of the live via the mediated (Auslander 2008b: 39). User reception of live streams remains akin to and informed by the embodied practice of watching live television events, or what Graeme Turner describes as 'the reality effect of television's "liveness" . . . as in what we are watching is happening right now!' (2010: 2), that has undergirded the appeal of television both 'live' and prerecorded. Turner describes the consumption of YouTube content as an 'experience of co-presence' but notes that this sensation derives from the communal watching of 'broadcast television' (2010: 93–4). YouTube instead offers 'an analogous co-presence, not necessarily simultaneous, but framed by transnational taste niches or by social networks' (Turner 2010: 94). While the live stream or its archived videos instil an awareness that other users are watching the content at the same time elsewhere, the mediatised fashion show nonetheless refocuses user attention *onto* the live event and its attendees. Bolter and Grusin (2000: 46) explain that the *newness* of new media, or remediated media, is often a selling feature, even as the new media contain trace features of their predecessors. Therefore, the temporal co-presence of the live stream has revolutionised consumer access to fashion content, even as the content itself remains familiar. John Tomlinson points out that the material nature and increased speed of our interactions with devices condition us to expect instant content, response and feedback (2007: 131–3). The spectator's experience of the live stream as immediate depends thus upon a perceptual media seamlessness.

The effect of seamlessness is the end result of elaborate technical production that both creates the illusion of presence but also establishes cinematic moments that remind the spectator that he or she is not *there*. Cameras are attached to tracks above the runway and to cranes and dollies in strategic locations at the corners – in addition to the traditional 'media pit' of press photographers located at the bottom of the runway. Franziska Bork Petersen notes that the frontal view from the media pit is offered in both 'look' photographs for print publications and 'the fashion show videos that fashion houses often release on their websites' (2013: 155). However, cameras also capture models at a diagonal or even from an aerial perspective; in all cases, the models stare straight ahead and, in most shows, remain detached. Live streams utilise continuous model shots similar to those of film and television, calculated to produce vicarious identification, but the camera can cut to alternate perspectives in a fraction of a second to maintain user interest. In one sense, the user possesses a superior view to that of an audience member, as they see multiple camera perspectives.[9] However, whereas spatial co-presence permits audience members to 'direct their own vision', cameras determine the user's focus in mediatised content (Auslander 2008b: 19). Camera shots operate in a pattern, consisting of a long, continuous, toe-to-head and/or frontal shot of the models as they start their march, and then a medium close-up of the upper torso, followed by a more full-body shot as the model turns. The model's walk is perceived as continuous, even as interstitial shots offer a closer look at ensemble and facial expression. Occasional extreme close-up shots permit the user to see details of a garment that are not discernible from the back risers, and aerial shots offer an omniscient, totalising view that is impossible to achieve in the performance space. Technical and aesthetic similarities between live streams and film, however, remind spectators of their position in front of a screen and often call attention to the presence of the elites as they take their seats or react to certain looks. In live streams for prominent fashion companies, a camera will often be placed so that models are seen from a diagonal or profile perspective with celebrities behind to enhance the exclusivity of the live event.

The first fashion show live streams

Victoria's Secret claims to have produced one of the first live stream fashion shows as early as 1999, before its move to television, in partnership with *Broadcast.com* and IBM. The event was advertised via a commercial that aired during the 1999 Superbowl, after which 'more than a million people immediately logged online after seeing the ad to look for the show – which wasn't airing for another week' (Storey 2016). Ed Razek, (now former) Chief Marketing Officer of parent company Limited Brands, admitted that the interface 'left a lot to be desired: it was about the size of two postage stamps in the middle of your computer screen' (as cited in Storey 2016). Nonetheless, 'Steve Jobs called it one of the 10 seminal events in the history of the Internet' (Razek, as cited in Storey 2016). Victoria's Secret streamed its 2000 show from the Cannes Film Festival, where it was held as an online fundraiser for Cinema Against AIDS. The event aired during the daytime in the United States and sparked concerns around lost work hours (Storey 2016). The show was produced by Alexandre de Bétak and was so 'successful' that users crashed the brand's website (Anaya 2013). The establishment of a televised fashion show in 2001 solved concerns around scheduling for a mass audience, at least in the United States. It is also probable that the live stream was not intended to sell lingerie so much as to respond to the Internet's usefulness as a medium for individual, scopophilic modes of spectatorship (see White 2006).

The end of the 2000s witnessed the first *concerted* attempts to live stream shows on the Fashion Month calendar. Alexander McQueen's 2009 attempt to live stream his 'Plato's Atlantis' presentation on *SHOWstudio* was botched due to a volume of web traffic that the site could not handle, but McQueen at the time expressed a hope 'to create special capsule collections for the public to buy immediately after seeing his collection' (Uhlirova 2013: 152). For Autumn/Winter 2010, Burberry became the first brand to fuse the live stream and its e-commerce platform: it streamed the fashion show for its ready-to-wear line Burberry Prorsum on its website and on Twitter and connected users to its website to purchase collection pieces for a limited window, six months prior to their arrival in stores (Uhlirova 2013: 152). Burberry estimated that 'more than 100 million users' witnessed this event (Amed 2010: n.p.). Despite numerous technical problems with the stream documented in the press and in social media posts, the press heralded the initiative as the future of fashion communication and observed that the e-commerce integration would offer the company invaluable 'consumer data' to inform its retail operations come autumn (Amed 2010: n.p.). Burberry went on to win the Digital Innovation award at the 2010 British Fashion Awards.

The live stream as cinematic

Despite companies' production investments, in their depiction of clothes in motion, most fashion show live streams read as more informational rather than performative or aesthetic. Companies have responded to this conundrum with a return to cinematic effects. The use of slow motion had, as of the late 2010s, infiltrated the full live stream broadcast, completing in a certain respect a circular process of remediation in which the live transmission assumes all of the technical capabilities that rendered film the ideal medium to represent fashion shows. The live stream for Raf Simons' debut for Calvin Klein Collection, at Fall/Winter 2017 New York Fashion Week, transmitted on Facebook Live but filmed with professional cameras, showed continuous shots (at disparate distances) as each model paraded down the first section of the two-aisle runway. As the next model turned towards the second aisle, however, the stream cut seamlessly to a slow-motion version of the previous model's walk. This kind of slow-motion effect can be achieved with the use of a high-speed camera in which recorded footage is run at normal speed to appear slow motion (Stark 2018: 176). The camera then reverted to the 'live' feed after a few seconds. The use of interspersed slow-motion effects within the 'live' stream allowed for increased time for visual assessment of each look and enhanced the effect of models' hair blowing out behind them – a throwback to the supermodel era. Transitions in speed also belied all sense of 'real time' as the user became aware that the slow-motion footage was repeating portions of the walk that we had witnessed seconds earlier, and that we were missing other looks that the live audience could see. Its use further created a curious sensation that the models' walks – and indeed 'real time' itself – had been intentionally slowed, which in effect it had. The most striking aspect of the slow-motion effect was how *familiar* it seemed to the user, conditioned to its reception from previous interactions with electronic media footage. This experimentation with cinematic technique indicates that footage remains intended to perpetuate a cinematic allure of fashion and an appreciation of fabric and bodies in motion.

Tommy Hilfiger's 'see now, buy now' spectaculars

While Burberry is credited with the first attempts to live stream its fashion shows concurrent with a hail to consumers to purchase the collection online, the more recent 'see now, buy now' business model has collapsed the seasonal time frame of promotion and retail, launching fashion collections in accordance with the 'real' temporal season rather than the calculated fashion season. American mainstream athleisurewear designer Tommy Hilfiger has become the most enthusiastic proponent of this model. His 'see now, buy now' fashion show series represents an apotheosis of the fashion show live stream as commercial spectacle, while its edits and overall production elements read as oriented towards a television broadcast, similar in aesthetic (and in casting) to that of Victoria's Secret. In September 2016, during New York Fashion Week, he produced his first TommyNow fashion show to launch a capsule collection (TommyxGigi) in collaboration with influencer/model-of-the-moment Gigi Hadid. To render the show simultaneously more elaborate and 'accessible', Hilfiger 'rented out a pier in New York's South Street Seaport neighbourhood' and produced a two-day branded carnival, making 1,000 tickets to the fashion show available to the public (Berlinger 2016).[10] Hilfiger followed this initiative with another TommyxGigi collection launched with a TOMMYWORLD carnival in February 2017 at California's Venice Beach, a location that bears more popular, celebrified associations. The live stream video archive, presented from FF Channel, reveals a similar circus-esque set-up with the runway and seating area adjacent to an amusement park stretch; the invited audience is demarcated with fences, but passers-by watch the production while the occasional cyclist speeds past. In a landscape opening shot, natural palm trees are interspersed with tall, round floodlights resembling moons, while a brief shot depicts attendees at a carnival booth. The camera cuts to the presentation *in medias res* as Hadid strolls down the L-shaped runway. A diagonal shot from far above zooms in on her walk, while a pit-level camera then lingers on her frame from her enviable torso on up; these shot distances then alternate as she rounds a corner to another runway section. The feed spends far more time focusing on Hadid than on the walks of the other (several dozen) models, most of whom are shown turning to and then strolling down the second section of the runway, with full-body frontal and toe-to-head shots intercut with more centred medium close-ups and then further diagonal shots from the front and back, in a disorienting succession with no more than ten seconds per shot. More than a minute elapses between Hadid's final walk and the finale, at which time the user sees a panoramic shot of the invited audience bifurcated by the runway – the first to indicate to the user the full length of the runway and that zooms out to reveal a lit-up, moving carnival ride behind, and the expansiveness of the boardwalk. The feed then cuts to a medium close-up shot of Hilfiger walking past with Hadid, taken, it appears, from a camera operated in the front row, and then back to a wider shot that centres the pair as the remaining models strut behind them in a lively cluster, waving their arms and prompting a celebratory atmosphere. Hilfiger waves his arms, extends thumbs up and blows kisses to the audience. A continuous shot is then taken from another camera operator that stands near the exit, showing the models from the waist up as they complete their parade, with certain models waving to the camera; the final shot is that of a performer near a fence, wielding devil sticks lit aflame.

Hilfiger has since taken his TommyNow fashion shows on an international tour to locations such as Milan and Shanghai, collaborating on capsule collections with celebrities like Zendaya and producing shows concurrent with official fashion weeks though not always on their calendar or even in the host cities. The brand's Spring/Summer 2020 collection, in collaboration with racing car driver Lewis Hamilton and R&B artist H.E.R., debuted during London Fashion Week in the cavernous Tate Modern in a hip-hop and hard rock-infused athleisure spectacle with a diverse cast of ninety-four models and influencers led by supermodel Naomi Campbell. While TommyNow's fashion extravaganzas represent the commercialism of the live stream taken to its extreme rather than the more informational (but still alluring) streams of most ready-to-wear presentations, these spectacles nonetheless demonstrate the way in which the camera captures the sense of the spectacular while mediating users' experience of immediacy to the production.

Conclusion

In the 2010s the live stream eclipsed film and television as the pre-eminent fashion show broadcast medium as it let consumers view the collections at the same time as the elite members seated in the actual presentation space. While fashion shows' 'real time' transmission represents a crucial shift in the time frames of fashion commerce, the practice should be read rather as an advancement in established mediatisation processes of a series of prerecorded fashion show scenes, transmitted to spectators via various screen interfaces. While this genealogy of fashion show transmission is divided up insofar as possible in order to elucidate media- and period-specific effects, it demonstrates too the manner in which online and digital media remediate earlier formats and now serve *as* a platform for streaming film and television content. Offering a context for the mediatisation of the fashion show via film and television illuminates how access to media and to fashion as a social institution has been democratised in increments over an extended period of time. Nonetheless, such an examination demonstrates that companies have continuously reinforced fantasies of aspirational consumerism under the rubric of trend forecasts, press profiles and entertainment. Discussions around the relation between the physical/material and the mediatised and around efficacious modes of fashion show communication were renewed at the turn of the 2020s due to the Covid-19 pandemic. The crisis did not simply shut down fashion shows (and resultant live streams) but forced practitioners to conceptualise new modes of communication, much of which blurred further the distinctions between fashion film and fashion show footage. In other instances, fashion critics were forced to watch live streams of social-distanced fashion shows in locations to which they were prohibited from travelling and assumed positionalities similar to that of consumers. The manner of the shows' transmission continues to evolve as affordances are developed and incorporated, and as devices permit intermediaries to stream short clips and/or entire shows concurrent with event producers. Still, the adoption of cinematic techniques of fashion transmission for online users has become evident in recent seasons, with the aim of showcasing clothes in as effective and enticing a manner as possible. Presentation streams, with audience members made visible due to the placement of multiple cameras, turn user focus to the fashion show itself as performance. The interface invites spectatorship of the total event and reminds spectators of a social exclusion to be rectified through 'immediate' purchase.

Notes

1. London Fashion Week was the first to centralise live streaming as part of the event, ensuring as of Autumn/Winter 2010 that all calendar shows could be streamed via its main website (Rice 2010: n.p.).
2. For purposes of scope, this chapter focuses on footage of real-life fashion shows shown in an informational albeit commercial context and brackets out the popular use of fictionalised or even real fashion show footage as glamourous additive in dramatic or

comedic cinema, a forum dealt with by scholars such as Stella Bruzzi (1997), Pamela Church Gibson (2012) and Charlotte Herzog (1990). Much of consumers' interest in live stream content is derived from its familiarity with these dramatised sequences in fictional narratives or narratives based on real life, as in the case of 2006's *The Devil Wears Prada* (see Gibson 2012). Discussion of the fashion show live stream also brackets out print media even as the technical apparatus and model walks still work in concert with the press (see Findlay 2017).

3. I credit Jennifer Braun, a student in my 2016 Master's course in Fashion and Popular Culture, whose collage-based research revealed the extent to which print magazines have co-opted social media phrases, using hashtags as heads or 'swipe right' to tell the reader to turn a page.
4. For a more detailed discussion of the 'real time' economies of the live stream, in relation to Tom Ford's fashion shows, see Halliday (2017).
5. I also, for reasons of scope, bracket out discussion of digital film as an alternative artistic/communication medium to fashion shows (see Uhlirova 2013).
6. This more journalistic fashion television is distinct from a more 'commercial' fashion television (so named) that arose in the late 1990s in which fictional or reality-format television series undertook fashion industry collaborations in order to outfit characters, and real-life fashion brands were invoked within the mimetic frame (Warner 2014: 29).
7. Arrington (2017) contrasts the more restrained aesthetic of *Style with Elsa Klensch* to MTV's later, more youthful and music video-oriented *House of Style* (1989–2000), hosted by supermodel Cindy Crawford.
8. Television broadcast innovation occurred parallel to the first uses of film to document athletic events. Leni Riefenstahl is credited with being the first documentary film-maker to use camera tracking to capture the fluid motions of athletes for *Olympia* (1938); the film also demonstrated advances in slow motion (Andrew 1999: 183–4).
9. As Rosie Findlay (2017) observes, the live fashion show spectator's view of a collection is often restricted by persons in front of them, if seats are not tiered, or if the spectator has to stand in the back rows.
10. The full video archive of the 2016 fashion show does not appear to be available at the time of writing.

References

Amed, Imran. 2010. 'Digital Scorecard | Burberry 3D Live Stream'. *The Business of Fashion*, 25 February. Available at https://www.businessoffashion.com/articles/digital-scorecard/digital-scorecard-burberry-3d-live-stream (accessed 4 July 2022).

Anaya, Suleman. 2013. 'Alexandre de Bétak, Fashion's Wizard Producer'. *The Business of Fashion*, 12 July. Available at https://www.businessoffashion.com/articles/creative-class/the-creative-class-alexandre-de-betak-fashion-show-and-event-producer (accessed 4 July 2022).

Andrew, Geoff. 1999. *The Director's Vision: A Concise Guide to the Art of 250 Great Filmmakers*. Chicago, IL: A Cappella Books.

Arrington, Deidra W. 2017. 'Elsa Klensch: The Inventor of Fashion Television'. *Film, Fashion & Consumption*, vol. 6, no. 2, 157–63.

Auslander, Philip. 2008a. 'Live and Technologically Mediated Performance'. In *The Cambridge Companion to Performance Studies*, edited by Tracy C. Davis, 107–19. Cambridge: Cambridge University Press.

Auslander, Philip. 2008b. *Liveness: Performance in a Mediatized Culture*, 2nd edn. London and New York: Routledge.

Bay-Cheng, Sarah. 2010. 'Theatre History and Digital Historiography'. In *Theatre Historiography: Critical Interventions*, edited by Henry Bial and Scott Magelssen, 125–36. Ann Arbor: University of Michigan Press.

Berlinger, Max. 2016. 'Tommy Hilfiger Brings the Circus to Town'. *New York Times*, 11 September. Available at https://www.nytimes.com/2016/09/11/fashion/tommy-hilfiger-gigi-hadid-collaboration-new-york-fashion-week.html (accessed 4 July 2022).

Berry, Sarah. 2000. *Screen Style: Fashion and Femininity in 1930s Hollywood*. Minneapolis: University of Minnesota Press.

Bolter, Jay David and Richard Grusin. 2000. *Remediation: Understanding New Media*. Cambridge, MA: MIT Press.

Bork Petersen, Franziska. 2013. 'Authenticity and Its Contemporary Challenges: On Techniques of Staging Bodies', unpublished doctoral dissertation, Stockholm University, Stockholm. Available at http://su.diva-portal.org/smash/get/diva2:661329/FULLTEXT02.pdf (accessed 4 July 2022).

Bruzzi, Stella. 1997. *Undressing Cinema: Clothing and Identity in the Movies*. London and New York: Routledge.

Chetty, Derick. 2012. 'FT Falls Out of Fashion; Fashion Television Cancelled After Decades of Influencing Trends'. *Toronto Star*, A3, 12 April.

Church Gibson, Pamela. 2012. *Fashion and Celebrity Culture*. London: Berg.

Couldry, Nick. 2012. *Media, Society, World: Social Theory and Digital Media Practice*. Cambridge: Polity Press.

Evans, Caroline. 2001. 'The Enchanted Spectacle'. *Fashion Theory*, vol. 5, no. 3, 271–310.

Evans, Caroline and Jussi Parikka. 2020. 'Introduction: Touch, Click and Motion: Archaeologies of Fashion Film after Digital Culture'. *Journal of Visual Culture*, vol. 19, no. 3, 323–39.

Findlay, Rosie. 2017. '"Things to be seen": Spectacle and the Performance of Brand in Contemporary Fashion Shows'. *About Performance*, vol. 14–15, 105–19.

Fulsang, Deborah. 2004. 'The Fashion of Writing, 1985–2000: Fashion-themed Television's Impact on the Canadian Fashion Press'. In *Fashion: A Canadian Perspective*, edited by Alexandra Palmer, 315–38. Toronto: University of Toronto Press.

Geczy, Adam and Vicki Karaminas. 2016. *Fashion's Double: Representations of Fashion in Painting, Photography and Film*. London: Bloomsbury.

Grusin, Richard. 2010. *Premediation: Affect and Virality after 9/11*. London: Palgrave Macmillan.

Halliday, Rebecca. 2017. 'Tom Ford and the Live Fashion Show as a Mediatized Spectacle'. *Comunicazioni Sociali: Journal of Media, Performing Arts and Cultural Studies*, vol. 15, no. 1, 119–28.

Herzog, Charlotte. 1990. '"Powder Puff" Promotion: The Fashion Show-in-the-Film'. In *Fabrications: Costume and the Female Body*, edited by Charlotte Herzog and Jane Gaines, 134–59. London: Routledge.

Low, Elaine. 2019. 'Why the Victoria's Secret Fashion Show Was Cancelled'. *Variety*, 22 November. Available at https://variety.com/2019/tv/news/victorias-secret-fashion-show-canceled-why-1203413186/ (accessed 4 July 2022).

MacAloon, John J. 1984. 'Olympic Games and the Theory of Spectacle in Modern Societies'. In *Rite, Drama, Festival, Spectacle: Rehearsals Toward a Theory of Cultural Performance*, edited by John J. MacAloon, 241–80. Philadelphia, PA: ISHI.

Rappaport, Erika Diane. 2001. *Shopping for Pleasure: Women in the Making of London's West End*. Princeton, NJ: Princeton University Press.

Rees-Roberts, Nick. 2018. *Fashion Film: Art and Advertising in the Digital Age*. London: Bloomsbury.

Rice, Simon. 2010. 'London Fashion Week to Be Streamed Live'. *The Independent*, 19 February. Available at https://www.independent.co.uk/life-style/fashion/news/london-fashion-week-to-be-streamed-live-1904888.html (accessed 4 July 2022).

Rocamora, Agnès. 2012. 'Hypertextuality and Remediation in the Fashion Media'. *Journalism Practice*, vol. 6, no. 1, 92–106.

Rocamora, Agnès. 2013. 'New Fashion Times: Fashion and Digital Media'. In *The Handbook of Fashion Studies*, edited by Sandy Black et al., 61–77. London: Bloomsbury.

Rocamora, Agnès. 2017. 'Mediatization and Digital Media in the Field of Fashion'. *Fashion Theory*, vol. 21, no. 5, 505–22.

Schneider, Rebecca. 2011. *Performing Remains: Art and War in Times of Theatrical Reenactment*. New York: Routledge.

Schweitzer, Marlis. 2009. *When Broadway Was the Runway: Theater, Fashion and American Culture*. Philadelphia: University of Pennsylvania Press.

Stark, Gill. 2018. *The Fashion Show: History, Theory and Practice*. London: Bloomsbury.

Storey, Kate. 2016. 'The Untold History of the Victoria's Secret Fashion Show'. *ELLE*, 29 November. Available at https://www.elle.com/culture/a40862/victorias-secret-fashion-show-timeline/ (accessed 4 July 2022).

Tomlinson, John. 2007. *The Culture of Speed: The Coming of Immediacy*. London: SAGE.

Turner, Graeme. 2010. *Ordinary People and the Media: The Demotic Turn*. Los Angeles, CA: SAGE.

Uhlirova, Marketa. 2013. '100 years of the Fashion Film: Frameworks and Histories'. *Fashion Theory*, vol. 17, no. 2, 137–58.

Warner, Helen. 2014. *Fashion on Television: Identity and Celebrity Culture*. London: Bloomsbury.

White, Michele. 2006. *The Body and the Screen: Theories of Internet Spectatorship*. Cambridge, MA: MIT Press.

Wissinger, Elizabeth. 2013. 'Fashion Modelling, Blink Technologies and New Imaging Regimes'. In *Fashion Media: Past and Present*, edited by Djurdja Bartlett, Shaun Cole and Agnès Rocamora, 133–43. London: Bloomsbury.

Wissinger, Elizabeth. 2014. '#NoFilter: Models, Glamour Labor, and the Age of the Blink'. *Interface/*, vol. 1, no. 1, 1–20.

Wissinger, Elizabeth. 2015. *This Year's Model: Fashion, Media, and the Making of Glamour*. New York: New York University Press.

Audio-visual references

Fashion File (1989–2009). CBC Television and CBC Newsworld, Toronto.
FashionTelevision (1985–2012). CityTV and CTV/FashionTelevision, Toronto.
Florence Rose Fashions (1916–17).
House of Style (1989–2000). Music Television (MTV), New York.
RAW (2005–12). FashionTelevision Channel and CHUM Limited, Toronto.
Sex and the City (1998–2004). Darren Star Productions and HBO Entertainment, Los Angeles and New York.
Style with Elsa Klensch (1980–2001). CNN.

Chapter 11

Documenting fashion in the era of Instagram: a critical reading of Asri Bendacha's *Follow Me* and Chiara Ferragni's *Unposted*

Marco Pedroni

Despite the variety of social, institutional and commercial actors that contribute to defining the meaning of fashion, scholars often postulate the existence of a fashion imaginary as a 'stock of images, values, practices and rules that dominate the western fashion industry and that its participants take for granted in their relationship with fashion' (Mora, Rocamora and Volonté 2016: 177). A social imaginary, according to Taylor's definition, is 'that common understanding that makes possible common practices and a widely shared sense of legitimacy' (Taylor 2004: 23). If such an entity exists in the domain of fashion (Mora and Pedroni 2017), digital media are a major contributor to its creation – not only via the activity of bloggers, Instagrammers and social media influencers (Rocamora 2011, 2012, 2018; Pedroni 2015, 2016) who have formed a new category of cultural intermediaries (Bourdieu 1984) able to define and legitimise cultural tastes and trends, but also due to their ability to attract the interest of the legacy media such as TV, cinema and magazines responsible for the diffusion of fashion imaginary.

Nowhere is this more visible than in recent documentaries on the rise of fashion influencers. This essay considers two documentaries produced in the late 2010s and distributed by two of the largest international video streaming platforms: Chiara Ferragni's *Unposted* (2019), directed by Elisa Amoruso and available on Amazon Prime Video, and Asri Bendacha's *Follow Me* (2017), included in the Netflix catalogue. My contribution is a comparative and critical analysis of both, investigating two aspects of each. One is the different status of the protagonists – Ferragni as a leading actor of the fashion and influencer marketing industry, and Bendacha as a film-maker not normally involved with fashion. The aims of each production are also examined, namely Ferragni's mission of self-consecration as a fashion icon and Bendacha's semi-ironic work, the first of its kind about the commodification of the digital persona.

The analysis, located in broader research on fashion influencers (Colucci and Pedroni 2021; Pedroni 2022), will highlight the main issues emerging from these documentaries, among them the commercialisation of the Self and the audience, the monetisation of everyday practices presented on social media, digital entrepreneurship, the democratisation of access to the fashion world, and the commodification of authenticity. These topics are evidence of the power of digital influencers to shape, directly or indirectly, the evolution of contemporary fashion imaginary. I conclude with a discussion on the legitimation of the digital turn in the fashion industry which results from both documentaries, despite their heterogeneous purposes.

Fashion influencers and the digital media

Social media influencers, also labelled 'digital influencers' or simply 'influencers', may be defined as people creating online content, distributed via digital platforms such as blogs, Facebook, Snapchat, YouTube, Twitter, Instagram and, more recently, TikTok, to an audience whose size can vary from a few to several million users, also known as followers (see Pham 2011; Marwick 2013; Findlay 2017). Business and marketing literature (see Backaler 2018) as well as influencer marketing companies have popularised the idea of classifying influencers according to the number of their followers. Launchmetrics, for example, defines influencers as micro (from 10,000 to 100,000 followers), mid-tier (100,000 to 500,000), mega (500,000 to 2 million) and all-star, with more than 2 million followers. Among the variations of this accounting method is the 'nano' category, as defined by Maheshwari in a 2018 *New York Times* article, and the 'celebrity' description for influencers with more than one million followers. The numbers are generally based on the total of the influencer's Instagram audience, considered the reference platform for influencer marketing in the early 2020s. For research purposes, the preference is to maintain a critical distance from these marketing-derived categories and the narratives promoted by 'marketing' (Zwick and Bradshaw 2016), focusing instead on the practices performed by individual influencers.

A *fashion* influencer is a media presence materially or symbolically tied to the domain of fashion, a person who regularly posts fashion outfits or who collaborates with fashion brands. An expanding contamination of the commercial areas an influencer is linked to is making it increasingly difficult to distinguish the fashion influencer from other categories. In addition to the 'pure' fashion digital practitioners who have gained an institutionalised position in the field of fashion by regularly attending fashion shows and events, occupying the cover of fashion magazines, and maintaining long-term relationships with established fashion brands, for example, there exists an army of influencers who appear on Instagram or other channels in association with beauty, travel, food and other products. This category may be more adequately described as *lifestyle* influencers, individuals who act as brands in themselves and who over time build a consistent editorial line spanning a range of product areas. The coronavirus pandemic, in particular during the 2020 lockdown periods, has seen many fashion digital practitioners evolve into beauty, home and food influencers. As *Wired* magazine has observed, 'everyone is baking bread, everyone's cat-cowing in their living rooms and everyone – if they have the time and means, of course – is turning to candles, baths, and cuddling' (Tsapovsky 2020).

Even if independent influencers with no commercial links to brands do exist, the label 'influencer' generally denotes a digital practitioner who is remunerated for the content they create and distribute online. Since the mid-2000s and the affirmation of fashion bloggers, fashion has become a field where the commercialisation of the digital presence is particularly evident (Findlay 2015). Typically, influencers begin their careers by posting digital content on one or more platforms in order to construct a 'fashionable persona' (Titton 2015). If an influencer's profile is able to attract a numerically significant audience, the interest of relevant brands may result in their investment in the influencer as a digital marketing tool. The production and circulation of this branded content on digital platforms has spawned a completely new industry, influencer marketing.

Practitioners of this new marketing world are asked to take part in promotion campaigns and are remunerated in various forms from 'gifting' (receiving products for free) to long-term collaborations ruled by formal contracts. Such remuneration is the influencer's 'price' for allowing brands to use the result of their digital efforts, the audience. The field of fashion has seen a progressive institutionalisation of the influencer character, its transformation from amateur to professional agent (Pedroni, Sádaba and SanMiguel 2017). Today, less than two decades after the emergence of the first fashion bloggers, influencing has been acknowledged as a form of labour made of digital, immaterial, promotional and aesthetic practices (Rocamora 2018).

Fashion influencers operate on multiple platforms, of which Instagram hosts the majority of content producers and followers. Conceived as a site for photo sharing, it is currently the most native platform for influencer marketing (Leaver, Highfield and Abidin 2020: 32). Clearly, the success of fashion on Instagram is linked to the visual nature of the platform. The original app has evolved and new tools and functions – for example videos, stories, IGTV and, more recently, Reels – have been added, features which fashion influencers are able to exploit to entertain their audiences. This perpetual updating of the software is in part the result of competition strategies. The introduction of stories was aimed at neutralising the similar functions offered by a competitor, Snapchat, while Reels is a response to TikTok short videos. The innovations allow Instagram to consolidate its monopoly. It would, however, be a mistake to portray fashion influencers as individuals belonging to an online domain, separate from the general field of fashion. Fashion bloggers emerged prior to the advent of Instagram (Rocamora and Bartlett 2009; Luvaas 2013, 2018; Findlay 2015; Lewis 2015) and the label of influencer first established itself in the second half of the 2010s as a self-congratulatory category which included all relevant digital practitioners, regardless of the platform on which they based their success. Influencers are an integral part of the tangible world of fashion. They sit in front row seats at fashion catwalks, appear on legacy media, publish books, work as fashion or marketing consultants, design capsule collections, open fashion stores, and manage e-commerce websites. They play a role in fashion that is considerably more significant than is suggested by the act of 'merely' posting pictures online.

The affirmation of fashion influencers may be explained by many factors both external and internal to the world of fashion. Important external considerations include the technological progress that has brought us social networking sites, as well as the labour market's transformation into a neoliberal arena rewarding self-branding and promotion efforts (see Duffy and Hund 2015). Internal factors include changes within the fashion industry such as the transformations of fashion companies affected by the crisis of brands (Klein 2000), and of the fashion editorial system where digital technologies have enhanced a bottom-up model of information flows and challenged the role of legacy media intermediaries.

What is clear to fashion professionals as well as to scholars is that, nowadays, it is no longer possible to consider influencers as a marginal or superfluous presence, since they are an active part of the commercial and advertising machine of contemporary fashion. And viewed as such, documentaries on influencers distributed by major streaming platforms may be read as further contributions to a cultural and symbolic legitimation of the business of influence.

Follow Me by Asri Bendacha

Follow Me is a 2017 documentary written and produced by the Dubai-based filmmaker Asri Bendacha and distributed by Netflix. In the film's opening scenes, Bendacha approaches two strangers and asks, 'Sorry, do you have Instagram? . . . I just need followers, so, like, I'm asking. I just need followers.' The strangers invite the film-maker to put his phone away and sit with 'real' friends instead of looking for followers. 'Come have a drink with us,' they say. The first few minutes of the film serve therefore to illustrate the distinction, grounded in common sense yet often misunderstood, between an authentic offline experience and a virtual online life.

Thirty-two-year-old Bendacha introduces himself in the film as a non-social media person interested in exploring the phenomenon of influencers after reading a newspaper article about Instagrammers being paid US$5,000 for posting a photo. Referring to these Instagram posters as social media influencers, his documentary attempts to answer the question, 'How can a person get paid to post a picture on social media?' In his quest for an answer, Bendacha presents himself as someone who, ignorant of the mechanics of an online presence, earnestly wishes to understand the logic of the influencer marketing industry and possibly earn a living from it. The documentary oscillates between the serious and the comic, alternating an investigation through interviews with successful influencers, photographers and PR and marketing agencies with scenes where Bendacha distributes flyers in the street or takes public transport with the plea 'Help me, follow me!' on his cardboard sign (Figure 11.1).

As both the director and the narrator of the film, Bendacha presents his audience with a critical yet ironic investigation into a recently established business form. Overall, the documentary lacks journalistic rigour and objectivity and on occasion displays a superiority complex towards his subjects, limiting his portrayal of influencers to young social media users able to monetise their ability to produce content for the web. The mechanisms of the influencer industry are not investigated in depth, and many of the interviews produce predictable answers which Bendacha fails to elaborate to an original interpretative framework. *Follow Me* focuses on a portrayal of the world of

Figure 11.1 Bendacha begs for followers on the streets of Dubai. *Follow Me*, Asri Bendacha, 2017. Screenshot by author.

young Middle Eastern influencers, despite an 'ethnographic' incursion in the United States in search of Instagram executives and Hollywood-based online celebrities. It also does not emphasise fashion over any other area of influencer activity. The first part of the documentary is the most effective, especially the interviews with influencers. The American excursion suffers from an excess of irony and a mockery of influencer marketing. The film's naive and somewhat prejudicial views present the business of influence as a world detached from reality. However, when seen as the attempt of a non-expert to understand the mechanisms of this new economy of visibility, the film has the merit of showing the point of view of several of the industry's protagonists.

At least four themes within Bendacha's film deserve mention. First, the battle to define 'influencer'. Lama al Akeel (@lama.alakeel, 579K[1]) personifies a common effort to maintain distance from the role. 'Personally, I don't like to call myself an influencer.' Similarly, Moudz (@mrmoudz, 184K) prefers being considered a blogger rather than an influencer, while Saufeeya Bint Goodson (@feeeeya, 208K[2]) opts for 'content creator'. Jamie Wilks, a digital marketing expert, stigmatises the army of irrelevant influencers under the label of 'blaggers' instead of bloggers, 'normal people who want things for free or want to be paid for posting about stuff'. In a similar vein, he also compares influencers to 'human billboards' because they can be used to advertise anything as required. The influencer marketing industry is implicitly presented as a hierarchical domain where several levels of professionalism – and success – exist.

But the process of commercialisation and monetisation, and this is the second issue, is seen as problematic at any of these levels. Influencers' words are generally intended to frame their work as a cultural enterprise detached from economic interests. Akanksha Goel, general manager of Socialize Agency, describes influencers as a source of inspiration for consumers, and when required to outline how the collaboration with brands works, two young YouTubers explain that brand advertising should not be direct, in order to avoiding damaging the relationship of trust with the audience. While it is clear that influencers monetise their audience and performance by promoting products and services for companies which target their followers, the economic dimension is denied or presented as a non-core aspect of the work, which is an activity based on a passion and alignment with the public.

A third key issue of the documentary, and of the influencer marketing industry, is the commodification of the influencer's labour. Bendacha's investigation of the commercial services designed to boost follower numbers and engagement rates is eye-opening. After contacting one of these service providers, he is asked, 'Are you interested in buying real followers or fake followers?' The company then offers to provide the wannabe influencer with bespoke audiences targeted by age, gender and location. Bendacha subsequently decides to pay US$33 per week to discover how the service functions. Sue B. Zimmerman, the founder of *Insta-Results*, explains in an interview how to grow an audience, offering further evidence of the existence of professional consultancy services promising success through numbers on Instagram.

The fourth and final theme worth mentioning relates to influencer labour and the ensuing fatigue. The viewer is led to question co-founder and COO of *Contend* Philip Alberstat's insistence that there are low or no barriers to entry to the online world and digital content production. 'We all are content creators,' he says in typical marketing lingo as if referring to a known, obvious fact. Why, then, is Bendacha unable to garner more than a hundred or so followers during the shooting of the documentary, despite all his efforts? The answer, clear to the viewer, is that despite the frivolity and narcissism of some protagonists of the industry, and despite short cuts such as buying fake followers, achieving success as an influencer is just not as easy as it appears. YouTuber HaylaTV (@haylatv, 1.7M) offers an explanation: 'It's really just about selecting the right brand for my brand.' Influencers are themselves a brand, one built through fatigue and determination, a brand equipped with an editorial consistency that obliges the influencer to negotiate the content and tone of the advertised posts with the investor, rather than passively posting whatever the external, vendor brand has chosen. This (partial) independence is linked to the mythology of authenticity (Rocamora 2018; see also Peterson 1997, 2005; Banet-Weiser 2012). The success of an influencer on social media is presented as the result of 'being real', being true to their own brand: 'Showing how you live, showing the real you,' as another interviewee states, to demonstrate to followers that 'we are all the same'. A narrative of this type places sincerity and passion at the core of influencers' work through a de-emphasis bordering on denial of the presence of economic motivations and strategic behaviours.

Unposted: Ferragni as a pop icon

Chiara Ferragni – Unposted is a documentary directed by Elisa Amoruso focusing on the life and career of the world-famous Italian influencer. It was presented in September 2019 at the Venice Film Festival, given a limited screening in Italian cinemas on 17, 18 and 19 September, and then made available on Amazon Prime Video streaming services. Critics gave the film negative reviews and dismissed it as 'propaganda' and 'a long commercial disguised as a movie' (Mereghetti 2019; Ravarino 2019). Despite this, the film was the most-watched documentary ever released in the history of Italian cinema, grossing more than €1.6 million over three days of screening.

Unposted was designed as an event rather than a movie, one aimed at drawing the attention of fans and generating related online content, interaction and engagement. As such, it should be contextualised by taking into account Ferragni's professional past. With an Instagram account exceeding 20 million followers in 2020, she is unanimously recognised as one of the most influential fashion digital practitioners in the world. A 2019 publication by Launchmetrics and WGSN regarding the numbers of millions of dollars in media impact value (MIV) influencers are individually able to generate ranked Ferragni at the top of their listing of global influencers and celebrities. The economic value of her MIV in the 2019 report, more than US$18 million, can only have increased since then.

The high number of collaborations, initiatives and events that have made her famous in the fashion field and in popular culture make the compiling of a concise history of Ferragni's entrepreneurial evolution difficult. Her career, first as a blogger, then as an influencer, began in 2009 when she launched her blog *The Blonde Salad* while a law student to publish photos of herself with a description of the clothing and accessories she was wearing. In the first post on 12 October, written in both Italian and in English and titled 'Here I am!', she introduced herself by saying,

> Here we are at the first independent blog driven by needs of communication and personalization. After years spent on Flicker and other different web communities, I felt like I had to move on and create a space for my own. The name is 'The Blonde Salad' because this blog is gonna be a salad of myself. The ingredients will be those which have always characterized me: fashion, photography, travel and lifestyle. (Ferragni 2009)

Ferragni launched the blog and was the front person with Riccardo Pozzoli as CEO, and within only a few months it had attracted the interest of thousands of web users and, consequently, that of commercial investors and fashion journalists. Fashion blogging in Italy in 2009 was still an almost unknown phenomenon. Internationally, however, several names had already established reputations, and the new activity's economic potential was clear. Only three months after opening the blog, Ferragni received her first invitation to Milan Fashion Week. National newspapers and television programmes then sought interviews with Ferragni, already labelled the 'fashion icon of the web' and a 'fashion blogger starting a new era'.

Ferragni's career from this point onwards moved from outsider to key player in the field of fashion communication through her collaboration with fashion brands such as Benetton and Yoox in 2010, Burberry and Yamamay in 2012, Vuitton and Superga in 2013; through awards, such as her nomination as 'blogger of the year' at the 2015 BlogLovin Awards; and through public acknowledgement of her importance in the fashion industry as well as in popular culture. Evidence is seen in her 2014 appearance in the popular TV show *The Simpsons*, as a character drawn by Matt Groening, or her stint as an appointed judge on the popular American talent show dedicated to fashion designers, *Project Runway*. In 2015, her photo featured on the cover *Vogue España*, the first blogger on a *Vogue* cover page. The *Financial Times* included her amongst the three biggest female names in the new digital luxury landscape in 2016, and *Forbes* named her in its prestigious '30 under 30' ranking. Ferragni was even the model for a Barbie doll.

However, her history cannot be understood without underlining the entrepreneurial character of Ferragni as a 'brand'. She was among the first Italian bloggers to understand the potential of Instagram. After registering two million followers in 2013, the blog was transformed into a lifestyle magazine site and the Chiara Ferragni Collection was launched. The blog further evolved into an e-commerce site in 2016. In 2017, the brand 'Ferragni' opened its first flagship store in Milan.

The move to Instagram made the label of 'blogger' obsolete, and it was replaced with that of influencer. Ferragni ended her sentimental and professional association with Pozzoli and became not only the face but also the CEO of her business activities. Her new personal relationship with the Italian rapper Fedez also opened a new season of storytelling which today continues to occupy a large part of her Instagram posts and stories, commencing with their 2016 engagement, through the pregnancy and birth of their son Leone and then the marriage-event in 2018, the most 'Instagrammed' Italian event ever with over 30 million interactions (D'Aloia and Pedroni 2021). Ferragni's uniqueness lies in her being not only a blogger and influencer of reference in the fashion field, but also a pop icon recognised as such by experts and non-experts alike, as a result of a series of initiatives including her 2015 visit to Harvard University where she was hosted and interviewed for a Business School case study (Keinan et al. 2015), the organisation of the exhibition *You: The Digital Fashion Revolution* at the Milan design and art museum La Triennale, the production of the 2019 documentary *Unposted*, to which I will return below, and the recent public commitment during the coronavirus epidemic in 2020 when she promoted a fundraiser for a Milanese hospital.[3]

This necessary premise may make it less surprising that a fashion influencer is able to become the subject of a documentary presented at one of the world's most important film festivals and then distributed on a popular streaming platform. This warrants a closer examination of the film, which alternates Ferragni's own words and the opinions of people who have a personal or professional relationship with her.

Unposting Ferragni

The title of the documentary is in itself a false promise, conveying the idea that a look behind the scenes in Ferragni's life will reveal information which has not already been converted into social media content. As such, the film is not offered to a spectator but to a follower, someone already familiar with the film's contents because it has already been revealed on Ferragni's Instagram profile or other media. The film consists of a series of interviews and footage featuring moments or events in Chiara's life. It makes extensive use of material taken from social networks, particularly Instagram, and includes vintage footage of her childhood taken during family holidays (Figure 11.2). The aesthetics of the film therefore conform to the aesthetics of social networks – an audio-visual diary made up of stories and interviews with Ferragni, people from her entourage and fashion professionals. It is a cross-media product made up of an assemblage of materials produced on different channels and platforms (D'Aloia and Pedroni 2021). *Unposted* offers a complete impression of Ferragni's personality and career through time through archival and previously unseen material produced specifically for the film which covers her entire life, becoming a 'reveal all' to anyone who has not previously heard of her. The documentary is effective insofar as it adds a filmic appendix to a narrative that has already built on social networks, describing how she built her blogger career by posting photos of inexpensive outfits and, through collaborations with fashion and luxury companies, how she evolved into an Instagram persona with a permanently impeccable, sophisticated wardrobe, even when at home, where she occasionally wears clothing from her own design collection.

Figure 11.2 This illustration is intended to show the use of low-resolution amateur videos from the 1980s (recorded by Ferragni's father) in the documentary as a visual strategy to emphasise authenticity. *Unposted*, Amoruso, 2019. Screenshot by author.

The 88 minutes of the documentary reveal at least four themes relevant to our analysis. First, the role of the blogger/influencer. Frequent references to her professional results underline the presentation of Ferragni as the personification of a successful blogger. 'When I was only 22–23 years old, I had a team of 10 people working for me – the blog generated 30,000 hits in the first month,' she says when referring to the origins of her blog. The invitation to the first fashion show was experienced as a consecration, and, in one of the less convincing passages of the documentary, where Ferragni's fairy-tale narrative turns into an unnecessary business case study, she elaborates on the company structure and boasts of the million-dollar supply chain and the eighty people she employs. From the opening scenes, the film responds to an implicit question typically voiced by anyone experiencing discomfort or surprise at the advent of this new digital profession: how is this possible? What explains the success of a young person, an outsider in the fashion field, in becoming a privileged interlocutor of major fashion brands and a public figure with a global audience on Instagram, as well as a digital entrepreneur? Interviews with fashion authorities such as designer Lorenzo Serafini and Dior's artistic director Maria Grazia Chiuri reveal possible answers. The former insists on influencers as a means to shorten the distance between the glossy presentation and the actual consumer in fashion:

> The role of the influencers was certainly to shorten the distance between the fashion world and the real people who looked at fashion as something unattainable ... The influencers really broke this pattern, this distance between real life and the reality of fashion ... Through Chiara, the public who did not previously approach fashion could really identify with an inspirational figure, a figure who became a model for millions of girls.[4]

Chiuri, on the same note, evokes the notion of authenticity, claiming that 'Chiara is authentic. She sends a message: if you want to, you can do it too.'

These statements from Serafini and Chiuri employ a rhetoric widely used by influencers themselves to support stereotypical mythologies of the digital practice of influencing. Similarly, Moira Forbes, the publisher of *ForbesWoman* and a *Forbes* columnist, evokes the widely disseminated theme of digital democratisation whereby anyone with a smartphone can have a global voice and impact. *Unposted* is therefore a quintessential example of the commonly held belief that social media are democratising tools because a previously unknown person, through the inversion of a previously top-down flow of information, may now become a valid source of information.

A second theme present in the film is that of labour. In addition to its intended confirmation of the glamorous patina of an influencers' workday, the film also emphasises the hard work required to position oneself in this new professional field. The thesis illustrated is that a career as influencer requires devotion, effort and sacrifice. Silvia Venturini Fendi, creative director of accessories, menswear and children at her family's brand, provides us with an example. While praising Ferragni as a 'visionary' person having the 'disruptive force of a popstar', she highlights the pressure the influencer is exposed to and the risk of feeling like a marketing product. This leads to the requirement to always be perfect; an influencer like Ferragni cannot risk a moment of failure.

Part of an influencer's labour involves being exposed to haters. Ferragni reveals that she has been the subject of harsh criticism since the creation of her Flickr account, even before *The Blonde Salad* was launched. Haters have accused her of 'polluting' a digital platform designed for professional photography with non-professional photographs, and in particular of appropriating a social media environment designed for other purposes. In fact, this is exactly what Ferragni has done, successfully, with any of the platforms she has used during her career. In noting the difficulties influencers face, at least at the beginning of their careers, in overcoming the prejudices of fashion professionals, Ferragni states that despite the positive results of her blog, 'I didn't feel accepted by people in the fashion industry . . . When I started out, I was really a fish out of water. When I arrived at an event and I was one of the few little girls and I didn't know anyone, and they did everything they could to make you feel uncomfortable.' The documentary's third narrative strand, centred on Ferragni's success, is built on the premise that she has been able to overcome these industry obstacles.

Evidence of this entry into the closed circles of fashion is shown in the film scenes of Ferragni sitting next to Paris Hilton during a fashion show. At this point in the film, the discourse regarding the figure of the influencer becomes less generalised and focuses on the peculiarity of the Ferragni case and the exceptional qualities behind her rise to fame. Ferragni presents herself as a digital entrepreneur 'who started out as a blogger in 2009' and the 'managing director of my company, which is TBS Crew. My blog, which used to be simply my diary, has become a full-fledged site [a company] with an editorial part . . . and an e-commerce part'. She also mentions further business activities, including her talent management company providing consultancy for digital projects and managing the profiles of other influencers, among them her two sisters; the development of digital courses such as the *Beauty Bites Masterclass* series; and the company producing the

Chiara Ferragni Collection of footwear, clothing and accessories. During this parenthesis within the documentary, a quasi-LinkedIn description of activities, Ferragni gives freely of business-related data, listing the number of worldwide retailers of her collection, the industries connected to and the number of people employed by her company, in what seems a desire to give validity and substance to her self-description as an entrepreneur.

This narrative, supported by Ferragni's interview with Diane von Fürstenberg, underscores her striving to be recognised as an icon of female empowerment in a world traditionally dominated by men. 'You don't need a man to do all this,' she says, referring to Pozzoli, her former boyfriend and manager. The statement, however, unintentionally ends up relegating even her husband to an ancillary role. The celebration of the self-made woman is completed with the repetition of a follower's comment, more or less the same sentence pronounced by Chiuri quoted above, which Ferragni presents as proof that in life you can do what you want.

These three themes intertwine and prepare the ground for the fourth area worthy of analysis in the documentary and expressed by several of the interviewees, namely the mythologisation of Ferragni. According to the editor-in-chief of *Vanity Fair Italia*, Simone Marchetti, 'Chiara possesses the contemporary Esperanto, the natural language of social media ... The medium is her talent ... She is her medium.' The Italian artist Francesco Vezzoli states that Ferragni's normality becomes universality, that the influencer is 'the elective daughter of Marina Abramovich and Big Brother, Chiara is a concept, she is the idea of exposing herself day and night: pain, pleasure, failure, success, tripping, heel'.

The inclusion of interviews with writers, artists and creative workers serves to ennoble reflection on the Ferragni phenomenon. Screenwriter Chiara Barzini states that there is no conflict in Ferragni's storytelling on Instagram because 'she reinvented the genre of storytelling on social media'. It is perhaps the only sentence in the documentary, presented as a contribution to the construction of the Ferragni myth, in which an implicit criticism can be glimpsed, one related to the removal of the conflictual dimension from a digital storytelling. The myth lies in the apparent contradiction between Ferragni as a celebrity and Ferragni as the girl-next-door. Her Instagram feed alternates glossy pictures of the influencer in the model poses typical of fashion and lifestyle magazines with amateur-like photos and videos taken at home or in the car to document daily life with her family.[5] Ferragni also continues to post selfies made in front of a mirror, in the style of early fashion bloggers,[6] thus evoking a hobbyist ideal of the influencer practice.

Both on social media and in *Unposted*, the references to origins and everyday life function to feed the rhetoric of authenticity, so that the glossy collaborations with the institutional field of fashion do not call into question the spontaneity and realness of the influencer.

Consecrating influencers

The two documentaries are very different in terms of objective and position of the protagonists. The titles reveal two opposing perspectives: *following* is the activity of those who watch and admire, *posting* is that of those who produce content. While Bendacha invites other people to follow him because he has no audience, *Unposted* is presented by a leading influencer who has millions of followers and who 'reveals' content which is neither new nor secret. There are also significant differences with regard to stylistic elements. *Unposted* is not devoid of amateur material, such as Ferragni's childhood videos shot by her parents, but it is in *Follow Me* that we find the rawest aesthetics. Interviews are often conducted in public, noisy locations with several scenes, particularly of the trip to America, filmed with cameras hidden or mounted on bicycles or by hand-held mobile phones. In contrast, the settings that form the backdrop of *Unposted* seem to have left no detail of light, framing or furnishing to chance. Bendacha's insistence on amateurish scenes serve to emphasise his naivety as an outsider in the world of influencer marketing, while Ferragni's amateur content is designed to underline her authenticity or to evoke the aesthetics of Instagram stories as discussed above.

Despite these differences and the diametrically opposed tones of Bendacha's ironic curiosity vis-à-vis Ferragni's self-celebration, the two films can be read as an agenda of key topics to be addressed in any present and future analysis of the influencer marketing industry. This list includes the ambiguity of a monetisation legitimately pursued by influencers even while they euphemise it under the guise of producing a cultural content undistorted by the commercial pressures of brands; the claim of authenticity despite sophisticated levels of exposure and sponsored content; the presentation of digital platforms as factors aiding a democratisation of the rapport with normal citizens and of the empowerment of an individual's abilities; the tension between the glamorous life stories related on Instagram and the considerable effort required for success. Of most importance for the purposes of my analysis here is the role played by each of the documentaries in the consecration of influencer marketing.

Follow Me contributes to the external legitimisation of influencers. The director and protagonist's lack of links to the field of fashion or any other cultural industry to which the development of influencing is linked reflects the perspective of the man-in-the-street, someone alien to the logic of social media functioning but who is nevertheless aware of the existence of a new and curious category of digital practitioners and who wants to understand how this world functions. Bendacha as 'researcher' occasionally mocks his subjects, lingering on the frivolity of some influencers and denouncing the existence of commodification of likes and followers. However, his film does reveal how highly developed the recently founded industry already is, and its potential to replace the traditional advertising methods of legacy media.

On the other hand, *Unposted* presents itself as a muscular display of strength by the world's leading fashion influencer. Ferragni demonstrates a proven competence in the contextualisation of the (commercial) activities of a digital practitioner as an expression of cultural, technological and social innovation, for example in the case of initiatives such as the *You* exhibition. With a social media following unachievable for most of her colleagues, the economic power assured by her companies, and the support both in terms of recognition and financing of relevant fashion brands, Ferragni has accomplished a double objective with her autobiography, namely a simultaneous consecration in the temples of high culture and of the mass market through the release of the film at the exclusive Venice Film Festival and its immediate distribution through the attainable Amazon Prime Video.

Both films are implicitly weighed down by the sedimented prejudice that the commercial world precludes cultural value. Although neither Bendacha nor Ferragni attempt to measure themselves against the theses of the Frankfurt School, the two documentaries do give the impression of a self-defence of a nascent cultural industry. When Simone Marchetti states in *Unposted* that influencers are 'living advertising pages', he does not intend to condemn the lucrative dimension of influencing, but rather to pave the way for the subsequent statements from David Craig, professor at the University of Southern California, who explains the Ferragni phenomenon as a culture construction process. According to Craig, creators and followers are united in a social bond through which the interests and the community of the latter are transformed into a source of income for the former. Similarly, the naturalness of the teenagers and young influencers interviewed by Bendacha when they claim to have turned a passion into a professional and profitable business is impressive.

In the final part of *Unposted*, Ferragni talks about the possibility of media overexposure of her son Leone. 'For me, it would have been really impossible not to do it, it would have been a too strong deprivation for me not to publish my reason for living, also because what I am talking about is an absolutely positive message.' Her husband Fedez also intervenes, stating, 'Leo is the son of two public figures who are exposed and have decided to be exposed mediatically, and he would inevitably have lived through this exposure by osmosis. Having to hide it at all costs for two people who relate their lives would have been a more cumbersome force than hiding it.' Fedez underlines that Leone has never been commercially exploited, meaning that he has not been used for sponsored collaborations. Once more, naturalness is the key theme. As Fedez states, 'We tell the experience of the parenthood of two young people who are entering this world.' The couple denies that there is a business logic behind every choice of which content to publish. What is striking here is not whether or not the claim is true – an assessment beyond the purposes of this essay – but its naivety. Even if a video about the private life of an influencer does not involve direct and immediate monetisation, the content does allow the influencer to potentially attract new followers, building the audience that may later be exposed to brands and lead to a subsequent improvement of the influencer's value.

Conclusion

Both documentaries in fact reveal the lofty ambitions of an influencer, and indeed, that it is permissible to boast of one's success – influencers combine a lack of denial regarding the economic and commercial dimensions of their work with a claim to a wider cultural role. They see themselves as builders of online communities, producers of entertainment and dispensers of authenticity, all as part of a (seemingly) horizontal relationship with their followers. The almost hyperactive Bendacha fails to give us a completely negative view of the influencing phenomenon, and ultimately provides an external legitimacy, albeit with critical cues. *Unposted* pursues and achieves the obvious goal of placing the fashion influencer par excellence, Chiara Ferragni, in the quintessential role of the protagonist of the changes, both technological and cultural, and the opportunities presented by digital media. This filmed consecration of the influencer marketing industry reverberates to further audiences through its distribution by two global entertainment players, Netflix and Prime Video. The cultural processes underlying the emergence of digital influencing as a social practice are obviously more complex, as a recent but already well-established body of scientific studies demonstrates (for example, Abidin 2017; Duffy 2017; Rocamora 2017). However, future studies should closely study how influencer marketing is related and then transformed into 'common sense', including through high visibility media products such as documentaries distributed by major streaming platforms.

Notes

1. Here and in the rest of the section, I give the name of the influencer with their Instagram nickname and the number of Instagram followers registered in December 2020.
2. At the time of writing, the Instagram account appeared to be disabled. The reported number of followers refers to July 2016 (see Ghanem 2016).
3. The October 2016 exhibition in Milan was organised by the fashion magazine *Grazia* and *The Blonde Salad* to aid 'shedding light on the revolutions and changes that web influencers implement and have implemented in the world of all-round communication', according to the event's press release. The exhibition focused on two aspects of fashion: first, the centrality of the consumer/user in the alleged bottom-up revolution of which fashion blogs are an expression, presenting Ferragni and bloggers in general as ordinary people with a direct relationship with other ordinary people, and hence the emphasis on the *You* in the title; and second, the reconstruction of a history of fashion blogging capable of providing social and cultural legitimacy to the phenomenon.
4. The Italian interviews reported in this section have been translated into English by the author.
5. An example of this contrast is the branded post for Pomellato (11 December 2020, https://www.instagram.com/p/CIputxHhTCF) which is immediately counterbalanced in the blog by a video of Ferragni the mother playing with her son Leone (7 December 2020, https://www.instagram.com/p/CIdXt99qzQX/?hl=en).
6. One example being a post from 29 November 2020 (https://www.instagram.com/p/CIK7LjXB0Vz/).

References

Abidin, Crystal. 2017. '#familygoals: Family Influencers, Calibrated Amateurism, and Justifying Young Digital Labor'. *Social Media+ Society*, vol. 3, no. 2, 1–15.

Backaler, Joel. 2018. *Digital Influence: Unleash the Power of Influencer Marketing to Accelerate Your Global Business*. Cham: Palgrave Macmillan.

Banet-Weiser, Sarah. 2012. *AuthenticTM: The Politics of Ambivalence in a Brand Culture*. New York: New York University Press.

Bourdieu, Pierre. 1984. *Distinction: A Social Critique of the Judgement of Taste*. Cambridge, MA: Harvard University Press.

Colucci, Mariachiara and Marco Pedroni. 2021. 'Got to Be Real: An Investigation into the Co-Fabrication of Authenticity by Fashion Companies and Digital Influencers'. *Journal of Consumer Culture*, online, 1–20. DOI: 10.1177/14695405211033665.

D'Aloia, Adriano and Marco Pedroni. 2021. '#Ferragnez. Anatomia di un sincretismo mediale'. In *SuperTele. Come guardare la televisio*, edited by Luca Barra and Fabio Guarnaccia, 81–92. Rome: MinimumFax.

Duffy, Brooke Erin. 2017. *(Not) Getting Paid to Do What You Love: Gender, Social Media, and Aspirational Work*. New Haven, CT: Yale University Press.

Duffy, Brooke Erin and Emily Hund. 2015. '"Having it all" on Social Media: Entrepreneurial Femininity and Self-Branding among Fashion Bloggers'. *Social Media+Society*, vol. 1, no. 2, 1–11.

Ferragni, Chiara. 2009. '"Here I am!" *The Blonde Salad*'. Posted online 12 October 2009. Available at http://www.theblondesalad.com/talents/chiara-ferragni/here-i-am.html (accessed 31 July 2017).

Findlay, Rosie. 2015. 'The Short, Passionate, and Close-Knit History of Personal Style Blogs'. *Fashion Theory*, vol. 19, no. 2, 157–78.

Findlay, Rose. 2017. *Personal Style Blogs: Appearances that Fascinate*. London: Intellect Books.

Ghanem, Khaoula. 2016. '5 Hijabi Fashion Influencers On Our Radar'. *Vogue Arabia*, 21 July. Available at https://en.vogue.me/archive/culture/hijab-fashion-influencers-instagram-dina-tokio-zozoliina-ruba-zai-amaal-said-feeeeya-modest-muslim-style/ (accessed 4 July 2022).

Keinan, Anat, Kristina Maslauskaite, Sandrine Crener, and Vincent Dessain. 2015. *The Blonde Salad*. Harvard Business School Case, 515-074, pp. 1–25.

Klein, Naomi. 2000. *No Logo*. London: Flamingo.

Launchmetrics and WGSN. 2019. 'Data on the Runway '19: The Voices Dominating Fashion Week'. Available at https://www.launchmetrics.com/it/risorse/whitepapers/fashion-week-donna-analisi-dati (accessed 4 July 2022).

Leaver, Tama, Tim Highfield, and Crystal Abidin. 2020. *Instagram: Visual Social Media Cultures*. Cambridge: Polity Press.

Lewis, Reina. 2015. 'Uncovering Modesty: Dejabis and Dewigies Expanding the Parameters of the Modest Fashion Blogosphere'. *Fashion Theory*, vol. 19, no. 2, 243–69.

Luvaas, Brent. 2013. 'Indonesian Fashion Blogs: On the Promotional Subject of Personal Style'. *Fashion Theory*, vol. 17, no.1, 55–76.

Luvaas, Brent. 2018. 'Street-Style Geographies: Re-mapping the Fashion Blogipelago'. *International Journal of Fashion Studies*, vol. 5, no. 2, 289–308.

Maheshwari, Sapna. 2018. 'Are You Ready for the Nanoinfluencers?' *New York Times*, 11 November. Available at https://www.nytimes.com/2018/11/11/business/media/nanoinfluencers-instagram-influencers.html (accessed 4 July 2022).

Marwick, Alice E. 2013. *Status Update: Celebrity, Publicity, and Branding in the Social Media Age*. New Haven, CT: Yale University Press.

Mereghetti, Paolo. 2019. 'Chiara Ferragni Unposted, la recensione del Mereghetti: sembra un film di propaganda nordcoreano, voto inclassificabile'. *Il Corriere della Sera*, 5 September.

Mora, Emanuela and Marco Pedroni. 2017. 'New Frontiers of the Fashion Imaginary'. In *Fashion Tales: Feeding the Imaginary*, edited by Emanuela Mora and Marco Pedroni, 13–25. Bern: Peter Lang.

Mora, Emanuela, Agnès Rocamora and Paolo Volonté. 2016. 'Editorial: Feeding the Imaginary'. *International Journal of Fashion Studies*, vol. 3, no. 2, 177–84.

Pedroni, Marco. 2015. '"Stumbling on the Heels of My Blog": Career, Forms of Capital and Strategies in the (Sub)Field of Fashion Blogging'. *Fashion Theory*, vol. 19, no. 2, 179–99.

Pedroni, Marco. 2016. 'Meso-Celebrities, Fashion and the Media: How Digital Influencers Struggle for Visibility'. *Film, Fashion & Consumption*, vol. 5, no. 1, 103–21.

Pedroni, Marco. 2022. 'Two Decades of Fashion Blogging and Influencing: A Critical Overview'. *Fashion Theory*, online, 1–32. DOI: 10.1080/1362704X.2021.2017213.

Pedroni, Marco, Teresa Sádaba and Patricia SanMiguel. 2017. 'Is the Golden Era of Fashion Blogs Over? An Analysis of the Italian and Spanish Fields of Fashion Blogging'. In *Fashion Tales: Feeding the Imaginary*, edited by Emanuela Mora and Marco Pedroni, 105–24. Bern: Peter Lang.

Peterson, Richard A. 1997. *Creating Country Music: Fabricating Authenticity*. Chicago, IL: University of Chicago Press.

Peterson, Richard A. 2005. 'In Search of Authenticity'. *Journal of Management Studies*, vol. 42, no. 5, 1083–98.

Pham, Min-Ha T. 2011. 'Blog Ambition: Fashion, Feelings, and the Political Economy of the Digital Raced Body'. *Camera Obscura: Feminism, Culture, and Media Studies*, vol. 26, no. 1, 1–37.

Ravarino, Ilaria. 2019. 'Chiara Ferragni-Unposted, il film alla Mostra di Venezia è solo un lungo spot pubblicitario'. *Leggo.it*, 5 September. Available at https://www.leggo.it/spettacoli/cinema/chiara_ferragni_unposted_venezia_ultime_notizie_oggi-4713983.html (accessed 4 July 2022).

Rocamora, Agnès. 2011. 'Personal Fashion Blogs: Screens and Mirrors in Digital Self-Portraits'. *Fashion Theory*, vol. 15, no. 4, 407–24.

Rocamora, Agnès. 2012. 'Hypertextuality and Remediation in the Fashion Media'. *Journalism Practice*, vol. 6, no. 1, 92–106.

Rocamora, Agnès. 2017. 'Mediatization and Digital Media in the Field of Fashion'. *Fashion Theory*, vol. 21, no. 5, 505–22.

Rocamora, Agnès. 2018. 'The Labour of Fashion Blogging'. In *Fashioning Professionals: Identity and Representation at Work in the Creative Industries*, edited by Leah Armstrong and Felice McDowell, 65–80. London: Bloomsbury.

Rocamora, Agnès and Djurdja Bartlett. 2009. 'Blogs de mode: les nouveaux espaces du discourse de mode'. *Sociétés*, vol. 104, 105–14.

Taylor, Charles. 2004. *Modern Social Imaginaries*. Durham, NC and London: Duke University Press.

Titton, Monica. 2015. 'Fashionable Personae: Self-identity and Enactments of Fashion Narratives in Fashion Blogs'. *Fashion Theory*, vol. 19, no. 2, 201–20.

Tsapovsky, Flora. 2020. 'Could the Coronavirus Kill Influencer Culture?' *Wired*, 14 April. Available at https://www.wired.com/story/coronavirus-covid-19-influencers/ (accessed 4 July 2022).

Zwick, Detlev and Alan Bradshaw. 2016. 'Biopolitical Marketing and Social Media Brand Communities'. *Theory, Culture and Society*, vol. 33, no. 5, 91–115.

Audio-visual references

Follow Me. 2017. Directed by Asri Bendacha. Written by Asri Bendacha. Netflix.
Project Runway. 2004–present. Created by Eli Holzman. Buena Vista Television/Disney-ABC Domestic Television (2004–10), The Weinstein Company (2005–17), Lantern Entertainment (2019–).
The Simpsons. 1989–present. Created by Matt Groening. 20th Television.
Unposted. 2019. Directed by Elisa Amoruso. Screenplay by Elisa Amoruso. Amazon Prime Video.
You: The Digital Fashion Revolution. 2016. Exhibition organised by *Grazia* and The Blonde Salad. 7–13 October, Milan, La Triennale di Milano.

Index

Page numbers in italics are illustrations, and those followed by n are notes

Abruzzese, Alberto, 186
academic fashion scholars, in documentaries, 179n
activism, 26–7, 29n, 33–6, *36*
Adams, Mary, 159–60
advertisement, 4, 15, 28n, 81–2, 87, 88–92, 95–9, 184–6, *196*
affect, 203–23
affective experts, 215–21
affective trans-temporal remembrance, 174–7
affordable clothes, 72–3
Agel, Seller and Masius, 186
Agente Segreto (Lionello Massobrio) [Cori-carousel], 189, 190, *190*
Agnew, Vanessa, 165
The Agronomist (2003) [documentary], 114
Ahmed, Sara, 208
Air Jordan sneakers, 27
Aktiv Hushållning, 85–6, 97
al Akeel, Lama, 253
Alberstat, Philip, 254
Alex James: Slowing Down Fast Fashion [documentary], 26
Alexander McQueen: Savage Beauty [exhibition], 14
Allen, Robert C., *New Film History*, 59–60
Amazon Prime Video, 248, 255, 263, 264
Americana, 212–14
Amoruso, Elisa, 248, 255–7
Anderson, Fiona, 125

Annabelle Serpentine Dance (Edison film 1895), 42
Antonaglia, Federica, 17
Antoni & Gehlin, 86
'Archaeology of Fashion Film' (2017–19) project, 2, 228
Architectural Digest [magazine], 219
archival footage, 18, 19, 35, 124, 126, 127, 129, 133, 144–7, 160, 172, 174
archive aesthetics, 165–7
archive effect, 167
Archivio Nazionale Cinema d'Impresa, 183–202
Armani, Giorgio, 14, 29n
Arrington, Deidra W., 244n
artisans, 21–3
Arts and Humanities Research Council (AHRC), 2, 228
ARWA, 71
Assmann, Aleida, 164
Assmann, Jan, 164
Atelier Versace, 132
Aufderheide, Patricia, *Documentary Film: A Very Short Introduction*, 120n
Der Augenzeuge [newsreels], 60–8, *66*, 69, 72–4
 East German fashion in, 65–7
 East and West German fashion in, 67–8
Auslander, Philip, 229–30
Austin, Thomas, 11
Australian Fashion Week, 229–30

Austrian fashion, 71
Auteliano, Alice, 188
autobiographical film-making, 218

Balençiaga, Cristóbal, 128–9
Ballerina: Fashion's Modern Muse [exhibition], 135–6
ballet, 135–6
Bande à part [podcast], 178
Bangladeshi factories, 24
Banton, Travis, 48
Barbie dolls, 256
Barnouw, Erik, 112, 120n
Baron, Jaimie, 166–7
Barzini, Chiara, 261
Baudelaire, Charles, 159
Bay-Cheng, Sarah, 230
BBC fashion history documentary, 159–81
Becker, Bessi, 70
Beckman, Anders, 86, 96
Beckmans College of Design, 86, 91, 95, 96, 98
Beesley, Philip, 151–2
behind the scenes, 13, 39, 41–3, 54, 234
Beker, Jeanne, 234
Bell, Erin, 162
Bendacha, Asri, 248–68, 253
Benjamin, Walter, 107–8, 168
    The Arcades Project, 168
Berlin Olympics 1936, 236
Berlin: symphony of a Metropolis (Walter Ruttman, 1927) [film], 110
Bétak, Alexandre de, 234, 239
Bide, Bethan, 169–70
BIG [exhibition], 151
Biki, 187, 189–90
Bill Cunningham New York (Richard Press, 2010) [documentary], 13, 102–21, *104*, *107*
Binder, Pearl, 159–60, 178n
binding technique, 219
Bint Goodson, Saufeeya, 253
biographical documentary, 15–17
biopics, 178
Biossance, 216, *217*

Blanks, Tim, 234
Blessed Sacrament Mothers' Club, 49
Blick in die Welt [newreels], 60
blockbuster fashion exhibition, 14, 141n
bloggers, 15, 120, 229, 250, 251, 253, 255–7, 259, 265n
BlogLovin Awards 2015, 256
The Blonde Salad [blog], 256, 265n
Blow, Isabella, 19–20
blue jeans, 22–3
Bolter, Jay David, 228, 230, 237
Bonniers Månadstidning [magazine], 86
Bonwits department store, 103
books, 216
Bordwell, David, 60
Bormann, Heinz, 66, 66, 67, 73, 77n
Bourdieu, Pierre, 209
Boxer, Posey, 144
Bra Bohag, 86
brand websites, 231–2
Braun, Jennifer, 244n
Bravo, 203
Brettkelly, Pietra, 22
Breward, Christopher, 167, 171
Britannia franchise (BBC) [TV], 162
British Fashion Awards 2010, Digital Innovation award, 240
British Film Institute, 36
British Style Genius series (BBC2) [TV], 161, 172–3, 175–6
Broadcast.com, 239
Brown, Helen Gurley, 50
Bruzzi, Stella, 14
Burberry, 239–40
Burnham, Dorothy K., 149

Calabrese, Omar, 184
Caldwell, John, 42
    Production Culture: Industrial Reflexivity and Critical Practice in Film and Television, 42–4
call to mind-images, 187
Calvin Klein Collection, 240
camera equipment, 69–70

Camilleri, Izzy, 148–9
Campbell, Naomi, 242
Canada, 144, 149
Canadian Broadcasting Company (CBC), 144
Cannes Film Festival, 239
Caoduro, Elena, interview, 32–8
Capucine, 188, 192–4
Carnaby Street, 48
Carosello [TV], 182–202
Carosello. Pubblicità e televisione 1957–1977 [exhibition], 199
carousels, 182–202
Carrozzini, Francesco, *Franca: Chaos and Creation*, 16
Cartier-Bresson, Henri, 116
catwalk footage, 123, 132–3, 138, 154
CBC, 145
CBC Newsworld, 234
celebration of iconic garments, 27–8
celebratory approach to fashion documentaries, 15–17
celebrities
  television, 189–90
  young, 194–7
A Chanel Tie Embroidered by Joseph Wong, ROM, 2020, 149
Chapman, Harold, 116
cheap clothes, 25
Chez Ninon, 103–6, 115
China Blue [film], 22–3
Chiuri, Maria Grazia, 259–61
Christian Dior: Behind the Scenes at ROM (2017) [exhibition], 134, 140, *140*, 146–7, *147*
Christian Dior: Designer of Dreams [exhibition], 141n
Church Gibson, Pamela, 14, 16, 17
Cimorelli, Dario, 199
cinema, early, 44–8
Cinema Against AIDS, 239
cinema attendance, 45, 76n, 232–3
cinema of attractions, 13–14, 45
cinéma verité, 16, 109–10, 112–13, 119

cinematography, 37, 59–60, 62–4, 75, 87, 110–11, 119, 126, 129, 132–3, 192–3
  work reports, 77n, 78n
CityTV, 234
civic clubs, 46, 49
Clark, Judith, 134–5
Clayburgh, Jill, 47
close-ups, 14
Clothes to Die For (Zara Hayes, 2014) [documentary], 25
Clothes-Line (BBC) [TV], 159–60, 178n
CNN, 234
Cohen, Bernard, 77n
Cold War, 71
collective memory, 163–5
comedy shorts, 187–8
commentary, 63, 65, 66, 67, 68
Condé Nast Entertainment, 29n
confidence, 214
Confino, Alon, 164–5
The Container Store, 209
Contend, 254
content creators, 253
contextualization, 123–5, 127, 135, 183, 228, 255, 263
cooperative savings and housing, 83–4
co-presence, 237–8
Cori-carousel series, 182–202, *190*, *196*
Corner, John, 166
Cosgrave, Bronwyn, 15
Cosmopolitan [magazine], 50
costume design, 39
Costume Institute of the Metropolitan Museum of Art, 108
Couldry, Nick, 236
The Courtship of Eddie's Father (Vincente Minnelli, 1963) [film], 42
Covid-19 pandemic, 243, 250, 257
Craig, David, 263
Crawford, Cindy, 244n
cues, 60, 71, 75, 77n
cultural intermediaries, 209–10, 248–68
cultural memory, 58, 75–6, 163–5, 168–72, 178
cultural remembrance, 159–81

Cunningham, Bill, 102–21, *104*, *107*, *116*, *117*
Czechoslovakia, 65

dance, 69
Darcella, Aria, 'Chic Report,' 111
Davidsson, Bengt, 81–2
day-to-day lifestyle documentation, 218–19
Dean, Jodi, 219
DEFA, 77n
Demme, Jonathan, 114
demo tapes, 43
democratisation of fashion, 234, 249
democratisation of luxury, 182–202
department stores, 39–42, 46
Designer DIY, 120
designer monograph exhibition, 128–33, 138
Designing Woman (Vincente Minnelli, 1957) [film], 40–2
Deutsche Film AG (DEFA), 60–1
Deutsche Wochenschau GmbH, 77n
development triad, 83–4, 86
The Devil Wears Prada (David Frankel, 2006) [film], 21
Dhaka garment factory collapse, Bangladesh 2013, 25
Diana Vreeland: The Eye Has to Travel [documentary], 17
@diarmuidferry, *213*
digital media, 226–68
Dior, 13, 22, 134, 146, 150, 259
Dior, Christian, 78n
Dior and I (Frédéric Tcheng, 2014) [documentary], 13, 22
Dior Archive, 146
direct cinema, 112–13
documentarian of clothes, 104
documentaries
 academic fashion scholars in, 179n
 interactive, 112
 observational, 112–13, 132–3
 talking heads, 20, 26, 130, 135, 138, 171, 174
documentary
 biographical, 15–17
 industrial, 185
 modes of representation, 112–13
 process, 102–21
documenting the ugly truth of fashion, 23–7
Dominique, Jean, 114
Dorfles, Piero, 187, 192
Drago, Eleonora Rossi, 188–91, *190*
Dralon, 70
Dressed: The History of Fashion [podcast], 178
Duke of Windsor, 113–14
durational design, 166
DVD, 12

East and West Germany
 differences and similarities of, 72–4
 fashion in Der Augenzeuge, 67–8
East German fashion, in *Der Augenzeuge*, 65–7
East German newsreels, 57–80
Eaton's archives, 144–6
Ebba von Eckermanns Textilier, 95
Eckert, Charles, 'The Carole Lombard in Macy's Window,' 48
Edgar, Robert, 16
edutainment, 125, 184–6, 198
Edwards, Sam, 162
Ehrenreich, Barbara, 209
Eleonora Rossi Drago (Anton Giulio Majano) [Cori-carousel], 189
Elite Elegance: Couture Fashion in the 1950s [documentary footage in exhibition], 127, 133, 144, 145
Elsaesser, Thomas, 188
Emporio Armani, 29n
environmental cost of fashion, 1, 11, 22–3, 33–4
Erll, Astrid, 163–5
 Cultural Memory Studies, 161
Etsy, *218*
Ettedgui, Peter, 20
Evans, Caroline, 13–14, 44–6, 168, 228, 233
exceptionalism, 82
exhibiting
 a certain historical movement, 133–4
 theory and the conceptual underpinnings of fashion, 134–6

exhibition narrative, 122–43
exhibitions
    and moving images, 126–7
    in museums, 14, 178n
    themed, 133–4, 147
exploitation of labour, 22–3

Fab Five, 203–23
fabula, 76n
Facebook Live, 232, 240
family, 19–20, 29n, 114–15
fashion
    Austrian, 71
    and beauty as self-care, 204, 210–14
    blogs, 229
    as commodity, 22–3
    designers, 15–17, 73
    East German, 65–7
    education, 86
    environmental cost of, 22–3, 33–4
    French, 73, 74
    fur, 68–9
    gender equality in, 105–6
    as high art, 17
    historian, 102–21
    history in museums, 178n
    houses, 73
    hubs, 64
    human cost of, 22–3, 24
    illustrators, 68, 82, 86
    as important subject for newsreels, 61–3
    increased literacy of, 14
    industrial shorts on television, 186–91
    Italian, 182–202
    labour, 22–3
    in the live stream, 237–8
    luxury, 18
    Made in Italy, 29n
    making of, 13, 21–3
    in motion, 227
    Paris, 68, 69, 73, 74
    production of, 13
    ready-to-wear, 182–202, 227, 236
    shorts, 45
    on the street, 103, *117*
    teenage, 81–101
    on television, 233–6
    ultrafast, 1
    West and East German, 67–8
    West German, 68–71
    western in West German newsreels, 71–2
fashion, memory and time, 167–71
fashion documentaries, 2, 13–15
    celebratory and critical approaches, 11–31
    celebratory approach to, 15–17
    critical approach to, 21–3
fashion exhibitions
    and moving images, 126–7
    in museums, 14, 178n
    themed, 133–4
fashion featurettes, 39–56
Fashion File (CBC Newsworld, 1989–2009) [TV], 234
fashion film, 14, 39–56, 55n
Fashion Follows Form [exhibition], 147–8, 152
fashion history documentary, 159–81
fashion influencers, 248–68
Fashion Institute, 126
fashion journalism, 2, 4, 84, 86, 96, 136, 235
Fashion Month circuit, 227, 239
fashion photography, 69, 103–6
fashion shows, 13–14, 39–56, 77n
    commercial and civic function of, 48–9
    department stores, 39
    on film, 232–3
    filmed, 45, 54
    live stream, 227–47
    mediatisation of, 228, 229–30, 235, 242–3
    as sites of industrial reflexivity, 39–56
    and/as sporting events, 236–7
Fashion Theory [magazine], 122
Fashion Unpicked: The 'Wet Collection' by Mary Quant [film in exhibition], 131, *131*
fashion websites, 229
Fashion Week Online [website], 231–2
fashion-moving-image culture, 54
fashiontainment, 235–6

FashionTelevision (CityTV, 1985–2012) [TV], 234–5
fashion-themed television, 234
fast fashion, 1, 22–7, 29n
    Fath, Jacques, 57–8, 71, 78n
Fedez, 257, 264
@feeeeya, 253
female identities, 187–8
female spectatorship, 45
femininity, 192
feminism, 35–6, 43
Fendi, Silvia Venturini, 260
Ferragni, Chiara, 248–68, 258
FF Channel, 241
film, 10–157
    commissioned, 15–16, 19, 29n
    in-house production, 124, 128, 131, 137, 155
    industrial, 188
    museum film, 123, 124, 128, 137, 139, 149
film degradation, 18
film rolls, *107*
film truth, 119
filmed fashion shows, 45, 54
filmed interviews, 69–70
film-within-film, 88–90
Finamore, Michelle, 45
The Financial Times [newspaper], 256
Finding Vivian Maier [documentary], 111
Findlay, Rosie, 229–30, 244n
Firclough-Isaacs, Kirsty, 16
FitOn, 216
Flickr, 260
Follow Me (Asri Bendacha) [documentary], 248–68, 253
followers, 252–5, *253*, 262
Fontana sisters, 187
Forbes, Maria, 259
Forbes [magazine], 256, 259
ForbesWoman [magazine], 259
Foucault, Michel, 165
Fox Studios, 40
Fox tönende Wochenschau [newsreels], 60
Franca: Chaos and Creation [documentary], 16
France, 13–14
France, Tan, 203–23
    Naturally Tan: A Memoir, 216
Frankfurt School, 263
free world, 71–3
French fashion, 68, *69*, 73, 74
French newsreel, 68
French tuck, 212, *213*, 217
Frisk, Ragnar, 87–8
Fulsang, Deborah, 235
functionalism, 91–2, 93, 96, 98
Functionalism and the International Style, 86
fur fashion, 68–9
Fürstenberg, Diane von, 261

Gable and Lombard [biopic], 47
Galliano, John, 150–1
gender equality in fashion, 105–6
German Wirtschaftswunder (economic miracle), 57
GFT Archive, Turin, 182–202
Gianni Versace Retrospective [exhibition], 131–3
Gilda (Charles Vidor, 1946) [film], 58
Gill, Rosalind, 205
Giuggioli, Livia, 26–7, 29n
'The Glamorous Wonderful World of Helen Rose' [fashion show], 46
glamour labor, 120
Godall, Eric, 68–9
Goddard, Molly, 128
Goel, Akanksha, 254
Goffman, Erving, *The Presentation of Self in Everyday Life*, 50–2
Golden Bayer Schere, 74
Gomery, Douglas, *New Film History*, 59–60
Gomorrah (Matteo Garrone, 2008) [film], 29n
Google search, 35
Gorman-Murray, Andrew, 206
Granny Takes a Trip, 175–7
Granzotto, Emiliana, 187
Grasso, Aldo, 185
Gray, Ann, 162
Grazia [magazine], 265n

The Great British Sewing Bee (BBC 2013–present) [TV], 14
Greenpeace, 36
Gregg, Ronald, 52
grooming, 212
Gruppo Finanziario Tessile (GFT), 182–202
Grusin, Richard, 228, 230, 237
Guardian [newspaper], 26
Guo Pei, 22
Gyllene Gripen, 89–90, 94, 96

H&M, 29n
Hadid, Gigi, 241–2
Halbwach, Maurice, 163–4
Halligan, Benjamin, 16
Halston (Frédéric Tcheng, 2019) [film], 37
Hamilton, Lewis, 242
happiness, 208
Hård, Mikael, 83, 86
Harper's Bazaar [magazine], 17
Hartnell, Norman, 144
Harvard University, 257
haute couture, 21, 28, 82, 89, 91, 96–7, 99, 102–3, 108, 129, 133, 150, 233, 236, 237
@haylatv, 254
Hayworth, Rita, 58
Head, Edith, 39–56
  The Dress Doctor, 49
  How to Dress for Success, 49–50
Heavenly Bodies [exhibition], 141n
Hediger, Vinzenz, 185
Heim, Jacques, 72
Hemmens forskningsinstitut (Household Research Institute) (HFI), 86, 97–8
Hepburn, Katharine, 37–8
H.E.R., 242
Herzog, Charlotte, 45, 233
Heumann, Joseph K., *Film and Everyday Eco-Disasters*, 23
Hilfiger, Tommy, 'see now, buy now' spectaculars, 241–2
Hindson, Catherine, 45
Hollywood, 39, 46, 48–9, 136
'The Hollywood Story' [fashion shows], 49

homosexuality, 115, 203–25
Horne's department store, Pittsburgh, 46–8
Horsley, Jeffrey, 137
Houlès, Pierre, 116
House of Style (MTV, 1989–2000) [TV], 244n
housewives' films, 81–101
How Was It Made? Constructing Balenciaga's Historically Inspired Evening Dress [exhibition video], 129
HSB, 84
human billboards, 253–4
human rights, 22–3, 33
Husmors Filmer AB, 81, 84, 97–8
Husmors-Journalen (Housewife's Magazine), 82
Huyssen, Andreas, 169
hypermedia, 230

IBM, 239
Ice Follies, 40
IGTV video, 217
IKEA, 84, 86, 97
immediacy, 227, 230, 233–5, 242
industrial documentary, 185
industrial fashion shorts, on TV, 186–91
industrial film, as an event, 188
industrial reflexivity, 39–56
influencer labour, 254–5, 260
influencer marketing, 251, 253–4, 262
influencers
  consecrating, 262–4
  fashion, 248–68
  Instagram, 220
  lifestyle, 250
infomercial film, 15
in-house film production, 124, 131
Inspired by Balençiaga [vignette], 128–9
Instagram, 210, 216–20, 248–68
Insta-Results, 254
interactive documentaries, 112
intermediaries, cultural, 209–10, 248–68
International Exhibition, Paris 1900, 126
international fashion show, Warsaw 1956, 67

International Newsreel Association (INA), 77n
internet spectatorship, 229–32
interview-style featurette, 40–2
Iris van Herpen: Transforming Fashion and *Philip Beesley: Transforming Space* [exhibition], 151–2
Italy, 29n, 182–202

James, Alex, 26
Japanese designers, 105
Jenss, Heike, 167–9
Jones, Dan, 37
Jong, Wilma de, 11
@jvn, 216, *217*, 220

Katja of Sweden, 96
Kavka, Misha, 204
Kelly, Patrick, 219
'Kenny Kenny', 108
Kino Pravada, 119
Klein, William, 53
Klensch, Elsa, 234
Koda, Harold, 108
Koivunen, Anu, 167
  Theatres of Memory, 162–3
Kondo, Marie, 209
Konfektions AB Zober, 88, 89, 94, 95, 96
Konsthögskolan, Stockholm, 86
Konsum (state-owned shops), 73
Kraftwerk, 'Das Model,' 58
Kubrick, Stanley, 111
Kyaga, Ulrika, 82

La Casa dei Vip (Luciano Emmer) [Cori-carousel], 195–7, *196*
Lacarbona, Roberto, 199
ladies' lunches, 48–9, 51, 52
@lama.alakeel, 253
Landsberg, Alison, 167, 169, 178
Larella, 89
Larella Young Lady, 88, 94–5
Lascity, Myles Ethan, 15
Launchmettrics, 249, 255
Laver, James, 159–60

Laverne, Lauren, 173–4, 177
Lefebvre, Germaine, 192–4
Lehmann, Ulrich, 168
Leipzig trade fair 1957, 68, 69, 77n
Lesmoir-Gordon, Nigel, 176–7
Lester Costume Company, 40
Lewis, Tania, 219–20
LGBTQ, 118
Liberty, London, 126, 176
lieux de mémoire, 164
Life and Debt (Stephanie Black, 2001) [documentary], 25
lifestyle influencers, 250
lifestyle television, 219–20
Liljevalchs art gallery, Stockholm, 96
Limited Brands, 239
Lindbergh, Peter, 132–3, 138, 140
live stream, 227–47
liveness, 237
Livingston, Karla, *140*
Loane, Scott, 148
Lokrantz, Kerstin, 99
Lombard, Carole, 47–8
London Fashion Week, 242, 243n
The London Look: 1960s British Fashion Youth Quake [film], 130, 138
Long, Paul, 162
Look [magazine], 111
Lopez, Antonio, 116
Loren, Sophia, 190–1
Los Angeles fashion week, 1
Los Angeles Times [newspaper], 26
Lucarelli, Noemi, 187
Lumière brothers, 13–14
Lyberg, Anna-Lisa, 85–6

MacAloon, John J., 230
McCartney, Stella, 27
Macdonald, Sharon, 163, 165
McQueen (Ian Bonhote and Peter Ettedgui, 2018) [documentary], 17–21, *19*, *20*
McQueen, Alexander, 17–21
  'Plato's Atlantis', 239
  skull symbol, 18, *19*
McRobbie, Angela, 209–10

Made in Italy fashion, 29n
Made in Milan (Martin Scorsese, 1990) [documentary], 14, 29n
Made in Paris (Boris Sagal, 1966) [film], 42, 43
magazines, 99, 229, 244n
Maheshwari, 249
Maier, Vivian, 111
makeover culture, 14, 203–23
'making of' fashion, 13, 21–3
Mamber, Stephen, 112
Man with a Movie Camera (1929) [documentary], 109–11, 119
Mandelli, Elisa, 123–4, 126, 137, 139
mannequin parade, 126, 146–7, 159, 160, 169, 233
Manolo: The Boy Who Made Shoes for Lizards (Michael Roberts, 2017) [documentary], 15
Marchetti, Simone, 261, 263
Margiela, Martin, 155
Marker, Chris, 109–10
Marklund, Tore, 95
AB Märthakonfektion, 95, 96
Märthaskolan, 91, 93, 95
Marucelli, 194
Marwick, Alice E., 219
Mary Quant, 130–1, *131*, 138
Marzotto, 183
media archaeological approach, 228
media impact value (MIV), 255
media overexposure, 264
media rituals, 236
mediatisation of fashion shows, 228–30, 235, 242–3
Metropolitan Museum of Art (MOMA), 14, 108, 124, 141n
MGM, 40–2
Milan Fashion Week, 256
Minney, Safia, 26
Modeinstitut (fashion institute), Prague, 68
Modellkonfektion, 82, 99
models, 32–3, 44, 47, 63, 66, 66, 72, 78n, 102–3
Montez-Creations, 52–3
Morgan, Andrew, 23–7

movie costumes, 47–8
@mrmoudz, 253
MTV, 235–6, 244n
Muller, Pieter, 13
Murray, Robin L., *Film and Everyday Eco-Disasters*, 23
museification, 17, 18
museology, 5, 122
 and moving images, 123–5
 new museology, 122–5, 127, 128, 137, 139, 149, 152
museum as cinematic space, 123–5
Museum of Fashion Institute of Technology, New York, 135–6
music, 19, 37, 58, 63, 69
The Music Documentary: Acid Rock to Electropop, 16
music videos, 58

Nathanson, Elizabeth, 220
National Archives, Ottawa, 144, 145
National Programme, 184
Naylor, William, 172
neo-formalism, 60, 76n
neoliberalism, 25
Netflix, 203, 218, 248, 252, 264
Neue Deutsche Wochenschau (NDW) [newsreels], 57–8, 60–2, 68, 70, 70–2, 74
new centre, 83
New Look style, 87, 96
new museology, 122–5, 127, 128, 137, 139, 149, 152
New York Fashion Week, 240, 241
New York Gay Pride parade, 105, 115
New York Times, 102–6, *107*, 109, 112, 113, 115, 118, 120, 249
newsreels, 14, 45, 48, 54, 61–5, 76n, 126, 146, 227–47
 fashion in East and West German, 57–80
 French, 68
 inserted footage of audience, 64
 in West and East Germany, 60–1
 and women, 62, 65, 67–70, 73–4, 77n, 79n

Nichols, Bill, 11
   Representing Reality, 112–13
Nora, Pierre, 164–5
Nordiska Kompaniet (NK), 95, 99
Normal Love (Jack Smith, 1963) [film], 52–3
Notebook on Cities and Clothes (Wim Wenders, 1989) [documentary], 14
Nyman, Michael, 19

Object Lessons, 149
observational documentaries, 112–13, 132–3
Oestergaard, Heinz, 70
Oh! You Pretty Things: The Story of Music and Fashion (BBC4) [TV], 161, 173–6
Olympia (1938) [documentary], 244n
One Man and His Shoes (Yemi Bamiro, 2020) [documentary], 27
O'Neill, Alistair, 172
Opal, 71
Ouellette, Laurie, 205, 215

Packard, Vance, 184
Palais du Costume, Paris, 126
Palmer, Alexandra, 122, 125, 127, 133–4, 138, 144–56
Pangalos, Stylianos, 151–2
Paquin, Jeanne, 126, 233
Paramount Studios, 48, 49
Parigi è sempre Parigi (Luciano Emmer) [Cori-carousels], 193–4
Parikka, Jussi, 228
Paris, Ivan, 182, 187
Paris fashion, 68, 69, 73, 74
Partington, Angela, 96–7
Passebois-Ducrois, Juliette, 17
Passion Films, 35
Pathé newsreels, 54, 126
Pathé-Frères, 'Florence Rose Fashions', 233
Patou, Jean, 44–5
Patrov, Julia, 170
Paul, Gerhard, *Visual History*, 59, 75
Pearse, John, 176
People Tree, 26
performativity in the everyday, 49–53
personal appearances, 95

Petersen, Franziska Bork, 238
phenomenological time, 166
photographers, 53, 102–21
photographs, 47, 99
   still, 19–20
plastic surgery shows, 204
Plate, Liedeke, 177
podcasts, 178
   Getting Curious with Jonathan Van Ness, 216
Poiret, Paul, 126, 233
Pontén, Gunilla, 99
Poopourri, 216
posting, 213, 218, 262
powder puff promotion, 45, 233
Powell, Benjamin, 25
Pozzoli, Riccardo, 256, 257, 261
Prentice, Rebecca, 25
presence, 230–1
print advertising, 82
production cultures, 42–4
Project Runway [TV], 256
prosthetic memory, 167, 170, 178
Puritan Fashions Corporation, UK, 130
PVC plastics, 131

#qehiptip, 212, 213, 215
Queer Eye [TV], 203–23
Queer Eye for the Straight Guy [TV], 203, 205–6

Radio Times [magazine], 171–2
RAI channel, 184–5, 187
rationalisation, 98
RAW [TV], 235
Razek, Ed, 239
Ready to Wear series (BBC2) [TV], 161, 171–2, 175
ready-to-wear fashion, 182–202, 227, 236
real time, 229–32, 242–3
reality television, 2, 14, 204–10
'the Red Dior', 73
Rees-Roberts, Nick, 13, 15, 227
   Fashion Film: Art and Advertising in the Digital Age, 2
refugees, 78n

remediation, 227–47
Renov, Michael, 218
re-wearing, 169
Riche restaurant, Stockholm, 95
The Ridiculous Theater Company, 52–3
Riefenstahl, Leni, 244n
Rigney, Ann, 165
Rizzo, Mary, 209
Rocamora, Agnès, 168, 229
Roffi, Stefano, 199
Rose, Helen, 39–56
    The Glamorous World of Helen Rose, 46
    "Just Make Them Beautiful": The Many
        Worlds of a Designing Woman, 46
Royal Ontario Museum (ROM), Canada,
    127, 134, 138, 140–1, 144–56
Rumba (1935) [film], 48
Russia, 109–10
Russian Formalism, 76n
Ruttman, Walter, 110

Sahlins konfektionsfabrik, 88, 89, 94, 95, 96
Samuel, Raphael, 162–3
Sandrew-Week, 82
sartorial remembrance, 168–9
Save the Arctic campaign, 36
Saviano, Roberto, 29n
Scatter my Ashes at Bergdorf's
    [documentary], 15
Schneider, Rebecca, 230
Schuberth, Emilio, 71, 72
Schulze-Varell, Heinz, 63, 70, *70*
Schwerin, Marg, 95
Se magazine, 96
seamstresses, 21–2
Seaport Gallery, New York, 'immersive
    exhibit' of Bill Cunningham's work
    2021, 111
SED party, 61, 79n
see now, buy now, 227–47
self-care, 203–23
self-celebration, 249, 262
self-help genres, 204–5
Sender, Katherine, 204, 220–1
The September Issue (R. J. Cutler, 2009)
    [documentary], 29n

Serafini, Lorenzo, 259
serpentine dance, 42, 45
Serra International Convention, 49
Serres, Michel, 173
Sex and the City [TV], 236
Shaping Fashion: Balenciaga's Legacy
    [video], 128–9
SHEIN app, 1
Shein X: 100K Challenges [TV], 1
SHOWstudio, 239
Siegel, Lucy, 26
Simmel, Georg, 50
Simons, Raf, 13, 22, 240
Simpson, Wallis, 113–14
The Simpsons [TV], 256
A Single Man (Tom Ford, 2009) [film], 37
SIPRA advertising agency, 184–6
size revolution, 183
Sklovskij, Viktor, 76n
slimming tips, 212
Smelik, Anneke, 177
Snapchat, 251
sober advertising, 82, 97, 98
Social Democrat politics, 82–4, 97
social imaginary, 248–68
social media, 1, 210, 216–19, 244n
socialist countries, 73
socialist 'new people,' 66
Socialize Agency, 254
soft promotion, 233
Soviet economic model, 65
Sozzani, Franca, 16
Spaak, Catherine, 188, 195–7, *196*
Spears, Britney, 38
spectacle, 230
spectatorship, 45–7, 52–3, 58, 85, 90, 189,
    228–9, 238, 243, 244n
    female, 45
    internet, 229–32
    scopophilic, 239
'Springtime Fantasies', fashion shows, 49
Stallybrass, Peter, 168–9
Steele, Valerie, 122, 125, 126
Steorn, Patrik, 84–5
stereotypes, 192, 194, 205–6
A Stitch in Time (BBC) [TV], 169

Stockholm Exhibition 1930, 86, 91
Style with Elsa Klensch (CNN, 1980–2001) [TV], 234, 244n
Sundance Film Festival, 36
Superbowl 1999, 239
supermodels, 33, 132, 242, 244n
supply chain, 22–3
Svenonius, Brita, 85–6, 91, 97
Svenska Dagbladet [newspaper], 86
Svenska Slöjdföreningen, 96
Svilova, Yelizaveta, 109, 110
SVOD, 12
sweatshops, 25
Sweden, 81–101
synthetic fibres, 58, 64, 70, 73, 74
syuzhet, 76n
Szymanski, Adam, 12, 13, 21
    '*Bill Cunningham New York* and the Political Potentiality of the Fashion Documentary', 107–8

tableaux, 126
talking heads documentary, 20, 26, 135, 138, 171
@tanfrance, *213*, *218*, 220
Taylor, Charles, 248
Taylor, Lou, 178n
TBS Crew, 260
Technicolor, 145
teenage fashion, 81–101
Tekniska skolan, Stockholm, 86
television, 49, 158–225
    celebrities, 189–90
    and/as cultural remembrance, 162–5
    lifestyle, 219–20
    as time machine, 165–7
    voter-based reality, 236–7
textile industry, 64, 66, 73, 84
textile machine industry, 65, 67
Textile Museum, Borås, Sweden, 131–3
textile techniques, 153–4
theatrical costumes, 40
Thierry Muegler: Couturissime [exhibition], 141n
third way teenage fashion, 81–101
Thompson, John, 161

Thompson, Kristin, 60, 76n
TikTok, 120, 251
The Times of Bill Cunningham (Mark Bozek, 2018) [documentary], 102–21, *116*
Tomlinson, John, 238
Tommy Hilfiger, see now, buy now spectaculars, 241–2
TommyNow fashion show, 241–2
TOMMYWORLD carnival, 241
Tonårsmodet, Husmors Filmer 1954 [short film], 81–99, *94*
Tonner doll, 47–8
Tonnie-modeller, 94, 95, 96, 99
Trade Organisation (Handelsorganisation, HO), 73
Trägårdh, Göta, 82–91, 95–9
transgender, 118
transparent media, 230
The True Cost (Andrew Morgan, 2015) [documentary], 23–7, *24*
Tsai, Martin, 26
Tucker, Lorna, 32–8, 36
Tuffin & Foale, 130
Turner, Fred, 83
Turner, Graeme, 237
Twiggy's Frock Exchange [TV], 172
Twitter, 36, 239

Ufa-Wochenschau [newsreels], 60, 62, 69, 70–1
Uhlirova, Marketa, 42, 54, 55n, 228, 232
Ulfsdotter, Boel, 144–56
Una scelta sicura (Antonio Moretti) [Cori-carousel], 189
United States, 71–2
Universal, 48–9, 52
Unposted (Amoruso, 2019) [documentary], 248–68, *258*
AB Upsala Kappfabrik, 89, 95–6
Uricchio, William, 165–6
useful cinema, 124, 129, 131, 133, 137, 138, 139

Valentino: The Last Emperor [documentary], 14, 21–2
van Herpen, Iris, 151–2

Van Ness, Jonathan, 203–23
  Over the Top: A Raw Journey to Self Love, 216
Vanity Fair Italia [magazine], 261
Veneziani, Jole, 187, 193–4, 198
Venice Film Festival, 14, 255, 263
Verfahren, 76n
Versace, Gianni, 138
Vertov, Dziga, 109–11, 119
Vezzoli, Francesco, 261
VHS videos, 18, 114
Victoria and Albert Museum (V&A), London, 125, 128–9, 130, 134, 138, 139, 141, 141n, 159–60
  How Was It Made? films, 128, *129*, 139
  YouTube, 130
Victoria's Secret fashion show, 236–7, 239
Victoria's Secret Model Search, 236–7
video, 18, 114, 150, 258
Viva Mexico! [exhibition], 148–9
vloggers, 15, 120
Vogue [magazine], 17, 29n, 49, 53, 105, 109, 115, 219, 233
Vogue España [magazine], 256
Vogue Italia [magazine], 16, 194
Vogue US [magazine], 29n
voice-over, 23, 26, 63, 88, 89, 90, 106, 115, 118, 136, 160, 166, 175, 184, 194
volkseigener Textilmaschinenbau, 67
Vonderau, Patrick, 185
voter-based reality television, 236–7
Vreeland, Diana, 17, 29n, 126
The Vulgar: Fashion Redefined, Barbican Art Gallery, London [exhibition], 134–5

Wall, Tim, 162
Ward, Paul, 113
  Documentary: The Margins of Reality, 119
Warner, Helen, 43
Wasson, Haidee, 124, 129, 137, 155
wearability, 70–1, 73
Weber, Brenda R., 206, 207
welfare society, 82, 83, 85, 90–5

Welt im Bild [newsreels], 60, 62, 68–9, 71, 72
Welt im Film [newsreels], 60, 62, 71, 73
West and East Germany
  differences and similarities of, 72–4
  fashion in Der Augenzeuge, 67–8
West German fashion, in West German newsreels, 68–71
West German newsreels, 57–80
Westberg, Margareta, 95, 99, 100n
western fashion, in West German newsreels, 71–2
Westwood, Vivienne, 32–8, *36*
Westwood: Punk, Icon, Activist (2018) [documentary], 32–8
WGSN, 255
What Not to Wear (BBC, 2001–7) [TV], 14
Who Are You, Polly Maggoo? (1966) [film], 53
Who Do You Think You Are? (BBC) [TV], 162
Wildfeuer, Elfi, 78n
Wilks, Jamie, 253
Willis, Emma, 171
Wilson, Elizabeth, *Adorned in Dreams*, 170
Wintour, Anna, 29n, 105, 109, 115
Wired magazine, 250
Wissinger, Elizabeth, 235, 236
  This Year's Model: Fashion, Media, and the Making of Glamour, 120
#wokeuplikethis looks, 217–18
Woman's Weekly [magazine], 175
women, and newsreels, 62, 65, 67–70, 73–4, 77n, 79n
Wood, Stephanie, 131
Worby, Robert, 19
Worn Stories (Netflix, 2021) [TV], 27
Worth, Charles, 126, 233

Yamamoto, Yuhji, 14
Yellow is Forbidden [documentary], 22
You: The Digital Fashion Revolution, La Triennale, Milan [exhibition], 257, 263, 265n

Young, Ernie, 40
young people, 68, 70–1, 81–101, *117*, 194–7
YouTube, 1, 35, 120, 136, 231–2, 237, 254
   Dressing Funny, 216
   GFT Archive, Turin, 183

Victoria and Albert Museum (V&A), London, 130

Zimmerman, Sue B., 254
Zober, 89, 96
Zwickau, Saxony, 66

EU representative:
Easy Access System Europe
Mustamäe tee 50, 10621 Tallinn, Estonia
Gpsr.requests@easproject.com

www.ingramcontent.com/pod-product-compliance
Lightning Source LLC
Chambersburg PA
CBHW050840230426
43667CB00012B/2075